Heralds of Revolution

Heralds of Revolution

Russian Students

and the

Mythologies

of Radicalism

SUSAN K. MORRISSEY

New York   Oxford
OXFORD UNIVERSITY PRESS
1998

Oxford University Press

Oxford   New York
Athens   Auckland   Bangkok   Bogota   Bombay   Buenos Aires
Calcutta   Cape Town   Dar es Salaam   Delhi   Florence   Hong Kong
Istanbul   Karachi   Kuala Lumpur   Madras   Madrid   Melbourne
Mexico City   Nairobi   Paris   Singapore   Taipei   Tokyo   Toronto   Warsaw

and associated companies in
Berlin   Ibadan

Library of Congress Cataloging-in-Publication Data
Morrissey, Susan K., 1963–
Heralds of revolution : Russian students and the mythologies of
radicalism / Susan K. Morrissey.
p.   cm.
Includes bibliographical references and index.
ISBN 0-19-511544-9
1. College students—Russia—Political activity.   2. Student
movements—Russia—History—20th century.   3. Left-wing extremists—
Russia—History—20th century.   4. Political socialization—Russia—
History—20th century.   5. Russia—Intellectual life—1801–1917.
6. Russia—Politics and government—1894–1917.   I. Title.
LA838.7.M6   1998
378.1'981'0947—dc21   97-2262

9 8 7 6 5 4 3 2 1

Printed in the United States of America
on acid-free paper

Acknowledgments

During the years this book has been in the making, I have accumulated countless professional, intellectual, and personal debts for which I offer my gratitude and thanks. Many institutions have generously supported this project. Research in Russia and Finland was funded by the International Research and Exchanges Board, the Fulbright-Hays Commission, and the University of California at Berkeley. Grants from the Social Science Research Council and the Berkeley Slavic Center enabled me to devote my time to writing. I am particularly indebted to the helpful staffs of the following institutions: the Slavonic Library at the University of Helsinki, the Russian National Library in St. Petersburg, the Russian State Library in Moscow, the Russian State Historical Archive (especially Serafima Varekhova), the Central State Historical Archive of St. Petersburg, the Museum of St. Petersburg University, the State Archive of the Russian Federation, and the Bibliothèque Nationale in Paris.

It is also a pleasure to acknowledge the many people who have supported and encouraged me. I thank my former teachers at U.C. Berkeley, especially Reginald Zelnik, Boris Gasparov, Nicholas Riasanovsky, Martin Malia, and Irina Paperno. Special thanks are due to Reggie, whose critical and personal support have made this book possible, and to Boris, who spurred me to fortify my argument by calling an earlier version "watered down." I would also like to mention my fellow graduate students at Berkeley, whose friendship and spirit of intellectual community have been important to me: Simmy Cover, Robert Geraci, Sue Grayzel, Paul Harvey, Benjamin Nathans, Robert Vieira, Theodore Weeks, and Glennys Young. In addition, I am grateful to my former colleagues at the University of Kentucky who all warmly welcomed me, and especially to Daniel Rowland, who encouraged me to pursue the "story." As a not-so-secret reader of the manuscript, Richard Stites bolstered me with his knowledge, enthusiasm, and critical suggestions. Only a friend would eat sushi followed by Christmas goose; my gratitude goes to Catherine Evtuhov for helping me at times to maintain my perspective. The annual visits of David Myers have accompanied the making of this book; I thank him for long summer evenings on the balcony and his friendship. At Oxford University Press, Thomas LeBien and Lisa Stallings have been exemplary editors.

Many individuals have welcomed me both professionally and personally in Germany. I would like to thank Helmut Altrichter as well as the staff and students of the Lehrstuhl Osteuropäische Geschichte in Erlangen. Mark Edele, who devoted three days to critiquing a much longer version of this manuscript, deserves extra acknowledgment. In Munich, Wolfgang and Bele Jüngling have backed my opposition to a certain Bavarian dress and shown me the pleasures of hiking to (and from) Andechs. In very different ways, Bernhard Chiari and Dieter Weiß have both helped me to appreciate the languages and cultures of the "South." I owe a singular debt of gratitude to Reinhold and Hilde Jahn and Heidi Jahn-Müller for warmly accepting me into their family. In Russia, I thank the people who have made me want to come back again. Ksana Kumpan and Albin Konechnyi have always had a place for me at their table, and I am especially grateful for Albin's "side job" in Phoenix. Konstantin and Svetlana Azadovskii have opened their hearth to me and showed me by example the importance of determination and élan. The art of Valentin Gerasimenko and Elena Figurina has watched over the writing of this book; so has their spirit. Niina Melanen has helped to make Helsinki a destination rather than just a stopover on the way to St. Petersburg.

Hubertus Jahn has read various stages of this book and helped me to move. Without him, an Oachkatzelschwoaf would have been a mere Eichhörnchenschwanz, which, as I now know and can even pronounce, is not the same thing at all. To Hubs, my heart. Finally, my special gratitude belongs to Brenda, Charles, and Mike Morrissey, who have given me a lifetime of encouragement. I dedicate this book to my family.

Note on Transliteration, Dates, and Translations

In transliterating Russian titles, quotations, and names, I have used the Library of Congress system and partially modified old-style orthography to conform to modern usage. Place names reflect conventional spelling. All dates until February 1918 are given according to the Julian calendar, which was behind the Gregorian (Western) calendar by twelve days in the nineteenth century and by thirteen days in the twentieth century. Dates thereafter follow the Gregorian calendar. All translations are my own unless otherwise noted.

Erlangen, Germany   S.K.M.
December 1996

Contents

Heralds of Revolution

Narrative and Identity in Russian Radical Culture

> Nachdem ich etwas erfahren hatte, kam es mir erst vor, als ob ich gar nichts wisse, und ich hatte recht: denn es fehlte mir der Zusammenhang, und darauf kommt doch eigentlich alles an.
>
> —Johann Wolfgang von Goethe, *Wilhelm Meisters Lehrjahre*, Erster Teil

The Russian revolution has been written as both an epic and a tragedy: the heroic struggle of the working class as the agent of history, and the Bolshevik seizure of power diverting Russia from the natural path of liberal reform. Both versions represent dramatizations of a complex and contradictory tangle of events and of the chaotic and unordered experiences of participants. Yet those confronted with making sense of the past, such as memoirists and historians, must select, reject, and then organize the "relevant" facts into a narrative form. In this task, they are assisted by the metaphors, structures, and conventions of their cultural context, which, in the case of the historian, includes the various practices of a scholarly discipline. For both memoirists and historians, "making sense of the past" can also serve to legitimize or delegitimize aspects of the present. This is especially true in the history of revolutions.[1] Yet narratives are also an important part of the historical terrain itself, for it is through them that individuals and collectives, ranging from nations to professional groups, order experience and articulate identity. Though these kinds of stories inevitably influence the subsequent writing of history, too often historians discard them as subjective, biased, or simply unimportant.[2]

This book is about one story of Russian radicalism that would prove particularly flexible and enduring: the story of consciousness. The concept of "consciousness" was omnipresent in the political culture of late imperial Russia. It connoted the Marxist-influenced dialectics of historical development, class formation, and class struggle. With the founding of political parties, consciousness was generally considered something either reflected in or possessed by the party. As an adjective describing a person—a "conscious worker," for example—it referred to an individual who was aware of his class identity and consequently took an active role in the historical process; that is, it indicated a specific kind of politicization. After 1917, the unfolding of consciousness would form the master-plot of countless memoirs and monographs of the revolutionary era, thereby grounding Soviet power in the processes of history. By the 1930s, socialist realism would appropriate the pattern and depict the individual's growth to consciousness under the guidance of a party member as an allegory for revolution and progress. A parallel trend in the West operated largely within the same categories and assumed the task of revealing the absence of consciousness, the will to power of the Bolshevik Party, and hence the illegitimacy of Soviet rule.

My intention here is neither to expose the fictions of consciousness nor to evaluate its relative levels in various revolutionary actors. It is, rather, to examine the development and fate of its particular "stories" for a specific group of people over the revolutionary era. I emphasize the quality of narrative because, by definition, consciousness is thought to develop over time in a person or a "class" of persons, and the process of development is typically represented as a kind of "story." At issue, therefore, is how consciousness became a meaningful narrative in revolutionary Russia, its functions as such, and how the story of a story can be historically significant.[3]

Students form an ideal subject for a case study of the narrative of consciousness. As many historians have documented, they were central figures in the history and development of Russian radicalism. Students played an important role in the populist movements "to the people" of the 1870s as well as in subsequent ventures into the worlds of both workers and peasants.[4] Student protests and demonstrations likewise occurred with a chronic regularity between 1857 and 1921, and, beginning in 1899, assumed the form of a broad student movement, with six nationwide strikes in addition to innumerable local confrontations both in the universities and on the streets. During this period, the student milieu provided one of the most important settings for the education of revolutionaries, for it was as students that many young people first became acquainted with radical ideas and were baptized into politics. At the root of this radicalism was the ethos of the student corporation or *studenchestvo*, which successive generations of Russian youth joined upon their journey to the city and enrollment in the university.[5]

Any history of an "imagined community"—to adopt Benedict Anderson's famous term—raises important methodological questions.[6] Indeed, to pursue the parallel, *studenchestvo* is better understood as a phenomenon analogous to both class and nation, because, like these other categories of identity, *studenchestvo* existed through the consciousness of its members. It linked a group of individuals through time and space—over six decades, from St. Petersburg to Kiev to

Tomsk—by a process of self-identification with an abstract collective rather than by personal acquaintance or particular shared experiences. In this specific case, the *studenchestvo* was also connected to a similarly amorphous group (as well as its "adult" counterpart), the intelligentsia.[7] Although contemporaries (and later historians) attempted to define both groups through socioeconomic or ideological criteria, neither group was limited to a single social class or political platform. Cultural identity was instead paramount, for *studenchestvo* and intelligentsia shared a self-definition as the antithesis and archfoe of "bourgeois philistinism" *(meshchanstvo)*. Despite this similarity, *studenchestvo* remained singular and distinct for a practical reason: a student is inherently a transitional identity. After a certain number of years, he or she either graduates or drops out, thereby becoming something else—a bureaucrat, a doctor, a teacher, a revolutionary, and in many cases a member of the intelligentsia. For this reason, the institutions of *studenchestvo*, including illegal organizations of mutual aid and self-education as well as rituals and songs, played especially important roles in transmitting ideals and symbols, new and old, to successive cohorts of students. As historians have documented, this student culture was a primary factor in the emergence and persistence of an organized protest movement.[8]

The ethos of *studenchestvo* did not remain static over the course of the nineteenth and early twentieth centuries. Various political ideologies and philosophical fads coexisted and occasionally supplanted one another in popularity. Continuity was provided, however, by the institutions of *studenchestvo* and the distinctive notion of education that developed within and through them. For many students, the true purpose of the university experience, which included academic studies and participation in *studenchestvo*, was not the accumulation of factual knowledge and skills but the formation of ethical and intellectual character *(vospitanie)*, often described in terms of a unified "world view" *(mirovozzrenie* or *Weltanschauung)*, from which all principles and actions could be derived. According to this notion, education would produce a new kind of person dedicated to the enactment of social and political change. This concept, which guided radical, liberal, and, by the twentieth century, even conservative students in their understanding of identity and politics, developed in an ongoing conflict with two other views of the university. Many professors propounded an ideology of *nauka* (science), according to which the university, as a force of social progress, should be devoted to scholarship and the teaching of a "pure" science quite separate from politics or practice. These aspirations contrasted with those of the government, which regarded higher education as a form of professional training. Students thus advanced their own version of *nauka*—the moral and intellectual cultivation of the individual and, ultimately, of the collective.[9]

In the 1890s, the story of consciousness began to unfold for students and within *studenchestvo*. Because it built on the well-established notion of education and was characterized by a strong pedagogical metaphor, I call it the revolutionary *Bildungsroman,* or novel of formation. In its most formulaic version, as expressed in a typical memoir of the 1920s, it recounts the coming of age of the author in the midst of the gathering revolutionary storm. The scene opens on a provincial youth, suffocating in the repressive atmosphere of the classical gymnasium that symbolizes all of the darkness of Russia's old regime. The story then traces his political awakening from his journey to the city, through his enrollment in the university, disappointment with "official" science, discovery of the student subcultures, and, ultimately, to his participation in political protests and achievement of political consciousness.[10] One might dismiss this story as a simple fiction, a highly formulaic epic hardly reflecting the reality of the 1890s. This is right, of course, but only partly so. In this study, I will argue that this story began to coalesce into a narrative in the late 1890s and achieved a mature form during the Revolution of 1905–1907. It evolved thereafter as one important and flexible interpretative model of autobiography (or politicization) for the revolutionary left until the canonization of a subsequent version into socialist realism during the 1930s.

This broad pattern extended beyond students with only minor structural modifications to other social groups, most important the revolutionary intelligentsia—who were often former students—and workers. Because of the differences in social background, the parallel to workers is particularly striking. In an article and a translated volume of memoirs, Reginald Zelnik has explored the stages of personal and political development of Semen Kanatchikov, whose memoirs were first published in the Soviet Union in 1929. Though Kanatchikov presents his life story from peasant to worker, skilled worker, conscious worker, and professional revolutionary as a natural progression toward adulthood and consciousness, Zelnik stresses the important choices made by Kanatchikov over this long and difficult process and provides a convincing portrait of the many faces of workers' identity in late imperial Russia. Kanatchikov had the option, after all, of stopping at one of any number of points: for example, as a skilled, literate, and urbanized worker.[11] Yet the linearity of Kanatchikov's reconstructed life story presents a noteworthy parallel to student memoirs and suggests not only the shared conventions of the Soviet memoir but also particular understandings of identity and consciousness among workers, a hypothesis supported by a recent study of the worker-intelligentsia.[12] But the narrative of consciousness among workers has not been addressed as such, with labor historians at times adopting the category by tracing the emergence of political consciousness (or its failure to emerge) and, more recently, inverting it by looking at "unconscious" workers.[13] A hurdle for such a study lies in the character of the sources. Most workers' memoirs were published after 1917, and contemporary documents such as proclamations and leaflets were often written by the radical intelligentsia. The contrary is true for students.

When a nationwide student movement that encompassed the vast majority of students exploded in 1899, *studenchestvo* seemed to become an historical actor in its own right. Over the course of the movement of 1899–1905, the story of consciousness would unfold as a new dimension of *studenchestvo*. This does not imply that the story preexisted the student movement or that it existed separately from real students. It means, rather, that certain categories structured students' interpretation of their collective experiences, categories which appeared in hundreds of strike resolutions, speeches, pamphlets, poems, and songs, and which acquired an increasingly narrative character over the course of time. The underlying plot has been identified by scholars in somewhat different contexts as the "spontaneity-consciousness dialectic." [14] According to this dialectic, historical progress (in a Marxist sense) occurs through the interaction of the forces of spontaneity (elemental, unorganized, mass action) and those of consciousness (political awareness, control, discipline). In the specific context of student radicalism, this dialectic appeared in the rhetorical conflict between the spontaneous "academic" protests of the student "masses" and the conscious "political" movement directed by student leaders. It culminated by 1905 in the official, if inaccurate, story of student radicalism as a progression from the spontaneous academic protest of 1899 to the conscious political movement of 1905. This dialectic was also personalized into an ideal of consciousness to be instilled within each student as a member of *studenchestvo;* in other words, it became the goal of *vospitanie*. The revolutionary *Bildungsroman* (for students) developed over the course of the student movement. [15]

The narrative of consciousness shaped the historiography of the student movement and even of the Russian revolution. Predictably, Soviet historians claimed to find a linear process of politicization that ended in the conscious activity of student-Bolsheviks and the overall bourgeois aspirations of students as a whole. Recent Western scholarship has attempted to unveil the "real" story behind the contemporary and historiographical fictions by discounting the various stories as biased. While such studies provide a valuable corrective and a refreshingly nuanced view of the student movement, they struggle, perhaps inevitably, within the categories of their subjects (especially the academic-political opposition) and thus tend to come down on the side of academic moderation. [16] Finally, the historian Richard Pipes has recently argued that the student "disorders" of 1899 marked the beginning of the Russian revolution. With his linkage of lower-class background to political radicalism, his stress on the politicizing role of student leaders over the masses (who really just wanted to study), and his identification of a progressive displacement of academic interests by political ones between 1899 and 1905, Pipes appropriates many of the categories of his Soviet opponents but inverts their value. Unlike them, however, he thereby links the Russian revolution to its intellectual (rather than socioeconomic) heritage. [17]

The reasons for the vigor of the narrative of consciousness are manifold. Constantly looking to the West in order to interpret their own world, educated

Russians were highly sensitive to the various possible lines of historical development they believed open to Russia. Hegelianism, positivism, populism, and
Marxism were all narratives of history. The important role of "self-education" in
the culture of Russian radicalism likewise shaped an understanding of progress
in which individual and historical development were closely, even causally,
linked. Yet the recurring motifs of the *Bildungsroman,* a narrative form well-
known to Russians from nineteenth-century literature, suggest that formal reasons may also have played a role. The cultural theorist Franco Moretti has
likened the *Bildungsroman* to "the 'symbolic form' of modernity" because, he
argues, "youth, or rather the European novel's numerous versions of youth, becomes for our modern culture the age which holds the 'meaning of life': it is the
first gift Mephisto offers Faust." The narrative of formation, thus, can express
the dynamism of modernity (of youth), yet also impose a final order (the fully
formed adult). Though Moretti largely limits his purview to central and western
Europe and circumscribes the era of the *Bildungsroman* from the late eighteenth
to the mid-nineteenth century, his words could fit as well for the Russia of
the 1890s, "when status society starts to collapse, the countryside is abandoned
for the city, and the world of work changes at an incredible and incessant
pace. . . ." [18]

To be sure, the revolutionary *Bildungsroman* is a fiction like any other story;
it helped to organize experience by the process of selection and exclusion. Occasionally, however, such widely accepted stories are also revealed to be fictional,
and such was the case for students. The pivotal event for them was the Revolution of 1905, when the first fully formed examples of the narrative appeared. The
(apparent) achievement of consciousness, combined with the revolution's at best
problematic accomplishments, disrupted the story. In the revolution's wake, students could no longer articulate a single coherent story for themselves and endured a "crisis of *studenchestvo*" that persisted with highs and lows from 1907 to
the final demise of *studenchestvo* in 1922. In this period, the public and personal
images of students underwent a dramatic reversal. From principled participants
and even leaders of the liberation movement, students became drunkards and
syphilitics. What had changed, however, was less students' actual behavior than
the interpretive framework. While the story of consciousness had highlighted the
political identity and activity of students, its demise, so to speak, raised disturbing questions regarding other nonpolitical aspects of students' lives. To extend the metaphor of *Bildungsroman,* if the 1905 Revolution marked fully formed
adulthood, it was now time for students to get on with "real" life. And it was
precisely real life that so plagued students after 1905.

Heralds of Revolution is divided into two parts of four chapters each, organized around the making and unmaking of the story of consciousness. It opens
with a survey of student radicalism from the 1860s to 1899, with particular concern paid to the development of its defining mythologies—the interwoven con-

cept of the new person and the new student, a socioeconomic determinism, the *studenchestvo,* and a pedagogical model of identity and consciousness. Attention shifts in chapter 2 to the emergence and development of the student movement. It will show how the notion of individual "upbringing" leading to consciousness both motivated and shaped student radicalism between 1899 and 1904. Indeed, the rise to consciousness became a means to understand the political evolution of a mass movement and the politicizing function of student protest within society.

The deviations and exclusions from the story of consciousness form the topic of chapter 3. The Russian language lacks an adequate translation of the concept of "private" life, with *chastnaia zhizn',* or "particular" life, forming the closest equivalent. *Chastnaia zhizn',* however, has a negative connotation of egoism, of something existing in opposition to the "common" good.[19] In tracing the shifting boundaries of the "particular" within student radicalism, this chapter discusses the marginalization of conservative and women students, both of whom qualified their common identity as students with political and gender factors respectively, and both of whom developed their own stories of identity and politics. The chapter concludes with a review of the "particular" lives of male students—in taverns and brothels—and the challenge this posed to their claim to consciousness. Despite a few lonely voices critical of the everyday behavior of male students, it was only the Revolution of 1905–1907, the topic of chapter 4, that ended the story.

The confusing and sometimes liberating new environment of post-1905 Russia sets the scene for part II. As students became the focal point of unprecedented public debate, a number of new stories competed for attention without, however, ever attaining the success of their glorious and teleological predecessor. Likening 1905 to the 1848 Revolution in Europe, some commentators declared the onset of capitalism in the university, which was to mark the death knell not only of a student movement but also of the old idealistic *studenchestvo.* This controversy helped to shape new stories of student life that substituted the particular for the political, or corruption for consciousness: the provincial youth travels to the university but is tempted by alcohol, prostitutes, and careerism. The resonance of this story spanned the political spectrum. The experiences and public images of women students—the topic of chapter 6—form a rhetorical counterpoint. As educational opportunities expanded for women around 1905, women students came increasingly to be viewed by progressive Russians as forces of moderation, morality, and social progress, though, to be sure, modernity posed potential hazards for them as well.

The story of consciousness and of the fall from consciousness are analyzed through the prism of suicide in chapter 7. In the late nineteenth and early twentieth centuries, Russian students developed a tradition of "heroic" suicide in which the act of suicide became a heroic feat: a symbol of political resistance against despotism. Though disrupted by the Revolution of 1905, this tradition did not disappear. When the suicide of students seemed to take an epidemic form by 1908, students found that the political symbolism of suicide had acquired new ambiguities. Indeed, suicide implicated at once the spiritual poverty of state, society, and *studenchestvo*. The failure of the various scenarios to pin down the new realities was exposed by the events discussed in chapter 8. As students rediscovered their political power in 1911, the last nationwide student strike led to the arrest and exile of thousands of students, the mass resignation of hundreds of professors, and a broad political crisis. Though they had clearly not renounced political activism for the pleasures of the market, their protests now had only a symbolic value, and students found themselves isolated from both liberals and radicals. A new story was found only after the October Revolution, when the old prerevolutionary *studenchestvo* would join its final battle with the new regime.

At the outset of this project, it was clear that the tremendous amount of archival and published sources would require that I limit my study in space or time. I was hesitant to do either because *studenchestvo* was a group that existed throughout the Russian empire, and its story seemed to have logical beginning and ending points. With these considerations in mind, I decided to focus my archival research on students studying in the city of St. Petersburg, but to read widely in published sources relating to students throughout Russia. This approach has had both advantages and disadvantages. As the capital, St. Petersburg acted as a magnet, drawing a wide variety of students from all across the country—including women—to its prestigious institutions. Consequently, I was able to integrate such factors as gender into this study. The issue of ethnicity, however, proved a tantalizing but elusive topic, thereby suggesting that the investigation of student culture in the borderlands remains a promising avenue of research.

Not only practical factors, however, but also cultural ones influenced my choice. Precisely as the political center of the Russian empire (though itself without a sacred center), as the proverbial "Window to the West" (indeed, almost a Western city in its "rational" plan), St. Petersburg occupied a central place in nineteenth-century Russian radical culture.[20] The pivotal literary texts—Ivan Turgenev's *Fathers and Children* and Nikolai Chernyshevskii's *What Is to Be Done?*—both hinge on the symbolism of St. Petersburg, the first as imagined from the provinces and the second as experienced from within. This positioning of the city, suspended between Russia's provincial "darkness" and Western "enlightenment," was a pivotal rhetorical device in both the story of consciousness and its successors. There is some evidence from 1903 that Petersburg students were more advanced, to take a contemporary expression, along the path to consciousness; that is, the categories of the narrative may have been more pronounced there than in other cities. This extremity is hardly a disadvantage, because this study has not sought to reconstruct a detailed history of the student movement, a task already accomplished, but to trace its resonance through its guiding story. While the reader will find some traditional social and political history, this approach has led me to investigate such formerly unresearched topics as student suicide and to put the occasionally familiar event under a new light. In endeavoring to situate cultural myths into the geography of St. Petersburg and to explore culture without artificial geographic limits, I hope that this study gains in contextual depth what it may have lost in geographical breadth.

At the turn of the twentieth century, Russia possessed nine universities, located in St. Petersburg, Moscow, Kiev, Kazan, Odessa, Kharkov, Tomsk, Warsaw, and Iurev (better known by the German name Dorpat or today, the Estonian Tartu); in 1909, a tenth was founded in Saratov. In 1899, 16,497 students were enrolled in universities across the country, a number that would grow to more than 35,000 by 1908.[21] Admission was limited to men and contingent on the completion of the eight-year classical gymnasium or its equivalent. Under the controversial 1884 University Statute, which remained in force through 1917, the Ministry of Education administered the university system through curators appointed in each academic district. The government possessed wide powers over the appointment of faculty and deans, curricular offerings, the state examinations necessary for graduation, and, through appointed inspectorates, the activities of students.[22]

A university education represented a tremendous opportunity for upward social mobility for young men (women were officially admitted into universities only in 1917), for entrance into the Table of Ranks, as well as careers in civil service, secondary school teaching, law, and medicine, all were predicated on the university degree and official state examinations. Acceptance into a university had the additional benefits of a deferment from the military draft and, not to be underestimated, the chance to move out of the provinces and into one of Russia's major cities. The financial burden of higher education was a major hurdle for most students, who generally came from provincial backgrounds, neither wealthy nor poor. To restrict the admission of poorer (and, in its view, politically suspect) students, the government set tuition costs high and tied financial aid to academic performance and political reliability. It also forbade all independent student organizations, even those with a purely economic function, thus forcing these organizations underground and keeping many students in relative poverty. This situation would worsen after 1905, when enrollment increases made the already competitive search for side jobs as tutors still more difficult.

Though founded relatively late in 1819, St. Petersburg University was—along with Moscow University, founded in 1755—the center of scientific life in the Russian empire. In 1899, it had 3,788 registered students in four faculties: law, with 2,192 students; mathematics and natural sciences, with 1,236; history and philology, with 178; and eastern languages, with 182. Though the number of students would increase to 8,224 by 1912, the breakdown by faculty remained relatively constant, with 4,218 studying law, 3,146 the sciences, 726 history and philology, and 154 eastern languages. Students came largely from middle groups in Russian society, with the majority being the sons of gentry and civil servants, (64.99% in 1899 and 56.95% in 1910). During this period, the number of students from the lower urban orders and peasantry increased from roughly 15% to more than 20%. Other groups, each composing less than 10% of the student body, included the sons of clergy and merchants. The predominant religious background of students was Orthodox Christian (more than 70% in 1899 and 1912), with other students officially registered as Armenian Catholic, Roman Catholic, Lutheran, and Jewish. The case of Jewish students requires particular attention, because the government set an official quota of 3% for St. Petersburg University. Due to the temporary relaxation of admissions during the 1905 Revolution, however, the number of Jewish students increased beyond the quota, reaching a high point in 1908 with 1,200 or 12.5% and falling again by 1912 to 605 or 7.36%.[23]

In addition to the university, St. Petersburg possessed many specialized institutes, which were administered under various tsarist ministries. These included the Technological Institute (with 1,292 students in 1905) under the Ministry of Education, the Mining and Forestry Institutes under the Ministry of Land Management (550 and 540 students, respectively), the Institute of Civil Engineering and Electrotechnical Institute under the Ministry of Interior (1,008 and 381 students, respectively), the Communications Institute under the Ministry of Communications (849 students), and the Polytechnic under the Ministry of Finances (835 students). Finally, the Military-Medical Academy (766 students) stood under the jurisdiction of the Ministry of War.[24] Given the many employment opportunities for specialists in a rapidly expanding economy, competition was fierce for entrance into these technical institutes, and some of those who did not make the cut enrolled instead in the university. The social background of technical students across the nation differed slightly from that of university students; by 1914, more than 50% came from the lower urban orders and peasantry, as compared with fewer than 40% of university students.[25]

The experience of women students presents a special case.[26] Though women were admitted in 1860 as auditors at St. Petersburg University and the Medical-Surgical Academy (the predecessor of the Military-Medical Academy), the government banned women from men's educational institutions in 1864. The struggle of Russian women for equal educational opportunity then began in earnest. Under the leadership of a group of powerful and articulate society women, permission was finally obtained to open the Liubianskie Courses in Moscow and the Alarchinskie Courses in St. Petersburg by the end of the decade. Due to the weakness of the secondary school system for girls, the level of instruction of these new courses was closer to that of a gymnasium than a university. Nevertheless, a precedent had been established. Over the next decade, both girls' gymnasiums and university-level women's courses were founded in many cities across Russia, with medical courses founded as well in St. Petersburg. The new women students were called *kursistki* after the Russian word for "courses" *(kursy)*.

In 1878, the most important of these new programs, the St. Petersburg Higher Women's Courses—often nicknamed the Bestuzhev Courses after its first director, professor of history, K. N. Bestuzhev-Riumin—were officially opened. This was the first institution of higher learning for women with a full university-level curriculum. Faculty members were drawn from St. Petersburg University, and many agreed to teach for only a nominal fee. Admission required the successful completion of a full course of study at a girls' gymnasium. Within several years of their opening, the courses moved to an independent site on the tenth line of Vasil'evskii Island—walking distance to the university—where they remained until their closure in 1918. Because of the proximity of the courses to the university and the shared faculty, the Bestuzhev Courses were considered a kind of women's university, and the students of both institutions tended to associate with one another.

With many government officials still opposed to higher education for women, the successes of the 1870s were reversed during the 1880s. In 1882, the Women's Medical Courses stopped admitting new students, and the last class graduated in 1887. In a similar decree from May 1886, new admissions were not allowed in any women's courses while the government considered its policy. When the final class was graduating in 1889, permission was granted only to the St. Petersburg Courses to admit a new cohort of students. It remained the only institution of higher education open to Russian women until the establishment of the St. Petersburg Women's Medical Institute in 1897 and the Moscow Higher Women's Courses in 1900. Several restrictive provisions were also introduced. The curricula of the two faculties—history and philology, and mathematics and natural sciences—were henceforth to be approved each year by the Ministry of Education, and the teaching of human and animal physiology and natural history was strictly forbidden. As in the universities, an "inspectorate of students" was appointed by the district curator to supervise students. And, unique to the courses, admission now required not only appropriate academic preparation but the written permission of parents or husbands.

Beyond the clear imperative to keep Russian women from seeking their higher education abroad, the government recognized little purpose in promoting women's education in Russia. Unlike male students, women had few career choices. Upon graduation from the courses, women students received only a certificate of completion, because an academic degree required passage of the state examinations, which were restricted to men. With women legally precluded from the bureaucratic Table of Ranks, they were effectively barred from careers in civil service and law as well. Pedagogy remained their one official career path. For women who studied abroad, at one of the less prestigious midwifery and paramedic schools, or, after 1897, at the Women's Medical Institute, medicine represented an alternative.

PART ONE

The Making of Revolutionary Heroes

CHAPTER ONE

Myths and Memories

The New People in the University

Studenchestvo—the keeper of sacred traditions, the defender of the people's liberty, the leader of social movements, the hope of Russia!

—Mikhail Osorgin, "Posolon"

Georgii Nosar'—chairman of the 1905 St. Petersburg Soviet of Workers' Deputies under the name Khrustalev—first entered the political fray during the student strike of 1899 at St. Petersburg University. At the very beginning of the protests, before the movement had taken shape, Nosar' entered the drama from stage right—he was an orator for the moderate group at a *skhodka*, a prohibited general student meeting. When negotiations with the radicals revealed that he was acting out of "tactical considerations" rather than conviction, he resolved that "the masses were capable of a broader point of view," switched sides, and joined the strike committee.[1] As a first-year juridical student from Ukraine, Nosar' could not ground his claim to authority on the seniority and reputation conferred by previous participation in student protests. He instead improvised a radical persona and, thanks to his behavior rather than a specific platform or ideology, became a powerful symbol of radicalism in action.

With the passion of a convert, Nosar' dedicated himself during that spring to his new vocation as student radical, and in the process inspired the particular wrath of the rector of St. Petersburg University, V. I. Sergeevich. In a long report to his superiors, Sergeevich recommended that Nosar' be expelled from the university and conscripted into the army. "The quick removal of such a harmful element will undoubtedly facilitate the pacification [of students]," he explained. In his view, Nosar' had exceeded both his abilities and his station. "A university education is apparently not for him," the rector thus stressed, "the rigorous school of life will more quickly and accurately teach him intellect and reason." [2] Unlike any other student, Nosar' had drawn the specific antagonism of Sergeevich, epitomizing for him the extremes of student disorder.

Sergeevich and Nosar' probably had first met in February 1899, when a delegation of students that included Nosar' had informed the rector that students would no longer recognize his authority. They aserted that by calling police to quell the protests, Sergeevich had transferred his jurisdiction to the chief of police. With a seemingly minor gesture, Nosar' had also acted on this statement of principle: he lit a cigarette in the famous 400-meter-long corridor of the main university building—one of the students' most important social meeting points and, during protests, the favored site for mass processions with revolutionary songs. When a passing inspector reminded him that smoking was prohibited, Nosar' replied that nobody can forbid him a cigarette because students were the "masters" (khoziaeva) of the university. Nosar' then advised the inspector that should he wish to remain in the corridor and converse there with students, he must replace his own uniform with that of a student.

A second incident replayed this attempted inversion of authority, this time with the rector himself. Having been expelled in February and then, several weeks later, included in a general amnesty, Nosar' arrived in the university wearing regular clothing. Summoned to the inspectorate, he explained that his uniform had been confiscated and agreed to wear it as soon as it was returned. Upon discovering, however, that three (illegal) student pamphlets had been removed from the uniform's pocket, Nosar' rushed off to lodge a complaint with the rector, indignantly exclaiming, "You are not an inspectorate but a secret police." For his part, Sergeevich had just completed one lecture and was on his way to another, when Nosar' abruptly appeared. To Sergeevich's request to wait until after the lecture, Nosar' replied that he too must rush—to a student meeting—and could not afford the time. Nosar' then ordered Sergeevich's students, who were waiting in the auditorium, to disperse, so that he, Nosar', could speak with the rector. Under the threat of a student court, that is, the possible exclusion from the studenchestvo, all but one of the students complied.

For Nosar', student protest clearly entailed more than the discussion of tactics and platforms; it required the violation of convention and active rejection of established hierarchies. Sergeevich likewise experienced this behavior not as a simple personal affront, but as an assault on all relations of authority based on age, experience, and office. This case thus confirms the importance of "carnivalesque" inversions of authority, in both acts of protest and revolutionary movements, that has been described by numerous scholars in diverse fields.[3] In many respects, protest is inherently local and symbolic—it occurs on local territory (the university corridor, the marketplace, the factory floor) and depends on the association of local power structures with broader social, economic, and political structures. But the case of Georgii Nosar' is instructive for other reasons as well. From an unknown first-year student, he became not simply a student leader, but the consummate student radical—the single most "harmful element" in the student body in the eyes of Sergeevich. To maintain that Nosar' remade himself is not to imply deceit or hypocrisy, nor does likening him to an ideal-type belittle his individuality. His example instead offers a revealing glimpse into the phenomenon of student radicalism: Nosar' modeled himself after his conception of the student radical, which was fundamentally a style of behavior.

From the very beginning of his studies, Nosar' would have noticed a long-standing and oft-recounted characteristic of student life. Far from concealing their political convictions, radicals actually advertised them. In the 1870s, when the official student uniform was not required, clothing often took the form of a surrogate uniform. As one memoirist recalled: "Blue glasses, long hair, red shirts not tucked in but belted with sashes—those were surely medical students," then considered "the most advanced fighters for freedom." Radical women students likewise rejected fashion in favor of plain black dresses and short cropped hair.[4] Although the uniform again became obligatory for male students in the 1880s, dress continued to signify political attitude. With the term *belopodkladochniki* (literally, those with white-lining in their uniforms), radicals parodied their conservative comrades with a reference to their (supposed) wealth and concern for fashion. For their part, radicals favored a disheveled and "poor" appearance, often smoked, and typically sported long hair, beards, and glasses. They were known for the impromptu "audacious speech" *(derzkaia rech')* and for striking the tune of a radical song at student parties. From plebeian dress to disrespect for authority, students shared a set of commonly recognized acts that conferred a radical reputation and a moral authority within their community. During moments of conflict, such behavioral signs became more overt: in protest against the ending of the 1899 strike, Stepan Romanov attended classes at the Mining Institute wearing the traditional red shirt; he refused to change and was suspended.[5]

The theatrical quality of student radicalism traces its origins to the generation of students of the 1860s, a connection which Nosar' himself had made. When he refused to put out his cigarette at the request of the inspector, he stated that students were the "masters" of the university. In 1863, a well-known former student had coined this expression in his description of the new students of the 1860s, who, not unlike Nosar', were said to possess a self-confidence, an ability to make themselves known, a skeptical approach to established truths, and above all else, a lack of inborn respect for their elders. Musing over his recent experiences in St. Petersburg University, the radical publicist Dmitrii Pisarev recalled:

Already in 1858 and 1859 students entering the university no longer resembled us, students in their third or fourth year. When we entered the university, we were timid, inclined to veneration, disposed to look upon the words and lectures of professors as spiritual nourishment and as manna from heaven. New students, to the contrary, were bold and familiar, and very quickly became independent, such that in about two months, they found themselves the masters of the university; in the student discussion circles, they themselves raised the important questions and serious debates. They organized concerts to aid poor students, they invited professors to give public lectures for the same charitable cause, they built student libraries. . . .[6]

Although it is likely that Nosar' was familiar with the writings of Pisarev,[7] whether in fact he had read this particular work is of minimal importance, because these "new students" helped to define an era in Russian history that fundamentally shaped the character and values of student radicalism at the turn of the twentieth century.

THE BIRTH OF STUDENT RADICALISM

The death of Nikolai I and the ascension of Aleksandr II to the throne in 1855 ushered in a decade of transformation in all spheres of life. Along with the abolition of serfdom in 1861, the Great Reforms enacted fundamental changes in the legal, administrative, and social structure of the Russian empire. The changes in Russian society and culture were equally revolutionary. With the expansion of the universities, the rapid growth of newspapers and journals, and the organization of public lectures and professional societies, the 1860s heralded the emergence of a public sphere in which new social and professional groups advanced their right to independent opinion. From the "woman question" to the "worker question," no issue was off limits.[8] Essential to this new public was also a new type of person, heralded, mythologized, and ultimately exemplified by a group of young radical critics led by Pisarev, Nikolai Dobroliubov, and Nikolai Chernyshevskii.[9]

The "new person" was born on the boundary between literature and life, and the mediator was the literary critic. In 1860, Dobroliubov proclaimed that a new social type was about to appear in Russia, a type which had (unknown to the author) found shape in the character of a Bulgarian revolutionary in Ivan Turgenev's novel *On the Eve*.[10] Two years later, Turgenev immortalized the generational conflict between the "fathers" of the 1840s and the "children" of the 1860s in *Fathers and Children*. The novel provoked an extraordinary outcry over the authenticity of its hero, Bazarov, as a representation of the (real) new man. The son of a retired army doctor and a student of the natural sciences and medicine, Bazarov became famous for his rude manners, rejection of social convention, and passion for science over poetry—symbolized by his keen interest in dissecting frogs, which he considered the first step toward a scientific understanding of man. Critics on the right and the left judged the novel as if it were a mirror of life and its main character a contemporary social type.[11] While many conservatives regarded Bazarov as an accurate depiction of the younger generation and many radicals rejected him as a mere caricature, Pisarev not only recognized himself and his generation in Bazarov but proceeded to fill in the details of his "real" life and upbringing. For the "nihilist" children, as they were called after Turgenev's term, the fathers represented a generation of superfluous men, eloquent in their condemnation of the old order, but inadequate to the task of changing it. The new era required bold and rude new people—the products and agents of social transformation.[12]

At this time, while in prison, Chernyshevskii wrote a positive portrayal of the new generation, *What Is to Be Done? Tales about the New People,* that for decades was to be the bible for radical youth.[13] The novel recounts the life of Vera Pavlovna from her "imprisonment" in the home of her greedy and manipulative mother and "liberation" through a fictitious marriage with a poor young medical student of the "new" persuasion. It concludes with a veiled reference to revolution and a depiction of the new utopian society. The story of Vera Pavlovna was an allegory of revolution, and its power lay in its representation of revolution on the level of everyday life—from the "rational" living and sexual arrangements of the protagonists to the organization of cooperatives. The action was always local and particular, its implications utopian and universal. In the character of Rakhmetov, Chernyshevskii further invented the influential image of the ascetic professional revolutionary, willing to sleep, literally, on a bed of nails in order to discipline himself for the revolutionary struggle.

The polemics over the "new people," and especially the model advanced by Chernyshevskii, shaped the conventions of conduct and belief of Russian youth. But the influence was not undirectional, not simply from literature into life. The polemics coincided with the emergence of a new group into Russian society, the nonnoble *raznochinnaia* intelligentsia, literally "people of various ranks"; ostensibly, this group was the diametric opposite of the "gentry" intelligentsia of the 1840s, the generation of the "fathers."[14] Following a trickle of individuals in the 1840s, the first generation of nonnobles entered the universities, the professions, and public life during the 1850s and 1860s. Yet despite its name and reputation, the *raznochinnaia* intelligentsia was less a socioeconomic group than a cultural category defined by behavior, ideology, and an unequivocal rejection of the beliefs, traditions, and ideals of the past. Though aristocratic social graces had naturally been lacking in such early representatives of the *raznochintsy* as Belinskii and Chernyshevskii, the new people—no matter their true social origins—cultivated awkward manners and a plain style of dress as matters of principle. As rationalists and positivists, they espoused the superiority of science and labor over poetry and sentiment. They further attempted to enact their rational and socialist principles in all spheres of life. The complex interplay of the literary model and the historical embodiment forged an enduring and influential myth concerning the plebeian origins and democratic aspirations of the *raznochinnaia* intelligentsia. The linkage between a social identity and a pattern of belief and behavior (in which the latter certified the former) became a central motif of radical culture.

Considering the privileged roles of youth and scientific knowledge in the new model, it is hardly surprising to find a large number of students and former students in accounts of the new generation. The fictional Bazarov had been a student of medicine and the natural sciences in St. Petersburg. Vera Pavlovna ultimately chooses to study medicine as the best path for her personal development. The connection was more than incidental. Thick journals, filled with literary and critical polemics, provided one arena for the creation and transmission of images of the "new person." A second arena appeared in the university and the emerging student subcultures.

As in other parts of Russian society, the 1860s heralded the birth of a new era in higher education.[15] Upon his succession, Aleksandr II lifted many of the harsh restrictions placed on the universities by his predecessor. With the obligatory uniforms and military discipline abolished outright, curricular reforms heralded a new freedom in the thematic content and reading lists of academic courses. In addition to reforms from above, this period witnessed the birth of the student subcultures, as urban centers were flooded by thousands of youth, willing—even eager—to live in abject poverty in order to receive an education. These were the bold "new students" heralded by Pisarev. During public lectures and discussion circles, students passionately debated the anticipated abolition of serfdom and the broader transformation of Russian society. Even before the publication of *What Is to Be Done?*, they had organized an informal infrastructure of libraries, banks, cooperatives, courts of honor, and labor bureaus. Just as the government looked with some alarm at this thriving and independent community, students were equally quick to defend their newly won freedoms and institutions. Already in 1857, according to contemporary observers, a conflict between students and police revealed a "feeling of unity" and corporate spirit.[16] By 1861, stricter restrictions on admission and the prohibition of student organizations resulted in the first student demonstration ever held in St. Petersburg, which led in turn to the two-year closure of the university.[17]

The development of a corporate spirit and the consequent conflicts with the state were important factors in the chronic student protests over subsequent decades. Of equal importance was the students' new public image. The political engagement of students outside the university, which would become a central tenet of student radicalism by the 1870s, originated in the heady atmosphere of the early 1860s. Radical publicists described the special duty and mission of the student as such to spread the new word of liberty. Students were called upon to extend their freedoms into society, to repay the privilege of learning by serving the people, and to become, in Nikolai Ogarev's phrase, "apostles of knowledge."[18] The model was provided by the 1861 pamphlet, "To the Young Generation." "Only in you do we see people able to sacrifice personal interests for the good of the country," its then-anonymous authors, Nikolai Shelgunov and Mikhail Mikhailov, proclaimed. "We turn to you because we consider you to be the people most capable of saving Russia; you are her real strength; you are the guides of the people; you must explain to the people all of the evil done to them by imperial power." [19] During the next two decades, the universities produced a significant percentage of Russia's revolutionaries. According to prosecution records from the 1860s and 1870s, students were involved in more than one-half of all political offenses, despite their miniscule number in the population as a whole.[20]

The displacement of the gentry-student of the first half of the century by the *raznochinets* of the 1860s became the fundamental tenet of a cultural mythology of student radicalism. With the passage of time, the period between 1855 and 1861 came to be represented as an epic past, when the university had been democratized and transformed by the new *raznochintsy* students. Despite the suppression of legal student organization under the 1863 University Charter, the ethos of the new student continued to reveal itself in distinctive styles of dress and behavior, the flourishing underground of student organizations, and periodic "disorders." The relationship between politics and social identity was thus tautological. Notwithstanding the actual social composition of the student body (which remained dominated by the sons of gentry and civil servants through the end of the century), protest and radical behavior "proved" the existence of the new kind of student in a way statistics could never quite achieve. The poor student became a synonym for the rebel. By the twentieth century, these categories had shaped a dominant social explanation of student radicalism in which this type of poor student was associated with the birth of student politics, a movement to democratize education, and the development of radical movements in general.[21]

THE *STUDENCHESTVO*

Student radicalism developed through a complex interplay of literature and life that was itself mythologized over subsequent decades. Neither its character nor its persistence through succeeding generations of students can be explained, however, without examining the phenomenon of *studenchestvo*. During the late 1860s and especially the 1870s, *studenchestvo* acquired a normative meaning denoting the student corporation organized by study circles, mutual-aid societies, and other underground institutions. This *studenchestvo* evolved a unique and plastic ethos, which fused ideals of fraternity and solidarity with norms of ethics and behavior. While students were loosely united around such political principles as democracy, socialism (in its broadest sense), and women's rights, the ethos rather than a specific ideological platform united them into a group. For students arriving from the provinces, *studenchestvo* became a surrogate family, and upon joining, they claimed to share common values and endeavors which were embodied in the supra-individual collective.

Fundamental to these values and endeavors was a distinctive notion of education that emerged during the 1860s and 1870s and became the defining characteristic of the student ethos over subsequent decades. An offshoot of the exemplar of the "new person," this notion posited an ideal of "unified" and ethical knowledge as the basis of individual identity *(lichnost')*. One of its key sources was Pisarev's theory of "general education," which he advanced in an 1863 semiautobiographical article. Pisarev argued that the current system of secondary education fragments the personality due to its stress on rote memorization and classical languages. "The various subjects do not connect in a general cycle of knowledge," he stressed, they "do not support each other, but stand side by side, trying to crowd each other out." At St. Petersburg University, he had found the system in duplicate, a problem that he illustrated with an anecdote. Having decided to specialize in history, he asked a professor for advice regarding a program of study and was directed to begin by reading a multivolume German encyclopedia. This effort would have been wasted in his opinion, not only because it would have taken him ten years to read it, but because he lacked a general framework with which to order and understand the collected facts. Pisarev argued that students must first develop a unified, comprehensive, and scientific understanding of the world into which facts could then be integrated. On this basis, he advocated that education be based on the principles of observation, experiment, and universal regularity, that is, on the natural sciences. Once students had cultivated their new rational and materialist world view, they could also begin to replicate it into their social environment. Pisarev believed this process to be underway: having understood the primacy of the dissected frog, to take Turgenev's image, the "new students" of 1858 and 1859 had already thronged into the faculty of natural sciences.[22]

At the end of the 1860s, the populist theorist Petr Lavrov also depicted education as central to change but added an ethical and social component. The development and conscious activity of the "critically thinking individual," he argued, formed the basis of historical progress, because this individual would be able to uncover and ultimately to control the laws of human society and history. Lavrov's vision was inherently ethical. Because the dignity of the individual could exist only alongside the dignity of all, he believed, the individual would work to incorporate the principles of truth and justice into social institutions as well. The privilege of consciousness (i.e., education) thus included a moral debt, which could be repaid only in service to the people. In this manner, knowledge would transform reality.[23] Like Pisarev and Chernyshevskii, Lavrov placed the transformation of the individual at the heart of social change. Only a new kind of person would have the mental and moral capacity to make the future.

During the 1870s, these ideas of "education" shaped the primary institutions of *studenchestvo*—the *kruzhok,* the *zemliachestvo,* and the *skhodka*—which each

spread through the capital and provincial cities and thrived well into the twentieth century. In the *kruzhok,* or study circle, students discussed radical literature
and new ideas as a supplement to official university readings. This democratic
form of collective self-education, many argued, fostered not only independent
thought but also an ethos of fraternity and solidarity. The *zemliachestva* were
informal regional organizations that provided ready-made networks linking students from a single region with other students in the city and with both graduates and gymnasium students back home. From helping newcomers get oriented
to organizing charitable benefits and the occasional *kruzhok,* they provided an
important practical resource for members. Under the principles of mutual-aid
and self-education, they likewise aspired to shape collectivist and civic values.
The *skhodka* was students' impromptu representative body, modeled, they
claimed, on the assembly of the peasant commune. On matters of common concern and collective action, it was the final source of authority and judgment for
all students. It was, in theory, the most pure expression of democratic community and collective responsibility, indeed, the "general will" of *studenchestvo.*
Taken together, this characteristic subculture shaped the experiences and attitudes of successive generations of students, lending continuity and form to the
student ethos.[24]

The purpose of education embedded in student institutions was not the accumulation of factual knowledge and skills, but the formation of ethical and intellectual character *(vospitanie),* or, in other words, the development of a comprehensive world view from which all principles and actions should be derived. This
notion was revolutionary and dialectical: education was to produce both personal and political transformation by fostering the development of a rational
world view, a sense of solidarity, a social conscience, and a moral duty of practical application. That is, education would produce a new person, capable of enacting broad social and political change.

During the populist movements of the 1870s, in which they took a leading
role, students passionately debated the goal of their education and began to explore the problem of how individual transformation would lead to social revolution. The central debate revolved around the platforms of Lavrov, who advocated
a gradualist path of cultural development, and of the famous anarchist Mikhail
Bakunin, who called upon students to leave the university and go to the people.
One memoir recounts the two arguments:

> It is a debt of honor before the people we want to serve that we receive a
> solid, scientific, well-rounded, and serious education; only then can we
> assume with a clear conscience the spiritual leadership of the revolution.

> "Continue to study!" others jeered. [That means] to remove yourself from
> the revolutionary cause. Your aspiration for a "solid, well-rounded educa-
> tion" is only a self-deception. In our eyes, you are only careerists. It is not

in the university or from books but in immediate interaction with the people and the workers where you can receive the knowledge useful to the revolutionary cause.[25]

This controversy over tactics contained different interpretations of education. In the first case, education meant the creation of an educated individual, who would dedicate himself to social progress as a doctor, scientist, or teacher. The second view rejected book learning in favor of a revolutionary fusion with the people and sometimes a life devoted to labor. The goal of education was viewed as the creation of revolutionaries.

This conflict would prove enduring and flexible. It characterized the expectations of gymnasium students—some of whom dreamed of science and others of politics—and colored the recollections of memoirists. The historian and liberal politician Pavel Miliukov thus remembered his feelings upon enrolling in Moscow University in 1878: "I entered as if it were a 'temple.' "[26] The revolutionary activist N. V. Vasil'ev recalled a different mood as a gymnasium student: "To become a real student, that is, a fighter for freedom and truth, this is my passionate dream." [27] The contrasting tones reflect ideological beliefs, molded by time and memory: Miliukov embodied the moderate aspiration for scientific study, and Vasil'ev, the radical passion for the student corporation. The opposition of scholarship and politics would characterize memories, memoirs, and polemics well into the twentieth century, as students were repeatedly accused of renouncing academic studies in favor of political activism. "Political interests [and] extra-university life, rather than the interests of education or scholarship, linked students together," one such memoir characteristically recalled.[28] This politicized and purely rhetorical conflict obscured the principle common to both groups: science and self-education should lead to the formation of a new person.

The failure of the populist movement to ignite a mass uprising ushered in an era of terrorism and "heroic deeds" that culminated in the 1881 assassination of Aleksandr II. During the next decade, which was marked by political repression and the disintegration of populism, the ideology of "small deeds"—of education in preparation for social service and of evolutionary rather than revolutionary change—dominated the social mood. The University Statute of 1884 extended political reaction throughout the academic world by curtailing the rights of the professoriate, instituting an inspectorate of students, and requiring state examinations for all graduates. Although the statute termed students "individual visitors" (otdel'nye posetiteli) to the university (again denying them corporate recognition and the right to organize), the reinstituted student uniform seemed to indicate the opposite, indeed to be a "spaika" between students, that is a connection, a symbol of solidarity and cohesion.[29]

Memoirs of student life during the 1880s depict the studenchestvo as the upholder and heir of the revolutionary tradition, the crucial link between the more heroic generations of the 1860–1870s and the 1890s. They thus contrast the darkness of political and social life in general to the light still shining in the university: "[P]eople strove [to prevent] the spark from being extinguished, [the spark] that could only burn again in another time, a more favorable epoch." This spark took several forms, including study circles and the occasional protest. In St. Petersburg, the Student Scientific-Literary Society, which had been founded in the early 1880s "to struggle with sedition by [exercising a] scientific-literary influence on students," became by the mid-1880s the meeting point for an entire generation of political and intellectual luminaries, until it was closed down in 1887. Such circles nurtured a new generation on a shared intellectual heritage.[30]

Protests demonstrated a different kind of connection to the already legendary exploits of populism. In the decade after 1881, the memorials and funerals of well-known radicals allowed students to mourn individual deaths while celebrating the continuity of generations in the ongoing struggle for liberation. In the words of one participant, the decision to mark the twenty-fifth anniversary of Dobroliubov's death in 1886 was motivated by the need "to remind Russian society of the radiant image of the great publicist, [who had bequeathed] to us the idea of struggle for the freedom and happiness of the people."[31] According to another memoirist, the 1891 funeral of Shelgunov prompted the spontaneous desire "to affirm that we had not reconciled ourselves to the horrors of lawlessness, in which reaction endeavored to confine the Russian citizen." After the speeches, students toured the cemetery, pausing at the graves of Dobroliubov and other writers. "We youth felt wonderful thanks to the consciousness that we had openly showed the government how the spirit of freedom had not been tamed."[32] Although memoirists acknowledged that many students were passive and apolitical, they depict the study circles and protests of the 1880s as the "living" bonds uniting generations of students and radicals. In their view, the *studenchestvo*, if not all students, had carried the torch.

RADICALISM AS *BILDUNGSROMAN*

Not only for students did the 1890s seem to be an era of infinite possibility and mass movements. In 1891–1892, educated society mobilized to provide famine relief for millions of starving peasants along the Volga and in other regions. Rapid industrialization brought thousands of peasants into cities, transformed the urban landscape, and, by the second half of the decade, forged the conditions for a labor movement. While populists feared the rise of capitalism, Marxists glorified the new city, its factories, and its workers, and in their famous polemics, the Marxists often won the upper hand. Just as the utopian image of the enduring peasant commune was slowly displaced by the dynamism of modernization, the one-time beacon of knowledge and progress—positivism and the natural sciences—was superseded by political economy, history, and social science. The

poetry and art of the modern also began to challenge the literary canons established during the 1860s.

In this self-conscious leap into modernity, a new generation came of age in
the university. During the 1890s, memoirists tell us, the *studenchestvo* experienced
unprecedented self-organization and a reinvigorated sense of community. Unlike
earlier generations of student radicals, this one perceived the ethical *studenchestvo* as a category denoting not just the progressive few but potentially the entire
aggregate of students. The experiences of this generation read as a story of political education leading to the formation of both individual and group consciousness, the evidence of which would be the 1899 student strike. Generational thinking is hardly new in Russian cultural history—witness the romantic fathers of
the 1840s and the materialist sons of the 1860s, the heroic feats of the 1870s and
the small deeds of the 1880s—and such labels inevitably contain both elements
of insight and oversimplification. The generation of the 1890s is no exception.
Yet the historian of this era faces particular difficulties, because most memoirs
are indelibly stamped by the teleology of revolutionary history as reflected in its
larger outcomes of 1905 or 1917. The story of growing up in the revolutionary
era is often difficult to distinguish from the story of the revolution itself; both
rely on a pedagogical metaphor of consciousness, the one for the individual and
the other for the collective. The self-representations of this generation nevertheless are crucial to an understanding of student radicalism at the turn of the
century. Though it is impossible to uncover the reality of generational experience, narrative structures within autobiographical writings point both to common motifs of shared experience and to a particular understanding of the collective called *studenchestvo*. Let us take an example.

Nikolai Iordanskii was a student at St. Petersburg University during the 1890s
and a leader of the 1899 strike. In 1907, he published a memoir about the 1899
student movement, entitled "The Mission of P. S. Vannovskii." The title refers to
a little-known commission formed by the tsar in 1899 and headed by Petr Vannovskii, Minister of War under Aleksandr III, to investigate the causes of the
protests. In his introduction, Iordanskii asks that this commission be given "a
little corner in history" because it "[awakened] the political consciousness of
Russian democracy" and "helped democratic souls tear themselves free from the
psychological umbilical cord binding them to the old order." As the commission
was short-lived and its recommendations disregarded, these claims seem pecu-
liarly excessive. In his conclusion, Iordanskii states further that the failure of the
commission discredited the paternalism (*serdechnoe popechenie*) of Vannovskii,
and "after minor vacillation, the *studenchestvo* turned to the left and quickly
went the path of revolution." From the introductory to the concluding para-
graphs, Iordanskii thus proceeds from a symbolic birth (cutting the umbilical
cord) to the rejection of paternalism and achievement of revolutionary consciousness (adulthood?); in the process he equates *studenchestvo* with "Russian

democracy," and the student strike of 1899 with the Revolution of 1905. Despite its title, Iordanskii's article does not focus on the Vannovskii commission, which figures only in some sections, but rather chronicles the development of group consciousness among students. It recounts a process of maturation beginning with the arrival of the naive gymnasium student in the city and proceeding to his education into a radical, all told from the point of view of "we"—the *studenchestvo* of the 1890s.[33]

The contemporary generation of students, Iordanskii begins, stumbled into higher educational institutions after enduring the classical gymnasium during its most "accursed period," 1885 to 1895, when "a holy war" was waged against "the red phantom, or more accurately, the phantom of the red phantom." The rote memorization, harsh discipline, and strict supervision enforced in the secondary school had long been criticized in Russian society, and Iordanskii's critique presents nothing new. More important for his purposes was the intellectual isolation of youth in the provinces. With their reading strictly limited to approved works, students had to fall back on the inadequate libraries of their parents, an occasional journal, and the rare opportunity to join a shadowy study circle.[34] The pervasive "gloom" of provincial life prevented youth from becoming acquainted with the outside world, assuring that when "we came together in the university, we would be political infants, in the full meaning of the word."

This was Iordanskii's rhetorical point: real "learning" began with higher education. "Fortunately, we found ourselves in a good school," he continues. "This school was not, of course, the university as such, but life in a large industrial city, which had just then begun to awaken itself from the reactionary hibernation. The profound currents in the depths were felt first by students before [reaching] the heights of bourgeois democracy." Iordanskii lightly dismisses the academic learning of the university in favor of the school of life, which he equates with the city but by which he really means the student subcultures. He cites the Marxist-populist debates, a central site for which were student parties, a series of minor conflicts over student rights in the university, and labor strikes in St. Petersburg that students discussed among themselves. Over a few years in this "school," according to Iordanskii, the *studenchestvo* matured and grew, such that by 1899, the "student mass" had experienced too much "to preserve its primordial innocence." [35]

According to Iordanskii, the most important collective experience for Petersburg students occurred in 1897, when the suicide in prison of Mariia Vetrova, a woman student and populist activist, triggered a demonstration at the Kazan Cathedral in the center of the city. News of her self-immolation led student radicals to decide "unanimously" on a demonstration; most students, however, hoped to arrange a memorial service at the Kazan Cathedral and did not consider their actions to constitute a demonstration—even when church officials refused to conduct the service and police raided the gathering, citing the 1,200 students who had failed to get away. Iordanskii notes the strange punishment for demonstrators: "a three-day incarceration in the *Kresty* [a notorious prison], which undoubtedly played a nice role in the development of the political consciousness of *studenchestvo*." [36]

After his brief survey of the generational experience of the 1890s, Iordanskii turns to student organization, which, he stresses, was also expanding at this time. In his view, the various "levels" and "types" of organization reflected the political "age" of members. At the lowest end was the *zemliachestvo*, an inferior "zoological" grouping, one whose only value was in mutual-aid and a modicum of conspiratorial training. Because it united students by the principle of chance (that is, by regional origin) it was a lesser, more "spontaneous" group than a *kruzhok*. The latter represented a higher form in Iordanskii's hierarchy, because it organized students according to their ideological convictions rather than by the geographical accident of birth and provided the intellectual forum necessary for further self-development. An organization unique to St. Petersburg, the *Kassa vzaimopomoshchi*, stood at the pinnacle of Iordanskii's ladder of consciousness. Though in its origins a mutual-aid society espousing the conventional principles of self-help and self-education, the *Kassa* had evolved a conspiratorial structure in which its 300–400 members were distributed among numerous circles that elected delegates to a representative assembly. In 1898, the assembly also began to elect a five-member board. Students joined the *Kassa* upon their admission to one of its circles. In Iordanskii's eyes, the *Kassa* constituted the most advanced and organized part of the *studenchestvo* and was, therefore, its central political and ideological force. Organization was thus a metaphor of maturation and politicization for Iordanskii, the path to consciousness from the "masses" to the leaders:

> Each year, youth joining [a *zemliachestvo*] distinguished themselves by their complete political freshness, and only by the path of more or less complex experiences could they approach the point, beyond which stood the most inexperienced members of the *Kassa*. Therefore, the *zemliachestvo* always remained one step behind the *Kassa*. New trends were first mastered in the *Kassa*, and from there disseminated among the remaining students.[37]

Having divided *studenchestvo* into two parts according to relative consciousness and organization, and having identified himself with the advanced group, Iordanskii addresses the question of student politics. Paradoxically, he suggests that both groups had arrived at a dead end. Under the influence of Marxism (and particularly economism), the *Kassa* largely dismissed student protest as inconsequential to the real struggle, which was to be led by the proletariat. While some members ventured into the working class suburbs to lead workers' circles,[38] the *Kassa* denounced student "disorders" as parochial and insignificant. In contrast, students in their so-called *zemliachestvo* stage believed that the *studenches-tvo* must protest injustice within the university as both a defense of human dignity and a means to inculcate civic values. Yet, as Iordanskii points out, almost every year, students protested aspects of the university regime—its arbitrary rules and prohibitions on student organization—and demanded changes in the reactionary 1884 University Statute, to no avail. The statute was never amended, nor did the university regime change.[39]

Rejecting both the preoccupation of the *Kassa* with the proletariat and the limited nature of student protests, Iordanskii resolves this stalemate dialectically. On the one hand, the failure of protests to compel reform revealed the complicity of the political regime as a whole and had a pedagogical-politicizing function for the "student-masses." On the other hand, the *Kassa* was developing the ideological constructs with which to direct a mass movement. The 1899 strike marks the first synthesis and is an analogy for the liberation movement as a whole. This underlying structure allowed Iordanskii to make the grandiose claims about Russian democracy and *studenchestvo* in his introductory remarks. By defining education as the striving for and achievement of consciousness, and then locating consciousness in organization, Iordanskii associates individual with collective experience, and the organization of the *studenchestvo* with the growth of its collective consciousness. The spontaneous protests of the student-masses become organized and directed, student protest becomes social protest, and the student strike of 1899, which did in fact mark the entrance of educated society into the political struggles of the twentieth century, becomes a symbolic precursor of the 1905 Revolution.

This account could only have been written shortly after 1905, for it narrates a coherent, teleological, and optimistic story of revolution, a fact that Iordanskii frankly acknowledges. In a section about the different levels of political consciousness among students, he self-consciously notes:

> The schematic nature of this sermon *[propoved']* is now evident to everyone. One can even add a theoretical question mark regarding the relative level of development of class contradictions within the *studenchestvo,* formerly, by and large, a petty-bourgeois mass. But then [in the 1890s] this blueprint *[skhema]* did not seem artificial and dry. To the contrary, it inspired the heart.[40]

This quotation is extremely revealing. With the word *propoved',* Iordanskii highlights the sermonizing quality of his article, and, reinforced by the adjectives "artificial" and "dry," he demonstrates his awareness that his readers in 1907 (not to exclude later historians) easily recognized the "schematic" story of consciousness he retold. Yet Iordanskii underlines something else altogether: in the 1890s, this blueprint had inspired the heart. Though his memoir clearly enjoys the benefits of hindsight, he claims to "remember" the pattern itself.

This contradiction can be resolved if this article is treated as autobiography. Although Iordanskii's individual experience is seemingly absent, dissolved into the various collectives of conscious students, *studenchestvo,* and democratic forces, the hero of the story is the narrator—Iordanskii's mature authorial voice. From the darkness of the gymnasium to the light of the university, from self-education to politicization, Iordanskii had recounted his own "rise to consciousness" as a generational and historical phenomenon. The unfolding revolution serves as an allegory for his own personal and political development. In its general outlines, Iordanskii's story thus can be interpreted as a kind of *Bildungsroman,* in which the emergence of the heroes (Iordanskii and *studenchestvo*) occurs within the context of historical progress. While the story as a cohesive whole dates to the period after 1905, many of its motifs and cognitive structures can be traced back to the 1890s, explaining the paradox of his memory.

As massive changes transformed urban centers across Russia during the 1890s, Marxism provided a dynamic framework for understanding personal experience and social change alike. As Russian Marxists struggled to understand (and direct) the forces of change, they too developed strategies (and narratives) not unlike those recounted by Iordanskii. In the influential pamphlet "On Agitation," for example, Iu. O. Martov, the Marxist leader (and student at St. Petersburg University in the early 1890s) among others, argued that the failure of the day-to-day protests of workers on local issues, combined with the agitation of revolutionaries, would lead them to generalize their situation in social and political terms, at which point a Social Democratic movement would emerge. The parallel with student politics is striking, and it is not the only one. In the factional disputes between Bolsheviks and Mensheviks, the seemingly mundane question of organization acquired critical ideological significance and likewise came to be almost synonymous with "consciousness." [41]

Yet, while a few students were Marxists and many Marxists had once been students, most students in the 1890s did not commit themselves to an ideology or party. They did, however, listen to the debates and live in a rapidly changing world. The broader influence of Marxism lay in its dynamic conception of individual, collective, and historical development, its faith in the unity of all life and experience, and its optimistic teleology. This was not just the theoretical Marxism of objective historical forces, but a Marxism that seemed to explain the transformative dynamism of Russia in the 1890s. As Marshall Berman has pointed out, Marxism was an ideology that celebrated the great nineteenth-century principle of progress; it was a panegyric to the birth and formation of modernity.[42] As a story of humanity's own maturation, its plot is also a *Bildungsroman* of the dialectical unfolding of consciousness and revolution.

Iordanskii's generation of students had a second inspiration. Along with the popularization of Marxist ideas appeared a renewed interest in the role of the individual in history, and in part, the heroic individual heralded by Nietzsche.

Throughout the 1890s, publicists and writers debated the concept of the *Übermensch;* the populist theorist Nikolai Mikhailovskii, for example, praised Nietzsche's elevated concept of the individual but sought to combine it with ideals of the social good.[43] The most influential advocate of a Nietzschean individual was the writer Maksim Gorkii. With his glorification of individual rebellion in his early works, Gorkii presented the "warrior-hero" as the new "new person" of the 1890s. Stressing such character traits as strength, will, daring, and courage, Gorkii asserted that the individual must "strive" toward a goal to give purpose to life. Gorkii's fictional characters and, more important, the writer himself were idealized by many Russian youth as the embodiment of the new ideal.[44] This hero also proved compatible with the story of "formation" embodied in the principle of consciousness. In Gorkii's 1906 novel *Mother,* the strands of heroic individualism and political education unite in what would become the prerevolutionary prototype of the socialist realist novel.[45] But like Iordanskii's memoir, *Mother* would suffer from superficial characters rising to consciousness and enacting revolutionary teleology. After 1905, the literary model also became drier, more artificial.

In the 1890s, the quest for self-education, long integral to student culture, overlapped with the drama of modernity. As students sought to interpret their individual and generational experiences, a narrative understanding of individual and historical development joined with the traditional conception of *studenchestvo* as the torchbearer of revolutionary activism, and the master-plot of "consciousness" began to form. Though the story of consciousness as a cohesive and teleological unit emerged after 1905 and evolved over the decades thereafter, its scattered motifs each have a history in radical culture. In his memoir, Iordanskii simplified, homogenized, and some would say even falsified the experiences of his generation into a typical "student" autobiography, but he did so with reason. For him the story of consciousness was the real drama, for it was both his own story and the story of the Russian revolution.

STUDENTS' STORIES

Autobiographical writings depicting the student generation of 1899 duplicate many of the motifs and structures found in Iordanskii's memoir. Predictably, those written after 1917 tend to be the most formulaic, and those before 1905 the least. The parallels suggest that there were indeed certain "typical" experiences, such as the highly negative recollection of the gymnasium, that students either shared or believed they shared. They suggest in addition that a particular genre of memoir, which can be called a "student memoir," evolved out of such precursors as Pisarev's writings and provided potential memoirists with expressive forms and structures, including the age-old contrast between "darkness" and "light." An example is the 1924 memoirs of Mikhail Mogilianskii, a contemporary of Iordanskii at St. Petersburg University. By focusing more closely on his own experiences, Mogilianskii fleshes out some details of student life and occasionally conflicts with the portrait painted by Iordanskii. However, the memoir shares the teleological biographical structure, except that, in his case, the narrative of formation is predetermined and predictably culminates in his graduation into a full-fledged revolutionary.[46]

As a gymnasium student, Mogilianskii had more exposure to radical ideas than the typical student described by Iordanskii. While participating in a circle dedicated to "moral-social questions," he recalls reading Dobroliubov, Pisarev, and Lasalle. Despite this difference, he too placed all his hopes on the university and, in 1892, entered the juridical faculty. Like Pisarev, he was soon disappointed with the official world of the university. "The lectures of Professor [A. A.] Isaev (political economy) and the seminars of [M. I.] Sveshnikov provided a few elements for the future answer to the question about revolutionary method," he noted; "other courses widened [my] intellectual horizons but were dryly academic, somehow irrelevant to the moral and social questions then troubling youth." By the end of his first year, Mogilianskii recalls, he had understood that most lectures were unnecessary and had moved into the next phase, that of self-education and political activism. He joined the *Kassa vzaimopomoshchi*, where he found "a consonant atmosphere." As Mogilianskii describes various small protests, his narrative becomes increasingly formulaic. Pointing out that the *studenchestvo* was not yet ripe for protest, he separates himself and his "conscious" comrades in the *Kassa* from the "mass" of other students (and is more condescending toward them than Iordanskii). Soon his character receives its final form: "Marxism answered the search for a practical program of action, it taught the mind to find [its] bearings in the laws of historical necessity." The subsequent recitation of student protests and his role in them shows Mogilianskii struggling to impart his (conscious) vision to a "politically innocent" mass.[47]

Arrest constituted the culminating stage of personal development for the young radical. Even overplaying the symbolism, Mogilianskii recalls how imprisonment finally allowed him to read Marx's *Das Kapital* (although release prevented him from finishing the third volume). Prison thus confirmed his revolutionary identity.

> I think that the main reason was the spiritual equilibrium and feeling of moral satisfaction. It is funny to say, but I felt myself to be a free man [because] I had said my word, I had expressed the next task of the New Russia. . . . We [revolutionaries] knew, that many comrades. . . were losing their [political innocence] and following us. The old [assumptions] were dressing themselves in new flesh, warming themselves with new blood. . . . As I entered conscious life, the certitude became firm, that our generation would see the fall of autocracy.[48]

Mogilianskii creates a romantic view of the student turned revolutionary. Like Iordanskii, he relies upon the experience of student protest to portray the parallel achievement of individual and generational consciousness. By using similar biological metaphors and likening the rise of consciousness to maturation into adulthood, he too unites biographical into historical time. By the 1950s, the economist Stanislav Strumilin found the paradigm so well established that he could describe revolutionary history and his own biography by evoking the legendary ordeals of the *bogatyr'*, the mythical Russian knight. Expelled from the Electrotechnical Institute in 1899, he "entered upon the path of *long wanderings and ordeals* altogether typical for the Russian revolutionary intelligentsia. The soldier's barracks, prisons, and exile were, of course, practically unavoidable interim stages" (italics added).[49]

In three humorous and ironic autobiographical fragments from the 1920s, the well-known writer Evgenii Zamiatin plays with the story line, which Mogilianskii romanticized and Strumilin cast in such epic dimensions. He instead paints an impressionistic landscape of his student years at the St. Petersburg Polytechnic Institute at the turn of the century that nonetheless culminates with the standard ending:

> All that time seems like a whirlwind today; demonstrations on Nevskii Prospect, cossacks, student and workers' circles, love, huge mass meetings at the universities and the institutes. I was a Bolshevik then (today I am not) and was active in the Vyborg district. At one time my room was a clandestine printing shop. I fought the Kadets in the Student Council of Class Representatives. The outcome of all this was, of course, a solitary cell in the prison on Shpalernaya.[50]

Though Zamiatin does not give his character its "final" shape or construct a heroic past, many of the details he recalls conform to the standard formula. Like other memoirists, Zamiatin stressed his strongly negative memories of the gymnasium, "school, as gray as the cloth of our uniforms," and recounted the following anecdote. On his last day there, the school inspector showed him a brochure inscribed by Pavel Shchegolev, then a student leader and later an important historian and publicist, "To my alma mater, about which I can remember nothing good." "Fine isn't it?" The inspector warned Zamiatin. "He also finished with a gold medal, and what does he write? Of course he ended up in prison. My advice to you is: Don't write. Don't follow this path." Zamiatin notes that the admonition had no effect: his gold medal soon found its fate in a St. Petersburg pawnshop, and he landed in prison.[51] Zamiatin combined motifs of exhilarating chaos and predictable outcomes into an amusing and fresh picture of student life.

The 1922 memoirs of Viktor Chernov, a student at Moscow University in the 1890s and later a leader of the Socialist Revolutionaries, confirm the pattern in

Moscow. Although he was hardly an innocent provincial youth upon enrolling—he had already participated in study circles—he recalls his excitement at his first lecture and the inevitable disappointment. The good professors had proven the exception rather than the rule. "No, once again it was necessary to search for science outside the walls of the university," Chernov writes, and devotes the bulk of his subsequent recollections to the underground life of student radicals. In this respect as well, his portrait of Moscow University in the 1890s provides important parallels to the situation in St. Petersburg. He too depicts students as divided into leaders and masses, he too discusses the problems posed by the "spontaneous disorders" and the lack of interest of Marxist students in student politics altogether. Not unexpectedly, organization proved to be the critical political issue in Moscow.[52]

Unlike Petersburg, where the *Kassa* occupied the pinnacle in the student underground, Moscow students—with Chernov at the forefront—were organizing a United Council of delegates from ultimately dozens of *zemliachestva*.[53] The principles of the United Council and the *Kassa* were similar, for both provided leadership for the student body and a home for the student radical. Thus, it was in the United Council where Chernov found "what he needed": "a group of the most active and intellectually alive students from all the provinces"—his "we," so to speak. And it was the council that tried to teach the masses to take their protests outside of the university, that is, to give student protest clear political meaning and direction. The dream of council members, Chernov recalls in utopian terms not unlike Iordanskii's, was to seize the moment when the entire student body was enraged to make a university-wide movement, which would become in turn a general civic movement, and even a social movement. The method was organization. Considering the *zemliachestvo* too narrow a forum, Chernov's group sought to "weave threads" between the *zemliachestva* by organizing various intermediary groups and seminar series. Partially in response to the criticism of Marxist students, one such forum was devoted to the history of the intelligentsia and *studenchestvo* in Europe. Its product was a new justification of the *studenchestvo* as the leader of the revolution, which was based on Russia's supposedly unique historical experience and lack of a bourgeoisie: "Thanks to the particular conditions of [Russia's] development, a national student movement and a single student organization in Russia was not a myth, and our work corresponded to the purport of the historical moment!"[54] Like Iordanskii, Chernov focused his memoir on the emergence of a *studenchestvo* conceived as a single politically active body and a subset of society as a whole. He too saw organization as a method of instilling consciousness and a reflection of the relative stage of collective development.

A rare personal document from before 1905 provides another perspective on the dynamics of personal and generational development. At his March 1901 trial,

P. V. Karpovich was asked to give his reasons for assassinating the Minister of Education, N. P. Bogolepov.[55] To explain he told the story of his generation of students:

> During the last years of gymnasium, I and my comrades, along with the majority of Russian youth, were avidly interested in various social questions. Not finding the answers. . . either in the bureaucratic gymnasium science or from the bureaucrat-teachers, we searched for the solution to these questions in books and journals.

But censorship left much undecided:

> All the hopes of our young fiery heart, passionately searching for truth, were placed on the university, which seemed to us—youth who still hadn't grasped all the secrets of the autocratic regime—the well of knowledge and the repository of truth; [the university] would resolve all the questions troubling us, explain everything dark and incomprehensible, provide us with the desired knowledge, and teach [us] conscious participation in social life. But this all turned out to be a dream. Professors were simply bureaucrats in the Ministry of Education. . . .

After condemning government harassment of students and professorial indifference in general, Karpovich turned to his own experience at Moscow University during the 1890s when the rector had been Bogolepov. Harshly denouncing Bogolepov's overall callousness toward students, he focused on several specific incidents of an academic nature, most important, Bogolepov's intervention in a matter that ended with the conferral of a degree on a student whose dissertation had been rejected by a specialist. "How could we, young people who placed so much faith in science, truth, man—how could we remain indifferent to such a flouting of science, to such mocking of the elementary rudiments of justice?! We wanted to protest openly, but more experienced comrades held us back." Karpovich drew his political lessons not from ideology, not from an available master narrative, but from the disjunction between his dreams and his experiences. He then universalized them through his evocation of both his generational experience and the concepts of truth and science. But he was clearly not a student leader (an "experienced comrade"); instead, as he notes, "Step by step, I began to cross from the abnormality of university life, to another, broader anomaly." Karpovich was suspended from Moscow University and later Iurev University before going to Germany to complete his studies. But the conscription of student protesters into the army in 1901 drew him back to Russia and led to his decision to assassinate Bogolepov. He had appointed himself the spokesman of his generation. Although Karpovich's story lacks ideological closure, it too shows the unity of collective autobiography, the "we" of *studenchestvo*.[56]

FROM A FEMALE POINT OF VIEW

According to women students, the St. Petersburg Higher Women's Courses gave them the opportunity to develop "their spiritual personality" *(dukhovnaia lichnost')* and to satisfy their desire to be "not only honorable but also intelligent and cultivated worker[s] [in] society." Students who had since entered the Women's Medical Institute recalled how their studies at the Bestuzhev Courses "disciplined us for independent work, awoke in us the desire to go further on the path of self-education, [and] awoke the aspiration to comprehend the all-around nature of man and to lessen his suffering as much as possible." [57] While these sentiments do not differ widely from those held by many male students, they possessed special meaning for women and cloaked their particular difficulties. Denied both the career choices of men and the academic degree of a "real" university, many women experienced education more as a personal than a professional opportunity. Even as women shared many of the same experiences as men, their stories reveal how gender shaped their student experiences.

In her unpublished memoirs dated January 20, 1931, the schoolteacher Mariia Miliukova recounts her political coming of age at the turn of the century. Joining her life to the advancing revolutionary storm, Miliukova tells a story of personal development in highly enthusiastic if formulaic language. Although she describes the collective of male and female students without noting any particularities to one or the other sex, her account possesses a decisive feminine voice. As a student, Miliukova sought to develop herself politically and intellectually; as a woman, she looked to other women as role models. She unites these two strands in an ideal of the revolutionary heroine.[58]

In ritual form, the memoirs contrast the darkness of the provinces to the light of St. Petersburg's student life. As with other young people from the provinces, Miliukova came to St. Petersburg in search of the answers to the accursed questions of Russian reality. Both a circle of university and Bestuzhev students and her work on behalf of political prisoners for the underground Red Cross nurtured her personal development and self-education. "In the arguments [of the study circle]," she recalled, "the principles of a revolutionary world view gradually formed in us, in the youth, who had gathered here from the far corners of the provinces, where life was then so difficult, where civil society *[obshchestvennost']* was mostly lacking [and] crushed, and where living even temporarily was somehow suffocating." With the provinces symbolizing stagnation and the circle the path to enlightenment, Miliukova sets up the dominant motif of her story: the development of consciousness as a student and the subsequent application of its principles to life. Miliukova and her circle organized workers' circles, and she likewise describes them and the "friendly relations" of students and workers in glowing terms. The only group to surpass the fire of student youth at that time, she proudly notes, was worker youth.[59]

As a woman student Miliukova was sometimes greeted with skepticism. She recounts a conversation with a prison official, who, having condemned the Higher Courses as especially useless (noting that at least the Medical Institute provided practical skills), related a family drama. When his daughter had expressed interest in the courses, his wife had immediately ruled this out as wholly unsuitable. Gradually the daughter had accepted this decision, had since married, and was raising children. Miliukova rose to defend the courses: "Your poor daughter! It would have been better to allow [her] into life" *(propustit' v zhizn')*. The language is important, for Miliukova did not censure motherhood, but the enclosure of women in the home. For her, education symbolized and assisted the entrance of women into public life without affecting their private roles as wives and mothers. She mentions the birth of her own son in passing, treating it as a purely private matter.[60]

Alongside such personal scenes are the "stock characters" of Soviet fiction and revolutionary history. They include the revolutionary—a Russian student studying in Freiburg, Germany, who would come through St. Petersburg bringing illegal literature and organizing contacts with workers, and who ultimately dies young and tragically. She describes him as "unusual," "developed," and with a "sharp intellect." She also recalls the "spiritual purity" of a fellow woman student from a poor background who struggled to get to Petersburg to receive an education but was arrested and exiled for leading an illegal workers' circle. After her father's death and despite her tremendous thirst for knowledge, the woman accepted a low-paying job in order to support her mother and orphaned nephew. She was "someone who actually gave her life to others." As products of the interplay of memory, popular culture, and revolutionary mythology, such idealized characters enhance the formulaic quality of the memoir.[61]

Ideal types can nonetheless be revealing. Miliukova dedicates her memoirs to Vera Mikhailovna Velichkhanova, the first wife of the Bolshevik V. D. Bonch-Bruevich, and the heroine of Miliukova's youth. While bringing food and messages to political prisoners, she had the opportunity to become acquainted with Velichkhanova, who at the time was imprisoned, pregnant, and writing for a legal Marxist journal. Miliukova describes her as "strong, kind, and serious," possessing "a firm sense of purpose, duty, and social responsibility." Velichkhanova's great influence on Miliukova moved her to "[strive] to develop [herself] with reading, to move forward without stopping halfway. . . to struggle for human truth, and not to become discouraged by life's misfortunes." In her transformation from a provincial girl with an undeveloped world view into a grown woman, Miliukova used Velichkhanova as her model—the "ideal of the real, intelligent, educated Russian woman," who combined motherhood and radical activism without apparent personal conflict.[62]

Just such a conflict runs through the diary of Elizaveta D'iakonova.[63] Ever since her childhood, D'iakonova had known that she would study at the Bestuzhev Courses. At the age of 14, she recalls, she had noticed the narrowness of women's conversation compared with that of men, and understood that "education was necessary for intellectual development." But while life opened up for men after gymnasium, the doors of the university were closed to women, who sat at home and waited. When she reached the age of majority and received a small inheritance from her father, D'iakonova resolved that she too would go to St. Petersburg. Due to the active opposition of her mother, she was initially refused admission—her mother had believed the rumors that women students were "public" women. Only special dispensation from the Ministry of Education counteracted her mother's resistance, and she enrolled in the fall of 1895.[64]

From the very beginning of her studies, D'iakonova struggled to escape not only the "darkness" of the provinces, but also the legal and spiritual claims of families on their daughters. Education represented a dual opportunity for intellectual development and personal freedom, as illustrated by one particularly enraptured diary entry:

> January 1, 1896. . . For the first time in my life I meet the New Year as an independent person, more or less free. . . . The New Year finds me a student at the courses, and in part—a new person. If only I could really remake myself into a new person, a person in the best sense of the word.[65]

For D'iakonova, the process of "remaking" herself depended on the promise of knowledge. The first lecture seemed to fulfill this promise. In her diary, she describes in some detail the lecture of Professor Ivan Grevs, a popular history professor who had just returned from a year abroad. He addressed the audience of excited and expectant students as representatives of the educated society of the twentieth century, as women who would enact their learning in public or family life. He spoke of the role of the individual in society, and proclaimed science to be the guiding light of social progress. "I left the courses and walked for some time without seeing anything before me," D'iakonova wrote. "We had heard from the podium the voice not only of a professor, but of a man, who had addressed us with such wonderful words—words, which we had so hoped to hear upon entering here; he had explained to us our life's task, which the majority of us had not yet clearly seen." [66]

Though D'iakonova grew increasingly skeptical of such beautiful words, science and scholarship rather than politics continued to play a central role in her personal development. Having read illegal brochures and participated occasionally in circles, she dismissed the rhetoric of radical students as abstract and useless to the people. Although she questioned whether science could solve all the problems of Russian society and was very disappointed with the low level of intellectual discourse among students of both sexes, she also doubted whether a few brochures could prepare workers or peasants to take power. In contrast to her feelings of disillusionment regarding her peers, she was genuinely impressed by the students she met during a visit to a night school for workers run by the Imperial Russian Technical Society. The three-year course covered the curriculum of a boy's gymnasium without classical languages, and she found its students much more serious and articulate than her usual company. Feeling more commonality with them than with Bestuzhev students, she saw once again how knowledge could liberate the personality and thereby serve as the foundation for useful work and real social change.[67]

Unlike Miliukova, D'iakonova perceived a conflict between female physiology and higher education, a conflict embodied in the institution of marriage. As children, D'iakonova and her younger sister Valia had dreamed of coming to St. Petersburg together. During D'iakonova's first year at school, however, Valia had gotten married with the intention of coming with her husband to St. Petersburg, where she would also begin her studies. The plan did not come to fruition. The husband failed to find a position in the capital, and the wife was forced to abandon her quest for education. D'iakonova could only feel intense pity for her sister—and guilt that she had not persuaded her to prolong the engagement. In her eyes, marriage resembled the renunciation of both personal autonomy and the aspiration for self-improvement. This theme repeats itself. Several months later, she recounts the words of a friend who had recently had a baby, had just begun to nurse it, but had once again become pregnant: "Well you see, getting married means that we can not determine ourselves freely—we have husbands." Ruminating about the moral and legal position of women in society, D'iakonova noted how the unrelenting cycle of male desire, pregnancy, and birth ruled a married woman's life. Since the husband would not curb his desire, the wife was not even able to raise her children properly, much less have independent interests. Male desire, she concluded, was ruining the health of women and subverting the institution of the family.[68]

In many respects, the importance of sexual autonomy for D'iakonova derived from her own family experiences. Having struggled to achieve her independence through education, she saw marriage as another form of slavery. Even worse in her view was the fact that marriage seemed to many young women the only "liberation" from a restrictive family environment. Over the course of the diary, she self-consciously notes how her own interests are developing in very different directions from those of her sister, who, incidentally, becomes pregnant. As she remembers their closeness during childhood and their shared desire for education, she increasingly depicts marriage and personal development as two incompatible life paths.[69] For D'iakonova, the choice lay between the domestic world governed by husband and children and a life devoted to meaningful public activity. Her sister had taken the first path, while she herself searched for the second.

D'iakonova had to confront the absence of career opportunities. As she contemplated graduation in the fall of 1899, she realized the paucity of her options. Her highest legitimate ambition was to direct a girl's gymnasium, but D'iakonova had little interest in pedagogy. Her real interest—a legal career—was legally closed to her, as she was informed when she petitioned the Ministry of Justice for the right to study law. Ruminating over the different horizons of men and women, she sardonically concluded that at least it was less offensive to be a woman in autocratic Russia than in a Western democracy. Because men had so much more freedom in a republic, she reasoned, women would feel their dependency and disenfranchisement much more. With both men and women in Russia denied civil and political rights, the gender gap was somehow less extreme.[70] The next year, she left for Paris and enrolled in the law faculty of the Sorbonne.

Both Miliukova's memoir and D'iakonova's diary recount the aspiration for self-development shared by many Russian students, and both show how women's experiences often differed from those of men. Yet Miliukova softens the rough spots of life, resolving the conflicts of personal development, political activism, and motherhood into an ideal type of the revolutionary woman. In this respect, the stylized formula of the student memoir allows her to reduce life to recognized types and utopian solutions. In contrast, D'iakonova's diary provides a rare glimpse into the day-to-day struggles and aspirations of a woman who mostly rejected the claims of student radicalism and failed to find community with her fellow students—hence the absence of a strong "we" so central to most memoirs of student life. She perceived rather a fundamental conflict between the ideal of self-development and women's traditional role, a conflict that culminates in her decision to leave Russia and search for a plot of her own.

Autobiography is a constructed representation of the self, and as such, it relies on the principle of internal coherence. That is, an autobiography tells a story through the perspective, intention, and memory of its author. While this story can be more or less factually accurate, it cannot be an accurate representation, because its "truthfulness" is always relative and mediated. The problems inherent in all autobiographical writing are particularly evident for the memoirs of Russia's revolutionary era, a situation that has understandably led many historians to dismiss their utility outright. These memoirs tend to construct the individual life story as the reflection of historical teleology, making the formation of the author-hero predetermined; both the personal and historical story lines are often formalized into teleological epics. To distinguish clear layers of experience, memory, and literary-autobiographical convention is impossible. Yet this would also have been difficult for contemporaries, because many of the formulas and clichés that governed their writing were accessible and sometimes even expressive conventions in revolutionary and Soviet culture.

The autobiographical writings examined in this chapter are highly diverse. Written over the course of some fifty years, they include the memoirs of Marxists, populists, and nonparty members; a court statement; and a diary. All of the memoirs are teleological, in Zamiatin's case mediated by self-irony. Some focus on the development of consciousness, others state its achievement and recount its subsequent application into life. In contrast, both D'iakonova's diary and to some extent Karpovich's court statement lack ideological and biographical closure. Yet despite such differences, these documents belong to a generic tradition of the student memoir, in which "typical" student experiences play an important narrative role as plot motifs—the repressive gymnasium and occasional secret circle, the high hopes placed on the university, the disappointment in professors and "official" science, the discovery of the student subcultures, the process of self-education, the striving to develop a world view, participation in student protests, and so forth. Is this narrative accurate? The answer must be no. There were many good professors, radicals were often excited by the intellectual world of the university, and some students complained of dead and uninteresting student organizations. In other words, the world of the Russian student in the 1890s was more complex and variegated than its representations in memoirs suggest. Is the portrait truthful? The answer here is equivocal. Many of these motifs date back at least to the 1860s and would soon be represented in hundreds of student proclamations as the shared experiences of students, indeed, as the foundation of *studenchestvo*. Though the genre is inherently teleological, many students did experience several of its moments if not always its outcome, for its story could have meaning even for those former students who did not become revolutionaries. Memory, as Stefan Zweig once noted, must be understood "not as an element which accidentally retains or forgets, but rather as a consciously organizing and wisely exclusionary power." [71]

The generation of 1899 built upon the institutions, practices, and mythologies created and transmitted by students over the decades since Pisarev had first heralded the "new students" of the 1860s and called them the "masters" of the university. Just as Georgii Nosar' drew on this rich legacy when he fashioned himself into the consummate student radical, so too did Nikolai Iordanskii when he recounted his generation's search for enlightenment through the stale order of the state-run schools. The entry of the "new people" into the university as the *raznochinnoe studenchestvo*, the construction of the student subcultures around the principle of self-education, and the public image of students as revolutionaries all shaped a rich and sometimes contradictory ethos, which would form the basis for a national student movement in 1899. Confronted by the social, economic, and cultural transformations of the 1890s, a generation of students found its social identity in a collective narrative of "formation" that began with the darkness of the provinces and the quest for light.

CHAPTER TWO

The Rise of Consciousness

The Student Movement, 1899–1904

One crocodile affirmed to us, not long ago
That the country is ruled by "law."
Little Whip, Little Whip, of February Eighth,
Little Whip, Little Whip, we will bring you fame.

      —*The Little Whip (Nagaechka)*, Student Song, 1899

In response to an incident of police brutality in February 1899, Petersburg students called a strike that quickly spread across the country. At its height, 25,000 students boycotted the classroom under the banner of human dignity, personal inviolability, and rule of law. This strike inaugurated a period of mass protest in higher education that marked the entrance of educated society into the political struggles, which would culminate in the 1905 Revolution. For students, the explosion of a nationwide movement confirmed the existence of *studenchestvo* as one body, united by an ethos of honor and solidarity. They had some reason to believe this: appeals to *studenchestvo* galvanized mass protest through 1905. The causes of the student movement were largely structural, arising from the conflict between an authoritarian government and a proud *studenchestvo*, both with definite ideas about education, science, and individual rights. Its dynamics were influenced at times by government policy, police repression, and the agitation of revolutionary parties. Of central importance, however, was the character of students' new political community. Between 1899 and 1905, students repeatedly tried to understand their collective experiences by historicizing them, and student leaders even began to see the evolution of the student movement as a reflection of the political maturation of *studenchestvo*. In this process of self-exploration, two interpretive strategies coexisted and occasionally competed with one another. I call them "epic" and "history" (although both were equally mythical), because the first represented student protest as episodes within a heroic tradition and reflective of eternal values, while the second assumed a historical dynamic.

The epic depicted the student movement as a perpetuation of the radical traditions of the 1860s and 1870s that were reenacted on a universal level during the 1899 strike. After the strike, "1899" came to signify a mythical past, a moment of total solidarity, absolute honor, and pure community. During times of conflict, "1899" served as exhortation, as the ideal by which students should organize their behavior. Though such exhortation was not always successful (and could never be, because the ideal was utopian), the epic sustained the image of *studenchestvo* as a carrier of high ethical principles and of students as leaders of cultural progress.

The strategy of history built instead on the model of *Bildungsroman* and divided student radicalism into discrete stages of historical development that began with the paradise myth of 1899 and would conclude with the professed achievement of consciousness in 1905. The roots of its underlying plot were evident in 1899 in the dialectical use of the categories "academic" and "political" and in the equation of organization with consciousness. When a historical narrative first emerged in 1903, however, student leaders drew an unexpected conclusion: the *studenchestvo* itself, as an archaic and spontaneous form of social identity, must dissolve. This outcome reflected widespread ideas about class development, the emergence of organized political parties, and the depiction of the party as the highest form of political organization, the reflection of mature class consciousness. The death of *studenchestvo* would, in theory, mark students' achievement of consciousness and the differentiation of their community into classes and parties.

For many students, the epic *studenchestvo* remained a glorious ideal; for many student leaders, the historical model helped to explain their failure to organize a disciplined movement. And despite the growing dominance of the historical model, the practices and language of student protest were imbued with an epic style. Just as the *skhodka* remained an intrinsic celebration of the particular ethical unity and collective honor of *studenchestvo*, the teleology of the historical narrative lent the student movement an epic tone. In the end, these two strategies did not exist independently, nor did they reflect the views of particular groups. They rather gave language and structure to the inchoate experience of student protest and ultimately wove its scattered threads into a story. Though students would find that neither epic nor history explained real life adequately, they used their categories and cliches to confer meaning on their experiences.

THE 1899 STRIKE

The anniversary of the founding of St. Petersburg University on February 8 was an annual event of some importance, when the elite of official Petersburg would join professors and students in the main hall of the university for a ceremonial assembly. On this one evening each year, students were permitted to throw huge parties, which by the mid-1890s had become notorious for their radical speech-making and a central site for the Marxist-populist polemics. After the assembly in 1898, students had noisily paraded down Nevskii Prospect and clashed several times with police. Later that evening, the parties had become especially turbulent with inflammatory speeches on the political role of students. To prevent a repetition of that scandal, the Ministry of Internal Affairs formally advised the Ministry of Education in January 1899 that appropriate measures must be taken. In a notice published on February 4 in a conservative newspaper, rector of St. Petersburg University V. I. Sergeevich consequently condemned these habitual disorders. Curtly citing the traditional excesses of students on this day—the crowds in the streets, drunken intrusions into restaurants, and disorders at the theater or circus—he wrote: "Although only a small minority actually participate, the capital's society. . . is exasperated, and censures the university and the entire *studenchestvo*." He pointed out that the police were obligated to maintain public order on February 8 as on every other day and detailed the various legal penalties for disorder. "Students must obey the law," he concluded in a condescending tone, to "preserve the honor and dignity of the university." With its emphasis on legality and threat rather than appeals to student honor, this notice set the tone for the subsequent confrontations.[1]

Sergeevich judged the student mood very poorly. Insulted by the notice and the humiliating fact of its publication, students resented the implication that they were an embarrassment to the university. As February 8 approached, students discussed their options together and ultimately agreed to maintain public order as evidence of their dignity. By posting monitors to prevent large crowds from exiting the university after the assembly, they hoped to forestall even the appearance of a street demonstration. However, no such measures were taken to preserve order within the university.[2] The stage was set; the audience included government and church dignitaries.

During the opening ceremonies, students remained quiet, but every time Sergeevich tried to speak, they erupted with shouts and whistles. When the assembly was finally canceled, students sang their anthem "Gaudeamus," resolved once again to avoid conflict with the police, and left the building in small groups as planned. They were greeted with an unexpected sight. Expecting protests, the police had completely surrounded the area, blocked the bridges to the city center, and stationed reinforcements across the river on Senate Square. As students continued to exit the university only to find all the streets blocked, the crowd grew larger and increasingly disoriented. Without apparent provocation (beyond several much-disputed snowballs), mounted police armed with whips rushed the crowds. Cornered between police divisions, students, as well as some professors and passersby, were unable to flee the beatings.[3]

The traditional student parties were well attended that evening but surprisingly uneventful. Rationalizing that in a police state one should expect the arbitrary use of police power, student radicals dismissed the incident. Nikolai Iordanskii recalled how they intended to use the beatings for purposes of political agitation, that is, to argue that students were powerless and must join with the proletariat in conscious revolutionary struggle. Neither he nor another student leader, Mikhail Mogilianskii, expected any significant response. To their amazement, however, the "thirst for protest" spontaneously erupted the next day, when thousands of students broke into the main auditorium, elected a chairman, and created an "Organizational Committee" to provide leadership and coordination for the still amorphous movement. Iordanskii was actually in the cafeteria when he was informed of the unusual events. Though ascribing the determination of students in large part to their leaders ("soldiers of the student old guard. . . torn from their organizations and thrown to the top of the deep mass wave"), Iordanskii did acknowledge their unprecedented self-organization and seriousness. While one student beat himself on the chest, demanding that students protest the desecration of their uniform, the general mood was sober. The meeting continued for three days.[4]

Upon reviewing potential tactics, students were forced to acknowledge the legal constraints on their actions. Pointing out that Russian law prohibited collective action, speakers argued that a moderate proposal to gather a petition demanding changes to the reactionary 1884 University Charter was not only ineffectual, it was illegal. Others questioned the relevance of the charter to an incident of police brutality. Students soon realized, moreover, that lodging a judicial complaint was equally senseless, because the courts lacked an established and regulated authority over police. The debate went full circle. Students sensed that the police had arbitrarily violated their "right" to personal security, but found they had no legal protection. They had stumbled against an indisputable fact: Russia was not a *Rechtsstaat*.

The only way to draw attention to the issue of legality, students finally resolved, was through a nonviolent academic strike, which they hoped would not give the police a pretext to intervene. Because nobody could ever pinpoint who exactly made this suggestion, this decision seemed to express the "general will" of *studenchestvo*.[5] With a balanced tone and specific propositions for reform, a proclamation laid out the strike conditions, which all centered on the problem of personal inviolability and police arbitrariness. It demanded, first, that the courts be empowered to respond to a complaint against the police in an independent and public fashion; second, that the legal procedure be given a defined term; and third, that rules regulating police procedure for the maintenance of public order in general and with regard to students in particular be published as the basis for judicial opinion. The proclamation virtually demanded an independent judiciary and the rule of law.[6]

Denying any "political" intent to their movement and describing their strike as a "social movement" *(obshchestvennoe dvizhenie)*, students depicted themselves as battling for the law rather than against the state. They steadfastly refused to acknowledge any political dimension to the beatings, their demands, or their method of protest. This rejection of political language was neither a tactical maneuver to avoid repression nor an unconscious avowal of liberal ideology (as Marxist students claimed at the time).[7] Drawing on their own version of customary law, students instead derived universal principles from the affront to their personal and corporate dignity. When Sergeevich had accused students of sullying the image of the university, he had enumerated the legal punishments for public disorder and described the police as the guardian of the law. The incident of brutality had reversed these roles, revealing that students lacked all remedies of their own. With their sense of honor offended by the notice and then the beatings, students framed their demands in the same language of legal principle. Although it was never clear whether the strike demands applied only to students or to all Russians, students implied (but never stated directly) that the rights of the student should be equivalent to those of the citizen, and that the rights of the citizen needed to be defended. This blurring of identity between the student and the citizen became a constituent part of the "student" movement, lending it a certain universality from its very beginning.

Having called the strike, students took over the university, replacing lectures and seminars with a new kind of education. In the main auditorium, a meeting remained in perpetual session as a forum to debate policy and principle. Unsure at first how to respond, most professors declined to hold their classes, which students mistakenly interpreted as support for their movement. If a professor did attempt to lecture, "obstructionists" engaged him in a discussion of the strike, police brutality, and the rule of law. If this tactic failed, he was disrupted with noise and whistles. The other innovation of the strike, and central to its success, was the hectographed daily bulletin, written by the Organizational Committee, which was now acting as a strike committee. With summaries of the day's events and statements of common purpose, bulletins informed, interpreted, and exhorted. By studiously avoiding any discussion of politics, the Organizational Committee hoped to capture the general mood; by evoking principles and norms, it strove to direct it. As a reflection of the movement in its various stages and a creative force within it, the bulletins developed the rhetorical forms of student protest.

The strike transformed St. Petersburg University into a battleground. Discerning an assault on its natural order, one official report stressed how students adopted "unfriendly relations to all figures not belonging to the student corporation and, in particular, to members of the inspectorate." It concluded with an allusion to Pisarev: students behave as if they are "the full masters of the university," as "rebels, who apparently set the goal of taking the university into their own hands."[8] For their part, students saw a struggle for moral right. Contrasting their pacifism to the violence of the state, their demand for rule of law to official arbitrariness, bulletins defined norms of behavior for students and personalized "the other" in the figure of the rector. Counterpoised to the "orderly," "united," and "principled" conduct of the strike and the "maturity," "seriousness," and "dedication" of the strikers stood the petty, self-seeking Sergeevich. Bulletins repeatedly praised the levelheadedness of the students in the face of many provocations, and the students' seriousness and dedication came to signify the validity of their demands.[9]

On February 12, repressions began in earnest. Police occupied St. Petersburg University, noting the names of all students present within the building. The following day Sergeevich himself called in the police—sparking jokes about his transfer to the interior ministry—and the university was closed. By this time, highly critical of police actions, students across St. Petersburg had affirmed their solidarity, demanded personal inviolability as "that basic principle of all civilized societies," and joined the movement. Over the next week, confrontations with police occurred in and around educational institutions throughout Petersburg. Carried by student emissaries and word of mouth—for censorship was almost total—appeals to join the movement found sympathetic ears across Russia. By the middle of February, twenty-five thousand students were on strike, thousands had been cited, and hundreds arrested. Higher education had been shut down.[10]

With bulletins continuing to link "the quiet but firm mood" of students to the justice of the common cause, the unprecedented size of the movement and police repression helped to introduce new rhetorical elements. As one bulletin noted, students now possessed not only a noble goal, but also "a great responsibility before our comrades and all of Russian society." Aware that their strike was the first mass movement in educated society since the populist movements of the 1870s and famine relief of the early 1890s, students placed themselves on the stage of history. Traditional revolutionary images of embattlement, self-sacrifice, and moral purpose also entered their language. "Our protest is a protest of the human personality, profaned in its most elementary rights," another bulletin proclaimed; "human dignity is incompatible with the Cossack's lash." Recounting the decimation of student ranks and the imminent arrest of the authors, it asked students to pick up the fallen banner: "Beyond the awareness of fulfilling one's duty, those of us who will be thrown out of the battle will find moral support. . . . To those who remain, we transfer the cause, a cause which is not only for students but for all of society [obshchestvennoe delo]."[11] Depicting themselves as citizens and their strike as historically significant, students portrayed their movement as a struggle for freedom and dignity in all of Russia.

Both the strike and the language exalting it strained the relationship between faculty and students. Although only a handful of professors actively opposed the strike, students seem to have expected more active support, especially in light of their moderate demands. But professors did not condone the strike as a method, and their initial acquiescence to obstructions had not meant approval, as most students had assumed. Like the noted jurist A. F. Koni, many were simply perplexed. "I understand that students were insulted by the actions of the police," Koni explained to Mogilianskii, "but I do not understand why they want to close the university; I would understand them better had they closed down the police." But, of course, that was not possible, Mogilianskii noted.[12] With bulletins encouraging students' resentment, the conflict between students and conservative professors accentuated the dilemma. "Honorable professors" should continue to lecture even in a "time of war," one professor was quoted. Another bulletin blacklisted five professors, asserting that they must no longer "appear in the university."[13] Such tactics also alienated those liberal professors who sympathized with students but valued collegiality and scholarly independence.

The strike had created new tensions between students and professors that revealed two different and even incompatible understandings of *nauka,* or science. For many professors, the university represented the sanctity of scholarship and the transmission of progress and enlightenment through teaching. Despite their dissatisfaction with government policy, most believed the university to be an inappropriate arena for protest. For their part, students argued that autocracy had long corrupted the university (along with the ideals of progress and enlightenment) by controlling admission, tuition, and curriculum. Their disappointment with official science had led them to idealize the unofficial learning of self-education and the student subcultures.

Despite these differences, faculty vainly attempted to convince the Ministry of Education to let them handle the protests as an internal university matter. But when they were finally allowed to convene an emergency session of the faculty council on February 16, the ministry limited their options to "moral cooperation" in the pacification of students. Although professors condemned the beatings and the subsequent repressions, they could not turn back the clock and reverse the damage already done.[14] Some professors worked behind the scenes in an attempt to defuse the situation. Professors N. N. Beketov and A. S. Famintsyn collected signatures and evidence for a report to the tsar, in which they contended that students would not deserve to be called Russians had they not protested the police insult. When informed of this action taken on their behalf, students were somewhat surprised by its patriotic tone, an approach which they had never considered. "Now is the most critical moment," one student stressed in a personal letter after Beketov's audience with the tsar; "everything depends on how students behave themselves."[15]

Only ten days after the strike vote, the unprecedented dimensions of the nationwide movement spurred a conciliatory gesture. On February 20, the tsar appointed General Petr Vannovskii, Minister of War under Aleksandr III, to head a commission charged with the investigation of the "reasons and circumstances of the disorders." In their initial response, student leaders took exception to the characterization of their movement as "disorders," pointing out its orderly con-

duct and unprecedented size, but they acknowledged the importance of the commission as confirmation of its historical significance. Noting the conservative
reputation of Vannovskii as well as the mass repressions continuing unabated
in the provinces, the Organizational Committee concluded, however, that the
commission was inadequate reason to halt the strike.[16] But for many students,
especially those in St. Petersburg's elite technical institutes, the appointment of
the commission was sufficient, and by February 24, most had voted to reopen
their schools.[17]

As university students gathered on March 1 to reconsider the strike, the last remaining issue involved the principle of solidarity: the full pardon of all students
who had been arrested, suspended, or exiled. Proclamations signed "Those who
have not forgotten about the suffering," "The Group of Unity," and "All for one,"
argued that the strike should continue until amnesty was granted. Others countered
that further protests would mean death for arrested comrades. One suggested a
two-week grace period, after which the strike would be resumed should students
not receive amnesty. On the third day of the meeting, students voted 563 to 554 to
resume their studies.[18] The government responded swiftly, allowing the return of
most of the seventy-eight university students exiled from St. Petersburg. The situation in the provinces proved more volatile, and continuing repression in Moscow
and Kiev fostered resentment over the "capitulation" of Petersburg students.[19] In
February, provincial students had answered the call from St. Petersburg; in March,
the provinces would demand that they not be forgotten.

A Bourgeois *Studenchestvo?*

"Our protest was *a protest against the reigning arbitrary rule in Russia,* the one
guarantee against which we saw in the *law* and its inviolability," proclaimed a
manifesto distributed by the Organizational Committee that March. "We thus
protested in the name of right and law against arbitrary rule and violence."
Although its language and tone were reminiscent of the daily bulletins, this manifesto was the first statement of the political character of the strike. Students had
not been protesting the beatings of February 8, it stressed, nor had they been
struggling for the enforcement of existing law. By rejecting the traditional suppli-
cant petitions and instead going on strike, they had in fact protested the entire
political order. The need to preserve unity and to avoid repression had precluded
such open political language earlier, but the Organizational Committee now criticized students' capitulation following Vannovskii's appointment, decried their
political innocence, and advocated fundamental political change in Russia.[20]

The strike nonetheless marked the birth of a new generation of students, the
manifesto asserted, who had renounced the habits of the imperial subject by
claiming the rights of the citizen. Describing the decision of students to rely
upon the Vannovskii Commission as a throwback to the era of favors, appeals,

and petitions, it derisively contrasted the will of the "emasculated" students of the 1880s and 1890s with the new student of 1899. The subtext was clear. By actively protesting the arbitrary system that denied them their rights, students had transformed themselves into individuals and citizens. Defined by his sense of dignity and rational purpose, this "new student" required systemic political change for his full development. "Science and enlightenment, as well as their carriers, the universities, cannot survive alongside an order [of arbitrary rule]," the manifesto warned. "There will always be a muffled battle between them, accompanied by frequent explosions, so long as this order is not changed."

Members of the Marxist-dominated *Kassa vzaimopomoshchi* greeted the manifesto of the Organizational Committee with a mixed response, with the majority believing that an additional commentary from a Marxist perspective was necessary.[21] In the *Kassa's* manifesto, which appeared two weeks after that written by the Organizational Committee, students were described as the idealistic youth of the Russian bourgeoisie, who had risen in defense of their class interests with demands for human dignity, freedom, and property.[22] Though it praised the "spontaneous" movement as a potential factor in raising social and political awareness in general, it condemned the "naive" trust students placed in the Vannovskii Commission. Indeed, students' "liberal opportunism" had revealed their "inadequate revolutionary mood." Calling for "organization" in the struggle against autocracy, this manifesto drew a very different conclusion from its predecessor: students must understand that they were fighting in the name of the bourgeoisie.

When the *Kassa's* manifesto appeared in mid-March, students angrily shredded, slashed, and trampled it. Even the report of the Ministry of Internal Affairs (which usually overstated the revolutionary cast of students) remarked upon the dissatisfaction it caused. When students mistakenly accused the Organizational Committee of baseness *(delaet podlost')* in giving their cause "undesirable [political] coloring," the Organizational Committee formally disavowed any participation in the preparation of the *Kassa's* manifesto.[23] While Mogilianskii attributed this hostile reception to students' political immaturity—that is, their unwillingness to accept the term "revolutionary movement"—Iordanskii's appraisal is more subtle and illuminates the self-image of students. Iordanskii noted that the manifesto of the Organizational Committee had not generated controversy, although it also called for political change at a moment when students had just resolved to end the strike. He instead blamed the tone of the *Kassa* manifesto (described, quite aptly, as doctrinaire, sharp, and authoritarian), and, more important, its language of class. True to their intelligentsia tradition, students "despised bourgeois-ness in all its aspects" and thus rejected such a qualification of their movement.[24] Although Iordanskii concedes that students feared the word "revolutionary," his brief digression suggests a more fundamental dynamic. Students themselves viewed the character of their movement as ethical and beyond

class, seeing it as an expression of the universal principles of dignity, enlightenment, and progress.

THE CALL OF SOLIDARITY

Under growing pressure from provincial appeals and emissaries, university students assembled on March 16 to consider a proposal to renew the strike. Although fewer people attended than in February, those who did were more "serious, thoughtful, and conscious," in Iordanskii's words. These words may be
interpreted to mean that the movement had entered a "higher" phase of consciousness, because students now understood its political significance. At this
assembly, the elected chairman spoke directly of the political character of a renewed strike, the lack of social support, and the inevitable repression. Other
speakers pointed out that the repression of provincial students was a direct result
of their solidarity with Petersburg students. It was, consequently, a moral duty
to renew the strike. Russian students abroad sent letters of "comradely sympathy" for "the courageous, united battle against the violence of Russian power,
and the rude police hand placed on science and its free development." [25] The
strike was approved with dissent, and it adopted the slogan of February: "Students consider themselves compelled to begin the strike and continue it until
such time that all comrades, including students at provincial educational institutions, are amnestied, because their return is, in the given instance, the first guarantee of personal inviolability, [which is] the fundamental principle of our movement." [26]

Other schools had hesitated to join the movement, but then the government
suspended all university students, rendering the duty of solidarity clear. On
March 18, technological students voted 367 to 351 against the strike but reversed
this decision the next day and were all expelled.[27] The politically modest demand
of an amnesty thus unleashed the powerful emotions of honor, solidarity, and
collective responsibility, ideals that permeated the language of student protest
over the next decade. When the daily bulletins reappeared on March 16, they
thus criticized the least sign of "liberalism," which was defined as anything contrary to group solidarity. Although the Vannovskii Commission was included
among liberalism's discredited representatives, professors received the brunt of
the attack. "Once we awaited [their] support," students were reminded; "now we
know the value of their positive statements and smiles." This resentment derived
largely from the ongoing refusal of the faculty council to treat students as a
collective, a policy students interpreted as a direct assault upon fraternal solidarity and collective responsibility, which they now considered the foundation of
the movement.[28]

Despite Vannovskii's personal assurances of their safety, police quickly arrested student leaders. By late March, sixty-three members of the Organizational

Committee (which was reconstituted several times), had been arrested, requiring forestry and mining students to assume leadership of the strike. The most common fate of activists was suspension for periods lasting up to two years; in some cases, expulsions were made permanent. This was not an insignificant punishment, because suspended students could suffer exile from St. Petersburg and become eligible for the military draft, due to the loss of residency permits and draft exemptions. At the very least, they lost a semester's tuition and credit. In March and April, 225 students of the Women's Courses, 294 forestry students, 346 technological students, and almost seven hundred university students were suspended.[29]

As arrest and suspension became facts of everyday life, honor became the only sign of victory. No longer portraying personal inviolability as a modest demand, bulletins and other proclamations idealized "heroic" resistance and depicted the strike as the first skirmish in a longer war, a war of principle. "Once again, we firmly hold our old banner, and we are ready to sacrifice everything in order to pay our debt to you," Petersburg students thus wrote in an open letter to their provincial comrades. "With new courage. . . we enter the *final* battle, and true to our honorable student traditions, we will either achieve [our goals] or fall; and we will all fall unto the last [man], preserving our purity, and charging our younger brothers to remember us and follow our path." [30] Martyrdom— the model for the "younger brothers"—was the only projected victory. As with earlier generations of Russian radicals, transfigurative religious imagery became central to self-presentation. It highlighted the individual transformation—even salvation—achieved through personal dedication, struggle, and self-sacrifice.

If the bonds of *studenchestvo* had linked students across the empire with common traditions and ideals, then the collective experience of the strike had forged a new bond, a new expression, and a new duty of fraternal solidarity. In this struggle, each student was called upon to place the good of the collective above his own. Bulletins described the duty of the student to pick up the banner of a fallen comrade, who, sure of support, had boldly "risked himself, and carried our movement on his shoulders." The only evidence of virtue was personal self-sacrifice: "Surely a student cannot be found [who is] ready to end his participation in the movement and, at the price of the destruction of his best comrades, purchase his own petty well-being?" [31] If victory was thus to be achieved through honor, defeat could result from egoism or corruption but not from the arrest of every single student. Those who did not join the strike were disgraced: students of the Military-Medical Academy and the Women's Medical Institute were excluded from the *studenchestvo*.[32]

This ideal had a tremendous resonance. A student at the Technological Institute distributed his personal philosophical statement, signed "The Voice of a Comrade," in which he called upon students to reject the theory and practice of Russian life—the experience of the fathers—and to live instead according to conscience. To be true to student traditions, he argued, was to be guided by principle, not by the "rational" acceptance of power and fate. In rejecting the authority of their elders schooled in Russian reality, students would transform life itself. They would live according to their consciences, dedicate themselves to serving the people, and, in this way, mold reality to their own image. Reworking the ideals of the 1860s and 1870s, this student called for a new "new generation" to enact revolution.[33] Other students expressed both their frustration and their sense of history. On March 22, one St. Petersburg student mused in a private letter, purloined by police: "Now when the movement actually has meaning, we must wonder. . . at the stupidity of society. The movement is historic, nothing like it has ever happened before, and if now our fathers and elder brothers watch and curse [us] for raising the banner of liberty, then. . . they would rather teach us [to be] fools." [34] Confiscated materials of Kiev students include photographs inscribed, "In memory of our struggle for the rights of man," and "Boldly, friends, do not lose courage in the unequal battle." [35]

Examples abound of students publicly recording their support of the strike. Many students disrupted final examinations, reported themselves as prepared to do so, or simply returned their examination tickets. All such displays resulted in suspension. Vera Voronina announced during an examination that to participate under current conditions was shameful *(podlo)*. When she personally delivered her exam ticket to the director after refusing to give it to the professor, she was promptly expelled. Sometimes students were arrested en masse. On March 31, 481 students were taken to prison and cited because they had congregated outside of their locked institutions and refused to leave.[36]

Although the arrest and expulsion of students inevitably depleted the ranks of activists, the overall success of the strike can be assessed by examining attendance figures at final examinations. All students were clearly ill-prepared and for this reason alone unwilling to take their exams. Nevertheless, absence from an exam to which one was personally invited—known troublemakers were not invited—can be seen as a sign of passive respect for the strike. Reports from individual institutions show that less than half of technological students and only 284 of 960 enrolled students from the Women's Courses took at least one exam. At the university, 1,803 of 3,867 scheduled examinations took place in late April and early May.[37] These figures suggest that the strike maintained a deep if not full resonance.

As the semester wound down, student leaders around the country began to assess the movement. They were united on three points. First, the protests were objectively political. Second, by exposing the fallacy of reform from above, they had helped to discredit the government in the eyes of society. Third, students had proven it possible to fight for one's rights in a country without the rule of law. The question of future tactics proved more divisive. Whereas *Kassa* Marxists argued that students had accomplished nothing concrete and must join the struggle of the working class—the one truly revolutionary group—Kiev's United Council argued that the *studenchestvo* constituted a viable political force, even the prototype of a new form of political organization based on broad principles of civil liberties.[38] Here we see an early expression of the conflict between the historical and epic models of student protest.

The clear imperative to develop consciousness within the student "masses" and the related dynamics of "political education" posed new organizational difficulties. This problem was to form the primary topic at the first national conference of student leaders scheduled for late April in Moscow. Although their discussions were disrupted by a police raid, their program suggests that some students were conceptualizing tactics according to a hierarchy of academic and political categories. It distinguished those causes of student dissatisfaction based on the academic regime from those based on the political regime; the academic demands, goals, and tactics of the movement from the political ones; and the spontaneous "academic" student "masses" from the ("organized") political leadership. For the first time, the task of a national student movement was described according to the progression from the academic to the political.[39] As student leaders groped for a way to guide the incipient movement, the academic/political dialectic thus shaped their perspective from the outset.

The strike of 1899 had forged the ideals and practices of a new political community. The beatings of February 8 had offended students' sense of corporate dignity, prompting them to demand their personal inviolability, and they had articulated their corporate rights through the principles of human rights. The movement consequently blurred the boundaries between the person of the student and that of the citizen. Thousands of hectographed bulletins, manifestos, leaflets, poems, and songs appeared in every university city across the country. Itself a phenomenon without precedence, the explosion of print helped students to fashion a repertoire of values and practices that would guide them over subsequent years. Throughout the strike, students depicted their steady adherence to principle as evidence of the seriousness of their movement and their dignity as citizens. At the same time, their style of politics glorified the individual feat of heroism culminating in self-sacrifice. Contrasting their action to the passive resignation of their "fathers," students claimed to be acting as citizens, only this time they defined citizenship through the "civic virtue" of struggle. The strike had marked the birth of a new kind of student, they believed. But it had also produced two different conceptions of citizenship, the one based on dignity and the other on boldness. The second conception increasingly dominated students' political rhetoric through the Revolution of 1905.

ASSESSMENTS OF 1899

With the long semester finally over, government officials also evaluated the unprecedented events of 1899 and ultimately chose a tough stance over several alternatives. These other options would subsequently be tried as well, but government policy would consistently fail to contain the movement born in 1899. This was partly due to the tendency of officials to respond more to long-held stereotypes of student unrest rather than to the real dynamics of protest. Instead of addressing the discrete grievances of students, they defined the problem in terms of authority and attitude. Students did not study enough, it was concluded, nor did they take a properly serious approach toward their specialization. Many officials argued (accurately, in this case), that students were influenced by their comrades and illegal organizations. Corrective measures focused on increased supervision and a heavier workload. Members of the inspectorate were also instructed to become personally involved with students by helping them with their studies and personal problems. Such "moral bonds," it was hoped, would displace the subcultures. The Temporary Rules of July 29, 1899 offered added incentive. Without any exceptions, students found to have participated in disorders would be drafted into the military as privates for up to three years.[40] The government had chosen to rely on threat to restore its authority.

For its part, the report of the Vannovskii Commission forwarded a paternalist solution, which also stressed the need to bond students closer to their superiors through supervision and academic reform. According to Vannovskii, the reasons for the disorders lay in "the complete neglect of student-youth, their self-reliance, the absence of supervision on the part of the academic authorities, and their extreme alienation. . . from members of the professoriate and inspectorate." In contrast to other officials, and citing his military background, Vannovskii sympathized with the corporate solidarity displayed during the strike, and argued that students should be allowed to organize on a "purely academic basis" and for economic self-help. He cited the example of the Military-Medical Academy, which had not joined the second strike and had long allowed limited student organization. His conciliatory recommendations would not find a sympathetic audience until the threat of conscription failed to suppress student protest two years later.[41]

With the government vigorously asserting its authority over higher education, professors agitated for increased autonomy. In the eyes of many professors, the cause of unrest was a combination of government policy and student extremism, both of which politicized the academic environment. In this spiraling confrontation, many faculty members felt that their potential influence and moral authority had not been tapped. One memorandum from Moscow University called for internal mechanisms of trial and punishment for students, the legalization of student organization, and the repeal of the 1884 charter in matters concerning the professorial corporation. This last requirement was considered most important. Professors argued that their authority over students would be strengthened if the state restored their privileges granted under the 1863 charter and revoked in 1884.[42] This middle road was also rejected until several years later, when a professorial disciplinary court was instituted, but like the Temporary Rules and Vannovskii's paternalism, it too would fail in its appointed task.

Throughout the spring of 1899, Russian society clearly feared the conse-quences of supporting students; a mildly phrased petition, which circulated for a month in St. Petersburg, garnered only two hundred signatures. Due to strict censorship, moreover, only the émigré and underground press covered the story openly.[43] One anonymous report (written in March by a well-educated man with liberal views from St. Petersburg) suggests that support was high—at least in the capital. He likened the futile attempts of students to find a street free of police lines on February 8 to "the prototype of Russian life and our society, blocked on all the most legal paths of action." Repeatedly praising the "restraint" and "disci-pline" of students, which he contrasted to the behavior of Sergeevich, the author not only duplicated students' own representation of the movement but even romanticized it into a confrontation of a "bureaucratic Mephistopheles" with a "young agitated Wagner." Likewise terming it a social (rather than a political) movement advocating the rule of law, he compared its significance to the Drey-fus affair in France. The injustices of Russian life had raised a new generation of youth who believed in justice.[44]

The most prominent supporter of students was the writer Lev Tolstoi. In both February and March, students sent representatives to Tolstoi's estate at Ias-naia Poliana to explain their movement and ask for his blessing, which he gave both times. Recounting his pilgrimage of March 1899, Pavel Shchegolev, later an important publicist and historian, recalled Tolstoi's great interest in and praise for students' solidarity and nonviolent methods. Several student bulletins de-scribed these meetings in some detail, which in turn apparently prompted the conservative publisher Suvorin to inquire about their truth. (It is in itself note-worthy that Suvorin was reading student leaflets.) He confirmed that Tolstoi was "for the strike."[45] Until Tolstoi's death in 1910, students would send emissaries to him during moments of crisis. Vladimir Chertkov, the émigré publicist and follower of Tolstoi, noted the tendency of Russian youth to overestimate the significance of their actions but likewise praised the protests as "the first gleam of a new era in the life of Russian society."[46]

TURNING TO THE STREETS

Although two years passed before student protest again erupted on a national level, the events of 1899 had given students a new language with which to inter-pret their day-to-day experiences in the university. As students thus debated whether and how to mark the first anniversary of February 8, the dismissal of several professors who had been supportive of students' aspirations provided ammunition for a fresh attack on the "university regime." Playing upon the three anniversaries—official science, official arbitrariness, and student solidarity—stu-dents' leaflets likened the state's utilitarian attitude toward higher education to its use of arbitrary police force. "The government strives to turn the university into an institution for the production of bureaucrats," one proclamation asserted, and "to eradicate all manifestations of living and independent thought, that is toward unlimited arbitrariness." This image provided a rich contrast to the "real" education defended by students and described in the same proclamation as "the broadening of the intellectual horizon and the development of consciousness in a person." Though the first commemoration of February 8 was ultimately unorchestrated, it was effective: the ceremony was again cut short by shouts and whistles. Students lingered to sing "Gaudeamus" and "The Little Whip," the anthem of 1899, and left the hall without further incident. The official anniversary of the founding of St. Petersburg University had become a student holiday.[47]

Despite this incident, large-scale protest did not recur, a problem that dominated attention at a national student conference that June in Odessa, which was raided by police. As they grappled with the vicissitudes of student protest, student leaders employed categories of analysis very different from the universal and heroic images associated with February 8. Focusing instead on the differing levels of consciousness among students, conference participants outlined the functions of student organization, beginning on the lower levels with mutual aid, followed by self-education and limited "academic" protest, and culminating in mature political protest against the governmental order. The purpose of organization was defined as political education to raise the collective level of consciousness.[48] The rift between organized and unorganized, leadership and mass, consciousness and spontaneity was thus resolving itself into a dialectical process of "education" based on the opposition of the academic to the political. To bridge the academic and the political was in fact to transcend the academic in order to achieve a political movement.

During the fall of 1900, however, most students continued to draw on the categories of 1899 to interpret and politicize the day-to-day conflicts of academic life. When a student was expelled from the Women's Courses without apparent cause or a chance to appeal, one leaflet asserted that this "violation of the natural rights of the individual" mandated a "protest against the reigning system of violence and arbitrariness." [49] In November, students were arrested for disrupting a theater performance of an anti-Semitic play, "The Sons of Israel." Evoking the "principles of 1899," a leaflet supplemented description with interpretation: "In the events of November 23, as in the events of February 8, students recognized that same fact of violence upon the individual—the [same] flouting of one's most elementary rights." Students again demanded a legal review of the incident and an independent judiciary. The university administration instead expelled thirty students, both for the incident at the theater and for participation in illegal meetings.[50] As the semester thus drew to a close, students charged a new Organizational Committee with leading a movement in the spring and went home for their winter vacation, free to ponder both their obligation to defend the principles of 1899 as well as the path toward consciousness and an organized student movement.

Nationwide protests were sparked by events at Kiev University. Like their Petersburg comrades, Kiev students had called a series of meetings during the fall of 1900 to discuss such minor local concerns as the poor lectures of one professor and the dishonorable behavior of several students. However, in their case, the protests had escalated, resulting in the conscription that December of 187 students under the provisions of the 1899 Temporary Rules. As students across Russia resumed their studies in January 1901, they faced a difficult decision. That students were drafted on such a minor pretext documented the government's intention to counter protest with repression of unprecedented severity. It seemed imperative to defend themselves against this new assault.

Already politicized from their experiences of the previous fall, many students in St. Petersburg argued that an organized response was necessary to prevent the annihilation of both the *studenchestvo* and the "last vestiges of freedom" in the university. But when three hundred university students convened a meeting in late January, the depth of the crisis became clear: the threat of military induction was undermining students' collectivist principles. Citing the potential danger of active protest, some speakers suggested that students determine their actions as individuals—thereby ensuring the easy elimination of activists and the collapse of the ideal of solidarity. Other measures put forward for consideration included the individual return of university entrance cards and an appeal for the intervention of the Grand Duke Konstantin. Although a majority resolved upon collective protest, settling once again on the strike, the absence of broad consensus made the resolution difficult to enforce. Several lectures were disrupted, but the strike never caught fire.[51] Even when twenty-eight students from St. Petersburg University were drafted, organized protest failed to develop, and doubts grew over the viability of the movement.[52]

Exalting the heroic past as a challenge to the present, dozens of leaflets censured this atmosphere of uncertainty and fear. One poem entitled "Then and Now (1899–1901)," which circulated in late January, contrasted the honorable students of 1899, who boldly defended their ideals and tied their fate to the collective, to the cowardly students of 1901, who cleansed their hands "in the fraternal blood. . . like Pilate":[53]

> Comrades! Is that really you?
> Is that you I now see?
> Where are the aspirations for truth, for light—
> Where is our former family?
>> If thus you have changed in two years,
>> What will happen after twenty—
>> When the adversities of the world
>> Shatter "youthful delirium"?!

Dirtied in the mire of life,
Your "useful labor" toppled,
Will you not find the torture chamber, the whip
Useful for the motherland?
   Will you not say: We are not well-developed
   And therefore are slaves,
   Who must be beaten:
   Such is already the law of fate.
But no! I do not believe in that!
Is it possible that therein lies happiness—
Is it possible that the thirst for truth, light
Are but words, words, words?!
   Comrades! Take courage!
   The black clouds may surround us—
   But together brothers,
   We will boldly enter the unequal battle.

This poem used a generational metaphor to contrast idealism and struggle with the egoism and progressive degradation of everyday life—careerism leading to compromise and even complicity with the regime. Though fearing the corruption of student values, this anonymous author likened the gulf between the heroism of 1899 and the betrayal of 1901 to an unfilled promise and a historical obligation. Students had the choice of following their fathers into the "mire of life" or transcending the mundane through heroic self-sacrifice.

The "glorious past" of student protest referred less to concrete achievements or tactical successes than to the myth—mediated by the printed word—of absolute solidarity and heroic resistance. "The memories of 1899 are still fresh," one leaflet asserted, evoking the well-known slogans; "The carriers of noble principles and humane intentions do not have the right to remain silent when the most sacred rights of the citizen are flouted, when the basis of every government—the law—is violated." [54] Other leaflets drew on older traditions: "We are enduring a critical moment," the Organizational Committee admonished students. "Will that *studenchestvo* survive which for decades has been the only living spring among the horrors governing Russia? Remember comrades, with your gentle silence, you disavow those great traditions—the struggle in the name of right and freedom—bequeathed to us by our predecessors, the students of the 1860s." [55] With such passionate appeals to a primordial testament of *studenchestvo* the Organizational Committee both mythologized a heroic past and represented student protest as the "living spring" of Russia herself. Although such leaflets initially failed to spark a new round of protest, the power of epic should not be underestimated. Thousands of students were still believers in *studenchestvo*.

It was soon realized, however, that a strike would fail under current conditions. Searching for an alternative mode of protest, one student cited the 1897

Vetrova demonstration and suggested a similar memorial for February 19, 1901, the fortieth anniversary of the abolition of serfdom. Proponents of this tactic argued that the demonstration was an ideal form of protest, because it did not require unanimous support and, moreover, would bring students out of the university and on to the streets. Although some Marxist students rejected the proposal on principle, most activists saw the demonstration as a means to raise public interest and political awareness. As final plans were being made on February 16, the police raided the meeting of the citywide protest committee and arrested twenty-five student delegates. Despite the disruption, several hundred protesters appeared as scheduled at the Kazan Cathedral, and 244 people were arrested. According to one participant, the crowd seemed disoriented at first and was beginning to disperse when someone cried out "To Nevskii" and began to sing "The Little Whip." At that point, mounted police swept into the square, beating those in their path.[56]

Over the next few days, student leaflets described the demonstration as well as other notable events, including the assassination of Education Minister Bogolepov, the demonstration and beatings in Kharkov on February 19, and the mass arrest of 358 Moscow students on February 23.[57] These pamphlets emphasized the expansion of the student movement through the "walls of the academy" into the street. The meaning of "the street" depended on the point of view of the author. One leaflet from the Technological Institute described the support of "masses" of workers and the joint "resistance" of workers and students. Another linked students and educated society: "Having progressed thus far with lonely and timid steps, the protest of the living part of society against the obscurantist state—against personal rightlessness and slavery—is beginning to stand on a real basis." [58]

The heightened mood led to a second and more important demonstration on March 4 that later came to symbolize the first public joining of the academy and the street, educated society and the working class, and even consciousness and spontaneity. During the days preceding that Sunday, meetings, strikes, and proclamations filled academic life, and on the appointed morning, a crowd gathered at Kazan Cathedral. Although the vast majority of those present were students, both male and female, representatives of Petersburg's educated elite, including the political economist Mikhail Tugan-Baranovskii and the publicist Petr Struve, also attended. The exhilarated crowd was just lifting placards and beginning to read proclamations when Cossacks attacked, indiscriminately beating those unable to flee: 672 students—349 men and 323 women—were arrested.[59] Numerous accounts of the chaotic and bloody scene appeared in leaflets, the underground press, and, later, memoirs. The two main organs of Russian Marxism and populism, *The Spark* and *Revolutionary Russia,* heralded agitation within society and the (thwarted) efforts of workers (in reality, a very small number) to join student demonstrations in Petersburg and other cities. Despite continued apathy in some quarters, the lesson seemed clear: "the student movement was becoming a social movement." [60] The demonstration also entered a select canon of significant events that would lead to the triumph of Bolshevism. Soviet historians later argued that it played a "serious role in the growth of political consciousness among workers and revolutionary Social Democrats." [61]

The success of the demonstrations and the accompanying public outcry reinvigorated the student strike movement in St. Petersburg and other cities. Deciding not to apply the 1899 Temporary Rules, the government temporarily closed many educational institutions and chose the path of compromise. The appointment of General Vannovskii that March to the post of education minister signaled a new intention to placate students through the promise to legalize some organization. As bulletins were quick to point out, however, Vannovskii had also advocated increased supervision over students, close controls over professors and curriculum, and restrictions on admission, particularly of Jewish students.[62] Though many students believed that substantive reform was on the way, storm clouds were gathering on the horizon already that April. When students formally requested the delay of exams until fall, in light of the prolonged unrest, Vannovskii refused to sanction a general postponement, favoring individual petition instead. On April 9, university students then passed a resolution expressing their distrust in government intentions.[63]

Faced with apparent defeat in early February, students ended the spring semester with a victory over the state and renewed confidence in *studenchestvo* as the catalyst and leader of social protest in general. With their decision to take student protest outside the university, they had shown a new willingness to recognize the political implications of their movement. In its final bulletin, the Organizational Committee also identified a "spiritual connection" between 1899 and 1901: "In the historical chain, the accomplishment [of 1899] was the form of our protest—the strike with obstructions. We can now add the demonstration, which, [as a tactic], is old, but as a broad social movement is new." The demonstrations of 1901 were important, the leaflet continued, because "students had no other option than to bring their protest on to the street and. . . before society, and to include under their banner all who are oppressed." By uniting people from various social groups, the demonstration had given the student movement new historical significance.[64] In reaching out to both educated society and workers, most student activists were hoping to build an extra-class movement based on traditional conceptions of the *studenchestvo* as the bearer of the principles of freedom, human rights, and social progress. For this reason, they continued to bemoan the passivity and treachery of "liberals," equating liberalism with petty-bourgeois philistinism, and to glorify the ideal of active protest. Refusing to link class and ideology in a Marxist schema, they believed that large segments of Russian society—following the example of *studenchestvo*—would be able to transcend bourgeois passivity in the struggle for political change.

Though some Marxist students had proved unable to see beyond the ideological visor of economism and continued to dismiss the student movement as
irrelevant to the struggle of the working class, this faction, along with the *Kassa*,
soon disappeared. A new branch of Russian Marxism associated with Vladimir
Lenin had introduced a different strategy. In 1901, Lenin called upon workers to
join students' demonstrations, reminding them that students had in the past
renounced their bourgeois origins to dedicate themselves to the socialist-workers'
movement. For Lenin, the very fact of political protest required support.[65] The
factional struggles within Russian Social Democracy and the defeat of economism would facilitate closer cooperation between Russian Marxists and student
radicals. Although the student movement remained independent from revolutionary parties, Marxist conceptions of class slowly began to penetrate students'
political world.

THE BOUNDARIES OF COMMUNITY

When nationwide protests again erupted the following academic year, students
openly declared their movement a political struggle against autocracy. Although
their declarations echoed the vision articulated in the late 1890s of a *studenchestvo*, that would grow to consciousness as a single body, the protests of 1902
marked the culmination and disintegration of this vision. As new conservative
groups challenged the authority of the radicals and their conception of *studenchestvo*, radicals could no longer explain political differences among students
solely with reference to a conscious "political" leadership and spontaneous "academic" masses. By the spring of 1902, therefore, the epic of the student movement began to unravel.

Fully expecting official recognition of their corporation from Vannovskii, students attempted to establish their corporate rights by practicing them—in particular, by holding meetings as a normal part of academic life. Students thus gathered over the fall of 1901 to discuss a conservative publicist's tirades about
women students, the fortieth anniversary of the death of Nikolai Dobroliubov,
and issues related to the anticipated reforms. The mood radicalized as their expectations were progressively disappointed. Vannovskii refused, for example, to
facilitate the amnesty of students exiled the previous spring or to consider a
liberalized admissions policy for Jewish students. Consequently, Petersburg students formally met on November 13 to demand freedom of speech, assembly, and
organization, and they defined the function of student protest in the following
revolutionary terms: "the catalyst of the disintegration *(ferment razlozheniia)* of
the contemporary absolutist-bureaucratic order." The following week, they formulated a "declaration of the rights of students." Defining the *studenchestvo* as a
single autonomous corporation, it demanded the right to self-administration,

individual freedoms, the right to a judicial hearing on extra-university matters, and university admission without regard to sex, religion, nationality, or secondary school. Students also called for a constitution—amid much laughter at the form of the resolution: "We, the students of St. Petersburg University, demand. . . the introduction of a constitution into Russia." [66]

Over that same fall, however, fissures within the student community deepened as a new group calling itself the "academics" also claimed the mantle of student history and traditions. According to them, students were united only by their academic interests, and should, therefore, pursue academic reform through legal and academic methods. The role of the university in matters of culture and enlightenment precluded the activities of radicals, who, they argued, really sought to transform the university into a political club. In separate meetings of their own, the academics repudiated the introduction of politics into the academy, protested the political resolutions, and welcomed the expected reforms "as the first step of the government in the granting of autonomy to the university." Their opponents, calling themselves the "politicals," countered that academic autonomy, including the constituent tasks of culture and enlightenment, could not be achieved without substantive reform of the political order. Autonomy without democracy, they asserted, would at best transform the higher school into a "foreign island in the ocean of absolutist institutions." The "moral obligation" of the student movement was "to strive for the freedom and rights of the entire people." The theoretical opposition between the academic and the political had now taken an organizational form.[67]

When Vannovskii finally introduced his Temporary Rules on Student Organizations in December 1901, they were met by a chorus of criticism. The unfortunate product of political compromise, the new rules legalized some student organization but prohibited the general *skhodka*. The proposed surrogate—elected student elders by course and faculty—did not include a general assembly. Other organizations were legalized with strict limitations. Not only were publications and meetings to be banned from student dining halls, but the administration claimed the right to censor and supervise libraries and discussion groups. Under the guise of paternalism, the reforms eliminated rights already established in practice.[68]

The widespread disillusionment engendered by the chimerical reform politicized many students, who united in opposition to the Temporary Rules under an openly political banner. The emblem was the right to consciousness. On February 5, university students voted 1063 to 5, with 26 abstentions, to call a strike in defense of the *skhodka*. Once again, the strike spread across the city and the country. More than a legislative organ, the *skhodka* symbolized the right to conscious thought and public opinion. As students explained at the time, the right to have economic and academic organizations without the right to meet would be akin to a "torso without a head." In rejecting the Temporary Rules and all forms of "legal" organization, students thus defended their corporate rights by demanding civil rights—free speech, free assembly, and personal inviolability. Moderate students also criticized the reforms because they desired academic autonomy, not paternalistic interference in their education. Hoping to avoid direct confrontation, the government closed the university and other educational institutions for three weeks and arrested many student leaders.[69]

At this time, a new organization, the *Kassa radikalov* (henceforth, the Radicals), offered fresh leadership. Its introductory leaflet of January 1902 advocated an independent and activist role for students in the broader revolutionary movement: in particular, to forge social coalitions and to foment unrest under the banner "Down with Autocracy."[70] According to the Radicals, the unique task of the student movement was the infusion of political consciousness into society. Having renounced the special status of the university as an oasis of relative freedom and privilege in the desert of despotism, students had begun the struggle for the political liberation of Russia. "Is it conceivable that we could be citizens with rights inside the walls of the university, but upon our entrance into life become slaves without any rights?" one proclamation queried. "Do not criticize students for taking the initiative in the responsible matter of political struggle. IT IS FOR YOU. We will quickly give you this honor and welcome the day when all of Russian society, the entire Russian people, demands its rights."[71]

The Radicals thus applied the lessons learned over the last years of the student movement—and the story of consciousness—to society as a whole. Just as student leaders had led the student masses, *studenchestvo* would guide society. The recurrent strife in the universities was educating society on the repressive nature of the state, Radicals argued, and students had formulated a model for fighting back. There is "but one right which neither the law of god nor man can revoke," they stressed, "the right to struggle—to struggle for your rights, which you do not have, to struggle for the right to call yourself a citizen." By linking citizenship to struggle, Radicals proclaimed the student radical the prototype of the citizen and struggle the precondition of citizenship. Students in the university, workers in the factory, scholars at conferences—all Russians were called upon to struggle together for their political freedom.[72]

In 1902, most students recognized that "student rights" could only be guaranteed under a constitutional order, and that the student movement was political. In a February bulletin, the newest Organizational Committee heralded this mood of conscious social protest: "We are able to assert that the student movement, which has always been a general-political movement, has only now been accepted as such in the consciousness of its participants." Two days later, a motto began to head every bulletin: "We demand freedom of speech, freedom of assembly, guarantees of personal inviolability."[73] Student leaders interpreted the determination of students to do battle with autocracy in expansive language: "People

will perish but the idea will live, its echo spreading across the Russian land. . . .
For the Russian people are gathering with strength and studying to be citizens.
That is the goal of the movement, the dawn of a new day." [74]

This so-called "achievement of consciousness" initiated a reevaluation of the
student movement, in which the 1899 protests began to be described as "academic," that is, spontaneous disorders with demands limited to the student corporation. In this narrative of historical development, 1899 signified the birth of
consciousness with its spontaneous protest. Radicals thus depicted their movement as an objectively "higher" stage in the evolution of collective consciousness.
Nevertheless, the images of heroic solidarity and self-sacrifice associated with
1899 still dominated the rhetoric and practices of student politics. With leaflets
contrasting the "moral force" of students with the "physical force" of the state,
the third anniversary of February 8 was marked with a public demonstration
ending with the arrest of almost one hundred students.[75]

The most distinctive aspect of the 1902 movement was the almost exponential
growth of student organizations and the mass production of leaflets. Almost
every institute in Petersburg formed an organizational committee, appointed
representatives to a citywide Delegates' Conference, and produced bulletins in
addition to those of the university's Organizational Committee and independent
student groups. For the first time, students opposing the strike formed shadow
organizations that printed bulletins and proclamations of their own. Petersburg
was consequently flooded with an unprecedented number of pamphlets, poems,
and proclamations. From January 30 through March 13, at least 174 locally produced and distributed leaflets appeared.[76] As diverse groups thus competed for a
hegemonic voice, the strike exposed unprecedented disunity.

The two most explosive sites were the university and the Technological Institute, where the "University for Science" and the "Unorganized Group of Technological Students" led antistrike movements. The chosen names illustrate both
their platform (the defense of science as inherently pure, objective, and apolitical) and their initial tactic (organization to counter the "organized," that is, "political" *studenchestvo*). In its first bulletin of 1902, the Unorganized Group announced: "Considering the transformation of educational institutions into
weapons of political struggle to be inappropriate, we decided to struggle against
the extremists." The new academic movement appropriated not just the categories but also the activist tactics of their opponents. Countering violence with
violence, antiobstructionists turned radicals over to the police. Although some
moderate students initially were involved, the extreme right soon dominated and
espoused an anti-Semitic explanation for the student movement. While the nu-
merical strength of the militant-academic groups was vastly inferior to the politicals, who could claim the passive sympathy of a majority of students, the vocal
and active presence of dissenters spotlighted the real disunity of *studenchestvo* at
a time when its "conscious" unity had just been proclaimed.[77]

As the first anniversary of the March 4 demonstration approached, student groups called for new public protest as a symbol of historical continuity. Due to the arrest of student leaders, the quick action of the police in keeping groups of demonstrators apart, and the absence of broad public support, the demonstration did not attain the success of its predecessor, and the movement slowly fizzled out. By mid-March, dissent emerged within the leadership, and even the newly discovered and popular "chemical obstructions," or stink bombs, no longer disrupted the studies of those who remained in classrooms. The 1902 disorders wound down amid renewed debate over the methods and goals of student protest. The sacrifices seemed high, the community fragmented, and society unwilling to join a broad-based movement.[78]

In part, the spirit of protest had moved east. With the failure of the military draft to quell student unrest, the government instituted a new policy of mass Siberian exile—ordinarily the privilege of political prisoners. Student leaders from Moscow and St. Petersburg were deported to Siberia, while other students were banished to their hometowns or given short jail sentences. The train journey to Siberia foreshadowed the fate of this policy as well. Demanding a certain standard of treatment, which they considered to be their right, students protested a substandard train car and greeted the crowds en route with revolutionary songs and a red flag, which they had insisted on keeping with them. As letters from the exiles soon appeared in hectographs and the oppositional press, their tales circulated around European Russia. By the summer and fall of 1902, the government even sent a high-ranking envoy to offer students an amnesty in return for an oral promise of good behavior. In telegrams and letters, students recounted how they had refused to agree to concessions, boycotted scheduled meetings with the emissary, and declined to accept anything but a general and unconditional amnesty. Ironically, the final amnesty divided the exiles into three groups—not according to their original actions, but to their reception of the envoy.[79]

THE PERIOD OF DIFFERENTIATION

Despite the dramatic events of 1901 and 1902, large-scale student protest did not recur until the outbreak of the Russo-Japanese War in 1904. In a period dominated by labor and agrarian unrest and the expansion of the liberation movement, students were clearly more interested in their own affairs, in particular, a new set of Temporary Rules that instituted a professors' disciplinary court. By involving professors in the internal discipline of students, the government hoped to contain disorders and to facilitate the "moral influence" of professors over students.[80] In the eyes of students, however, the reforms simply extended police functions to the professoriate. Rather than fostering a closer relationship between professors and students, the disciplinary court became a theater for the display of moral resistance.

Though the new decree had caused scattered protest in late 1902 and early 1903, events at the university brought tensions to a climax. When, in March 1903, a group of students attended an illegal meeting devoted to recent agrarian and labor unrest, sixty-eight participants were brought before the court. A hectographed transcript of the proceeding circulated in Petersburg before being reprinted in an émigré journal.[81] The courts were depicted as show trials—further proof of the absence of rule of law in Russia. Professor I. Ia. Foinitskii conducted the interrogation:

F: Bearing in mind that we already have sufficient material for your conviction, what do you have to say to vindicate yourself?

Accused: I have no doubt about your material and already realize that I shall not be acquitted.

Because students did not try to deny their actions, the court became an arena in which to probe attitudes and beliefs:

F: Do you consider the *skhodka* a good thing?

A: They have of course serious defects, primarily [because] they have the character of a *veche* [an ancient popular assembly] and lack forethought and discipline; but in general, I think it completely natural for people with similar attitudes living in similar conditions to gather and discuss questions of common concern.

F: But you know that they are forbidden?

A: Of course.

F: Then why did you go to a forbidden *skhodka?*

A: I consider that one of the ways to abolish norms standing in contradiction with popular consciousness is to disregard them. I consider such a nonobservance to be one of the factors [contributing] to the development of legal and governmental institutions.

The trial then turns into a debate on the nature of education and progress.

F: But why then do you students take it upon yourselves to discuss these questions? Wouldn't it be better to gain knowledge and ideas here in the university. . . and then introduce them to the kingdom of darkness?

A: Having fed on knowledge and ideas in the university (looking around at the board of judges), will people preserve them after graduation? I don't see it. You cannot imagine how truly difficult and painful it is for a student who truly loves the university to see his professors here in such a court. Alas, you do not understand that by judging or only interrogating me, you become the accomplice of the butcher who fires into an unarmed crowd.

F: How strangely you reason. You don't really think that the governmental order will change right away? That is the fruit of long and peaceful evolution. The peoples of the West are more cultured, and their governmental forms are better. Gradually progress will bring us toward them.

A: I don't see progress or the growth of culture *[kul'turnost']* in our governmental forms, quite the opposite.

Foinitskii, a political conservative, was particularly vilified after this exchange, and students portrayed the institution of the court as symbolic of the ideological and generational division between professoriate and *studenchestvo*. The following fall, students tried to disrupt sessions of the disciplinary court, portraying their actions as a "heroic struggle" in the name of students' "primordial testament." [82]

With most students thus occupied with events inside the academy, student leaders sought to explain the absence of large-scale protest. By December 1902, the *Kassa radikalov*—together with its conception of a unified and active *studenchestvo*—had dissolved. Foreshadowing its demise was its October leaflet, which distinguished that "active" part of the *studenchestvo*, "occupied with thought about the general struggle," from the "indifferent masses," concerned at most with the latest temporary rules. It identified a process of internal dissolution caused by the development of class divisions.[83] In 1903, student leaders named this process "differentiation" and gave it positive meaning. It was the product of historical progress: the evolution of political consciousness out of academic spontaneity.

Many student activists heralded the (illegal) political party as the organizational form of the future. By early 1903, Social Democratic (SD) and Socialist-Revolutionary (SR) groups had been founded in Petersburg University. While both party factions hoped to channel student protest and to recruit new members from the student population, they advanced conflicting theories regarding the nature and significance of student protest. The SDs led the acclaim for differentiation. Dismissive of nonparty politics, they called upon students to renounce their academic movement by aligning with the Russian Social Democratic Workers' Party (RSDRP). Together with other obsolete social groups, the *studenchestvo* must differentiate into its constituent social and ideological parts. The Social Democratic Group of Students presented party organization as a glorious alternative to bourgeois philistinism. Because Marx himself had recognized that some intellectuals could renounce their social origins by becoming conscious of historical processes, they asserted that students opposed to autocracy had two options: to become passive (e.g., liberal) spectators in the great historical drama, or to choose an active role on the side of the proletarian victors.[84] Rising in defense of coalition politics, the SRs attacked the SD position for underestimating the impact of student protest and promoting factional strife on the socialist left. Despite its fluid composition, they argued, the *studenchestvo* was a historically distinct group, and as such, must actively fight for both academic reform and political freedom.[85]

In the fall of 1903, a new nonparty student group, the Partisans of Struggle, presented a unique synthesis of traditional student ideology and support for political parties. In their first major leaflet, "What must we do?" they argued that "the *studenchestvo*, as such, [must] participate in the overall revolutionary struggle against autocracy." As champions of both academic and political freedom, students should be active in both student politics and revolutionary events such as workers' demonstrations. Yet the Partisans also acknowledged the process of political differentiation. Likening student protest to a prep school for real-life politics, they intended to foster students' ideological development in preparation for their entrance as individuals into the political party of their choice. The goal of student organization was, in their view, the production of (class) consciousness. Thus, one of their proclamations detailed a prescriptive ladder of organization from the unorganized apathetic masses, up through the archaic mutual-aid society, the higher study circle, the revolutionary group, and culminating with the revolutionary party at the top of the pyramid. Soon, the Partisans argued, the lesser organizations would die out, and students' central representative organ would be a "coalition council" composed of delegates from political parties.[86]

Other attempts to define a nonparty basis for the student movement likewise identified a process of political differentiation. In 1903, Grigorii Nestroev, a former student, founded the journal *Student* in Switzerland, which he introduced as the "revolutionary-social organ" of *studenchestvo*. Hoping to provide a nonparty socialist basis for the student movement as a distinct but integrated part of the revolutionary opposition, Nestroev argued that students should join the political parties of their choice but still collaborate within the university.[87] When representatives from nineteen educational institutions gathered in Odessa in November 1903 under the auspices of *Student*, the "sharp differentiation of the contemporary *studenchestvo*" was nonetheless the central topic of debate. Despite regional variations (St. Petersburg had apparently achieved the most advanced stage), this "inevitable process" was visible in the rift between active and inactive students as well as in the rivalry of progressive and reactionary political groups. With the *studenchestvo* "having lost the character of an organic whole and outgrown the basis of its militant-academic principles," the manifesto declared that "a mass student movement—a movement that is spontaneous, unconscious, and academic, is now impossible." Differentiation had instead facilitated "a conscious, organized, and universal movement with a social-revolutionary character." Strikes, meetings, and demonstrations would allow students first to gain a political education and then to transcend their student identity through a party affiliation.[88]

The manifesto was one of a growing number of documents reconceptualizing student social identity on the basis of a new narrative history, which was fully propounded in two long pamphlets by the Partisans. The first explored the institutional development of the *studenchestvo,* and the second marked the fifth anniversary of 1899. The story begins in the 1860s, when a new generation of students pioneered the circle of self-education and the mutual-aid society, which became enduring sites for the "passionate discussions of social questions, the perpetual debates between Populists and Marxists [sic], and the production of practical methods for the spread of the new world view." Having awakened and then sustained the *studenchestvo* with a "life-creating light," these institutions underwent a tremendous expansion during the 1890s, when students began to unite into a single community. The events of 1899 marked the culmination of this period, for differentiation had since precipitated the dissolution of the mutual-aid society, the circle, and their creators, the *studenchestvo.* "The time has passed when one could speak of a single *studenchestvo,* able to fuse in one harmonious cry of protest against everything bestial and reactionary," the Partisans thus proclaimed. A "fully conscious movement of the revolutionary part of the *studenchestvo*" had evolved out of the "spontaneous and disorderly movement" of all students. What was lost in numbers was gained in quality. "We invite you to look back to the past," the second pamphlet concluded, "to recall the long journey of the revolutionary *studenchestvo,* to consider all the twists and turns of the heroic battle of Russian youth, to analyze the tremendous evolution of this struggle." In this framework, student radicalism no longer reflected eternal principles, but points along a path of personal and collective development culminating in political consciousness and class differentiation. The past was a map of progress—the teleological unfolding of revolution.[89]

Although Marxist conceptions of class and history influenced these discussions, this new narrative was not a reflection of Marxism. More important was the imposition of dialectical categories upon a social movement—mass-vanguard, academic-political, spontaneity-consciousness—categories which themselves were translated into Russian Marxism and the labor movement. In addition, the motif of dissolution reflected students' inevitable failure to enact universal principles, indeed, to reproduce the mythical solidarity of 1899. The political fissures appearing by 1902 shaped a perception of disintegration, and the new historical narrative gave it positive meaning. Even as the expansion of party organizations and the lack of apparent interest in revolutionary politics on the part of most students seemed to confirm the process of differentiation, the dissolution of *studenchestvo* was undermined by those very groups who anticipated it. The SDs may have dismissed *studenchestvo* as archaic, but they still addressed students as a group uniquely able to overcome its objective bourgeois origins. They thus continued to define student identity by ethical rather than class standards and consistently highlighted the generational advantage—the idealistic youth not yet tainted by compromise. As a source of self-identification, therefore, *studenchestvo* still promised refuge from an unappealing class affiliation and the total commitment of a professional revolutionary. Radicals had simply recast the metaphor of individual and collective education embodied in students' striving for consciousness. The goal now entailed the overcoming of parochial "student" identity.

The student movement played an important role in the politicization of Russian society. Though censorship prevented public comment on the student strike of 1899, its impact was tremendous. The thousands of students who went on strike, many of whom were suspended, arrested, and exiled to their provincial homes, each had a story to tell to parents, siblings, and friends. The thousands of proclamations circulating through educated society and official governmental announcements each told a story of its own. These unprecedented events perpetuated the mythology of *studenchestvo* for the next generation of students. At the same time, the movement advanced an unstable mixture of powerful ideas, from the rights of man and citizen to the heroic struggle of youth, from the defense of science to social progress. That the student movement remained uncontrollable—an oft-lamented fact for student leaders and revolutionary parties alike—was perhaps an inevitable consequence.

Calling 1899 the birth of a new era of "active" protest, student leaders discerned a process of collective development as the *studenchestvo* embarked on a quest for organization, order, and consciousness. In the most schematic history of the student movement published shortly after the 1905 Revolution, two former student leaders identified four periods, each reflecting a particular stage in the development of political consciousness: the "spontaneous" academic movement of 1899, the "transition from academism to radicalism" in 1901, the period of "radicalism" in 1902, and the emergence of "conscious academic and conscious political movements" in 1903. With the academic or political character of these stages supposedly accompanied by academic or political methods of struggle, the 1899 strike was even termed an "academic" method. "Academism entered its natural channel," they summarized. "From a spontaneous movement it became a conscious movement," and, by 1905, "it had left its artificial channel and deserted the walls of the university." [90] Though this formula is hardly accurate, it was not an interpretive model imposed from without but an integral part of the student movement itself. The categories of *Bildungsroman* that later organized autobiography and the political mythologies of the Soviet period had developed within the context of a mass movement. With its compelling explanatory power, this model influenced the attitudes of an entire generation of students. In their quest to give order to their "disorders," however, students imposed a teleology that never contained the diversity of their experiences.

This "official" story is thus legendary. Though students had experienced a process of politicization between 1899 and 1904, various impulses could and did exist within one person or group, and the "necessary" end to the story would turn out not to be so necessary after all. Indeed, *studenchestvo* continued to provide a basis for shared identity, just as the metaphors of student protest— the school of dissent, the light of knowledge, and revolutionary education—all combined politics with science. The model of differentiation built on the false assumption that political consciousness develops in a linear and transparent fashion by the displacement of its antithesis, in this case "academic" interests (in the case of workers, "economic" ones). The continued vitality of traditional forms of student protest as well as the persistence of its metaphors decades later in autobiographical writings suggest that the proclaimed rift between the academic and the political could be reconciled. And despite its dialectical coherence, the official story was also incomplete. Strikingly absent from the political world of students was discussion of the private sphere, other than the various references to the "mire of life" leading to the corruption of ideals and the compromises of age and career. The grand narrative of consciousness had neglected everyday life.

CHAPTER THREE

Righteous Men and Sinners

Honor and the Politics of "Personal" Life

Where else indeed has [student] youth developed in and for itself—as it has here in Russia—almost all forms of creation, an almost complete little culture with its own righteous men and sinners, martyrs and "renegades," [and] with its own exclusive
songs, opinions, and even the rudiments of almost all the sciences?

—Vasilii Rozanov, "On Student Disorders"

Rumors that Leonid Ponomarev, a student at Petersburg's Mining Institute, was a spy had been rampant for years.[1] Fellow students recall that he was regarded as an "alien body in the organism of *studenchestvo.*" Long-simmering suspicions finally boiled over in 1901, when Ponomarev unexpectedly appeared at a party
in honor of the memory of the Ukrainian writer Taras Shevchenko. After being
tailed by several students calling him a spy, among other epithets, he quit the gathering only to appear several days later in the student cafeteria, the meeting place of
the radicals. This time, a student loudly accused him of being a spy and suggested
that after the events of the other evening, he should be more circumspect than to
show his face in the dining hall. Ponomarev feigned ignorance of the immediate
accusation and the circumstances of the party. Precisely this reaction confirmed
suspicions: a "real" student would have defended his honor. "Only spies conduct
themselves in this manner," one student remarked. Another elaborated, "If five
minutes ago I could still have doubts, you have just convinced me that you are indeed a spy. If you were an honest man *[poriadochnyi chelovek]* you would have
struck me *[dali mne po fisionomii].*" Only a spy would allow his name to be be-
smirched and not demand vindication. The charges against Ponomarev were formally levied, and a student court of honor subsequently indicted, tried, and con-
victed him. The mechanisms by which a spy was exposed provide a unique insight
into the criteria used to define both the spy and his nemesis, the honorable student.

The first step was indictment, that is, the collection of evidence for the court. Realizing the difficulties of finding direct documentation of Ponomarev's trade, the two students charged with the investigation focused their objective as follows: "to illuminate his character" (*osvetit' ego lichnost'*). Because identifying a spy was first and foremost a matter of character, no distinction was made between public and private life. During the next weeks, investigators were sent to Warsaw and Kharkov; others examined his living situation, finances, and personal life in St. Petersburg. The following "relevant" facts came to light: Ponomarev was the son of a police sergeant-major; he lived well but had no apparent employment or help from his parents; he had occasionally been supported by women and at least one time had sold "compromising documents" to the husband of a woman with whom he was living, presumably for use in a divorce case; he had stolen blueprints from a factory during a summer internship there. His actions among his peers were equally suspect: he often recorded the names of student-orators at meetings and asked who distributed illegal leaflets. More than any other single factor, his overall behavior provided the most damning evidence. By accusing one investigator of bias and continuing to feign ignorance of the long-term rumors, Ponomarev displayed the "moral physiognomy" of a spy. The psychological portrait was simply "not consistent with the psychology of an honorable unsullied man," but that of "a man capable of anything."

Any nagging doubts were erased at a general *skhodka,* which was constituted as the court of honor. While the presentation of the evidence convinced most students, the behavior of the accused again proved critical. With his "tendency to smear witnesses and prosecutors," "attempts to be evasive," and "threats and tears of powerless malice," Ponomarev did not display the "honorable and open reaction" of an innocent man. With a unanimous vote, Ponomarev was excluded from *studenchestvo* and from the institute, a decision apparently made official by the faculty council on the basis of evidence collected by students. The final "proof" emerged the following year, when the procurator of the trial was arrested. Soon thereafter, Ponomarev openly joined the ranks of the police.

This process and its recollection in memoirs illustrate how the social identity of the student and the spy were mutually sustaining—the spy was judged according to those tenets of behavior and psychology perceived as inherent to the "student." Such a conception of student identity relied upon a transparent congruence of public and personal life, honor and behavior—a semiotic idea central to students' conception of education and politics as well: the development of an integral world view was accompanied (and documented) by the application of its principles into life. That Ponomarev had stolen blueprints, betrayed the trust of a woman, and refused to defend himself to his accusers constituted sufficient evidence of his dishonorable character and, therefore, his extracurricular occupation as a spy. The ritual naming and exclusion of the impure element then restored the purity of the student community.

Other accounts of spying place a similar stress on the semiotics of behavior. One memoir of a student spy describes the general preoccupation of students with spies in their midst:

> Spy-phobia was developed to a high degree among students. Spies were seen everywhere. The imagination endowed him with definite external qualities. Without fail he had to be somber, taciturn, and incommunicative, and he had either to have shifty eyes or to go about in dark glasses. Someone with normal eyes—cheerful and communicative—was a good person and couldn't possibly be a spy.[2]

The semiotic counterpart to the spy was, of course, the revolutionary, who was likewise distinguished by his temperament. He always sang revolutionary songs, loudly applauded radical speeches at parties, hung out in the student cafeterias, and "had the mood" *(imel nastroenie)*. The revolutionary felt especially complemented when he noticed a spy following him in the street.[3] In a sense, the spy actually confirmed the selfhood of the revolutionary.

This memoirist also describes the consequences of a case of mistaken identity from 1901. A student at the Mining Institute had been accused of being a spy, and as rumors spread, a student activist at the university with the same last name came to be implicated as well. This second student initially had laughed off the rumors, but soon he came to feel himself the universal object of attention. "You know, he said darkly, it sometimes seems now that I am in fact a spy."[4] A cryptic archival source from 1903 authenticates such a scenario. One student accused of being a spy demanded a "public apology" in order to be "rehabilitated" in the eyes of his comrades. Because the accused also had his supporters, students debated whom to believe and how to react. Some proposed that if the accused was indeed innocent, then the accuser should be tried for slander.[5] The quick and indignant reaction of the accused student must have lent credence to his claim to honor.

Although the transparency of identity had been a characteristic of student politics since the 1860s, the boundaries of meaningful behavior in the early twentieth century are less clear. That the investigation of Ponomarev focused on his personal life suggests that the private sphere could have political significance for students. Yet if behavior made the spy, did it also make the student? In other words, to what extent did students organize their behavior according to commonly accepted conventions? How were "honorable" and "dishonorable" behavior constituted? Where did the public identity of the "student" end and private life begin? Did conventions differ within the student community? These questions proved especially important to conservative students and women students, who qualified their student identity with political or sexual criteria. Their examples suggest that an archetype of the radical male student was the norm against which students were measured; however, the rhetorical success of conservative students in appropriating the radical ethos points to some plasticity in its political content. For male students overall, the domain of "private" life began to raise increasingly political concerns.

THE POLITICS OF PURITY

At first it was easy to distinguish spies from real students. Stanislav Strumilin describes the atmosphere in 1899, when "mobilized spies, dressed in student uniforms" infiltrated the strike. According to Strumilin, all that was needed was an "elementary examination." Of a spy posing as a law student, one need only ask: "Ah, well then, you are acquainted with logic. Please identify the error in this syllogism: 'All geese are two-footed. You also are two-footed. Are you a goose?' " And before such a masterful display, the spy would acknowledge defeat and retreat in shame.[6] By 1902, however, the problem of the spy had become much more serious, because it overlapped with the entrance of conservative students into the political fray. For student radicals, the presence of political dissent posed a double threat of betrayal and contamination. The conservatives not only refused to play by the rules of the radicals but also claimed to be "true" students— in contrast to the radicals.

Lamenting the new milieu of dirt, degradation, and corruption in the university, daily bulletins from the 1902 protests stressed the narrow distinctions between students of order, infiltrators, and spies. One bulletin described a policy of "divide and conquer," according to which "representatives of order" and spies—but not real students—were allowed to enter the university. This bulletin carefully juxtaposed stories of betrayal and heroism: a certain "student Naumov" had turned an obstructionist over to the police, while imprisoned students continued a hunger strike. Decrying the defilement of the "temple of science" by spies and reactionaries, a subsequent bulletin described a university "purged" of true students, that is, those who value knowledge. It noted that spies had finally found a suitable milieu, because the "order party," which usually never set foot in the university, felt it their duty to attend classes during a strike. Overall, therefore, these bulletins linked the antistrike movement to both political betrayal and intellectual dishonesty. If students were to lead society by moral example, many argued, it was first necessary to purge *(ochistit')* the university and the student community.[7]

The appearance of conservatives in the academy did not threaten the dominance of the radicals, because their numbers were minimal. Their menace was symbolic: by their very presence they subverted any claim to a single, honorable *studenchestvo*. At the same time, and not coincidentally, the new conservative groups sought to undermine the unitary identity of the "student." The Unorganized Group of Students at the Technological Institute, which led the first active (and organized) resistance to the 1902 student strike, defended its program with a direct assault on the radical ethos: "We consider that the title 'student' does not impose any obligations relating to political conviction. . . . [E]ach student possesses freedom of conviction and action as a private person."[8] By reconfiguring the academic/political dyad in their own favor, conservatives defined the *studenchestvo* as an academic group, which should properly abstain from partisan politics—the domain of "personal," nonstudent life. They thus inverted the categories of the radicals into public/academic and private/political life. The group University for Science explained the new logic:

> We entered university for scientific improvement *[sovershenstvovanie]*. The *studenchestvo* is formed by this fundamental task—and we cannot stray from this [one] task of the university in service to any other idea, ideas of a political character. Therefore, each student as such cannot [also] be a political actor. We sternly delimit the person of the student from that of the citizen.[9]

This attempt to remove the political from student identity cut to the heart of a movement that claimed to embody the unity of principle and action, indeed, to struggle in the name of the citizen. Conservatives consequently focused their attack on the institutions of student protest, arguing, for example, that the *skhodka* trampled on the very principles proclaimed by the radicals: the freedoms of conscience, speech, and assembly. With all students obligated (in principle) to adhere to its decision, and hence to strikes, conservatives legitimately complained that they were excluded from participating and that the rights of minorities were disregarded.[10] It should be noted that these conservative groups nonetheless countered violence with violence in their antistrike activities.

A January 1901 memorandum to the rector of St. Petersburg University from a first-year student, Daniil Ianovich, provides an early elaboration of this counter-ethos. Writing out of the "duty of an honorable student," Ianovich decried the "violence in the name of academic freedom" and offered his own assessment of its causes. Ideally, he wrote, the student milieu should form the environment that inculcates *(vospitat')* "social instincts," the awareness of one's "duty before Tsar and Fatherland," and "an independent and firm view of one's calling." Thrust into an unknown city and forced to rely on their fellows for support, most students had succumbed to the temperament and passion of the radicals. To counter this unfortunate "seduction," Ianovich requested permission to form an academic organization designed to forge a different sense of family among students and in the university.[11] Ianovich had appropriated the metaphors of student radicalism and offered an alternative story.

The first academic organization was founded almost two years later. According to the rector, some three hundred students from the "party of order" wanted to form a student corporation, which he praised as a "measure against disorder." On November 13, 1902, the tsar approved the charter of "Dennitsa":

The corporation will facilitate the development of healthy comradely interchange and the consolidation of friendly ties between its members upon the basis of . . . love for science, respect for law, a spirit of order, and an honorable manner of thought. Uniting in the endeavor to prepare intellectually and morally for service to the fatherland, the members of the corporation may not pursue political goals.

The charter refashioned such traditional student principles as honor, science, and moral development into conservative-patriotic form. As the first cell of a parallel and alternative student community, Dennitsa was to counter the influence of radical underground groups. Membership was to remain small to foster internal bonds, and new corporations were to be formed as the number of interested students grew. Unlike those groups that claimed to advocate the elimination of politics from the person of the student, Dennitsa had simply inverted the formula. Conservative politics replaced radical, keeping behavior semiotic; except that now, a spirit of order and discipline (rather than boldness and dignity) was to signify a member of the corps.[12]

For student radicals, the existence of this group was most humiliating during January 1904. When war was declared against Japan, members of Dennitsa convened a meeting at St. Petersburg University to compose an address to the tsar. With a vote of 500 to 300, Dennitsa's version was approved, their opponents were kicked out, and the assembly sang "God Save the Tsar" before parading to the Winter Palace in a patriotic manifestation. According to the radicals, Dennitsa had simply timed its action well—at this very same time, they themselves were attending the funeral of the populist leader Mikhailovskii. Nevertheless, the picture of students behaving in this "dishonorable" manner—even cheering the chief of police—was shameful to them and by extension to the entire *studenchestvo*.[13] With its appropriation of student institutions in the name of political conservatism, Dennitsa formed a shadow world caricaturing the radicals. While radicals tried to laugh it off with ironic parody, their tone was always serious. At stake was their honor as students.

THE POLITICS OF GENDER

The language of student protest was strikingly masculine: the *studenchestvo* defined itself as a brotherhood. Leaflets, songs, and poems referred to brotherly love and brotherly graves, younger and elder brothers, fathers and sons. This fact raises the question of how women students understood their place in the student community. To be sure, women students consistently joined the countless protests, demonstrations, and strikes, and shared most of the same punishments. Indeed, the proportional representation of women students was often higher than that of male students. During the 1901 demonstrations at the Kazan Cathedral, for example, more than one-eighth of all Bestuzhev and women medical students were arrested, compared with approximately one-thirtieth of all university and one-twentieth of all technological students.[14] Yet female radicalism also had distinctive dynamics. Their gender fundamentally shaped their attitude toward education and their experience of student politics.

The histories of female education and female radicalism in Russia were closely intertwined. Since the opening of educational opportunity for women in the 1870s, women students typically had seen higher education as a means of liberation and development, because it facilitated their entrance into both public life and consciousness. During this same period, however, and despite the participation of hundreds of educated women, the populist movements of the 1870s all but ignored the "woman question" in favor of a concept of "the people." The liberation of the people, or so the argument went, would also bring about the liberation of women. Concern with women's issues, as such, was consequently dismissed by men and women alike as particularistic and egoistic.

This convention still held for the student movement twenty years later, but the status of women's education had fundamentally changed in the intervening period. By the late 1880s, all institutions of higher education for women had been closed except for the St. Petersburg Courses, which had been saved at the last minute. Although the Women's Medical Institute was opened in 1897 and the Moscow Women's Courses in 1900, women students strongly felt the precariousness of their position and were loath to act in any way that could threaten the survival of their institutions. As they were well aware, this problem was gender specific—the government could hardly close down the university system. From the very beginning of the 1899 protests, therefore, women students faced a dual loyalty—to the student movement and to that which enabled them to join the student movement: higher education for women.

On the surface, the experience of women students in 1899 largely mirrored that of their male comrades. After university students had called their strike in response to the police beatings of February 8, Bestuzhev students declared the solidarity strike, and within three days of the strike vote at the university, most lectures at the courses were cancelled due to the complete absence of the students (and occasionally the "illness" of a professor). Even an announcement threatening to expel anyone not attending classes failed to ameliorate the situation. After the end of the first strike, the twenty-one students (including nine in their last semester) who had actually been expelled were allowed to return. Notably, almost five hundred students threatened to request their own expulsion should they not be amnestied. On March 21, the strike was likewise renewed. During the next weeks, 225 were suspended or expelled for protesting the exams. Though many considered this second strike vote nonbinding, most students joined neither the opponents nor proponents, instead choosing a passive stance; by May 12, only 284 students had taken an examination.[15]

The strike at the Women's Medical Institute was less successful. Although a vast majority of students had resolved to boycott classes beginning on February 15, thirty students attended lectures on the first day of the strike, and more students showed up every day. By the time the strike was officially ended a week later, most had already resumed their studies. Their decision not to join the second strike that March was the only instance of nonparticipation in the student movement in the history of the institute. Even the director noted the ambivalence of students, correctly forecasting that they would join future protests. The weak reaction of medical students to the strike was undoubtedly related to the recent establishment of the institute. As in the Bestuzhev Courses, they feared that the Ministry of Education would close down their institution should the strike be called. These fears were amplified by the statements of academic officials, who, in an attempt to dissuade students from the strike, typically suggested that it would harm the cause of women's medical education. Some students also expressed concern that the scheduled opening of the Moscow Higher Women's Courses for the next year would be canceled or delayed as well.[16]

Despite these uncertainties, Bestuzhev students had supported the strike. Indeed, they were compelled to declare their position openly and individually, a step never taken by university students. On February 19, the administration declared that the courses would be officially closed for an oral interrogation of students to determine the real level of support for the strike. The inquiry consisted of six questions concerning support for and participation in the strike. Many students appearing before the board affirmed their support for the strike and then declined to speak more specifically. Those who did answer other questions expressed no regrets for their actions, declared that future protests would depend upon the will of the majority, and accepted "moral responsibility" for their actions. When results were tallied, it was found that a solid majority, 566 students, had gone on record in support of the strike. Many students unable to appear in person sent signed declarations of support and received an official reprimand in return.[17] In its interpretation of these results, the administration blamed the spread of disorders on the association of its students with male university students and cited such known factors as "female impressionability," their "dependence on male students," and the imperative to shield them from "harmful influences." What among male students was called solidarity, among females was "impressionability." [18]

For their part, many women students felt a moral imperative to declare their position. The case of Elizaveta D'iakonova is revealing. Although she had initially spoken out against the strike, believing it a potential threat to the continued existence of the courses, she wrote a letter to the administration of the courses on February 22 formally registering her change of heart. She explained that her absence from St. Petersburg during the beginning of the strike had led her to misinterpret its true significance. In supporting the strike, she cited both her sympathy for her comrades and the imperative to continue this struggle for "human rights." Her diary entries for this week likewise indicate an intense moral rather than political struggle. Although D'iakonova did not recognize the second strike vote of March, she likewise considered it immoral to take exams in the midst of such disorder and animosity. She delayed her graduation until the following fall.[19]

During the strike, women students had experienced a dual loyalty. As students, they tried to fulfill their obligations to *studenchestvo;* as women, they felt a personal responsibility to defend the cause of higher education for women. This conflict became the topic of two proclamations, the first written by women students, the second by men. The first struck a tone altogether different than the daily bulletins and other proclamations written by male students at this time. Whereas university proclamations likened the victims of exile and expulsion to martyrs and used their heroism as both evidence of and exhortation for solidarity, the leaflet produced by women students instead lamented the lack of solidarity among women. Addressed "To Students Who Are Taking Exams," it questioned these students' motives: "You don't really think that you are saving the honor of the courses?" it asked. "After all that has happened you must be convinced that their condition is sufficiently stable . . . that it is not necessary to sacrifice comradely feelings for their preservation. . . . How many have we already sacrificed thanks to your lack of camaraderie and solidarity?"[20] The proclamation implied an important contrast between the solidarity of (male) students and the egoism of women. That women feared the closure of the courses was depicted as nothing other than selfishness.

This difference was also the subject of the second proclamation, a poem entitled "To Women Students" *(Studentkam)* and dedicated to those expelled *(Iskliuchennym kursistkam)*. It was written during the early days of the examination period, when student activists in both the university and the courses attempted to disrupt exams, and many suffered expulsion and exile. With this poetic acknowledgment, the male authors accepted the woman student into their brotherhood—so long as she proclaimed her loyalty solely to the demands of student solidarity rather than to women's education. The poem opens with a panegyric to the heroism of women students:

> You did not disperse, true companions,
> With us you raised the flag,
> The hypocritical enemies did not overwhelm you—
> The decisive step was made.
>
> Quick, with the best inclinations of the times,
> You rose, as did we
> Against the heavy Russian burden
> Against violence and darkness.

The poem then turns to those women students who opposed the strike and were taking examinations, depicting them in gendered terms as submissive:

> Let she who is gifted with pitiful conscience
> Not carry her share,
> Let the well behaved children study (modestly)
> In happiness, under the rod.

> But you—do not disperse proud companions,
> All of us are linked as one:
> The dignity of the proud individual—
> The best feeling—is our bond.

Men opposing the strike were strike-breakers, while women who did likewise were modest, well-behaved children.[21]

D'iakonova briefly mentioned this poem in her diary, angry that students were describing the exams at the courses as "shameful events." Although she was herself boycotting them, she found their self-righteous condescension toward women students to be hypocritical, because male students were not only taking examinations but also had no fear that the university could be closed down by decree. Believing that male students had held women up to a different standard, D'iakonova turned the standard on its head. In her view, women had acted out a legitimate fear for their courses, whereas men had only feared for themselves. Archival records suggest that proportionally more university students than Bestuzhev students actually took their examinations that spring.[22]

As women thus navigated the treacherous waters of protest, they discovered that the government could not muster the courage to oppose public opinion and close down their schools. The Moscow Courses were opened on schedule in 1900. Although some students would oppose later strikes and protests under the banner of protecting the courses, this argument had become more of a rhetorical strategy than a heartfelt concern.[23] The further development of student protest among women was shaped by a factor already apparent in 1899. Responding to the condescension of officials and male students, women students increasingly framed their demands and goals in terms of the individual right to self-expression and self-determination. That is, the obligation of women students to join protests was a duty to the self as well as to the collective.[24] During the spring of 1904, this dimension of female student radicalism emerged fully formed.

In the days immediately following the declaration of war against Japan in January 1904, patriotic salutations were sent to the tsar from individuals and institutions across the country, including one sent by faculty of the Bestuzhev Courses in the name of both its faculty and students. Upon learning of this action, *kursistki* became indignant that as members of the academic community they had not been consulted. When approximately four hundred students gathered on February 3 to discuss this incident, attention centered first on the role of women in wartime. One position held that women were obligated to support the courage of their friends and family during this national crisis, whatever their personal convictions. Others countered by pointing out the great harm that this war would inflict upon the Russian people. As a group, they then resolved to protest the address signed in the name of the courses and to express their censure of those professors who had participated.[25] Women students were not obligated, it seems, either to remain silent against their conscience or to allow others to speak in their name.

On February 9, 1,066 of 1,473 registered *kursistki* attended a second meeting in order to work out a definitive position and an appropriate course of action. With a lopsided vote of 1,006 to 20 (plus 40 who refused to recognize the *skhodka*), they affirmed their dissatisfaction in principle with the actions of the faculty. By the time the final vote was taken almost twelve hours later, the few hundred remaining resolved with a vote of 290 to 116 that student deputies would read a statement of censure to each professor in his auditorium and that all students must share equally in any punishment. When the faculty had included the name of the *kursistka* in its address to the tsar, the resolution stated, it had displayed a "lack of respect for the elementary rights of the individual." It was further resolved that all relations with the forty students who had refused to accept the will of the majority be severed.[26]

The Bestuzhev Courses were immediately closed, only to reopen a week later after special entrance tickets had been distributed to "reliable" students. By this time, slightly more students (276) had gone on record in opposition to the resolution, daily attendance did not exceed 500 students, and the first 21 students had been suspended. When the deputies began to implement the resolution (expressing their moral censure in both oral and written form), they were suspended for a period of two years.[27] As the level of confrontation increased over the semester, punishment became harsher. Students demonstratively returned entry and examination tickets to the administration, disrupted exams, and verbally insulted professors. By April, 293 students had been suspended for returning their examination cards, and an additional 269 had been expelled for more active demonstrations.[28] These figures were simply unprecedented—representing some 38% of the student body.

The dynamics of this protest revolved around one particular question. At issue in leaflets on both sides of the dispute was not the morality or immorality of the war or comradely solidarity—though both issues were certainly raised. Rather, it was the meaning of *lichnost'*, which in rough translation means the individual, the integral personality. On February 9, students had asserted that the address sent by the faculty council to the tsar in the name of the courses had violated the rights of the individual *(lichnost')* to develop and express her opinion. Yet in addition, it had resolved that students were bound by the decision of the majority (a condition to which all but forty students had agreed) and were obligated to share the punishments imposed against the student delegates. The rights of the individual were to be defended through the united action of the collective. As opponents later stressed, a space for the expression of dissent did not really exist.

Those students opposing the protest organized into two groups, the Middle Party and the Women's University for Science. Their leaflets focused on the conflict between the rights of the individual and the coercion of the collective. One leaflet asserted that to adhere to the will of the *skhodka* against one's personal convictions was cowardly because it was easier to follow the crowd than to risk its censure. Turning the heroic imagery of student radicalism on its head, this proclamation asserted: "It is easier to be 'radical' than to be yourself." [29] Another proclamation noted a contradiction among the radicals between word and deed: "Certain phrases are often repeated among your enraptured and enthusiastic words: it is necessary to develop *lichnost'* in oneself, the striving toward the freedom of opinion, toward full equality. But we consider these words to be beautiful only when they leave the realm of theory and enter that of practice." The defense of personality, they argued, had resulted only in fanaticism and dogmatism.[30] Another leaflet observed that the confrontational tactics of the protesters reflected poorly on their high principles and concluded that "the path of rude deception cannot facilitate the development of *lichnost'* or ideals." [31]

On the opposing side, students argued that it was their moral duty to carry on the collective protest. It is not clear whether they acted out of indignation with the original action of the faculty council, respect for the principle of collectivity, or anger at the level of repressions, but it was probably a mixture of all three. When students returned their entrance or examination cards, they often wrote their reasons on the back. Many copied sections from the original resolution; others gave different but also standardized explanations:

> Your Excellency: I am returning my ticket to you, because I consider it impossible to attend classes by a ticket. In addition, I attest that I wish to share the fate of my expelled comrades.[32]

> Protesting the expulsion of [my] comrades and demanding their return, I refuse to take exams.[33]

> Being in agreement on principle with [my] expelled comrades, who were only fulfilling the resolution of the general *skhodka* of February 9, 1904, I demand their return to the courses; otherwise I will share their fate.[34]

This protest consisted of a series of individual acts—the demonstrative return of personalized examination and entrance tickets. Nevertheless, the vast majority of the written explanations copied one of the above formulas and lacked any truly individual comment.

The "individual" was nonetheless the real theme of their protest. In response to the accusations of opponents, leaflets focused on the function of both education and protest in the development of *lichnost'*. The most important such defense appeared in February 1904.

> We are told that we value neither science nor our [educational] institution. . . . This is not true. Science is valuable to us, but we believe that science and life must go hand in hand and mutually influence each other. Science must help us resolve the contradictions presented by life—we do not want to keep [science] in the laboratories and classrooms. But we do not believe that thanks to this same science we must give up our principles. Our first duty is to produce *lichnost'* in ourselves.[35]

According to this formula, the goal of education was not the accumulation of "pure" knowledge but the shaping of an ethical personality. On this basis, the leaflet criticized the attempt of faculty members to dissuade students from their protest, likening compromise to a violation of principle: "Instead of fostering [our] moral *lichnost'*, our teachers . . . are trying to break our determination and our principles." The decision to expel students was called a blatant attempt to threaten their "still-developing convictions" and "principled relationship to reality." The leaflet concluded by noting the positive aspects of the confrontation:

> These events facilitate self-definition, the development of conviction. They compel each of us to choose a position. . . . And now each must determine whether principle is valuable, whether the education of the moral *lichnost'* is necessary. . . . Each must determine whether he has the courage not only to speak his convictions but also to repudiate them.[36]

More than any other incident, the protests of the spring of 1904 reveal the central contradiction of the student movement as a whole. According to the theory developed among students of both sexes over the previous half-century, the primary goal of education and political protest was to develop moral and intellectual character, and, ultimately, to liberate the individual from the shackles (legal, political, and economic) of the old regime. Yet at the same time, the student was duty-bound to uphold the honor and will of the collective. Although the thorny question of the relationship between the rights of the individual and the obligations of the collective had also been raised by conservative male students, the question had been rephrased into the question of the health of the *studenchestvo* rather than the rights of the individual.

Women students had instead raised the ideal of *lichnost'*. Notably absent from leaflets produced that spring was the glorified word "*studenchestvo.*" One even used the neutral phrase "student corporation" (*korporatsiia uchashchikhsia*) to refer to the collective of Bestuzhev students. With education symbolizing for women their entrance into public life as full-fledged participants, even the original form of protest reflected this overriding concern to speak one's convictions. It is notable, moreover, that I have not found a similar case among male students. The student movement as a whole was characterized by mass actions and the grand act of heroism, rather than by the individualized gestures making up this particular incident. Out of the actual and potential conflict between gender and politics, women students had displaced the ideal of *studenchestvo* with a concept of an ethical individual.[37] Rather than rejecting the transparency of principles and behavior, they had thus reconfigured it.

THE POLITICS OF DAILY LIFE

"Honor" was a word often used by students to describe their behavior and their protests. Just as the honorable student would not have acted like the spy Leonid Ponomarev, the honorable student always stood ready to join his fate to that of his comrades. Internal disputes were likewise resolved by one of the original institutions of the student subcultures, the court of honor. With his ironic words about righteous men and sinners, martyrs and renegades, Vasilii Rozanov had recognized the fundamental role of honor in student culture, indeed, the centrality of polar values—sincerity and duplicity, virtue and corruption, dignity and abasement, principle and compromise. The rhetoric of student protest superimposed a variety of stock characters on these oppositions: students and liberals (i.e., professors), students and the state, students and the "party of order," (student) youth and adults. Because the concept of honor does not distinguish between public and private spheres, the question arises: Who, exactly, was the honorable student after the protest was over? Did student radicals translate their "politics" into their social environment as well? These questions are particularly difficult to address because of fragmentary sources. Unlike earlier generations of radicals, students rarely wrote about their private lives; this absence underlines the importance to them of their identity as public actors.

Despite the impression one might gain from their leaflets and published memoirs and even the publicistic writings of progressive Russians in general, students did not spend all of their spare time reading Marx and Chernyshevskii or propagandizing among workers. Indeed, by the late nineteenth century, students must have been rather notorious figures in St. Petersburg—and not just in a political sense. Police reports record numerous incidents of students disturbing the peace. In 1898, more than six hundred university students were noted in such infractions, and twenty-eight incidents (usually involving groups) occurred between September and November alone.[38] Most took place around taverns, restaurants, and public houses, generally those located on or around Nevskii Prospect or on Vasil'evskii Island, where the university is located. The offenders,

usually intoxicated, sang songs in the early hours of the morning, harassed passersby (both reputable and disreputable), tried to break into restaurants and
brothels, and got into fights—sometimes with one another but more often with
doormen and police officers.

The list of disorders for the fall of 1898 is repetitive, and a few examples will
suffice. At four o'clock in the morning on September 9, 1898, a crowd of fifty
drunk students tried to force its way into a public house in the Kolomna district
that was already closed; they broke a window and banged on the door with a
board. On the night of September 12, two drunk students were walking along
Nevskii Prospect with several (apparently disreputable) women and started a
fight with passersby. When police officers intervened, they were greeted with
"rude words." At 2:00 AM on September 20, ten students—including student
leader Nikolai Iordanskii—left the restaurant "Golden Anchor" on the Sixth Line
of Vasil'evskii Island and, with shouts and songs, headed to another on the
Eighth Line. When they were refused entrance due to their intoxication, they
broke their way inside and struggled with the doorman and police officers. On
September 26, a crowd of students paraded down Nevskii Prospect with shouts,
whistles, and songs. The list continues with students disturbing the peace every
few days with their indecent and improper *(neprilichnoe)* conduct. Alcohol and
prostitutes were clearly well-established parts of student life.

Behavior that would have been categorized as hooliganism had it involved
working-class or poor youth instead became a political act.[39] For the St. Petersburg Chief of Police, the reason was quite simple. In a report on the history of
student "unrest and disorders," he did not distinguish between disorderly behavior on the street and the political disorder of student protest, because, for him,
they were part and parcel of the same phenomenon. While he recognized that
most street disturbances occurred under the influence of alcohol, he stressed that
students spoke rudely to police officers and sometimes actively hindered them in
the execution of their duties. Whether by protesting the political regime or resisting the authority of police, students subverted public order. As he concluded:
"the Russian student is mostly an anarchist, and therefore he can not look upon
a 'pharaoh' [cop] with indifference." [40]

While such incidents were not initially acts of protest, students also colored
them with political tones. Despite (or perhaps because of) their drunkenness,
they often asserted that it was their "right" to be served in a restaurant (or
brothel); once the police intervened, they would likewise condemn the "arbitrariness" *(proizvol)* of police actions. Interpreting these experiences in the same language of principle they used in their better known protests, students transformed
an act of *poshlost'* (which translates as vulgarity, commonness, and philistinism)
into a heroic feat. To be sure, not all such incidents culminated in eloquent, if
slurred, defenses of human rights; indeed, many remained limited to drunken
and rude behavior.

Three of the disorders described in the reports from the fall of 1898 and an additional one from 1904 do not fit this general pattern—the students were apparently not drunk nor were they defending their own rights and persons. Rather, they show students actively intervening on behalf of individuals being arrested or cited on city streets. In one case, shouting "attention!" *(smirno)*, a student interfered with and struck a police officer who was questioning an unidentified man. In another, two students attempted to prevent a group of prostitutes from being taken to the precinct station. And in a third, a passing medical student helped a prostitute, who was being thrown off the street by a doorman.[41] The case from 1904 is similar: a student from the Technological Institute tried to prevent a drunk prostitute from being arrested.[42] On the one hand, such an ethical linkage between the student and the prostitute had long been a positive cultural stereotype, with students coloring their intervention with broad political and social significance.[43] On the other hand, not all interaction with prostitutes could be considered honorable. In 1903, a Petersburg University student was expelled for immoral behavior: he had been denounced for keeping prostitutes.[44] Nevertheless, the dynamics of these cases (and their inclusion in reports about student politics) underline the degree to which students and police shared an ideological view of students' public identity. While drunkenness did not constitute dishonor, a passive acceptance of the authority of police and doormen clearly did.

That drinking, brawling, and whoring occupied an evident place in the daily lives of many students is clear despite the silence of memoirists.[45] That such behavior could at times have a political meaning depended on the particular circumstances and individuals involved. Yet the two pictures of student life do not correspond with each other. Although student leaflets proclaimed the idealistic purity of the student movement—including its support for women's rights—a visit to a prostitute was hardly an act of political principle. The relationship between students' concept of honor and political activity on the one hand and their behavior in their daily lives on the other was manifestly contradictory and flexible. This issue provided the context for a major controversy in Petersburg's student community that erupted onto the pages of the periodic press and allows us a rare glimpse into the private lives and public images of students on the eve of the 1905 Revolution.

In 1903, Boris Gegidze, a student at St. Petersburg University, published fictionalized memoirs entitled *In the University: Sketches of Student Life.*[46] The book was met by a chorus of criticism. Angry students demanded an explanation from Gegidze, and some simply wanted to beat him up.[47] The reaction from critics was likewise impassioned and defensive. At issue was not simply the topic: a similar book published in Moscow earlier that same year had met with a subdued if also critical press.[48] With one critic likening its author to a lackey and another citing his cardboard characters and minimal talent, the earlier book was lightly dismissed as worthless and banal.[49] The intense response to Gegidze's book is not really surprising, upon closer examination. Gegidze replaced the image of the honorable student with one of dissipation and artifice and, in the process, called into question the basic tenets of the intelligentsia.

Central to the impact of Gegidze's work was its form. Using the genre of a journal, Gegidze gave psychological depth to his hero by writing in the first person and adopting the voice of an estranged narrator. He also appropriated one of the central motifs of student radicalism—the individual striving towards self-development and consciousness—and inverted it. The hero, like generations of student radicals before him, travels from the darkness of the provinces, symbolized by the hated gymnasium, to the light of the university. For him as for Pisarev, the dream of enlightenment fades into the unappealing reality of academic pedantry. Yet Gegidze's hero also rejects the long-idealized alternative path represented by the student subcultures. He instead scrutinizes both the academic and the political worlds of the university through the shadowy conventions of students' daily life and thereby repudiates the predominant narrative of students' collective and generational experience.

The story is framed by two letters from the hero, Volodia, to his friend, a young doctor and former student. The first letter marks Volodia's graduation from gymnasium as an idealistic youth who has focused all his hopes and dreams on the university.

> I am now entering into that period of life which all consider to be the most radiant and happy. . . . I will pass through the doors into that building called the "temple of science" and which has the most revered and sacred name "bountiful mother." . . . To be a student, to acquire [useful] knowledge, to struggle for lofty ideas—what position could be higher or more noble? [50]

The second letter marks Volodia's graduation as a superfluous man of the twentieth century.

> Do you remember four years ago I wrote you a radiant and enthusiastic letter? . . . Nothing at all now remains from those young hopes and expectations. . . . The university and everything connected to it is now repulsive to me. . . . I am losing here what few impulses to the good I had in gymnasium. With every year, I feel, I have sunk deeper and deeper into the mire of life [*tina zhizni*] and have become more narrow-minded and vulgar [*mel'che i poshlee*]. I drag out a pointless, boring, and drab existence. For pleasure, I fill my life with billiards and fallen women. I study without the joyous feeling of cognition but bear the burden of various sciences with thoughts about my future diploma. . . .

The language contrasts images of light and truth associated with the university from the perspective of the provinces, with the contrary values of darkness and vulgarity that, in Volodia's view, have pervaded his entire life as a student. The conventional light-darkness rhetoric is thus displaced. Though the hero presents his diploma as his sole remaining motivation for his studies, he has not deluded himself into believing that his future will be any different. Indeed, Gegidze has set up a conflict between the life of ideals and daily realities and given them the normative values of high and low, respectively. In so doing, he reproduces a well-known convention, recently analyzed by Svetlana Boym: "The opposition between *byt,* everyday existence (everyday routine and stagnation), and *bytie* (spiritual being) is one of the central common places of the Russian intellectual tradition. It is often understood as the opposition between everyday life and 'real' life, which is always everywhere." [51] An aspiration for such a "real" life comes at the end of Volodia's letter:

> I would so like to live my life well, brightly and joyously. But how to do it? Where is the exit from this tormenting condition? Where is the ideal which I can believe in and translate into life? I don't see that exit. . . . All around me everything is drab, boring, and banal, and my soul is cheerlessly dark and tormentingly sad.[52]

Volodia has not risen to political consciousness, but fallen into the "mire of life." Yet this is not the story about to unfold; it is, rather, the relationship between *bytie* and *byt.*

We learn of Volodia's disappointment in the second chapter, when the narrative jumps from the idealistic dreams of the schoolboy into the daily life of the student. The scene: Volodia, now a third-year juridical student, is waking up just before ten in the morning with a bit of a hangover. In this first sketch of student life, Gegidze introduces the central theme of sex. Two weeks earlier, Volodia had met a "nice-looking and, most important, an altogether still fresh milliner." He had taken her to a hotel and had visited her several times since then. Unfortunately, he had also boasted of her to a friend, who had now sent him a letter asking for an introduction: "Today I received money from home," the friend explains, "and it's been a while since I've been with a woman. It's necessary to revive the body in order to have a healthy mind." Resentful of the joking tone and recalling the young woman—"her simple blue dress, her figure, her face with big hazel eyes, her half-feigned struggle with him in the hotel, and her trembling hands as she took off her dress," Volodia decides not to make the introduction. After all, he concludes, she was really sweet, and he would perhaps still visit her.[53] The reader is left with the clear implication that her struggle was more serious than Volodia admits to himself.

That Volodia is also conscious of his compromised position does not affect his behavior. He joins his friends in visits to public houses—though he never confesses to anything more than conversation with the women at work; he describes an incident when a crowd of students tries to break into a closed brothel (highly reminiscent of the police report mentioned above), but he does not join them; he gossips over lunch about conquests and shapely legs. He records his observations throughout with a self-conscious irony and distaste. Though blaming the hypocritical sexual morality of Russian society for both his own and other students' debauchery, he primarily faults his comrades, who are oblivious of the moral implications of their behavior and confident of their high calling as students. Rather than the defender of the downtrodden prostitute, Volodia depicts the student as her equal in corruption, here in a description of a typical evening out, illuminated and energized by an important symbol of modernity in Russia—electric street lights:

> Nevskii [Prospect] was already full of people, mostly young women and students from every higher educational institution [in Petersburg]. . . . Brought here by one common instinct, the noisy, idle, and corrupt crowd drifts along the wide sidewalks lit by magnificent shop windows and electric lamps. Men look into the faces of passing women, and, having defined their profession, turn and rush after them. . . . Under the canopy of night, the atmosphere of sensual desires and trade is carried [by] the unnatural agitating light. . . .[54]

The crowd is one of Gegidze's most important images, and with it he links student behavior in the city, the university, and the student protest. The first description of the university thus highlights the "river of human bodies" all in identical uniforms flowing along the long corridor, an image that echoes the scene along Nevskii Prospect. These students are not rushing to lectures, moreover, but simply wandering the long hallway, killing time, gossiping with friends, and checking out the action. Likening them to two-legged cockroaches oblivious of their own insignificance and in love with themselves, he also ruminates about the fickle nature of this crowd: "you are capable of great feats but within a day you change and forget everything you had proclaimed, and you will peacefully serve that which you had earlier named arbitrariness." [55] In a later scene that takes place at a student party, Volodia again compares student radicalism to the politics of the crowd. Seeing only a momentary fascination with politics on the part of students, he records his doubts that many will stick to their ideals after they leave the university and begin some job in the tsarist bureaucracy.[56] Student ideals were fleeting, Volodia concludes; they last until graduation, when the demands of career and family *(byt)* displace them in practice and leave in their place the romanticized memories of middle-aged men. This criticism was no less biting for being familiar.

Gegidze did not limit his satire to academic and student life but dismisses the fundamental claims of science and progress as well. In an early scene, Volodia recounts how he had come to the university excited by "real science" and had attended lectures in all the different faculties. What he had found, however, were narrow and useless academic specializations and self-important bureaucrats called professors. Like other students, Volodia had quickly learned that attendance at lectures was not necessary to pass examinations; an hour or two of reading each day was quite enough.[57] In a continuation of this theme, a subsequent scene finds Volodia pondering the meaning of life and possible career pursuits. This time he casts out all of the main tenets of the traditional world view of the intelligentsia. First, he dismisses science as irrelevant and dry, reasoning "I want to live, not shut myself in books." Next, he rejects "the enlightenment of the people" as distasteful and potentially dangerous. Without a compromise with authority, one could lose one's position and even end up in Siberia. "But I am used to comfort, to clean linens," he laments. Questioning whether the people were even worth his personal sacrifice, he notes that "the people are rude and dirty. . . ." Finally, he discards a life devoted to human progress as unfulfilling to the present generation. "Would that require the renunciation of my own happiness? Does my personality have any less right to happiness . . . ?" Volodia thus ended up where he began: while other students blindly believed that they led useful lives, he perceived the absurdity of their common situation but could find no alternative.[58]

At the heart of this quandary, to take Volodia's words, was "the contradiction between consciousness and life," a contradiction that had several faces.[59] For the mass of students, in Volodia's opinion, it consisted in the disjunction between students' proud self-identification with an idealized *studenchestvo* and their aimless daily lives and future employment in the tsarist bureaucracy. For Volodia himself, who no longer believes in *studenchestvo* and casts a critical eye on his own activities, the contradiction lay in his own "consciousness" that "life"—sex, marriage, children, career—was his fate as well. Indeed, Volodia presents himself as more idealistic than the majority of students, in that he is searching for a broader morality around which to structure his life. Yet in one of the final scenes in the book, he discards the old model represented by Chernyshevskii. In a play on the plot of *What Is to Be Done?*, an acquaintance of Volodia, a sensitive and intelligent young woman, asks him for help, because her father is trying to marry her off against her will. Rather than coming to her aid, perhaps with an offer of a fictitious marriage in order to facilitate her entrance into the Bestuzhev Courses, Volodia dismisses the utility of higher education, points out the financial difficulties, and confesses that he sees no real options—either for her or for himself—to carve out a life truly worth living. The friend runs away in tears condemned to her unjust fate (an unrescued Vera Pavlovna?), and Volodia sinks further into helplessness and despair. There was no heroic feat to rescue her because Volodia could not find one. Life had triumphed over utopia.

Gegidze's story of student life deviated radically from the heroic battle of students against everything bestial and reactionary. To be sure, Gegidze's hero came to St. Petersburg with dreams about science, the professoriate, and student life. As in the conventional memoir, he is also disenchanted by science and the professoriate. But in a disruption of the pattern, he becomes just as bored with his fellow students, seeing student politics as little different than their other diversions—card games, drinking, and chasing women. In his own way, this hero nevertheless rises to a sort of consciousness, as illustrated in a discussion between Volodia and his closest friend, who says:

> "Students—they are some sort of band of dimwits and ignoramuses. And most important, such a self-confidence. They imagine that society needs them. . . . [They are] a most parasitic tribe."

> "And what is to be done? We come from the very same berry patch," I said sighing.

> "Yes, but I, at least, have the courage to recognize that—if someone asked, I would say so. But try saying that to them publicly. Good lord, what an insult. [I can just] imagine that if someone had the courage and honor to shout that we all live God knows how, that we are all libertines, that we play cards instead of study. . . . [I can just] imagine the tremendous discontent. . . . The entire crowd would shout that it is a lie, a reactionary [trick]. Our liberal gentlemen and ladies would eat such a man alive," he said ironically.[60]

In this brief exchange, Gegidze points to his motivation in writing this book. It is the expression of his own, albeit more cynical, achievement of consciousness. His prediction of its reception, moreover, was right on the mark.

Critics structured their response around one primary assertion: Gegidze had described his own "type," but not the contemporary student. Asserting that most students were in fact too poor for such a dissolute life, one reviewer likened Gegidze and his hero to a contemporary Hamlet, unable to find his answers (the ideal, the great) within himself.[61] In other words, he was condemned to *byt* because he had failed to find *bytie*. Another critic concurred. "Only the character of the observation point, from which the hero of Mr. Gegidze looked upon life," he asserted, "could explain everything he recounts to us about contemporary youth." Rather than defend the "fresh healthy powers, the honorably thinking and honorably living" *studenchestvo*—for one would have to be "blind" not to see this—he accused Gegidze of colluding with the "enemy," in particular, with the conservative publisher Suvorin and the reactionary publicist Prince V. P. Meshcherskii.[62] Even the one reviewer who did claim to see some degeneration among contemporary students from the high standards of earlier generations, stressed that the *studenchestvo* remained "healthy in body and mind."[63] Almost a decade later, a publicist would still passionately distinguish Gegidze's type from true *raznochintsy* students: "Wide circles of students thought and felt quite differently from this cultural neurasthenic," he emphasized.[64]

Naming him everything from a degenerate to a pawn of the reactionaries, critics united in their condemnation of Gegidze. Though they conceded that much of his portrait of the university order was accurate, they objected to his easy dismissal of all professors as bureaucrats and vehemently condemned his repudiation of science and progress. In their defense of students, they protested the heart of Gegidze's argument—the correspondence of personal vice with political artifice—and thus defined students' spiritual-political life as their "real" life. It was only Gegidze's type who frequented brothels and taverns, they asserted, and in distinct contrast, the majority of students remained true to their principles. In this same period, however, and citing the high levels of venereal infection among students, the Moscow docent Mikhail Chlenov would conduct the first survey of the sexual practices of students.[65] For some at least, the personal conduct of students had indeed become grounds for concern.

On the surface, the reason for the public defense of students seems clear. Blaming the fact of censorship for the dearth of public discussion of student life, one of Gegidze's reviewers stressed the need for "tact" and noted the political dangers of half-statements. Any one-sided discussion of the faults of youth would presumably provide ammunition for those conservatives seeking to discredit the political importance of the student movement, a topic that was heavily censored.[66] Yet a purely political explanation for the heated reaction to Gegidze's book would be overly simplistic. For decades, students had withstood the almost ritual accusations of sexual degeneracy made by conservative publicists, and by 1904, such swipes were offensive but hardly unexpected.

Any explanation must take into account the psychological importance and overall legitimacy of the student movement in Russian society at this time. Despite some minor criticisms, the uncensored oppositional press typically celebrated the student movement as one of the few examples in Russia of a "public opinion" and as a sign that Russian society (*obshchestvo*) was not an inert body. Indeed, the dominant narrative of student politics—the collective rise to consciousness—had found a wider resonance. The question at hand in 1904, according to the lead article in Petr Struve's *Liberation*, was whether a "conscious" and "organized" "public opinion" would rise out of "spontaneous" and "immature," if also important, manifestations of opposition such as the student movement.[67] At such a critical moment, the shrouded world of *byt* and its potential political meaning scarcely seemed relevant to the great historical drama about to unfold.

The story of the student movement of 1899–1904 had two primary sources: the mythical idealization of *studenchestvo* as the carrier of eternal principles and the historical narrative of consciousness as a metaphor for politicization. Both were critical to the persistence and character of student protest, and both shaped the understandings of "self" among students. The case studies examined in this chapter each point to some of the actual and potential contradictions in what it meant to be a student before the outbreak of revolution. In retrospect, the title of "student" appears both controversial and slippery.

It was first an object of dispute. Upon their emergence as an organized force in 1901 and 1902, students opposing the student movement called for the exclusion of politics from academic life; in this fashion, they attempted to reconfigure the boundaries of "student" identity. As the movement developed, "political" came to signify radicalism rather than politics per se, and the same categories used by the radicals appeared in a new guise. Although they rejected the historical narrative of progress (which in some fashion must lead to reform or revolution), conservative students retained the motif of individual development in their bid for the mantle of student honor. Their *Bildungsroman* inverted the value system of the conventional student story, replacing political with academic, audacity with obedience, citizen with subject, and posited the Russian patriot serving tsar and fatherland as its outcome. Yet if conservatives hoped to purge the student of politics, radicals hoped to purge the *studenchestvo* of conservatives. In their competing claims to embody the real *studenchestvo,* each group fashioned its opponents into an imagined "other." Sharing the same rhetorical oppositions, they assigned them contrary values.

During this period, the story of women students evolved its own peculiar dynamics as the process of self-definition led them toward an ideal of the ethical individual. During the 1899 strike, the potential conflict between student solidarity and the cause of higher education for women had lent a connotation of egoism to women's issues, a tendency with a long tradition within Russian radicalism. Though the conflict between radical and conservative women students consequently acquired an element of gender politics, the motif of purity characteristic of this conflict between male students was absent. This is hardly surprising, for male students remained the norm, and women students were often compelled to qualify their student affiliation. With women students lacking the career options enjoyed by male students, their understanding of education as a path to self-development was understandably more prominent. Indeed, the epithet of "careerism" could only rarely be relevant in their case. With the concept of the ethical individual, women students could retain the story of "upbringing" as a metaphor for both personal development and politicization but at the same time individualize political activism.

Boris Gegidze satirized students for what he perceived to be the disjunction between the public story and the conduct of private life, both before and after graduation. Though his portrait was certainly one-sided, he had raised important and sensitive issues. On the one hand, the rhetoric of student politics recounted the emergence of individual and group consciousness in universalistic categories; on the other hand, this generation of students lacked apparent interest in the reorganization of private life so characteristic of the generations of the 1860s and 1870s. Students rarely acknowledged, moreover, that they would end up working for that very same bureaucracy which they condemned in their protests. Outside of their collective political life, students thus applied their ethos more or less sporadically—during conflicts with authority figures and cases of apparent spying, for example. This is not to say that students were more corrupt than previous generations or indeed that their style of life differed that much at all; rather, their common value system was based on the political sphere and the importance of heroic political feats. Its great weakness, as time would tell, was that its language did not distinguish the personal from the political. When the public eye turned to the problem of private life in the wake of the 1905 Revolution, the story of the student would be transformed.

CHAPTER FOUR

When the Street Entered the University

The Revolution of 1905–1907

The street entered the universities and turned them into hearths
of the political movement. Each evening, newspapers were sold
in the corridors, drunks wandered through the open doors, and
lost dogs ran about. In a word, a new arcade was opened.

—Union of Students of St. Petersburg University and
Academic Union of the Bestuzhev Courses,
The University and Politics, 1906

The outbreak of the Russo-Japanese War in January 1904 proved a
catalyst to social revolution. Following scattered protests that spring, broad segments of Russian society united in the summer and fall into an organized opposition to the monarchy and its disastrous conduct of the war. Just as the assassination of the reactionary Minister of Interior V. K. Plehve and his replacement
in August with Prince P. D. Sviatopolk-Mirskii heralded a moderate "New
Course" in government policy, the opposition realized the inadequacy of piecemeal reform and its own potential strength. The progressive leader Petr Struve
proclaimed "no enemies to the left," the Paris Conference marked the collaboration of his Union of Liberation with the SR party, and the Union of Liberation
demanded the convocation of a constituent assembly and a program of universal
and equal suffrage. In November, the more conservative Zemstvo Congress also
called for constitutional reform.

Students joined the chorus of protest. By late October 1904, they were holding meetings parallel to the political banquets attended by their liberal and progressive elders. Dismissing the New Course, they demanded a constituent assembly, universal suffrage, unrestricted admissions to universities, and an end to the
war. During one meeting at the Military-Medical Academy, a staff officer ordered
students to disperse, but found their mood unusually defiant. A fifth-year student pointed out that since the *skhodka* was illegal, officers had no reason to be

99

present. Another student demanded that officers "stand when they speak with students." After throwing the officers out of the auditorium with an order to "march," the students barricaded themselves in and called for an end to the war, a constituent assembly, and revolution. By November, university students were lingering in auditoriums after the lectures of popular professors in order to sing revolutionary songs and listen to speeches. Protests also spilled into the streets with demonstrations at railroad stations against the exile of comrades.[1]

A growing strike movement among Petersburg workers struck the decisive blow. On Sunday, January 9, 1905, Father Georgii Gapon, the charismatic leader of a legal labor organization, led an enormous demonstration of workers and their families to the Winter Palace to present the tsar with a petition of grievances and demands for fundamental changes in the political order. At the entrance to the Narva Gates and at other sites in the city, soldiers fired on this excited but unarmed crowd, killing and wounding hundreds. In the year following Bloody Sunday, as this event came to be called, a wave of unrest and upheaval swept across Russia that almost toppled the monarchy. The pivotal month was October, when thousands of workers met each evening in educational institutions across St. Petersburg and other cities to debate politics and coordinate tactics. The Petersburg Soviet of Workers' Deputies was founded in the Technological Institute. By the time the government reacted and closed down the universities, a general strike had engulfed the nation, forcing the tsar to promise a constitution of sorts in the October Manifesto. By December, the social and political unity achieved during October would dissolve in the bloody streets of Moscow with the suppression of an armed uprising of workers. As the fear of social revolution—the uncontrolled violence and disorder of the street—polarized Russian society, the monarchy began to reassert its authority. Labor strikes, mutinies in the army and navy, and peasant rebellions were brutally suppressed, and the first legally elected parliament was disbanded. The revolution ended on June 2, 1907, with the dissolution of a second parliament and the enactment of a restrictive new suffrage law.[2]

The revolution in the university developed in three phases: a student strike in the spring of 1905, the transformation of the universities that fall into "revolutionary tribunals," and the struggle to defend the achievements of 1905 during the 1906–1907 academic year. These phases shared a common theme, which reflected a short-lived convergence of the academic and political dimensions of the student movement. Students construed revolution as the radical democratization of education—the admission of all who wished to study and the liberation of science and culture from the state. In October 1905, this vision of a democratic higher school inspired students to use the universities for mass political meetings that both then and retrospectively seemed to embody the utopian unity of intelligentsia and people (narod), the culmination of decades of division and struggle. The historical task of studenchestvo, as it was formulated in the 1860s and later reworked into the narrative of collective politicization, had been fulfilled. The story of consciousness had reached its teleological culmination.

In the view of a small but growing number of conservative students, the revolution had corrupted the "temple of science," and they called for politics to be purged from the academy. They equated the "people" with the "street," the revolution with social disorder. This critique became increasingly trenchant by 1906 as students, professors, and other members of Russian educated society began to rethink the political role of students and the university. With the establishment of a parliament for politics, perhaps it was time for the university to resume its rightful academic role.

STUDENTS ON STRIKE

In the aftermath of Bloody Sunday, labor unrest spread across the country, and students expressed solidarity with the revolutionary opposition and reaffirmed their demands of the previous fall. Within several weeks, a broad consensus had formed: students did not have the right to study in a time of national crisis but must instead join the struggle of the workers. Calls thus resounded for a semester-long solidarity strike.[3] At noon on February 7, student leader Aleksandr Zamiatin opened the most important *skhodka* at St. Petersburg University, where three thousand students had already gathered. Students sang a traditional revolutionary funeral hymn in honor of the slain workers and raised three flags: a black one of mourning, for the victims of Bloody Sunday, and two red ones, for the republic and the constituent assembly, respectively. The agenda focused on the contemporary political situation and the question of the strike.

Representatives of the professoriate addressed the assembly at its beginning. Forecasting a dire fate for cultural and scientific progress should the strike go forward, they defended the sanctity of scholarship and the neutrality of the university, even in times of national crisis. Students rejected this ideal. In a series of more than forty speeches, they hailed the proletariat, the constituent assembly, and the social revolution. Asserting that cultural progress required political change, orators argued that the strike would not harm science but would allow students to devote their cultural resources to the revolution. Pointing repeatedly to the portrait of the tsar hanging above the podium, naming him the "the silent gentleman" and "the vile autocrat," they resolved that Russia had entered a period of revolution, "when all minds are consumed by one thought, when all hearts burn with one desire, when all duties are displaced by one duty—the duty of the citizen." Voting 2,378 to 66 in favor of a semester strike, students demanded civil rights, political liberties, and a constituent assembly convened on the basis of equal and universal suffrage. Before the crowd dispersed, a "long-haired" student tore down the tsar's portrait, which was ripped to shreds with shouts of "down with autocracy." [4]

At first, the government tried to preserve a facade of normalcy, but most educational institutions delayed the first day of classes and ultimately failed to open for the entire spring semester. Citing the external causes of the strike and the environment of confrontation, faculty councils across Russia acknowledged the unanimous and defiant mood of students and voted against the resumption of studies. By March, the government had conceded its defeat and officially sanctioned the closures.[5] Although this strike was declared a precondition for mass revolutionary activism, without a struggle students had no common ground. During previous protests, students had banded together to enforce their strikes; the university, broadly defined, had remained a primary arena for their activism. In the spring of 1905, those who actively joined the revolution typically did so as individuals, and a student movement as such failed to materialize. With strike resolutions directing students, as "conscious citizens," to join the general struggle, activists abandoned student politics in favor of a party affiliation. Most students, however, were leftists with vague political ideas. Their potential activism was largely unexploited.[6]

Despite the absence of a coordinated movement over the spring, memoirs and police reports point to a process of politicization. With a considerable number of students remaining in St. Petersburg, libraries, dining halls, and dormitories remained open, and both scholarly and underground circles flourished. In contrast to previous strikes, few student leaflets appeared, and most underground publications produced by the various political parties reported on the spread of unrest across the country.[7] Students gathered daily to debate these publications and read clippings from the foreign press, which were openly posted in the dining halls.[8] University student Vladimir Voitinskii recalls the fascination with which students read about barricades and methods of armed resistance.[9] For other students, "politics" involved a range of more practical activities, including volunteer work in soup kitchens and literacy schools.[10] The uncontested strike thus exposed many students to new political ideas, with the vitality of the workers' movement attracting particular interest. In its apparent historical role as the revolutionary class of both the bourgeois and socialist revolutions, according to many theorists of Russian Marxism, the proletariat embodied the promise of both political reform and radical social transformation.

As students contemplated their options, some, like Voitinskii, underwent an accelerated political evolution, which, in his case, drew him toward Marxism. While Bloody Sunday had shown him the "heroism" of workers, the spread of labor strikes across the country and the elections to the abortive Shidlovskii Commission in St. Petersburg revealed what he considered to be their mature revolutionary consciousness. He remembers this period in eschatological terms: "It seemed as if all these events were swiftly leading us to the final encounter of the people with its enemy." By the fall of 1905, Voitinskii had decided to enter a political party as the best way to join the revolution itself, but he was hardly a partisan ideologue—during his initial interview with a Marxist student, Voitinskii failed to recognize the acronym "RSDRP." Manifestly ignorant of party doctrine and factional disputes, he became a leading agitator among both workers and students within several weeks.[11]

On August 6, the government made its first major, if inadequate, concession: it announced the formation of a largely consultative representative body to be elected on the basis of limited suffrage, the Bulygin Duma. The decree seemed designed to draw a wedge between liberals and radicals. Most non-Russians and all women were denied the vote outright, while its property qualifications would have excluded the vast majority of the urban and rural populations as well. By late August, the Union of Liberation had decided to participate in elections with the clear goal of transforming the duma into a genuine legislative assembly predicated upon direct, universal, and equal suffrage. Despite this important qualification, the Bulygin Duma represented the stark choice between reform and revolution. Both SDs and SRs called for a boycott.

Hoping to forestall a renewed student strike, the tsar also convoked a ministerial conference to formulate policy for higher education, and on August 27, just four days before the designated conclusion to the strike, new Temporary Rules were published. A strategic counterpart to the Bulygin Duma, the Temporary Rules made significant concessions to the professoriate in an attempt to gain an ally in the pacification of student unrest. While senior faculty were granted many long-coveted rights in academic administration, including the election of rectors and deans, the faculty also acquired the task of containing student protest, most important the obligation to summon the police and to close educational institutions altogether if disorders got out of hand. As a partial measure, effective until the enactment of a new general statute, the Temporary Rules remained vague on many specific issues, not the least of which were admission standards and the status of the 1884 statute. Predicated on fundamental miscalculations, this de facto grant of academic autonomy aggravated latent tensions within the university. In the midst of unprecedented social unrest, would students accept the professoriate's view of apolitical scholarship? Could the university function as an oasis of democracy and free thought when the country at large was still denied rudimentary civil rights? Instead of facilitating social pacification, the Temporary Rules laid the groundwork for the revolutionary climax.

THE POWERS OF *STUDENCHESTVO*

In late July, the Menshevik leader Fedor Dan called for an end to the student strike and the transformation of universities into centers of revolutionary ferment. The concentration of students in cities, he argued, would facilitate their participation in the revolution as an organized group rather than as individuals scattered across the country. He further invited students to liberate science from the shackles of censorship, to open the doors of the academy to all citizens, and to convert the university into a place for mass meetings.[12] As students gathered around the country in late August and September 1905 to define their new strategy, they largely followed this advice and resolved to open their institutions for both academic and political activities. This decision has been portrayed as evidence of both the hegemony of SDs over students (who renounced their studies in the name of revolution), and the absence of real revolutionary commitment among the majority (who really just wished to end the strike in order to resume their studies).[13] Both explanations fail to recognize the fundamental convergence between the academic and political dimensions of students' revolutionary aspirations. At issue was not the hegemony of a particular political party but a new conception of students' political role.

The question of tactics was first addressed at the Fourth All-Russian Conference of Student Delegates, which opened in the northern city of Vyborg on September 1 with delegates from twenty-three student organizations in attendance. These student leaders likewise advocated an activist role for students according to a revolutionary, rather than evolutionary, ideal. Their final resolution enjoined students to open their institutions and organize them into centers for revolutionary agitation and propaganda. Only when peaceful study precluded political activism, it advised, should a strike be called. With this recommendation, the conference not only followed Dan but acknowledged the failure of the spring's strike to define a positive and collective role for students in the revolutionary process. Several alternative propositions had garnered little support. On the two extremes stood the SRs, who considered the strike necessary to "total" revolutionary commitment, and the academists, who opposed any political role for the university. In rejecting these tactics, both of which placed academics in opposition to political activity, student delegates instead accented the interconnectedness of their academic and political goals.[14]

On September 13, two thousand students attended the first *skhodka* at St. Petersburg University. The debate focused on the SD and SR platforms, with the academists garnering minimal interest. The SRs argued that ending the strike before total victory would mean capitulation. The revolution was no longer bourgeois in its essence but already contained the seeds of socioeconomic transformation. Renewing the strike would therefore allow students to return "to the soil" and agitate among peasants and workers. Students were obligated, the SRs concluded, to renounce their studies and lend their efforts to the coordination of the conscious but unorganized protests of the peasantry. SD orator Voitinskii dismissed the "romantic" notion that the entire *studenchestvo* could devote itself to political agitation in the countryside. Indeed, the impending rupture of the radical bloc and the broad class differentiation of society indicated that the revolution would be a largely urban phenomenon led by the proletariat. It was therefore imperative, he argued, to concentrate students' energies in cities and to transform educational institutions into "hearths of revolutionary education and communication *[obshchenie]*." Conditions had changed since February, Voitinskii concluded, and tactics must change as well.[15]

After these initial speeches, a young worker named Petr Starostin asked for the podium. Calling upon students "to give us consciousness, development, ideas of socialism," he supported the SD program. As the first worker to speak at a *skhodka,* the impact of his appearance was tremendous. "The speech of the worker in all its simplicity and strength was greeted with thunderous applause," the chronicler A. A. D'iakonov reported.[16] When Voitinskii addressed the crowd for a second time, he knew that his position had triumphed. Yet even as he heralded the rapprochement of workers and students, he also detailed the diverse options available to students. Some might wish to work among the peasantry and others among workers, he stressed, and even those who wished to study retained their right to do so. It was necessary, above all else, that the *studenchestvo* affirm that the university as an institution would serve the cause of revolution. With a vote of 1,702 to 243 and 77 abstentions, students ended the strike. The resolution rejected the path of reform, proclaiming: "Let our open university become still more dangerous for autocracy than was the university-on-strike." Likening the open university to the "mobilization of the powers of *studenchestvo,*" it determined "to employ all means to increase students' revolutionary activism by holding popular meetings and organizing an academic legion as one division within the great army struggling for the freedom of the working class."[17]

The response across the country was strikingly uniform. Buttressed only by the recommendation of the Vyborg Conference and the example of their comrades, students resolved to open their institutions as political "hearths" and "tribunals." It is difficult to assess the motivation of the thousands of students (only a minority of whom were radical activists) who voted for these resolutions. The historians Samuel Kassow and Abraham Ascher have recently discounted the radicalism of these students. They argue that the rejection of the "total commitment" and "ultra-radicalism" of the SR tactic reveals a dominant motive to study and a general absence of personal commitment to the revolution. They also point to the fact that many resolutions, including one at Moscow University, rejected an exclusively political orientation in favor of a combined political and academic role for the university. Kassow concludes that the radical rhetoric constituted merely an "aura" and "gesture" of "opposition," arising from the conflict between self-interest (the real desire to study) and the strike. Both historians adopt the contemporary rhetoric built on the antithesis of academic and political interests and obscure the specificity of the revolutionary experience in higher education.[18]

Assessing the relative degree of radicalism among students according to a test of discrete academic versus discrete political interests would be a difficult task. Some students probably did, in fact, wish to resume their studies after a semester break, or at least to have the option to study in addition to joining the broader movement. But did these students wish to study under the same conditions and restrictions of previous years? As in the case of Russian workers articulating their economic and political aspirations, students rarely made such rigorous distinctions between their "objectively" academic and political goals. That demands for educational reform freely mingled with affirmations of revolutionary principle does not mean that students were more or less radical. Such an interpretation misses the main point: the relationship between academic study and political activism had changed.

Students described their academic and political tasks in strikingly similar language, which suggests that these were not mutually exclusive interests. Resolutions proclaimed the democratization of education and the "expansion of auditoriums" for all wishing entrance. "We open the institute's doors," technical students proclaimed, "as pulpits of political study and popular meeting." Students at the private Lesgaft Courses resolved: "you will study science in classrooms, but at *skhodki* and meetings you will receive a political education—you will get the opportunity to become citizens." Students at the Women's Courses argued that "scholarship has not only never interfered with political activity but will actually give the possibility of relating consciously to various social currents." To say that such resolutions merely conferred an "aura of opposition" legitimizing the return to studies is inadequate explanation for their content, at the very least because students intended to transform the very foundations of "academic studies." Though many of these ideas did seem abstract and even unrealistic to students, who had not found a way to bring them to life, they repeatedly condemned the strike as "passive" and consequently harmful. Above all else they searched for "active" and "collective" forms of revolutionary engagement, as one student argued: the *studenchestvo* must be "a collective force," not "dispersed to the far reaches of Russia." [19]

The decision to open the universities for academic studies and political meetings reflected a potent appeal to corporate traditions and to the experiences of the previous spring. When the SRs called for a renewed strike in the name of the mass activism of students as individuals in the countryside, they failed to understand the paradox that the strike had actually dissolved the common ground of student activism. That the strike was "ultraradical" seemed less important to students in the fall than that it was passive. The SDs may have proclaimed class differentiation, but they also supported the "mobilization" of the *studenchestvo* as such. They thus celebrated the heroism of corporate solidarity.

THE HEARTH OF DEMOCRACY

The first phase of the revolutionary process in the university occurred in September, when students resolved to revolutionize the entire university order under the slogan "democratization." These changes and this slogan facilitated the second phase of the revolution, the mass meetings of late September and October. Once students had voted to reopen the university, they first turned to the problem of academic reform. Demanding open admissions without regard for sex, religion, ethnicity, social background, secondary schooling, or political beliefs, they specifically called for the immediate enrollment of all Jewish applicants not admitted under the official quota. Several commissions were established to formulate proposals on long-coveted curricular reforms, for presentation to the faculty council. These included the introduction of an elective system and new courses on constitutional law, nineteenth century Russian history, and European history. The inspectorate, student uniforms, residency restrictions, and restrictions on organization were to be abolished outright. Finally, students resolved that a Council of Elders should be elected as their representative body and intermediary with the faculty council.[20]

These reforms reflected specific student needs as well as the broader intention to construct a new "democratic" university so potently symbolized in the proposal to delete "Imperial" from the official title of the university. Formulating their primary task as "the struggle against all oppression, whether against a class, party, nationality, or sex," students defined academic reform as essential to the democratic transformation of all social relations. Toward that end, it was proposed that "scientific-political meetings" be held during the evening to counter the elitism of higher education and to facilitate the entrance of workers into the universities. The words of one orator capture the atmosphere: "The grant of autonomy is mystification. We must strive toward a university for the people [*narodnyi universitet*], we must conquer [the university.]"[21] This ideal of a "university for the people" entailed internal structural changes and an expanded role for the university as a site for social interchange and political education. At its heart was a politicized conception of education and the educational environment.

Such ambitions presented a dilemma to the professoriate, which was still enjoying the new freedoms. In early September, the free election of rectors had resulted in the victory of many highly regarded moderate-liberal figures, including I. I. Borgman at St. Petersburg University and S. N. Trubetskoi in Moscow. Nevertheless, rectors and faculty councils proved reluctant to push the limits of the Temporary Rules and hesitated to apply their provisions when they conflicted with the 1884 University Statute. They instead petitioned the Ministry of Education on particular issues, such as the admission of women and the abolition of the Jewish quota. Although students and faculty shared many goals, including fundamental changes in admission and curriculum and the legalization of student organizations, students argued for immediate change, while professors hoped to construct a legal framework for academic autonomy. Moreover, students were also demanding a far-reaching role for themselves in the new "democratic" university, including the right to participate in designing a new elective system and course offerings and the right to be included on several faculty committees.[22]

A struggle for authority between professors and students emerged around the issue of faculty appointment. At a September *skhodka,* students demanded that all scholars who had lost their positions due to "political intrigues or [other] political reasons" should be reappointed, and they named nine scholars who, in their view, should be awarded professorial positions. Many of these individuals had been fired by the Ministry of Education—several due to their liberal attitude toward student protests. In addition, students instituted a boycott of five professors and two lecturers.[23] The faculty responded quickly and vigorously to this challenge. In a meeting with representatives of the Coalition Council, professors likened these demands to prior instances of state interference, arguing that students had supported or condemned professors solely on the basis of their political convictions. Adopting an ironic, even derisive, tone, one professor expressed his fundamental doubt that any scholar would accept a position if offered by students. This response was well chosen. When the issue was reconsidered a week later, the tactics of the professoriate showed some success. One of the popular professors who had been reappointed to his academic post independent of students' demands, L. V. Khodskii, defended the jurisdiction of the faculty council over appointments and pointed out that students could now invite scholars of their choice to give evening lectures. While students did concede on the issue of appointments, the boycott proved more controversial. Only under the pressure of the most popular student SDs did a majority vote to defer the boycott for further review by a student commission. It was nonetheless recommended that two professors remain under boycott.[24]

The episode has been cited as evidence of students' political moderation.[25] To the contrary, it instead illustrates the difficulty of establishing a new order within the university, a task which by late September was becoming more, rather than less, complex. Indeed, student leaders were forced to navigate between professors intent on preserving their authority and students hoping to shake up the system. Voitinskii recalls how he and fellow student activists perceived an absolute imperative to placate the professoriate so as not to threaten the closure of the university (as had already happened in Moscow) or in any way jeopardize their control over the evening meetings of workers and party cells (which were considered much more important than educational reform, appointments, and boycotts). While the deferral of the boycott was intended to mollify the professoriate, students called for its renewal over the next weeks despite the cautioning words of their leaders.[26]

The democratization of academic life culminated in the replacement of the underground Coalition Council with an openly elected representative body, the Council of Elders. The election occurred in the eye of the revolutionary storm, on October 12. During the campaign, SDs, SRs, nonparty socialists, Constitutional Democrats (Kadets), progressive-academics, and independents all agitated for student support. Indicative, perhaps, of students' interests, platforms tended to focus on broad political principles rather than limited corporate programs. In their speeches, the Kadets defended civil rights and constitutional rule, the SRs called for a democratic republic and land redistribution, and the SDs invited students to join the proletariat. Only the Kadets described current conditions in the university as temporary—until such time as other sites for political meeting and national representation could be found. At a separate meeting attended by some sixty or seventy students, academists denounced what they called the "dictatorship" of the Social Democrats and advocated a platform of "pure science." Though the SDs (an alliance of the Menshevik and Bolshevik factions) predictably won an absolute majority, significant successes were achieved by nonparty radicals advocating a combined academic and political role for the university. One such group of radicals, calling themselves the "Wild Ones," contended that the Council of Elders must defend all the interests of the university, from the political meetings to the "educational tasks." Another group put forth the ambiguous (and potentially far-reaching) right of students to representation on "all commissions" as part of a legal order within the university based on the principle of majority rule.[27]

Despite these differences, the ideal of a unified *studenchestvo* defending a free university did not lose its broad appeal across ideological boundaries. The proposal to establish the new council stated that "a university organization is necessary so that the conscious *studenchestvo* can act as the cement binding the unconscious students into one political whole." In combining political and academic leadership, the new student government was envisioned as a means to unite students in their struggle to defend the "university for the people."[28] Because they regarded the opening of their educational institutions as an opportunity to counteract decades of prior state control and to create a new educational system, students thus formulated the parameters of academic reform in a political language and with political intent. Many students did indeed wish to resume their studies, but in a democratized academy. They were searching for a new, active role for both students and the university.

THE PEOPLE'S UNIVERSITY

In September, technological students proclaimed "the participation of the *studenchestvo* in the political struggle both within the walls of the university and outside of them." University students hoped that their institution would "serve as a place for political meetings and gatherings."[29] In addition to the resumption of academic study and the transformation of the internal university order, the reopening thus entailed the revolutionary mobilization of the university. In this arena, the student movement played a decisive role. Beginning with small evening gatherings in late September and culminating in the tremendous mass meetings of the October Strike, educational institutions became central sites for the urban revolution. Yet, because September's radical resolutions detailed less a course of action than an abstract vision of a democratized university serving a revolutionary street, several questions arise. When did the *skhodka* become a mass meeting? How were the educational and revolutionary roles of the university reconciled in theory and practice? The answers lie in the ideal of the "university for the people" that shaped not only the internal academic reforms but also October's revolution.

When Fedor Dan enjoined students to open classrooms to all citizens and transform universities into "places for popular assemblies and political meetings," he had engaged a traditional student debate. Since the 1860s and especially after the 1899 strike, students had sought to define the relationship of their protests to the revolutionary movement as a whole; many of the images of students' political language consequently articulated linkages between the university and the street. The metaphor of the "oasis" suggested the fundamental disjunction between the freedom within the university and the autocratic "desert." The "hearth" indicated the source of liberation, the hotbed of radicalism and consciousness. The "barometer" implied the correspondence (and the possibility of measurement) of conditions in the university and in society. In 1901, students claimed a role as the catalyst of social unity and, in 1902, as the "ferment for the dissolution" of autocracy. In 1903, they had even called for a "popular meeting" *(narodnyi miting)*. Although the dominant image depicted students entering society (as "apostles of knowledge," following the mid-nineteenth-century radical Nikolai Ogarev), in 1905, workers entered the university, resulting in the mythical and long-awaited union of class with consciousness.

When students resolved to open the doors of the university to all who wished entrance, to establish civil liberties and democracy, and to construct, somehow, the metaphoric oasis or hearth, tactics had not been addressed. In September, Voitinskii had considered the formation of academic legions much simpler than the organization of mass meetings, which he regarded as complex and unrealistic.[30] Such doubts among student leaders justified the initial effort to enact internal change rather than to organize actual meetings. And once most internal issues had been resolved, professors began to lecture in the daytime while private gatherings occurred in the evenings. On September 20, for example, a group of Polish students and some nonstudents held a discussion of Polish autonomy and the Russian revolutionary movement. Most evenings as well, party cells met in relative safety to plan strategy, and students discussed issues and reforms of their own.[31]

Accounts of these gatherings sometimes note the presence of workers and the confusion of students, who seemed unsure of how to respond to them. Not uncommonly, students disputed the right of "outsiders" (mostly workers and students from other institutions) to vote on questions related to the end of their strike or to proposed changes in the internal academic order but did not continue such limitations when the meetings grew broadly political in content. Yet even in late September, some students continued to dispute both the presence of outsiders and their right to vote. In most such cases, uncertainties regarding the response of faculty to the (often illegal) activities of the evening hours caused these tensions. In the Mining and Polytechnic Institutes, for example, the faculty had forbidden the presence of outsiders at evening meetings and threatened to close the institutes altogether. For a short time, fearful of reprisals, mining students hesitated to transgress this prohibition; in contrast, polytechnic students voted to admit outsiders despite the warning. In the case of the university, so long as meetings were limited to the evening, professors were more willing to overlook the presence of nonstudent participants.[32]

The shadowy line, if it ever existed, between academic and political debate was often crossed. At an assembly of juridical students on September 25, attention quickly shifted from the official topic to recent events in Moscow: in particular, the closure of Moscow University by Rector Trubetskoi (due, incidentally, to the illegal presence of outsiders and his fear of clashes with police). Orators underscored the inherent contradiction of freedom existing within the walls of the university but not outside of them, and reaffirmed the need for meetings "with the goal of raising the consciousness of the masses." [33] Though party activists, students, and some workers were congregating in educational institutions, a meeting oriented specifically to workers had not yet taken place. By late September, change was nonetheless apparent. At a meeting on the elective system, Starostin, the worker who had spoken at the first *skhodka,* again ascended the podium, only this time to criticize the preoccupation of students with such trivialities. Students responded with applause, and the chairman thanked him in the name of the entire assembly. At this point, student leaders resolved to organize evening meetings for workers in accordance with their initial resolutions.[34]

Although students invited workers to attend lectures and meetings, workers themselves appear to have initiated contact with their impromptu entrance into educational institutions. Organization then fell to students, who drew inspiration from the ideal of a "university for the people" and the decades-old model of the study circle. The first meetings designed for workers, called, not insignificantly, "scientific-political assemblies," thus combined politics with pedagogy. In the absence of both a defined program and experienced orators, these meetings were quite disorderly. Voitinskii recalls the efforts to vary agitational speeches with lectures on history or politics, which suffered more from insufficient preparation than insufficient interest. In addition to debating political questions, workers read their poetry and compositions and described their lives and experiences.[35] One should not be too quick, therefore, to discount students' rhetorical combination of educational and revolutionary tasks. Polytechnic students had called for "evening lectures" and the enactment of "academic freedom in its broadest form." Students at the Institute of Civil Engineering invited "all those who wished to hear the voice of science and truth." Technological students described their institute as "a pulpit of political studies." [36]

Police files note the increasing number of outsiders and workers in attendance at student assemblies in late September. The first "meeting" seems to have occurred on September 25 in the Women's Medical Institute, located in an industrial part of northern Petersburg.[37] On September 28, another crowd gathered at the university: a Ukrainian group discussed the principle of federalism and Ukrainian autonomy in one auditorium; the SDs presented a paper in another; and the SRs sponsored a meeting attended by approximately fifteen hundred people, primarily workers, in the main auditorium. On September 29, the Mining Institute, located not too far from the university, hosted a meeting, and on September 30, the crowds, numbering by then approximately five thousand people including some three thousand workers, returned to the university.[38]

By this time, academic topics were completely absent from the discussions. With a student Social Democrat presiding, the program ranged from the class tactics of the bourgeois parties to preparation for an armed uprising. In his daily chronicle, D'iakonov describes in utopian language what he terms the "first meeting": " 'Guests' entered into the cloakroom feeling a bit shy, as if they were in some foreign place, but after a few minutes in the brightly lit hall, mingling with the lively crowd, they already felt like the best comrades of the youth." The university, a symbol of privilege and status, was a building most workers had never entered. Yet here, they were greeted with respect and often adulation: "The crowd quiets. The tremendous tension of the audience fills the hall. This is not the 'dark working mass' but people conscious of the tremendous task placed on them by historical destiny." Orators, who were typically, though not exclusively, student activists, were received enthusiastically: "As the speeches come to a close, shouts and applause ring out like thunder." [39]

A key moment in the unfolding of the urban revolution was provided by the sudden and unexpected death of Sergei Trubetskoi while in Petersburg on a political mission. Though a moderate liberal figure, Trubetskoi became a symbol the entire opposition embraced. On Sunday, October 2, several thousand workers, students, and other members of St. Petersburg society accompanied his coffin to the Nikolaevskii train station for the journey to Moscow. Because the station was located on Nevskii Prospect, the main artery of Petersburg, the procession took over the center of the city and became a demonstration, complete with red flags, placards, and traditional radical hymns. Despite the efforts of police to break up the crowd at the train station, a large number successfully headed back up Nevskii Prospect, pausing briefly at the Kazan Cathedral, and crossed the bridge to Vasil'evskii Island and the university. Although the doors to the university were locked and mounted police rushed the unarmed crowd, several hundred people managed to enter the building and assemble in the auditorium. The subsequent debate revealed that none of the established parties had planned this meeting. Although some interpreted the anonymous call to go to the university and the subsequent police attack as provocation, it seems much more likely, as many also claimed at the time, that the procession had been largely spontaneous.[40] The experience of the meetings at the university was forging a common ground for disparate social groups and creating a new sense of community across class lines that was displayed in this demonstration.

The funeral of Trubetskoi the next day in Moscow became the occasion for one of the largest demonstrations yet held in that city. Police violence again prompted public outcry and helped to spur the strike movement. The unrest that would culminate in a general strike had begun with a printers' strike in Moscow on September 20. The proximity of the printing works to Moscow University, then located in the center, had facilitated the growth of meetings slightly earlier there, resulting in the temporary closure of the university on September 22. On the day after the funeral, a general strike was set to begin on all the railways, and by October 10, service had stopped completely in Moscow. As the strike expanded, meetings in educational institutions in every academic center across the country grew larger and more radical. In a manner completely unforeseen by students only several weeks before, the universities were indeed becoming the hearths of revolution.[41]

With its elite institutes and centrally located university, Petersburg provided numerous sites for the almost daily meetings. During the daytime, entire factories sent delegates to reserve auditoriums for the evening. Concerned about the lack of space at the evening meetings, workers also began to request that students not present in the capacity of orators restrict their attendance to daytime lectures. Thus, on October 5, twelve thousand people gathered in the university. On October 7 and 8, the Women's Medical Institute and the Military-Medical Academy hosted thousands of workers. On October 11, railway workers meeting in the Military-Medical Academy voted to join the general strike.[42] A cross-section of Petersburg society attended the meetings, and placards directed the incoming crowds to reserved rooms. At the meeting held in the university on October 11, for example, railway workers met in the main auditorium, while anarchists, secondary-school students, printers, jewelers, Polish students, and other groups gathered in lecture halls.[43] University student Vladimir Zotov recalls the chaotic and exhilarating October days—the growing strike, the rumors from other cities, the closures of Tomsk University and the Institute of Civil Engineering, the lack of food in the student cafeterias, and the first time he heard a lecture open with the phrase "ladies and gentlemen." [44] Revolution, it seems, could be experienced in the classroom as well as the meeting.

The entrance of workers into the world of students engendered utopian images and social tensions. The size, social composition, and revolutionary character of the meetings led to their idealization as the enactment of revolutionary praxis. In the words of D'iakonov: "The 'autonomous' higher school has now for several days been transformed into an impassioned and stormy political tribunal. Tens of thousands of workers are holding general meetings. . . . As an independent body, the *studenchestvo* has merged with the tremendous proletarian mass, [students are] helping in word and deed, organizing and propagandizing." [45] This image is transformative and utopian: the merging of students with workers had combined consciousness with revolutionary force. When student radicals began to dress like workers, however, reactions undermined any claim to "merging." One police report described the "democratic" character of an early meeting—some thirty "shaggy" long-haired students, slovenly dressed in red and blue shirts and dirty jackets, the young chairman in a half-dirty white shirt, and the youth disguised in workers' clothing. [46] Although radicals cited their frequent excursions into working-class neighborhoods as the reason for their new clothing, other students considered such "proletarian suits" as high boots and traditional belted shirts *(kosovorotka)* to be a "revolutionary masquerade," intended more for the public display of radical consciousness than for its practicality. [47] The mixing of social groups under one roof had its ironic moments: when student Voitinskii rose to give a speech before the Academic Union, the organ of the professorial corporation, a faculty member protested: "We would like to hear the representative of the students, not the workers." [48]

Although the peculiar coexistence of daytime studies and evening meetings began to disintegrate after several weeks, the two pursuits occurred simultaneously, often with the same people participating in diverse activities. Student elections took place during the escalating strike, with Voitinskii, an organizer of the evening meetings, elected to the Council of Elders. Indeed, the continuation of "normal" academic life had become necessary to the evening meetings, because it allowed professors to disregard in large part the illegal activities. Voitinskii stresses the willingness of radicals to compromise on "daytime" issues in order to preserve this fragile equilibrium and their uncontested authority during the evening hours. By the time public meetings were formally prohibited on October 12 under threat of police intervention, a majority of professors had likewise acknowledged the political importance of the general strike and accepted the temporary political involvement of universities. In part following the advice of students, professors resolved that their particular civic duty was to continue lecturing in order to keep the universities open. Though fearing the violence and the precedent should the state close academic institutions by force, the Academic Union refused to prohibit meetings or to sanction the closure of educational institutions. Even General Trepov's notorious directive not to spare the bullets failed to halt the movement. Every school across the city—from the Academy of Art to the Mining Institute—was overflowing with thousands of people. At the

Technological Institute, early sessions of the Soviet of Workers' Deputies were held.[49]

The movement came to a climax on the evening of October 15, when soldiers surrounded the university and other institutes. The meeting in the university broke up in orderly fashion, with participants leaving in small peaceful groups; in contrast, the Technological Institute was placed under siege, with students remaining in the building to resist its "occupation." Meeting in emergency sessions, faculty councils refused to sanction the forced closure of their institutions, arguing that the meetings had not obstructed studies and that the demands of the population for civil liberties and political reform necessitated the temporary use of educational institutions for political meetings.[50] The crackdown came too late to check the wave of discontent. The General Strike had paralyzed the country, and the Soviet of Workers' Deputies was already functioning as much more than a strike committee.

Bowing to the pressure, the tsar grudgingly signed a manifesto granting civil liberties and a new Duma, based on an expanded male suffrage and possessing legislative powers. The next day, October 18, thousands poured onto the streets in tremendous demonstrations. The left condemned the concessions as insufficient and called for an armed uprising. Red flags were briefly raised over the university and the Military-Medical Academy and, for the last time, crowds gathered at educational institutions. Though dissatisfied with the manifesto, moderates hoped to transform the Duma into a democratic assembly, and the faculty of Petersburg University thus expressed its hope that freedom of speech and the new representative body would allow the universities to resume their rightful role in peaceful cultural development.[51] The celebration was cut short when the Semenovskii Regiment (famous for its rebellious role in the years before the Decembrist revolt) fired on the Technological Institute, where several hundred students had barricaded themselves. Five people were killed, with many others, including history professor Evgenii Tarle, wounded.

During the fall of 1905, the student movement had played a critical role in the revolutionary process. The politicization of universities had facilitated the organization and coordination of the workers' movement and the opposition as a whole. But this "hearth" also has a history. The interlocked images of the student as a revolutionary and the university as a source of consciousness dated from the 1860s and shaped the emergence of a student movement in the early twentieth century. The events of October 1905 marked the brief union of educated society and the people, because the university had served the revolutionary aspirations of the people. Although students did not anticipate the mass meetings, their September resolutions invoked a utopian vision uniting science and activism, intellectuals and people in revolution. As seems inevitable with utopias, however, this vision failed to produce lasting positive results.

THE SPECTER OF VIOLENCE

In the immediate aftermath of the October Manifesto, violence swept through hundreds of Russian cities. Sometimes it resulted from the confrontation of patriotic and revolutionary demonstrations; just as often, crowds went on a rampage unchecked by local police. In Minsk and Sevastopol, the military played a central role by firing on demonstrators. In Tver and Iaroslavl, the authorities looked away as crowds attacked intellectuals, professionals, and students. In Kazan, Cossacks fired on the university just as a meeting broke up. Many of the most virulent pogroms occurred in southern Russia and were directed primarily against the Jewish population, but also against intellectuals and students. The unprecedented extent of the violence spawned rumors of national organization and government complicity.[52]

Coming as they did in the first "days of freedom," the pogroms marked a transition into a new phase of the revolutionary period characterized by vastly increased violence: the bloody suppression of the Moscow Uprising, the summary executions of the military courts, and the repression of agrarian and national protests. The closure of educational institutions until the fall of 1906—despite protests by both faculty and students—reflected the extreme state of emergency. For students, who found themselves easy targets for both police and gangs, violence also became a fact of everyday life. Archival sources indicate that Petersburg students had been subject to unprovoked attacks as early as January 1905. In the aftermath of Bloody Sunday, the student uniform was an invitation for trouble as police and Cossacks began to beat up students who were simply walking along the street. The motivation for these attacks sprang from the association of students with radicalism. On the evening of January 9, for example, Napoleon Dobkevich and Aleksandr Shapirov were attacked when a group of twenty-five policemen spotted them and yelled, "There they are, the rebels [buntovshchiki]—Corner them at the alleyway!"[53] The problem was significant enough to warrant a formal protest on February 4 from the faculty council of St. Petersburg University.[54]

As the level of violence rose dramatically in the fall, students organized legions of self-defense. On October 24, the Council of Elders of St. Petersburg University requested money from the faculty council to purchase weapons but was instead provided with overcoats, intended—shamefully—to hide the uniform.[55] When Moscow University was placed under temporary siege on October 14, students there also organized an armed detachment. Many students likewise joined medical units, which were active during the Moscow Uprising. According to the Medical Union, 21 of the 788 men killed that December were students.[56] One incident in Moscow illustrates the importance of students' reputation in the escalating violence. On December 12, according to a leftist observer, five "provocateurs" presented a special brand of street theater. Two of the men played the parts of students and three the parts of Black Hundreds, a notorious right-wing group. In the performance, one of the Black Hundreds asked, "What will you students do if you are victorious?" The students responded, "Close churches, turn bells into cannons, shoot those who dissent." The Black Hundreds agitated in turn against students and revolutionaries. While the observer notes the failure of such propaganda, violence against students was clearly linked to their identification as iconoclasts, indeed, as symbols for the revolution itself.[57]

Such potent images helped create a legacy of martyrdom, preserved in the 1906 volume *In Memory of the Fallen: Victims from the Moscow Studenchestvo in the October and December Days.* A compilation of newspaper articles, portraits of individual victims, and a chronicle of events, this volume reads as pure hagiography. On the fly-leaf is a list of thirty-one student casualties, in whose memory the book is dedicated: "They were killed because they were students and had come to stand for freedom; they were killed for those beliefs and convictions, to which the entire *studenchestvo* subscribes, and which almost without exception imbue the *studenchestvo*." Accounts focused on the courage and dignity of the victims, unwilling to give their attackers the satisfaction of asking for mercy. With its genre-specific forces of good and evil, martyrology gave a different gloss on the violence. It situated individual experiences and losses in the context of eternal memory and final victory. The victimization of individual students demonstrated the vitality and purity of their community.[58]

TEMPLE OF SCIENCE OR BUILDING FOR MEETINGS?

In retrospect, the October Manifesto marked the turning point of the revolution. Although subsequent events revealed the absence of real commitment within the government to democratic processes, the manifesto drove a wedge between moderates and radicals. The attempted renewal of the general strike on the basis of radical economic demands and the Moscow Uprising raised the additional specter of a class-based social revolution. The short-lived unity of October also disintegrated in the universities, where new controversy arose over the proper role of the university in the postrevolutionary era. The debate revolved around two poles: should the university serve as a temple of pure science, a realm apart from the world of political interest and ideological conflict? Or, to the contrary, was the university as an institution obligated to respond to contemporary political and social conditions? Indeed, was science pure or political?

Although the professoriate had long criticized the student movement for politicizing the university, many professors had sympathized with students' aspirations for civil rights, if not with their methods. This state of affairs changed in 1905. With autonomy promised by the Temporary Rules of August 27, 1905 and with civil liberties and political representation pledged in the October Manifesto, the long-coveted dream of an autonomous university along the German model seemed close to realization. After October, most professors argued that political struggle no longer had any place in the university, the proper task of which was cultural development and scientific progress. Unlike such moderate proponents of academic autonomy, new conservative student groups argued that scholarship was antithetical to politics, and, indeed, that the events of 1905 had marked the spiritual death of the university. The student strike of 1899, they argued, had initiated a process leading to the complete renunciation of science in 1905. For them, there was simply no point of contact between academic and political interests.[59] In perhaps the most moderate account by a conservative group, the golden ages of Russian science and culture coincide with periods of political reaction, the 1830s and 1840s, and the 1880s. The authors of this work openly state their preference for an elitist basis for higher education and for a science separate from any form of practice. For them, the failure of the revolution heralded the rebirth of the university.[60]

The transformation of classrooms into sites for mass meetings also engendered the opposite conclusion. One leftist critic argued that the social and political role of universities in Russian history far outweighed their negligible cultural or scientific contributions:

> [T]o take the "hearth" out of Russian universities is to deprive them of their fundamental cultural significance. The university was the social-political club in which social senses and political ideas were developed. The circles of Stankevich and Herzen arose in the university; the activists of the 1860s and fighters of the 1870s were shaped in the university. The history of Russian higher educational institutions is the history of a "building for meetings."[61]

According to this logic, to take away the politics was to subvert the primary function of higher education in Russia. During the course of 1905, however, many students had seen, perhaps for the first time, a correlation between their academic and political interests. They had advanced a vision of a democratic university, which combined educational and revolutionary dimensions. Very few students viewed the university as an exclusively political or, conversely, academic institution.[62] During the 1906–1907 academic year, therefore, students searched for a new synthesis of the educational and revolutionary tasks of the university. These aspirations came into conflict, however, with those of a professoriate idealizing pure science and a government intent on reasserting its authority.

THE FREE UNIVERSITY

After almost a year-long break, students returned to their institutions in the fall of 1906 with the unequivocal desire to study. They discovered a new academic world. Reforms had already brought tremendous change to higher education, and the case of St. Petersburg University was typical. Due to the long closure and liberalized admissions policies, the overall number of students rose from 4,508 in 1905, to 8,090 in 1907, and to 9,630 in 1908. With the quota largely disregarded, the percentage of Jewish students increased from 3.28% in 1903 to 5.66% in 1905, 10.82% in 1906, and reached a high of 12.5% in 1908. The student body also became socially more diverse, with the number of nobles and sons of civil servants falling from 64.9% in 1899 to 58.7% in 1907, and the representation of lower social orders rising over this same period from 15.5% to 21.9%.[63]

On September 1, 1906, Petersburg University students formally resolved to open the university in the interests of the revolution and "to concentrate and mobilize the *studenchestvo* in urban centers." The tone of the resolution, however, reflected a new political world: "Considering it premature to organize mass meetings in the university, the *skhodka* expresses its faith that students' revolutionary traditions will compel the utilization of university buildings for meetings, when the interests of the revolutionary struggle so demand. Until that time, academic studies are allowed." In the eyes of many student leaders, the revolution had recast social relations in terms of class interest, with the events of 1905 inaugurating a new struggle between the proletariat, the autocracy, and to a lesser degree, the bourgeoisie. In this metahistorical encounter, a student movement as such was negligible—society no longer needed to be prodded into consciousness and action as it had before 1905. Students should continue to participate in Russia's political life, it was stressed, but as members of their class and party—as citizens, not as students. The new order had thus relegated the "glorious" leading role of the *studenchestvo*, "the solitary political fighter," to history.[64]

But what did this mean in practice? On the one hand, student leaders agreed that a politically unified *studenchestvo* no longer existed. Consequently, many sought to redefine *studenchestvo* in terms of "professional" interests rather than academic or political ones. Judging from discussions in early 1906, professional interests encompassed academic freedom, economic mutual aid, corporate organization, and free political expression.[65] On the other hand, socialist student leaders also intended to keep the university ready for any future revolutionary role. The SDs, in particular, chose tactics over theory. Although they considered the student body to be divided along class lines, they nonetheless believed it imperative to defend "revolutionary principles" and achievements.[66] That is, the SDs intended to preserve their own hegemony, in the name of the proletariat, over student institutions.

The contradiction between professional interests and revolutionary principles governed student politics during the 1906–1907 academic year, with controversy focusing on the Council of Elders. As a so-called professional institution modeled along the lines of a parliament, the council did not (and could not) have a political platform. Unlike the *skhodka*, which was conceived as the general will of *studenchestvo*, the council was intended to incorporate diverse currents of opinion. For this reason, its political resolutions would not be binding on all students.[67] Yet with elections conducted by public voting for party lists in faculty-wide *skhodki*, the council was in reality a hybrid. Predictably, the SD ticket dominated elections across the country, while voter participation hovered around 50%.[68] According to Aleksei Vilenkin, a Kadet council member, the council did not represent the will of all students but only the minority who voted according to the "reputation of radicalism," that is for the SDs. Arguing that elections should be conducted by a secret ballot, he advocated the replacement of the *skhodka* with a referendum. The dissolution of a unitary student politics, he concluded, required a new system of government.[69] In opposing both proportional representation of all parties and the replacement of the *skhodka* by the referendum, radicals continued to cite the imperative to keep the university in the revolutionary camp and played on romanticized radical traditions to garner votes.[70]

At issue in this dispute was the student ethos. Should student institutions develop revolutionary spirit, as had been advocated in the past, or a sense of civic values appropriate to the new era? Defenders of the old radical ethos argued that the referendum would shatter the collectivist spirit of student life, increase political apathy, and lead to the emergence of bourgeois values. The preservation of the *skhodka* was necessary to the revolutionary character of the university and *studenchestvo*.[71] Moderate-left students countered that the goal of student institutions was now the education of the citizen, not the revolutionary hero. Vilenkin thus depicted the *skhodka* as a revolutionary body from a bygone era. With its lack of structure and its tradition of bold and daring oratory, it was now an inappropriate forum for rational and orderly debate. The secret ballot would better teach students democratic values and practices.[72] Pointing to the low level of participation and the explosive growth in enrollments, another student observed that students no longer constituted a unified corporation but only an aggregate of disparate interests and social groups. The referendum, not the *skhodka*, would help students express themselves as responsible and politically educated citizens rather than as revolutionaries.[73]

Similar ideas shaped the ongoing aspiration of students to reform academic life. In addition to supporting democratized admissions, some students lobbied for the introduction of an elective system as a critical part of their "general education." The elective system, one student passionately argued, would create an autonomous university dedicated to the moral and cultural renewal of the country. It would free academic life from the dictates of the state and its civil service examinations, and, at the same time, allow individuals to tailor a course of study suited to their interests and needs. The new university must not limit its task to the preparation of civil servants or even scientists, this student believed. It must also educate conscious and educated citizens, develop broad philosophical-scientific world views, and begin to serve its great task in cultural enlightenment.[74] A parallel role was to be played by the study circle, hundreds of which were then being organized by students with the support of faculty members. Envisioned as forums to debate issues of contemporary relevance and to develop one's world view, circles formed around such subjects as the philosophy of law, political economy, the agrarian question, Jewish literature, mysticism, and anarchism. Titles of papers included: "The Psychological Basis of Utopia," "The Theory of Progress of N. Mikhailovskii," "The Class Relations of the Peasant and Worker," and "God." Excursions were organized to local factories.[75]

Other student institutions founded in this period promised new avenues of socialist experiment. They included a labor bureau and a committee to investigate the political arrests and exile of students. The labor bureau garnered particular interest for its attempt to regulate student intellectual labor throughout Petersburg. Students hoped not only to coordinate supply and demand but to control pay and working conditions, to allocate labor, and to distribute the common wealth to the neediest students. They also projected the formation of cooperatives and artels typical of earlier generations of Russian radicals.[76] With its combination of Marxist and utopian socialist ideas, the labor bureau reflected the ongoing interests of some students in the traditions of Russian radicalism.

Uniting the heterogeneous issues of student life was a vibrant student press, in which editorials, student poetry, short stories, literary criticism, and scholarly articles all clamored for attention. Chronicles of current events described everything from new study circles to political arrests and executions. Despite diverse political orientations, these newspapers aspired both to reflect the multifaceted interests of students and to educate students as citizens. One sought to provide a "full and exact picture of the life of the *studenchestvo*, its professional needs and endeavors, its political and ethical ideals." A Marxist journal aimed to promote Marxism yet still affirmed that the *studenchestvo* remained an "extra-class milieu," the "living source of the liberation movement." [77] As in the broader debates over political organization, differing conceptions of *studenchestvo* coexisted within and among student newspapers. Some looked primarily to the revolutionary tradition; others hoped to define a new basis of corporate identity on the principle of citizenship. Both perspectives built on the experiences of September and October 1905. Radical democratization had proved to be a uniquely flexible and powerful ideal.

The fragility of the new university order was all too soon exposed. Though many students assumed that freedom of speech and assembly had been achieved, this was not the case. The dilemma became clear on the first anniversary of the October Manifesto, when students in both Moscow and St. Petersburg held unauthorized memorials. In Moscow, Rector A. A. Manuilov closed the university for almost two weeks, called himself the "master of the university," and refused to sanction the use of university buildings for meetings. In St. Petersburg, Rector I. I. Borgman threatened to close the university should any lectures be disrupted. Both Manuilov and Borgman feared that students would imperil the achievement of academic autonomy by provoking police intervention.[78] In response, thousands of Petersburg students gathered to denounce their professors. Orators described their version of the history of student-professor relations, dwelling with particular relish on the participation of professors in the expulsion and military draft of students. A consensus quickly emerged: the class struggle had entered higher education. The professoriate was the defender of the bourgeois order, and students were aligned with the proletariat. Yet the parallel ended there. After all, *studenchestvo* was also divided by class. Though claiming the right to free speech and assembly, students lacked a means to defend their rights against the government and had simply lashed out at professors.[79]

Over the spring of 1907, the government acted with increasing vigor and confidence. To the futile objections of faculty councils, police conducted searches inside educational institutions and repeatedly objected to the presence of "outsiders" (usually students from other schools) and the "revolutionary character" of authorized student gatherings. The observations of police consistently conflicted with the experiences of professors. One police report on a literary-musical party sponsored by the Women's Courses, for example, described donations to illegal causes as well as revolutionary songs and poetry. The courses' director, who had been present the entire time, had reported the party a complete success and found the charge of a "disruption of order" completely unexpected.[80]

Even as professors implored students to refrain from any activity that could serve as a pretext for police intervention and threaten autonomy, the repressions of the government advanced without regard for the substance of students' activities. For their part, student leaders rejected the utility of protest out of hand. After an illegal police search in the Polytechnic Institute, students spontaneously gathered to discuss the incident, only to find their anger mocked: "What do you want?" their leaders asked, "What are you protesting? Are you not satisfied with current conditions? Then go fight—not as students but as citizens—in the ranks of that class whose point of view you share." [81] Several months later, the revolution ended in the university. A government decree banned student parliamentary organizations formed by universitywide voting and placed severe restrictions on the functioning of other student organizations. The presence of "outsiders" and the discussion of "nonacademic" issues at student gatherings were prohibited under threat of police intervention.[82] It was summer vacation, and there was hardly a whimper of protest.

The question of student radicalism during the 1905 Revolution has usually been formulated as one of degree. How radical were they? Was the student movement manipulated and controlled by the Social Democrats? Did students strive for (radical) political change or (moderate) academic reform? Was their radicalism just a verbal commitment, a smoke screen for their real goal of a diploma and comfortable position after graduation? Rather than engaging in this debate, I have explored how students understood and enacted the revolution in both their academic and their political lives. This approach has shown that the aspirations and activities of students were not antithetical but often interconnected.

Students articulated their political and academic goals in strikingly similar language, consistently associating the radical democratization of education with social and political revolution. This convergence of language allowed students with diverse political views to find common ground along a continuum of "academic" and "political" activity. Student radicalism did not follow the platform of a political party, but a historical vision that linked a broad conception of science to the achievement of consciousness and ultimately to social revolution. In the most radical phase, when the street entered the university during the October meetings, the utopia lay in the union of pedagogy with politics, intelligentsia with the people, consciousness with spontaneity. Paradoxically, the catalytic role of students in the revolutionary process led to their growing irrelevance to the movement as a whole. Indeed, their traditional self-image as heralds of revolution had been fulfilled and its basis disrupted. To paraphrase D'iakonov, in revolution, there are no students, only citizens and classes.

By 1906, most students were ready to resume their studies under the promised academic autonomy. Already reaping the benefits of admission and curricular reforms, students hoped to enjoy their new freedoms. As they considered the meaning of the revolution to their own lives in the university, however, an old conflict reappeared in a new guise and further dissolved the mythical unity of October 1905. While some students hoped to keep the university in the "revolutionary" camp, others envisioned a new democratic role for it. Should the university inculcate the heroic ethos of the revolutionary activist—the old *studenchestvo*—or the democratic values of the citizen? As political repression hindered the emergence of democratic structures, students were compelled to reevaluate the assumptions and lessons of the revolutionary heritage. As they confronted a heroic past, their revolutionary experience, and, with particular urgency, their supposed class identity, they began to ponder whether 1905 was a "bourgeois revolution." If so, were they the bourgeoisie?

PART TWO

The Mire of Life

CHAPTER FIVE

From Icon of New Order to Symbol of Disorder

Students and the End of Revolution

> Life does not follow along a single straight line. . .
> —Mikhail Gershenzon, "On Creative Self-Cognition"

The end of revolution inaugurated a prolonged crisis of authority in Russia. With its power reestablished through arbitrary and often bloody repression, the government lacked legitimacy among broad sections of society, from politicized urban workers to liberal professionals. At the same time, the specter of violence and disorder only polarized social and political groups, hindering the reemergence of a united democratic front. Though the State Duma remained a forum of opposition, it was a symbol of potential progress rather than a fully empowered constitutional body. In this new and ambiguous order, dominated by competing social classes, economic interests, and political parties, public fears rose over perceived increases in crime, disease, and disorder.[1] To a great extent, Russia seemed to have lost her moral ballast.

The failure of the revolution to live up even to more pragmatic expectations ignited new controversy about Russia's historical path, in which the social role of students became an important reference point. The European Revolutions of 1848 functioned as a historical parallel and a potential lesson. In an article dedicated to Russian students, Evgenii Tarle, the popular professor of European history at St. Petersburg University, explored the role of German and Austrian students in the Revolution of 1848. By depicting them as intermediaries between educated society and the working class, he invited an analogy with the events of October 1905. Indeed, Tarle deliberately portrayed student movements as prototypic components of bourgeois revolutions in general. This Marxist-influenced model of historical development presumed universal laws of class formation and political development, laws which Russia too would presumably follow. In France, students were thus a "progressive" force only in 1830, when they actively

struggled against the Restoration. Thereafter, according to the model, they followed the lead of the bourgeoisie by forming national guard units in 1848 to
suppress the workers' uprising. German and Austrian students belatedly took
this same path and abstained from radical political movements after 1848. "As it
became possible to breathe, move, and struggle, the blood, barricades and alarms
disappeared," Tarle pointedly concluded. "With an established 'parliament for
politics,' the 'university for science' peacefully resumed its work." [2]

The political neutrality and academic autonomy of German universities were
idealized by many professors, who sought to introduce these principles into the
Russian context. Hoping that their students would follow the established path,
they counseled the relative merits of evolutionary rather than revolutionary
change, cultural rather than overtly political methods. Though most students
could accept the idea that the university should, in principle, have a cultural
role, they watched helplessly as most of their hard-won freedoms were reversed
by ministerial decrees. In the fall of 1908, seeing no other option, they finally
called a strike in the name of academic autonomy. Repudiated by liberals for
their political methods and by revolutionaries for their academic goals, students
feared that this strike marked the death knell of the old *studenchestvo*. Their
public image had undergone a dramatic reversal. No longer were they considered
heroic fighters or even legitimate political actors. Distasteful as it was, the story
told by the bourgeois students of France and Germany appeared increasingly
relevant to the new era.

A Reappraisal of Values

By 1907, not just political questions but also personal ones had caught the public
eye. Concern and attention centered on the rumored predilection of youth for
pornographic literature and physical pleasure; the reputed bible of the new world
view was Mikhail Artsybashev's novel, *Sanin.* In contrast to the heroes of the
1860s and 1870s, who had proclaimed scientific rationality and social service as
their mottos, the new fictional hero, Sanin, pursued and propagandized sensual
pleasure as the basis for his ethical system. In his explicit rejection of the traditional ideals of the intelligentsia, Sanin seemed to embody the revolution in
values after 1905. Debates within Russia's educated society revealed both ideological dissension and a striking consensus. Describing Sanin as a by-product of
capitalism, which glorified individual freedom and consumer morality, radicals
rejected him as a positive hero. Citing his cult of the sensual, conservatives saw
him as the incarnation of the next stage of radical materialism, the logical and
perverted outgrowth of revolution. For their part, liberals regarded his sexual
liberation as a social evil and an inevitable path to disappointment. With Sanin
rarely seen as the herald of a courageous new historical type, controversy focused

on the all-important question: Were young people flocking to the banner of physical desire as a result of their political disappointment? [3]

For students, the controversy over Saninism, as it was called, became a means to grapple with the collapse of the "old" world view as it related to their own personal, as well as political, lives. Despite the tremendous public outcry, few students in fact praised the new hero, instead seeing him as emblematic of the dearth of new positive values and the moral "fall" of students in general into both sensuality and pessimism. Student leader Aleksei Vilenkin thus portrayed Sanin as the figure best articulating the predicament of modern Russian society. Arguing that the revolution had unleashed a new nihilism, he contrasted the pure love of Pushkin's nineteenth-century hero Evgenii Onegin for Tat'iana ("I love you with the love of a brother," Onegin had proclaimed), with the physical desire of Sanin for his real sister. But rather than condemning Sanin, he asked whether it was possible to prove it wrong to "love" a sister. After the revolution all values were suspect: "We experienced a terrible disappointment: the rise—the crazy thrilling spirit of ascent; the fall—quick, dark, and terrifying. There on the summit, at the crest of the wave where unlimited perspectives were opened, we came to disdain obstacles, prejudices, and conventionality. And this disdain has not deserted us below." In Vilenkin's view, the demise of the revolution and its dreams had left two options: the pursuit of personal pleasure or suicidal despair. Until society had defined a new ethical basis, youth would continue to live—and die—by the motto, "seize the moment." [4] He left the question open. Had sensuality replaced service as the credo of the new generation?

In defending Sanin as a positive hero, the student M. Greidenberg used remarkably similar language. He too described the "wide horizons" of limitless possibility but instead reveled in the pleasure of rebellion: "The former idols have faded, the old prejudices are mocked, and we, people of contemporaneity, no longer believe in those ideals, those life tasks and goals, in which our fathers until so recently believed." Suicide was the fate of the weak, Greidenberg suggested, of the people of the past, who had rejected the old values, yet could not adapt to the new conditions of life. In contrast, Sanin was "beautiful, strong, and full of the joy of living." He expected nothing from life but simply took what he wanted and could take. The new morality, according to Greidenberg, required the liberation of life "from all convention and prejudice, which impede living and make it difficult and boring." Yet Greidenberg admitted that Sanin was a transitional figure, because the novel had pointed out the path but not actually detailed the "new forms of life and love." Paraphrasing its end as "Sanin departs into the bright distance to meet the rising sun, new life, and a better future," Greidenberg pictured his own paradise "when life will not be a prison, when man can grow and develop freely—when he will not be broken or deformed by his upbringing, school, or society. There will be no struggle, no evil or hatred, no chains or scaffolds, no social inequality. . . . There will be only free labor and free love." [5] If Vilenkin feared the nihilism of limitless possibility, Greidenberg embraced the nirvana of total liberation.

Despite his impassioned defense of *Sanin,* Greidenberg had spotlighted one of the major weaknesses of the novel. Whereas Chernyshevskii had described the construction of the new society, Artsybashev had concluded with a vague promise. Most students seemed to reject the model for precisely this reason. At a public discussion of the novel at St. Petersburg University, they roundly condemned the absence of a broader program. At one extreme, some students asserted that all literature dealing with sexual themes was sick because the proper function of literature was to instill the social idea into the people. Even those who acknowledged that *Sanin* exposed the hypocrisy of bourgeois morality were critical of the hero. "If Sanin was to be a new 'new man,'" they asserted, the object of his slogan "I want" must "coincide with the general development of culture and human society." For them, the cult of pleasure seemed more an inversion of the traditional value of social service than a viable alternative to it.[6]

Though rejecting *Sanin,* students searched literature for ideological and spiritual direction, still hoping to find a new model and world view corresponding to the changed social and political landscape. In St. Petersburg University, opinion polarized around two groups, "Circle of the Young" (*Kruzhok molodykh),* later renamed "The Future Day" (*Griaduiushchii den'),* and "Circle of Realists" (*Kru zhok realistov).*[7] The dispute between the "Youth" and the "Realists," as they were called, focused on two issues: the relationship between personal freedom and social responsibility, and the didactic role of literature. Judging by the reviews appearing in student newspapers, the polemics between these two circles provided one of the more engaging and popular spectacles of the academic year.

The Youth affiliated with literary modernism and included such well-known poets as Sergei Gorodetskii. Their parties and lectures drew full auditoriums— perhaps because of the ritual attacks in the student press accusing them of advocating physical love as a world view. One letter to the editor thus argued that information about them should not even be published because their "melancholy individualism lacks all social instincts. . . and finds the resolution of life's problems in the exultation of a perverted sexual instinct." [8] Others criticized the conception of art as a servant of politics.[9] For their part, the Realists formed to struggle against this modernist "pornography" (although the sexual question was a constant topic at their sessions as well). At their first meeting in October 1907, the five founding members proclaimed: "We decided to struggle for the realistic current in literature, we wish to enact it into life." As the reviewer ironically pointed out, the group, though knowing its enemy, had problems defining itself. They could not decide whether realism meant that literature should copy life without coloring it or only depict its positive aspects.[10] This dilemma placed them midway between the critical realism of the nineteenth century and the socialist realism of the 1930s.

Despite the aesthetic-ideological opposition of these two circles, their members agreed that literature had failed to define a synthetic new world view as it had seemingly done over previous decades. Instead, literature—like the Revolution—was dismantling convention and subverting long-held assumptions. Interest focused on the popular neorealist writers Maksim Gorkii and Leonid Andreev. In a literary collection published by the Youth, B. Tikhomirov recalled how Gorkii had inaugurated the twentieth century by "singing a new song about the bold fighter-man, who thirsted for freedom and was full of anger and hatred for everything fainthearted and cowardly. He appeared before the storm, and in his songs we heard the call to relentless struggle, and we felt the ecstasy of struggle for a life worthy of man." These models had inspired students from 1899 to 1905, Tikhomirov recalled, but now Gorkii's heroes lacked such a clear message. "The old world view has collapsed, there is no new one, and attempts to create one have not been satisfactory." How is it possible to live, he wondered, when there is no meaning or goal? [11]

Other students likewise criticized the pessimistic message of Leonid Andreev's abstract new work. By depicting man as a "toy in the hands of fate" powerless to create or struggle with life, one anonymous reviewer claimed, Andreev had given mankind just two options, to reconcile itself to petty-bourgeois mediocrity (spiritual death), or to commit suicide (total death). This student concluded that such literature was harmful to the interests of humanity—there was simply no place in the world of scientific progress for those who talked about a crisis of meaning.[12] Another student, Iurii Krichevskii, countered that Andreev remained relevant because he now exposed the constraints and repressions of bourgeois society, albeit without shouting about his own freedom, as had Gorkii's earlier heroes. Yet Krichevskii did not dispute the conclusion reached by many of his comrades. Instead of creating new "new people," literature was destroying the last foundations of the old belief.[13]

REWRITING THE PAST

By the fall of 1907, student leaders shared a growing concern that most students had lost their sense of direction and ethical purpose, a concern that seemed to be documented in their political apathy. At the same time that literary evenings were attracting large and excited audiences, less than half the student body voted in student elections. This troubling phenomenon occurred at a moment when political reaction was gaining force. Following the dissolution of the Second Duma, most of the educational reforms instituted during the revolution were reversed. In August 1907, the Ministry of Internal Affairs ordered police to intervene should students gather within their schools without permission or refuse to disperse upon request. With the appointment of A. N. Shvarts as Minister of Education at the new year, the pressure increased. In a series of decrees, Shvarts excluded seminary graduates and women from the universities and reinstated the Jewish quotas. By reviewing course offerings and reading lists and instituting new civil service examinations for graduates, he successfully undermined the curricular reforms as well. Political reaction won by ministerial decree.[14] In its endeavor to hold back the assault on the university, the professoriate placed its hopes on legal appeal, moral persuasion, and the projected new university charter. Above all, many professors believed, it was imperative that students not provoke further repressions with their protest. And despite the threat to their hardwon privileges, students failed to define a viable course of action. This quiescence sparked heated debates in the student press over a "crisis of *studenchestvo.*"

A few students saw the crisis in a positive light. Petersburg University student Vadim Levchenko argued that the new era required a complete break with the past, "its false and naive faith in the omnipotence of external transformation, and almost complete disregard for the spiritual powers that create life." The heroic self-sacrifice and misplaced concern for social and political change, which had characterized the student movement, he argued, had destroyed successive generations of youth, obstructed the development of science and scholarship, and created a "despotism of the left" parallel to that of the autocratic state. Expressing his hope that the new generation would reject the traditional primacy of politics, Levchenko advocated the construction of a national culture as a new principle of social unity.[15]

With their faith unflagging, student SRs stood at the opposite extreme. Denying that 1905 marked a break of any significance, they asserted that the revolutionary struggle itself was the unifying principle of student identity. In order to put their principles into practice, the SRs staged an illegal meeting in September 1907 simply to protest the holding of an earlier "legal" gathering—in other words, to protest the fact that it had been authorized. A newspaper satire of the "socialist-romantics," as they were renamed, parodied the impassioned speeches of first-year students on the importance of oratorical eloquence and revolutionary behavior as well as the political courage of protesters singing revolutionary songs along the university's long corridor. Such open mockery of the old ethos was still an unsettling gesture. A letter to the editor demanded the author's name in order to bring him before a student court for defaming the honor of the *studenchestvo.* For its neglect of "serious issues," the newspaper was even accused of aiding the forces of reaction.[16] The revolutionary heritage retained its loyalists.

Most student activists remained averse to a complete break with the "heroic past" yet recognized that 1905 marked an important change. Fearing that the university was becoming what they considered a bourgeois institution, dedicated to the production of diplomas, they lamented the indifference of many of their comrades to university politics. Had the majority of students really renounced the traditional ideals of moral and intellectual self-education in favor of careerist advancement and sensual pleasure? In their search for positive lines of continuity, they developed a new narrative synthesis. Before 1905, the typical story of the student movement had recounted the progressive unfolding of political consciousness through spontaneous academic conflict. By contrast, the new narratives asserted that the struggle for academic autonomy—the democratic organization of academic study, political expression, and corporate institutions—had formed the foundation of student politics all along. Science and scholarship had legitimized political engagement in the past and would continue to do so in the future: "In their [past] struggle, students strove for academic autonomy—for the harmony of true politics and true science in the university. . . . In our day, *knowledge* has become the slogan. The political activist realized that he needed broad perspectives, scientific ballast, ordered thought, and a determined will." Academic freedom was a political goal because it facilitated the development of both the person and the nation, this student argued. From its origins, therefore, the student movement had been primarily concerned with the right to produce an individual—the right to *vospitanie*—and in this manner, with the construction of new social and political values within the nation as a whole.[17] Another student agreed, writing that "political education" *(politicheskoe vospitanie)* required scientific study. The function of the university was the production of "workers of democracy." [18]

From these writings, it was unclear whether students would have a larger political role. On the one hand, if the freedom of science and the right to personal development were the core values of the student corporation, political differentiation would not preclude a united student movement. On the other hand, the freedom of the university required the freedom of the country. If the old method of the strike was no longer appropriate in this new era, how then was freedom to be attained? Despite this contradiction, the attempt to "politicize" the academic—indeed, to place academic freedom at the center of student politics from its beginnings—was becoming a dominant motif in a new historical narrative.

In June 1908, Moscow student leader Rafael Vydrin provided a full exposition of the new "political academism." [19] Although Vydrin accepted that 1905 marked the end of a historical era, he managed to combine a Marxist class analysis with a defense of student radicalism. In dividing the history of the student movement into three parts, he predictably defined the first two by their dominant social group (the period of gentry dominance before 1855 and of the student *raznochinets*, 1855–1905), but refused to equate the period following the "bourgeois revolution" of 1905 with a bourgeois *studenchestvo*. This period, Vydrin asserted, would witness a new conflict in higher education: the "class" struggle of the "poorer" *raznochinnoe studenchestvo* against the "privileged" and "philistine" bourgeois students. The mix of class and estate categories allowed him to define a student political community outside of class. Students' "real" historical task—the democratization of education—remained unfulfilled, and the bourgeoisie was the new enemy. With his history, Vydrin claimed to find a social and ideological basis for a student movement.

By the spring of 1908, radical academism had entered student politics. When the Council of Elders was abolished by ministerial decree in February 1908, five thousand university students convened a *skhodka* to empower the council to maintain its authority underground and to lead the struggle for autonomy by legal and illegal means. The resolution did not advance any political demands beyond academic autonomy and student rights. Only the question of tactics remained divisive. The Kadets and the SDs rejected a strike, with the former opposing most strikes on principle and the latter arguing that students must follow the initiative of the proletariat.[20] By the next fall, in response to the long series of government decrees, students would attempt to defend their academic interests with political methods. The old hierarchy had been inverted.

THE LURES OF CAPITALISM

In the fall of 1908, a nationwide student strike closed down higher education. Having witnessed the systematic reversal of the reforms instituted during the revolution, students turned to their traditional weapon and demanded their rights. With its lack of explicit political demands, this strike was more purely academic in its rhetoric than any of its predecessors. But although the two-week strike was adhered to almost universally by students across the entire country, it would be perceived by students and society alike as an abject failure, indeed, a powerful symbol of the death of the prerevolutionary *studenchestvo*.

In early September, a group of St. Petersburg students wrote an appeal, "To Society and the *Studenchestvo*," which would form the basis for the strike resolutions in Petersburg, Moscow, and many provincial cities. With its moderate tone and conciliatory language, the proclamation appears designed to garner public support. As students were well aware, however, most professors had never supported a student strike, and the Third Duma was highly unlikely to be receptive to any protest. The appeal should thus be interpreted as an application of the new political academism. It opens with a brief and conventional account of the evolution of student politics before 1905 that emphasizes the rise of political consciousness out of academic experience. By the second paragraph, however, the political aspirations of the old student movement disappear. The Revolution of 1905—that utopian moment of enacted political consciousness—becomes a purely academic event; its central moment is not the October meetings but the August Temporary Rules. With academic autonomy rather than political change presented as the "true" goal of student protest, the appeal implied that this goal, almost achieved in 1905, was now under attack. Because all legal means had been exhausted, students had chosen the strike in a final effort "to defend culture and enlightenment." Demands focused exclusively on decrees restricting student rights: the exclusion of women, the reinstatement of the Jewish quota, the abolition of the Council of Elders, and the annulment of the elective system. Except for the brief mention of police controls and "dark forces," political discussion was absent.[21]

This strategy reflected an "academic" definition of *studenchestvo*. Assuming that corporate unity before 1905 had been a political unity destroyed by political differentiation, students attempted to build a movement on the basis of common academic interests. The appeal did not evoke the "academic" traditions of 1899, because even then students had rallied around civil liberties and personal inviolability. It instead placed the struggle for academic rather than political freedom at the heart of all student protest and implicitly posed a new question. If the democratization of education was students' ultimate goal, which then was more "conscious"—an academic or a political movement? Despite the absence of concrete political demands, politics in the broader sense was not lacking, and perhaps could not be in view of the movement's tactics. The strike as a method of protest, however limited its demands, connoted the imagery, rhetoric, and tactics of revolutionary struggle. From the very beginning, the strike subverted the new academism.

On September 13, Petersburg University students voted 2,398 to 77 (with 82 abstentions) to strike. In their resolution, they asserted that the policies of the Ministry of Education constituted the "full destruction of the university as a scholarly body" and a "strong blow against Russian enlightenment and Russian culture." They stated their firm expectation of the unanimous support of public opinion and the professoriate in this defense of culture. A debate over the implementation of the strike was scheduled for September 15.[22] On that day, several thousand students gathered with delegations from other schools at the university. After four hours of debate, they decided on a one-week delay in order to "spread the idea of the strike among the [student] masses." A citywide strike committee was formed, and agitators were dispatched across St. Petersburg and to other urban centers. Organized in this fashion, almost all of Russia's universities, institutes, and women's courses had joined the movement by late September. Only harsh repression in some provincial cities hindered its development.

The 1908 strike thus unfolded as a planned response to a series of ministerial decrees, rather than as a direct reaction to a particular event, which had been the case in previous years. It was led by students working independently of established political groupings. Kadet students, who had opposed the strike but agreed to adhere to the decision of the collective, could at best muster tepid support. Even SDs lacked real enthusiasm. At a separate meeting, they decided not to advocate a strike but, in the event of a prostrike vote, to lend their support.[23] Only the SRs, harkening back to an earlier era, hoped to use the "spontaneous excitement" of the strike for political education; that is, they rejected its academic banner and intended to explain its true political significance to those students who still did not understand.[24]

Prostrike sentiment reflected the powerful hold of student traditions. Student leader Aleksei Lozina-Lozinskii argued that a sense of guilt before the past, not a vision of the future, led to the strike. He cited the tremendous impact of a student at the *skhodka,* who had proclaimed: "If the university does not strike, then we will have the right to say: herein lie the deceased!"[25] This perceptive criticism touched upon the central contradiction of the movement: the relation between old revolutionary images and the new academic language. The complex place of remembered and reconstructed student traditions was reflected in a song written for the occasion, "New Dubinushka in the Old Manner" *(Novaia Dubinushka na staryi lad).*[26] Though the verse referred to glory and heroism, notably absent were images of the total eschatological transformation of darkness into light, old into new, slavery into freedom, so typical of the genre. In 1908, the revolutionary song instead celebrated student privileges. It opens with a reference to 1905 and lists the repressions of Shvarts, the Minister of Education:

> At great cost we won freedom
> We won freedom as well for our school,
> But the epoch of barracks has again commenced
> And the nightmare looms before us. . . .
> Shvarts hit beyond measure—
> He unexpectedly assaulted the student central organ
> Confined the professoriate,
> And . . . took away the right to the *skhodka.*

The verse closes with the swelling revolutionary wave: "First the capital, and then Moscow . . . /The banner of freedom will soar/And where there is a boldness of spirit and honor/They will proclaim: 'We rise for THE BATTLE!' " The equation of a "student central organ" with the "banner of freedom" highlighted, however, the transformation of the student movement—corporate rights rather than human rights had become its goal.

The most powerful image in strike leaflets was blood, especially the spilled blood of earlier generations symbolizing both the debt to the past and the continuity of generations. "The blood flowing in student veins has not yet congealed," the New Dubinushka proclaimed, "We will not cover our school with shame." "Are you not fighters for freedom?" another pamphlet asked. "Did you not sacrifice your lives and stain the barricades with blood? Has the flame of Prometheus been extinguished?" A third used a physiological metaphor: "You are the flesh of the flesh, the bone of the bone of the Russian *studenchestvo.* At the time of battle for the emancipation of thought, you were always counted on to be in our ranks."[27] The traditional repertoire of student protest—the verse, the leaflets, and indeed the strike—eulogized the living body of *studenchestvo* but subverted the moderate program. Although students demanded academic reform rather than political revolution, their movement raised the specter of 1905. The contradiction was perhaps unavoidable. To mobilize students as a collective, it was necessary to evoke their collective traditions. The result was a mixed message: the absence of political goals accompanied by the celebration of an eternal *studenchestvo*.

Despite these problems, the strike, which began on September 20 and continued through the first week of October, was extremely successful. After some early dissension, other St. Petersburg schools joined the movement. The boycott in the Technological Institute was total.[28] At St. Petersburg University, lectures were disrupted, and the crowd of students was at times so great that professors could not enter their lecture halls. As the strike spread across the country, students in many provincial universities were subject to arrest and repression, a rare occurrence in the two capital cities because the faculty of St. Petersburg University had persuaded government officials that repression would raise the level of confrontation. Despite Shvarts's resistance, a policy of restraint was implemented, classes were temporarily cancelled for a cooling-off period, and a possible escalation of the strike was averted. In a show of remarkably politic restraint, the police generally declined to enter university buildings without the permission of academic authorities.[29]

Despite its considerable dimensions and near unanimity, the strike began to lose momentum because of the lack of results and the weakness of outside support. Although the SRs praised the strike as a spontaneous sign of active resistance, the RSDRP attacked students for their political naiveté. In a letter to student party groups, the Petersburg Committee of the RSDRP noted that a free higher school was possible only in a free country, and until students defined general political goals for their movement, they should expect no support from the labor movement. A second letter was still more sharp, calling the original appeal (and by implication the entire movement), a product of the most "trite bourgeois liberalism."[30] Given its limited academic character and the disdain of the SDs, the strike did not capture the interest, much less the support, of workers in Petersburg, Moscow, or other cities. Yet in the eyes of all but the radical left, the academic strike was a confrontational and revolutionary tactic; the precise demands were immaterial. Moderate members of the Third Duma declined to intervene, and professors spoke darkly of the future prospects of education in Russia. Finding little support from either moderates or leftists, students were accused by the former of being too radical, by the latter of not being radical enough.

In an attempt to find common ground with professors, one student tried to articulate the parameters of the new academism in a letter published in (and disavowed by) a leading liberal newspaper. Freely admitting that students "no longer even pretend [to have] the role of the barometer of public opinion," he claimed that students were becoming "academists in the best sense of the word." Since the current crisis concerned the need for full academic freedom and the self-administration of both professors and students, he concluded, there was no conflict of interest. Both groups opposed the intervention of the state in the internal university order.[31] While many professors could agree on specific points, they correctly argued that the strike was the method of the old *studenchestvo* and would lead to increased state repression. Whether they offered another solution is a different question. In an attempt to counsel moderation, some professors turned their classrooms into discussion circles focusing on the merits of the strike. Expressing their fears of the destruction *(razgrom)* of the university from without (the state), and its dissolution *(raspad)* from within (the strike), they portrayed the strike as an assault on academic freedom equal to the recently announced draft of a new university charter. In appealing for reason, M. Ia. Pergament asked students to trust their elders, who had fought for years for autonomy. Professor F. A. Braun spoke of the dissolution of the "academic family" should students not return to class. As a potential cause of both destruction and dissolution, the strike was depicted as a fundamental threat to culture, enlightenment, and the social-generational order.[32] Only a few voices on the left criticized the professoriate's official position of embattled neutrality, pointing out that the circulars, the decrees, and the new draft charter were systematically destroying everything but the illusion of collegial independence.[33]

With the sole opposition of the SRs and the strong recommendation of the citywide strike committee, students voted to end the strike on October 7. Lending hardly a word in defense of the movement, orators claimed that students had shown their resolve and proved their opposition; continuation of the strike would result in the dissolution *(raspad)* of this resolve. To preserve solidarity, they argued (with an original twist of logic), students must call off the strike before it showed signs of collapse or drew serious repression. On the one hand, this argument was fully consistent. Students had chosen the strike as a last resort, only after most of the achievements of 1905–1907 had been reversed. And in its dimensions and unanimity, though not in its outcome, the strike had achieved greater success than any of its predecessors, excluding 1905. Moderate and radical students had displayed a willingness to work together on a corporate platform— indeed, in the case of the Kadets and the SDs, to support the strike against their better judgment and the criticism of their respective parties. In this instance, loyalty to the student movement had taken precedence over party allegiances. On the other hand, however, the strike had collapsed under its own contradictions. Despite signs of cohesion, students had gone on strike for the rights of students, and rather than provoking outrage or garnering support, they had been met with words of adult condescension. Even a conservative daily expressed its hope that the youth would be "spared."[34] The student movement had lost its meaning and its audience.

Soon after the end of the strike, Lozina-Lozinskii published an ironic and impassioned pamphlet, *Death of the Phantoms. (A Graveside Word Concerning Recent Events at St. Petersburg University).*[35] With the voice of a Greek chorus commenting on the action on stage, he parodied recent events:

> The curtain has fallen; until a few moments ago the stage radiated with fire and color; its boring and dusty ordinariness now divulges the falsity of the played-out tragedy. The many-headed, drab, and murmuring public hurries home, haggling with cabbies; behind the scenes, the actors—heroes and first lovers—wash off the bright paint, share their successes, count others' mistakes, and laugh and talk about their future professions. But the tragedy . . . actually there isn't one, and perhaps there never was. There were tragic words on stage, interested grimaces in the pit. . . but everyone knew that nobody really dies. . . . This tragedy, well . . . *ce n'est que pour rire messieurs!*[36]

Arguing that the strike was really an homage to the phantoms of past student generations, Lozina-Lozinskii contrasted its militant character (the legacy of the past) to its academic demands. Citing the words of September's resolution, "the individual determination of each and the strength of our mutual organization will lead us to victory," he parodied the final debates over the threat of "dissolution" from within and "destruction" from without, and disputed the claim to victory with open sarcasm. The strike had neither defended academic autonomy nor demonstrated student solidarity. True victory, he claimed, using the example of Caesar, required the genre of tragedy:

> Destruction? Yes the *studenchestvo* should have awaited it. . . . [Destruction] was the only defeat which [contained the seeds of] victory—victory because the *studenchestvo* would not have been defeated; [we] would have said that we did not end the strike but were arrested. It would have been victory because the act of destruction [could not be total]. . . . Victory, because history would record the moral victory.[37]

Only a tragedy could give protest real historical significance. By calling off the strike in order to avoid its "dissolution," students had simply staged a farce.

Lozina-Lozinskii did acknowledge a tragedy of a different order. In the concluding pages of the pamphlet, he drew on the biblical story of Samson and Delilah to provide his own morality tale. In the original, Delilah seduces Samson in order to deprive him of his source of superhuman power, his long hair. Just as her scheme appears to succeed, Samson pulls down the walls of the temple killing everyone within it. His suicide was his victory. The analogy could have been true down to the small details—the destruction of the "temple" of science, the "cutting" of the long hair (of the radicals). But this time, Lozina-Lozinskii concludes, Delilah was victorious. And who was she? Capitalism and the bourgeoisie. In choosing the path taken by their Western comrades after 1848, Lozina-Lozinskii argued, Russian students, like Russian society and the intelligentsia, had been seduced by the market. They no longer searched for scientific truth or studied Chernyshevskii and Marx; they preferred to read pornography, join athletic clubs, and receive their diplomas. "The traditional peasant shirt, the long hair, and the rude candor of the nihilist have been extinguished," he mourned, "lost among the neat jackets, high collars, clipped heads, and a reasoned deferential attitude." Instead of proving the vitality of corporate traditions, the strike had heralded the death of the "phantoms" in the university. The story of the *studenchestvo*, which had begun in the 1860s, had passed through Marxism and ended in "football-ism." [38]

Lozina-Lozinskii was not alone in his assessment. Despite the tribute to student unity with which the 1908 strike had ended, a series of articles in the student press detailed the social, political, and moral "dissolution" and "decline" *(raspad, razval, upadok)* of *studenchestvo*. In recounting how student X from the Technological Institute had stolen 188 rubles from the mutual-aid society, for example, one article suggested that the act of stealing from one's comrades showed the internal corruption of *studenchestvo*. [39] Others cited the financial bankruptcy of many mutual-aid societies (due to the nonpayment of loans by students and graduates) as evidence that the old bonds of community had been severed. [40] These articles contrasted a new concern for material well-being to the old ideal of mutual aid, the goal of a diploma to the aspiration of self-education, and the comfortable job upon graduation to the principle of self-sacrifice. For them, the failure of the strike had confirmed their worst fears. [41]

A few lonely voices counseled patience. In linking the dissolution, breakdown, and decline to the circumstances of political reaction, they discerned a temporary regrouping rather than actual political death, not unlike the 1880s. Adroitly turning the phantom motif on its head, one critic of Lozina-Lozinskii mused: "In an important way, all idealism and all love for the future is a love for 'phantoms,' and their power over humanity is almost limitless." He thus held out hope for the future: "Joke all you wish about the absurdities of people but leave the 'phantoms' in peace. It is impossible to bury them because phantoms do not die." [42]

THE TRIUMPHANT MARCH OF HISTORY

During the 1908 strike, a militant conservative movement claimed new prominence in Russian schools. Its roots date back to the "academic" movement of 1901–1902 and the founding in 1903 of the student corporation Dennitsa. Propelled by the politicization of the universities in 1905, academic unions formed that fall in the university, the Women's Courses, and several of Petersburg's specialized institutes.[43] Though they defined themselves as nonparty groups, united only in the opposition to politics in the academy, more notorious rightwing organizations also established branches in many educational institutions across the country and helped to propel the movement to the extreme right. As an eclectic assortment of monarchists, anti-Semites, and nationalists, the academic movement combined an opposition to participatory democracy with activist tactics.[44] Because it also developed in reaction to the dominant radicalism of student life, the movement appropriated many familiar rhetorical motifs, including the historical periodization based on the conjunction of 1905 with 1848. Indeed, if student radicals feared what the future held in store for them, conservatives celebrated themselves as the force of historical destiny.

A brawl between left- and rightwing students at a university *skhodka* on October 2, 1908 marked the coming of age of the academist movement. Over the preceding weeks, student members of the extremist Union of the Russian People, called *Soiuzniki* or Unionists, had actively struggled against the strikers and fully cooperated with the police. Having decided beforehand to disrupt the meeting, they apparently made an agreement with police stationed outside the building to break a window as a signal for them to enter (a charge they later denied). The meeting opened inauspiciously with a bomb scare and a general warning regarding the plan to break the window. Unionists congregated in one corner, next to the window in question, while student leaders formed a human barrier to prevent any clash between this group and the rest of the assembly. Events came to a climax, when Unionist leader Georgii Shenken began his speech with the words "Russian *studenchestvo*." This was a calculated exclusionary tactic, for he had used the word *russkoe*, denoting Russian national identity, rather than *rossiiskoe*, a nationally neutral adjective normally used to refer to the multi-ethnic "Russian" empire. Through the whistles and hisses, he warned against reprisals: "If you touch us, behind us stands the entire Union [of the Russian People]." The next speaker, who opposed the strike, though with peaceful means, was drowned out by the noise and tumult of Unionists protesting the reception of their leader. At this point, the window was broken by an unknown party; chaos and fistfights ensued.

In his statement at a disciplinary court convened by professors later that month, Shenken explained his group's philosophy: "Considering it our sacred duty to defend the banner of science and scholarship, [we] decided to repulse those 'students' who trample upon this banner." He then described their tactics:

I was in the fifth auditorium when Professor Grimm [of the Juridical faculty] was scheduled to lecture. Knowing that many students wished to hear his lecture, I also attended. Other students pointed out that I did not have the right to remain, being a student of the historical-philological faculty, but polytechnic students were also present. They all wanted to beat me up for using the word *"zhid"* [kike]. The lecture of Professor Platonov in classroom III also did not take place, and once again a confrontation occurred due to my use of the word *"zhid."*

As he recounted a series of such encounters, Shenken portrayed himself as a defender of order under attack by disorderly crowds of Jewish, Georgian, and Armenian students. He even censured the faculty council for allowing the situation during the strike to degenerate to such a level that "students must demand the intervention of police." [45]

Unionists reveled in confrontation, inciting other students in order to disrupt the strike and provoke police intervention. Despite their avowal "to act purely on an academic basis," they glorified their heroic stance against the "crude violence" of the strikers—just as students before 1905 had glorified their resistance to the arbitrary violence of the state. Shenken proudly referred to the results of his antistrike tactics: seven lectures had been held before an unspecified number of students. Others described their lonely struggle against the "hooligans" and the moral imperative to counter the terrorist tactics used by revolutionary students ("Jews and Armenians") against the nonrevolutionary (read "Russian") student body. Only a small number of statements bothered to mention the active assistance of student leaders in shielding the Unionists from physical violence throughout the strike.[46]

Despite the relative paucity of their numbers (perhaps twenty Unionists plus twenty nonparty activists), the experience of the strike with its unprecedented level of violence and confrontation spurred the development of academist groups in other educational institutions across the city and the country. Hoping to facilitate the movement, the Ministry of Interior waived the regulations imposed on student organization that prohibited any national or citywide student group and limited any meeting of students outside of educational institutions. By the fall of 1910, according to a ministry estimate, 578 academists in St. Petersburg were organized into a wide range of corporations, academic unions, and political clubs.[47] The movement was promoted as well by the financial sponsorship of the "Society for the Assistance of the Academic Life of Higher Educational Institutions," founded in December 1910 by the rightwing extremist and Duma deputy V. M. Purishkevich. The goal of his society was straightforward—to counter students' revolutionary mood—and was pursued in part through financial assistance. Its 1911 statement showed 39,191 rubles received and more than 16,000 rubles dispersed to academist groups in St. Petersburg.[48] Academists were also granted an audience with the tsar and patronized by such prominent government figures as Petr Stolypin (cf. figure 5-1).[49]

The new academic corporations formed according to several models, including the German *Burschenschaften,* the Baltic German student corporations, and

FIGURE 5.1 Banquet in Honor of Academists from Kiev. In addition to students from Kiev studying in St. Petersburg and a student delegate from Kiev, the photo depicts the well-known rightists and honorary members Count A. A. Bobrinskii, G. G. Zamyslovskii, and N. E. Markov. *Vestnik studencheskoi zhizni*, no. 6/7 (30.IV.1911). (Courtesy University of Helsinki Slavonic Library)

Dennitsa.[50] According to their charters, they aspired to create a community on the basis of explicitly nonpolitical values. "Friendship," for example, intended "to further the development of healthy comradely relations and the strengthening of [these] bonds between members on the basis of love for science and scholarship, respect for legality, a spirit of decency, and an honorable way of thinking."[51] Like their German counterparts, many corporations used Latin names, defended nationalist values, and stressed sport as a healthy alternative to politics. "Fraternitas Hyperborea" thus resolved to promote the "all-around intellectual, moral, and physical development of its members."[52] "Neo Ruthenia" likewise strove "to establish brotherly relations between its members, and to develop in them a feeling of proper dignity and respect for law and order in order to give honest, useful, and respectable professionals *[deiateli]* to the Fatherland."[53] This emphasis on the formation of character inverted the old radical ethos. The new corporation was meant to shape the loyal and patriotic subject rather than the citizen or the revolutionary. Yet the similarities in language were not coincidental. The corporations also founded courts of honor, mutual-aid funds, and libraries—in other words, the infrastructure of an alternate student subculture.

A second type of organization pursued a more stridently activist course. Building on the dual principle of academic purity and national culture, this wing of the academist movement defined the university as a national institution necessary to the development of Russian culture and identity. Unlike liberal proponents of an autonomous university, however, these groups equated Russian culture with the autocratic state and hoped to counter the influence of political radicalism with calls for national values. The charter of the Union of Russian Students thus aspired "to further the development of the academic life of the university on the basis of the ideals of Russian statehood: Orthodoxy, Autocracy, and Nationality, and to facilitate the dissemination of these principles among students." [54] An allied group, the All-Russian National Student Union, likewise sought "a) to assist the awakening and development of national consciousness in the Russian *studenchestvo;* b) to prepare future defenders of Russian statehood and nationality and devoted workers of the motherland in all fields of social activity; c) to make the Russian *studenchestvo* aware of the culture, tasks, and needs of its Fatherland; d) to unite its members into a close comradely family and provide them with moral support." [55] With their goal of raising consciousness, these rightwing groups again inverted the traditional task of their leftwing counterparts.

To link the various groups in each city, special "academic clubs" were opened for all members of established unions and corporations (excluding women, who were allowed only for balls and masquerades). The first club, founded in 1909 by the Academic Union of polytechnic students, occupied large premises with eight acres of parkland to the north of Petersburg. Open from morning till late into the night and generally furnished with a library, bar service, and billiard room, the clubs functioned as the social centers of academist life. A new student newspaper founded in 1910 further united the academist subculture and quickly became its most important vehicle in St. Petersburg. It chronicled the activities of academist organizations and campaigned against sedition in higher education. [56]

In addition to an institutional structure, academism also began to define new conventions and rituals. Again emulating their German counterparts, corporations petitioned for permission to wear pins and colored ribbons. "Neo Ruthenia," for example, requested black, white, and orange for its official colors, and the right to wear special clothing on ceremonial occasions. [57] To celebrate their patriotism, students sang the national anthem at their official gatherings, usually three times. [58] And because the international song of the student corporation, "Gaudeamus," had long been appropriated by the radicals, the Academic Union even wrote its own official anthem, "Forward, Academists!"

> Serving one idea and one sacred slogan, we will close our ranks, unite as a harmonious family. . . . Hands off aggressors! We will not give up the heritage of science and the kingdom of peaceful labor. . . . Away with

doubts! Forward, Union! Be firm and bold! Forward, Academists! Forward, Union! Forward to battle! For the temple of pure science, for the native university![59]

The traditional motifs of the sacred battle, the united family, and the courageous fighter were all reformulated into a counter-system.

The behavior of the academist was the subject of both internal discussion and external parody. In principle, the proper academist always displayed a chivalrous and respectful attitude to his fatherland and to his "second fathers," the professoriate. This behavior formed a clear contrast to that of the typical student, who, it was asserted, studied poorly, behaved disrespectfully to his elders and his nation, and followed the crowd rather than his conscience.[60] Despite such assertions, the academist's public image recalled that of the "gentry" students of the prereform era or those German students known for their drinking and dueling. His aristocratic disdain for studying (except during strikes) was coupled with his partiality for gambling, drink, and brothels. The facilities offered by the new academic clubs did little to counter this image and neither did his reputed behavior. When Russia's most prominent liberal newspaper took note of the new "type," it ironically described the infighting between groups, the overriding concern with pins, ribbons, and ritual, and the earnest pledges to uphold the honor of the corporation for one's entire life. The following incident was reported without commentary: When student "K" accused member "G" of the Russian Academic Corporation of police connections, G challenged him to a duel. "K agreed with one condition; should they be prosecuted for dueling, neither would appeal for leniency—to which condition *Korporant* G did not agree."[61]

The importance of the German model to Russian academism lay not only in the privileged place of dueling. Russian academists actually grounded their own legitimacy in what they saw as German historical experience. In an article entitled "The Inevitability of Academism," the student A. Belilin thus cited the German and Austrian experiences after 1848 as evidence that the academist movement was historically ordained in Russia. He identified three historical periods organizing the relationship between academic and political life in the German university and asserted that Russia was following the same pattern: the prerevolutionary student political movement, the moment of revolutionary synthesis, and the postrevolutionary academic period. Belilin argued that the academist movement would be a factor of cultural progress in Russia, as it had been in Germany, because it represented the inexorable path of history: "As soon as the corporation achieves its goal, i.e., when the *studenchestvo* has absorbed academism and politics have been extinguished from the higher school. . . [then] the [real] academic period commences. Academic corporations will cease to exist as separate organizations because the *studenchestvo* will already constitute one general corporation." Though Belilin depicted victory as historically assured, he espoused a familiar brand of voluntarism, if a different slogan. Consciousness needed to be actively instilled in the masses by those "strong and bold [individuals], who understand their debt to the motherland, and proclaim: *patriae et litteris*—for fatherland and letters." [62]

THE DECLINE AND FALL OF *STUDENCHESTVO*

The failure of the 1908 strike highlighted the crisis of student identity, and the rise of militant academism underlined its seriousness. In the public eye as well, the student appeared increasingly as a decadent figure, who had lost his high ideals in alcohol, sexual debauchery, and venereal disease. All signs seemed to point in one direction. Students had strayed from their old path and traditional ethos. But who was this new generation? And where was the new path? As the revolution faded into the past, the contours of student life and belief came under unprecedented scrutiny in a series of statistical surveys probing everything from sexual behavior and political views to the material conditions of daily life. These surveys were conducted by such respected organizations as the Pirogov Society, the central organization of the progressive medical community, as well as the statistical seminars of various universities. Students participated not just as subjects but also as authors by working on the definition of questions and the analysis of raw data.[63] The surveys did not, therefore, represent a single point of view but competing agendas, liberal and radical, within both the student community and Russian educated society.

Only their broader significance was beyond dispute. "To study the material and spiritual life of students will to a certain extent provide material for judging the entire intelligentsia," one survey's author characteristically asserted. "This is particularly important now. . . that a deep crisis threatens to turn the old gods into dust." [64] Woven into the very fabric of the questions was precisely this assumption. Modern youth was experiencing a moral and political "fall" from the standards of preceding generations. The goal of the surveys was consequently to diagnose the nature and causes—but not the fact—of this decline. With the character of the new student generation somehow signifying a deeper social truth, the interpretation of survey results became a politically charged endeavor. This discussion helped to develop a new collective biography of the student along with substantive critiques of both revolutionary and bourgeois values.

Most surveys first attempted to identify the critical factors in the upbringing of youth before they even became students, that is, to gauge social influences on individual development. A Moscow survey of student sexual practices thus claimed to reveal the abject failure of the contemporary family and school to instill enlightened values in children.[65] Intended to investigate the high rate of venereal disease among students and its connection to legal prostitution, the survey devoted well over one-third of its questions to upbringing, including students' early experiences at home and in school, and one-half to sexuality, under which masturbation and venereal disease were also grouped.[66] Although the vast majority of students reported healthy family relations, Dr. Mikhail Chlenov, the survey's author, criticized parents' failure to guide their children generally and to educate them about sexual hygiene in particular. He likewise assailed the wholly negative impact of the secondary school on the moral and intellectual development of youth. To solve the medical problem of venereal infection, he concluded, it was necessary to prevent the sexual corruption of the gymnasium student (in part by banning prostitution), and to encourage abstinence, which, in turn, required fundamental reform of the family and the secondary school. The moral failures of students reflected a moral failure within society as well.[67]

In the collective biography of the student, this early corruption was only the first chapter. Daily life in the city provided ample material for a second and third. Almost all surveys inquired about the student budget, often in considerable detail.[68] They examined the source and amount of income and expenditures on food, apartment, and other living needs. Without exception, a high level of poverty was documented. Up to one-half of students lived on less than thirty-five rubles per month, not a large sum, though higher than the average wages of a worker. In this case, however, student poverty resonated as a question of civic health. Many students—the next generation of cultural leaders—could not afford a regular dinner, much less three daily meals. In addition, their rented rooms were described as cold, wet, dark, and dirty.[69]

For most commentators, the moral consequences of poverty had paramount importance, as illustrated in the choice of "representative" quotations from the thousands of student respondents: "The landlady keeps prostitutes and sells them as bar-singers. The girls walk about half-naked, so it really is pretty much impossible to have guests." Another student had a similar experience: "Prostitutes live next door, so there are perpetual scandals, screams, and occasionally fights. Out of human decency, it is sometimes necessary to go for help and throw out drunken guests." Student poverty embodied short-term and long-term harm for the development of Russian culture and society, N. A. Kablukov argued in the introduction to his report on student housing: "The influence of [living conditions] on the character are strongest precisely in the student years. . . , when the personality takes its final shape and when the future orientation and activity of a person are defined." [70] Other specialists agreed. Poverty exposed students to the underside of urban life, formed an important cause of their moral corruption, and constituted a threat to cultural progress.[71]

Some students also blamed the conditions of daily life for their "fall." These stories lack the clear answers and teleological lines so common before 1905. "Circumstances push [you] along the path of drunkenness and kill all energy," summarized one student.[72] Responding to a question about the role of love in life, another recounted the experience of himself and two friends who had all arrived in Moscow together several years earlier. One had died of consumption after two months in prison—he had been arrested for participating in some meaningless "political" assembly. Out of loneliness, the other two students had tried to meet some women who were not prostitutes, but they lacked money and social skills. This student had returned to his studies, but his friend had visited prostitutes and been infected with syphilis. "The drama is not yet over, but I think that it will soon end," the student concluded. "I ask you to judge why all of this happened." [73] The fate of these three students seemed paradigmatic of Russia's own path since 1905. One had already perished due to political reasons; the second had been morally and physically corrupted; and the third was just barely getting by.

This student had raised the disturbing question of blame, a question which was also hidden within the correlation of behavior with economics. If students really were living in abject poverty, how then could they afford a life of dissipation? Indeed, the Moscow sex survey had found that 65.8% of students drank, and 26.2% of those with a sex life spent more than five rubles per month on their sexual satisfaction.[74] In a discussion of the hygienic conditions of student life, Dr. D. P. Nikol'skii condemned the poor diet and lodgings of students as an issue of public health, but also censured the high rate of alcohol and tobacco consumption among students. To spend precious rubles on such harmful diversions was clearly a practice to be discouraged.[75] There was only one possible conclusion: students were not simply passive victims but actively involved in their own corruption.

The investigation of daily life came full circle. The assumption that students had suffered a moral fall shaped the organization and elaboration of survey questions as well as their interpretation. The actual percentage of students who had contracted a venereal disease was immaterial, because everyone recognized the archetypical story, summarized here in a medical journal:

> One cannot study the sexual life of students without taking into account all of the circumstances of their lives. The inexperienced young, often already corrupted by the contemporary family and school, suddenly find themselves out of the provinces and in the capital. A half-starving existence, horrifying sanitary conditions, unhygienic circumstances, neighborhoods [filled with] prostitutes, cannot have a good effect. . . . [The high rate of venereal disease] is rooted in this material neediness.[76]

In the 1890s, the student's journey from the provinces to the city had symbolized the beginning of a longer journey toward enlightenment and consciousness. Now the mutual-aid society and the study circle seemed lost amid taverns and brothels.

Surveys also sought to gauge the influence of both the revolution and the conditions of daily life on political attitudes. Although surveys were conducted in different times and places, contemporaries compared the results and concluded that students were becoming more conservative. A 1907 survey at Iurev University revealed that 66.39% of the student body sympathized with leftist parties (including 38.47% with the SDs and 18.31% with the SRs), and 11.47% with the moderate Kadets, while the remainder either affiliated with rightist parties (6.25%) or declined to state their political preference.[77] By 1909, Jewish students in Kiev split almost evenly between leftist (53.5%) and moderate (46.5%) parties.[78] A survey at the St. Petersburg Technological Institute mirrored this trend, with just over 50% of students declaring their support for the left. While only 25.3% aligned with the formerly dominant SDs, 20.7% sympathized with the Kadets and 15.5% declared no political sympathies whatsoever. This survey also showed a peculiar inversion of roles: older students were more radical and younger ones more conservative.[79] In politics as well, students seemed either to be experiencing a fall from the proverbial heights of consciousness or at the very least to be emulating their bourgeois comrades in the West.

The most important task of the political surveys was the correlation of social background, income levels, and radicalism. This interest stemmed, of course, from long-held speculation regarding the relationship between social origin, socioeconomic conditions of life, and cultural-political attitudes. Poverty retained important connotations regarding the plebeian origins, principles of mutual aid, and high moral character of student radicals. It also had particular political resonance. The government had long fixed tuition rates high and restricted financial aid to discourage poorer (and therefore, in its opinion, politically radical) youth from attending university. The explosion in enrollments after 1905 and government repression of student organizations had further strained available financial resources. As studies thus compared the average monthly income and social origin of respondents to their political sympathies, they proclaimed an important statistical fact. Poorer students mainly from a clerical or petty bourgeois background—that is, typical *raznochintsy*—were more radical. Similarly, Unionists were almost exclusively from a gentry or bureaucratic background.[80] While such conclusions were not statistically valid, contemporaries were most interested in their polemical uses.

The logic thus extended to the "scientific" definition of the "academist type." Despite the paucity of data, several student newspapers were quick to publish the results of a 1909 questionnaire at the St. Petersburg Polytechnic Institute where only twenty-five of one thousand forms had been completed by academists. The academist, it was claimed, was wealthier than his leftwing comrades. The correlation was striking, indeed, a bit too striking: academists lived on forty-nine rubles a month, Octobrists averaged forty-four rubles, Kadets forty, both SDs and SRs thirty-three, and anarchists only thirty-one. Though his slogan was "Science and Fatherland," the academist was shown to be less interested in his studies. With thirty to forty examinations necessary for graduation, he took an average of four exams annually. And finally, the moral bankruptcy of academists was statistically documented—in jubilant tones. Despite their avowals of God, nation, and tsar, some 40% were heavy drinkers (as compared with 11.9% among all students), with the typical academist getting drunk thirty-one times per year (no general figure was provided). There were also proportionally more gamblers and fornicators among them, with 42.5% of all students virgins but only 36% of academists. Several representative quotations from survey results left little to the imagination. One 23-year-old responded in the following manner: How many bottles of beer do you drink each month? "When I binge, it's impossible to count." How often do you have sexual relations? "As many as God grants." Do you have any venereal diseases? "No, I don't take [prostitutes] from Nevskii Prospect" (figure 5-2).[81]

For some, the surveys confirmed what had been long suspected: the old *studenchestvo* had ceased to exist. One report in a student newspaper interpreted survey results at the Technological Institute as proof of a general decline: "Who knows what kind of seeds the new course has sown among the *studenchestvo*, and what the field of decay and disintegration prepares for us?"[82] The authors of this survey showed some disagreement among themselves. The academic sponsor and general editor, M. V. Bernatskii, concluded that it had documented the "reappraisal of values" among students but still had shown that their "general mood" had not really changed—they had not been tamed by political repression.[83] In contrast, M. Gusel'shchikov, a student of Bernatskii's Scientific-Economic Circle, which had conducted and processed the survey, concluded that an entirely new generation of students had appeared. He chose to end his report on a pessimistic theme by quoting a series of "representative" comments students had made on their future activity and ambitions. While none was optimistic, note the absence of a transition between the last quotation and the concluding words of Gusel'shchikov: " 'I don't imagine any future activity. I think more about suicide.' And this is a short overview of the results of our survey regarding the cultural-social life of students."[84]

The surveys seemed to reveal a *studenchestvo* in moral and political decline. Russian society was chastised for not providing moral guidance and material support for its children, but also instructed to examine youth as a mirror of itself. One viewpoint held that the corruption of youth was a social evil and a medical problem, with the solution lying in the reform of the family and the school. Another argued that systemic reform was impossible under current social and political conditions. Only a socialist society would remedy the ills and inequities of capitalism and destroy the lures of consumption embodied in the market for pornography and sex.[85] These two perspectives were mirrored in a broader debate over causality. According to some observers, the excesses of revolution and the traditional world view of the intelligentsia had led students into disease and despair. For others, this fate marked the victory of capitalism: stu-

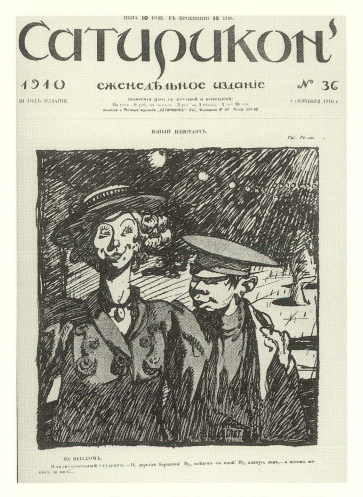

FIGURE 5.2 Cover Illustration of the journal *Satirikon,* entitled
"The Young Debutante." It depicts a student on Nevskii Prospect
inviting a woman "to come with him" and promising to marry
her. (Courtesy University of Helsinki Slavonic Library)

dents had sold out their heroic past for bourgeois pleasures and careerist ambitions.

The publication in 1909 of *Signposts,* a collection of articles by seven prominent scholars and publicists, drew the battle lines for this controversy over the
end of revolution.[86] In his contribution, the well-known publicist Aleksandr Izgoev cited recent surveys in a two-pronged attack on students' political and personal lives. Though he acknowledged the important political role played by students before 1905, he argued that students' faith in revolutionary values had led
to their current moral decline. With elaborate detail, he painted a portrait of

youth corrupted—by implication, wholly unfit to build and lead a democratic society. He recounted tales and statistics of sexual excess, masturbation, and venereal disease, students' lack of interest in academic study, and their disrespect for parents and teachers. In his view, the once lofty ideal of heroic self-sacrifice had degenerated into a kind of death instinct which prevented the emergence of a positive and constructive understanding of life. His solution to the crisis lay in the reassertion of parental authority and the development of a new ethos based on such "life-creating" values as moral restraint, self-discipline, industry, and knowledge. It was time for adults to guide the upbringing of youth, to shield them from harmful influences, and to establish a proper relationship between the generations. The revolution was over, Izgoev concluded, and youth must be taught to respect their elders.[87]

Paradoxically, perhaps, radicals cited the new behavioral patterns as evidence that students were in fact following at least some of Izgoev's advice. In his article "New times, New songs," the socialist S. O. Portugeis thus described a new "bourgeois" ethos:

> The old *studenchestvo* is being reeducated. The student has begun to study, or more correctly, to occupy himself with studies, or still more correctly, to pass exams, or most correctly, "to finish." In the university it is also understood that it is necessary "to live," to work, "to finish," to settle down. [That is,] it is necessary "to finish" with all dreams and fantasies and to begin in earnest one's practical work.[88]

Though lamenting the end to the Dionysian passion of revolution, Portugeis concluded that Russia was following the historical path of Western Europe after 1848. He adopted the same logic as student leader Lozina-Lozinskii. In assuming social and political authority, a sober-minded class of bourgeois specialists was beginning to shape its children in its own image.

The debate over the new generation of students revealed competing visions of Russia's future. The authors of *Signposts* depicted the autocratic state and the revolutionary intelligentsia as mutually sustaining forces, both of which had lost legitimacy during the revolution. They asserted that the development of a self-disciplined individual and the reconstruction of daily life was necessary for cultural and political progress in Russia. In contrast, radicals identified a new coalition between bourgeoisie (*Signposts*) and autocracy, and situated themselves in a dual struggle against bourgeois moral-ideological hegemony and autocratic power. They perceived the displacement of a revolutionary world view among students by a new bourgeois preoccupation with self and career. In both scenarios, the revolution had foundered on daily life, in the first case due to the dearth of attention paid to it, and in the second, due to its overwhelming tenacity. At issue was the old opposition between the political and the personal, between the heroic feat and the conduct of everyday life.

As the debate entered the press, a more wide-ranging conclusion was also drawn. Ol'ga Gridina, a columnist for a working-class daily, made fun of the current preoccupation with statistics but reserved her real sarcasm for the results of a recent student survey. "Our students, as children of the poor people, live poorly, sometimes even in destitution," she wrote, providing appropriate figures. "However," she continued, "among this half-starving mass, only 13 out of 100 are completely sober." To be sure, with only 71% "devoted adherents" to alcohol, Russian students had not quite achieved the heights of their German *"bursh"* comrades, who began to pour beer at 8:00 AM and by evening aimed to make a *"gros shkandal'."* Gridina then turned to the question of "students and love," noting that the results unfortunately did not indicate whether students found happiness in love, but only that 28 of every 100 caught "bad" diseases. Despite their leftwing sympathies, students' views of women clearly remained in the gutter. Questioning the depth of student principles, she castigated the corrupt cultural elite: "Unfortunately, there is not yet a statistic which can say how many of these fervent youth will grow heavy, [how many] will settle down with a belly, [how many] will partake in the spoils of government or social service, and [how many] will curse their idealism, and like pigs under an oak, begin to sing 'Down with enlightenment.' " [89] If the liberal and radical intelligentsia had examined the student as a mirror of themselves, the student could also be seen as a representative of a decrepit and decadent order.

With the long-awaited revolution now relegated to the past, many students feared that it was their collective destiny to follow the path already tread by their French and German comrades. In Russia as well, radicalism would be progressively displaced by conservatism, or at least a trite liberalism, and students would be domesticated: they would study to pass exams, play around with women and alcohol in their spare time, and, after graduation, begin their chosen career. The signs were all there. The 1908 strike seemed to document the shallowness of student radicalism and the coming of age of ultrarightist student groups who claimed historical legitimacy. Surveys likewise pointed to students' double political and moral fall. Yet, like the story of consciousness, this scenario of decline obscured as much as it revealed. Though students as a group were politically more varied after the experiences of 1905–1907, their overall behavior had changed very little. The old story had lost its explanatory value, and this scenario was an attempt to find a new one.

The fate of the student was much watched and discussed in Russia's educated society. Depicted as the unfortunate victim of either revolutionary or bourgeois values, depending on the point of view, students no longer embodied a positive example of political engagement. Before 1905, students' political identity had formed the basis for their public role—liberals and radicals had both appreciated the student movement and often defended students against their critics. After the revolution, the archetypal student was no longer the revolutionary, his place of activity was no longer the workers' circle, and his autobiography no longer replayed the narrative of consciousness. Instead, his story had overlapped with those other stories of urban danger contained in slums, brothels, and taverns. In the end, students did not conform either to the liberal ideal of an autonomous apolitical university or to a radical ideal of total revolutionary dedication.

In his contribution to *Signposts,* the historian and publicist Mikhail Gershenzon offered real insight into this shift. Though he did not discuss students in particular, he argued that the 1905 Revolution had disrupted the collective life story of the intelligentsia. By the late 1890s, he recalled, public opinion "categorically believed that the entire burden of life had political reasons: the political regime comes crashing down, and, right away, health and courage along with freedom are enthroned." With poverty, filth, and corruption blamed solely on autocracy, the role of individual responsibility had been disregarded. The proverbial "light" of revolution had made the darkness of real life bearable. Gershenzon further stressed the significance of this way of thinking for the intelligentsia-in-the-making: "A youth on the threshold of life was met by a strict public opinion, which showed him a lofty, simple, and clear goal. The meaning of life was predetermined, the same one for everybody without any individual differences." In his view, the failure of the revolution to transform life itself had finally ended the hegemony of politics: "Youth is no longer met with a ready-made goal, and each is left to figure out the meaning and direction of his life for himself." [90]

For Gershenzon, this was a positive development, one that even had the potential of a happy ending. He hoped that the high principles so long espoused by the intelligentsia would finally be realized in individual lives rather than degraded by the abstracted social cause. Yet his explanation is relevant beyond its immediate intentions. What he described was really not so different from the "official" story of the student movement. It too had stressed the unity of world view (and the *studenchestvo* as its carrier), the centrality of political change, the primacy of social service over individualism, and the utopian teleology of revolutionary consciousness. The difference was in emphasis. While Gershenzon condemned the hegemony of the old world view and heralded the possibilities offered by individualism, many students accepted that the old story had ended but searched instead for a new common principle consistent with the old ones. The revolution was over, leaving behind the chaos and routines of living as well as the many "phantoms" of the past.

CHAPTER SIX

The Promise of Education

Women Students in the Public Eye

> The guarantee of our culture [and] the guarantee of our rebirth
> lie in the education of women.
>
> —Vasilii Teplov, "Fifty Years of Women's Higher
> Education in Russia"

Sometimes the unconventional and atypical can illuminate social stereotypes. Such is the case with a 1901 article entitled "Homines novi" by Vasilii
Rozanov, a philosopher and publicist, best characterized as brilliant, iconoclastic,
and controversial. Claiming to recount how he came to support higher education
for women, he instead reveled in the contradictory persona of the woman student.

> I once had to consult with two old maid scholar-*kursistki* of the "sixties"
> and "seventies" on some literary matter. What could be more dull than
> this meeting. We all know what femininity is, and we all know that 1.)
> bluestockings, 2.) the sixties, and 3.) old maids, form the essence, the
> three particularities of [the fairy-tale witch] Baba Yaga, in whom the ten-
> derness, beauty, and interior depth of the woman has been eaten away.[1]

And indeed, the two women surrounded by their books were not attractive, and
Rozanov recalls thinking, "Ah, the hell with it, real women scholars, what could
be worse?" After several years, however, as he came to know the women better,
he noted their "astonishing friendship and closeness" and their "feminine calm,"
which he compares to that of Ivan Goncharov's fictional hero, Oblomov, the
prototype of the superfluous man. In the end, he decided that if these "truly
virginal" women had carried their scholarly identity any further, they would have
become the stereotype: "They stood on the very border of bluestocking-hood,
but remained the most pure women, little Jeannes d'Arc amidst billions of
books."

This clever, ironic, and highly ambiguous anecdote played with two competing fantasies about the woman student that had coexisted in various forms since
the 1860s and continued to shape the debate in the early twentieth century. These
women did not resemble a 30-years-later rendition of the stereotypical rude,
cigarette-smoking woman nihilist *(nigilistka)*, nor were they mannish and un-
feminine. In this regard, Rozanov downplayed the fears of many conservatives,
who believed that educating women would lead to their moral corruption, or at
the very least to the emergence of a "third sex," neither male nor quite female.
However, by comparing them to Oblomov, Rozanov implied that these albeit
womanly women and their scholarly labor were superfluous. They had rejected
procreation in the name of science. Yet it was precisely an ideal of enlightened
motherhood that was typically cited in defense of educating women. While the
first point of view held that education harmed women's moral character and
consequently reduced their qualifications as mothers, the second drew the opposite conclusion, that education better prepared women for motherhood. As Rozanov implies, these fantasies had produced antithetical conclusions built on a
single assumption: education fundamentally influenced femininity. Rozanov had
offered a third picture: the pure, but barren, woman scholar.[2]

The controversy over women's education reflected well-established assumptions regarding the social order as divided into the public (male) and the private
(female) spheres. In Russia, as in Western Europe and the United States, the
utility of educating women was often questioned because higher education had
been intended to prepare men for public life in government and the professions.
Many feared that the exposure of a woman to the university—a public institution—might lead to the corruption of her feminine essence as it was expressed
most fully in the private sphere, the home. For centuries, educated women in
Europe had been likened to public women, disorderly women, and prostitutes,
and this was the case in Russia as well.[3]

Despite these parallels, the public discussion of women students in Russia
was not a copy of the Western model. Over the last two decades of the Romanov
dynasty, an elastic concept of enlightened motherhood was particularly important in shaping the images of women students. It was used to defend the
principle of educating women in general and sometimes to advance the more
radical cause of equal education for men and women. Through a maternal metaphor, the education of women was also coupled to social and cultural progress.
Convinced that an educated woman would apply modern scientific principles to
the upbringing of children, many progressive Russians believed that reform of
the family and the school could be advanced through the education of women.
Despite the continued insinuations of some conservatives, this confidence in the
transformative power of enlightenment contributed to a positive public image of
the woman student within Russia's progressive educated society. Her public story
consequently differed in important ways from that of male students after the

1905 Revolution. When women students were subjected to the same scrutiny experienced by their male comrades, the results were startling. While male students were condemned for moral dissolution, female students were praised for moral integrity. Still, the new world of opportunity could also raise some disturbing questions.

PROSTITUTE AND MOTHER

The picture of the dissolute *kursistka* had some adherents in the twentieth century. In the fall of 1901, Prince V. P. Meshcherskii, a well-known publicist of the far-right active since the 1860s, published an article opposing the admission of women students to the university. He asserted that the *kursistka* was a debauched creature, lacking in basic feminine values and manners. Indeed, she possessed the sexual desire of a prostitute and was already a major source of corruption among contemporary (male) youth:

> Do we really think that by stuffing broads *[baby]* into universities, Russia will become more like Europe? [In Europe, women scholars and students] are modest and decent. But here, 9 out of 10 are recognizable by the vile absence of femininity, the vile expression on their faces, vile manners, and licentiousness. Have you ever seen a female student in Europe allow herself the least familiarity with male students? Never. But here. . . gatherings of students and *kursistki* have the morality of a den of debauchery.[4]

This article evoked the polemics over female education in the crudest fashion. The assertion that education corrupted the feminine character by supplanting modesty and subordination with sexual wantonness acknowledged no reason for women to pursue a higher education except to cavort with male students.

Despite the well-known political views of Meshcherskii, this double-edged attack on the morality and intellectual motivation of women students mobilized the entire academic community. Students clearly felt that such defamation must not go unchallenged. Throughout the fall semester, students of both sexes as well as many professors rose "to defend the honor" of the *kursistka* and the Women's Courses from the "dirt" and "slander" of the attack. Seeing these protests simply as disorders, the government refused to allow students to make any public statement. Hoping to defuse the situation and facilitate a compromise, Nikolai Raev, the director of the courses, suggested that an open letter in his official capacity would satisfy the students' desire to repudiate Meshcherskii's allegations. The government rebuffed even this conciliatory gesture and directed newspapers to reject any letter or advertising space on this issue. At an illegal gathering later that fall, women students demonstratively petitioned for the admission of women to the university.[5] The vitality of students' responses demonstrated their sensitivity to the traditional stereotype. That they thought it necessary to deny such clearly scurrilous words suggests that they still feared Meshcherskii would be believed.

The celebration of the twenty-fifth anniversary of the Bestuzhev Courses two years later in 1903 provided an unprecedented public forum for individuals and institutions to voice their support of women's education and allows the historian to examine the parameters of progressive thought. Hundreds of expressions of congratulations came from around the country and included addresses from the faculty and students of educational institutions, scientific establishments, academic and charitable societies, the editorial boards of journals, and a number of graduates and supporters of women's rights. The commemorative volume thus represents a cross-section of contemporary positive views of women's education and educated women.[6]

The volume can first be read as a celebration of the successful struggle of Russia's educated society since the 1860s against the forces of reaction that had almost emerged victorious during the 1880s. In praising the Society for Providing Means of Support for the Higher Women's Courses, a charitable organization led by feminists which had coordinated the funding of the courses and the financial aid of students since 1883, many groups applauded the role of "private initiative" in supporting the financially independent courses. The faculty council of the St. Petersburg Forestry Institute heralded the courses as "glorious proof of how much can be achieved in Russia with a sufficient reserve of energy, with faith in one's powers, with the hope for a sympathetic response among educated society, and with love for the realized dream."[7] The education of women here exemplified the untapped potential and growing self-awareness of Russia's emerging civil society.

Describing educated women as both the product and the engine of progress, many addresses equated the process of women's emancipation with the social and political progress of the country as a whole. That is, the education of women symbolized the enlightenment of Russia, and enlightenment was one of the motive forces of progress. The faculty of the Military-Medical Academy described this movement: "Having received a higher education within the walls of the courses and preserving its sacred behests, hundreds of women spread the light of true knowledge to the farthest corners of the motherland, and in their place under the roof of the courses, new young strength from all the corners of Russia gathers."[8] The St. Petersburg City Social Administration applauded the courses in similar terms, noting that 139 graduates currently worked in the city's primary schools.[9] While many addresses also called for the extension of women's legal and educational rights, including the designation of the courses as a full university with all appropriate rights and privileges, very few addresses called explicitly for the full legal equality of women.[10]

The images of educated women reveal an important dichotomy. One perspective highlighted the importance of education as preparation for motherhood and identified motherhood as an endeavor with a high civic value. A second stressed the entrance of women into public life, noting that women were serving the cause of progress and enlightenment alongside men. While these two formulas need not be mutually exclusive, they nevertheless illustrate an important ambiguity regarding the perceived object of women's education. The address of the Nikolaevskii Main Physical Observatory, for example, acknowledged the contribution of graduates to the development of Russian scholarship, but the primary beneficiary was the family: "As future mothers, the students will raise new generations, which will far surpass [our own]. May God grant you success in this sacred cause." [11] While such phrases as "the raising and education of the young generation" resonate through scores of entries, comparatively few addresses spotlighted the future professional activities of graduates. These addresses usually lauded the courses for fostering a "high civic spirit," "the high moral ideal of a public figure," and "the full and free development of activity in the scientific and social progress of the country." [12]

Most often, the role of women's education was discussed in dualistic terms as the preparation of citizens and mothers, as in this address from one of the first women's charitable societies in Russia: "[At the courses] hundreds of girls can satisfy their noble thirst for knowledge, and then become useful and enlightened social actors *[deiatel'nitsy]* and sensible and steady mothers, [who] instill true civic sentiments *[grazhdanskie chuvstva]* in their children." [13] The faculty and staff of a girls' gymnasium formulated the task of educated women in similar terms: "In the family and the school—in the role of mothers and educators, knowledge has given [graduates] the possibility to develop in the young generation a respect for the human individual and a glorious faith in a better future." [14] Maternal images thus shaped an ideal of the new educated woman as one who would disseminate "light and knowledge in both society and the family." [15] Though such ideals often included a belief in certain intellectual and spiritual qualities unique to women, supporters rarely endorsed women's education solely in terms of the education of future mothers.

The addresses of contemporary male students deviated from this general tendency, for they instead concentrated on the activism of women students and the common struggle for emancipation. With frequent references to "the darkness of ignorance oppressing the Russian earth," "the path of light and knowledge," and "freedom," their official words lightly veiled a more political agenda.[16] In an unofficial address, students at St. Petersburg University spotlighted the revolutionary obligations of women students. Praising their sisters as "selfless fighters for the great cause of the liberation of Russia from autocratic oppression," they called the *kursistka* a public figure *(obshchestvennaia deiatel'nitsa)* and stressed that a "woman is first of all a person, and her rights are human rights." But they also called on "conscious" women students to boycott the official celebration of the courses in protest of recent events at the university.[17] Loyalty to fellow students clearly superseded the celebration of women's right to education—and achievement of consciousness.

Though diverse and sometimes contradictory, the addresses contained in the anniversary volume show that social conditions had changed since Nikolai Leskov had suggested that women had two options in life, to reject all social values as a *nigilistka*, or to become the domesticated creature of family life.[18] The positive visions of the educated woman contrasted with the various female "types" of the old patriarchal order—the shielded and naive product of a finishing school, the society woman, or the maternal Natasha of Lev Tolstoi's *War and Peace*. They also stood in direct opposition to that much-abused icon of total ignorance, backwardness, and darkness, the superstitious peasant woman. As the product of a rational scientific education, the educated woman was to become an agent of social and political transformation charged with the dissemination of enlightenment in the family and the school. Yet this agency was in fact highly ambiguous, because the rights conferred on this woman by knowledge were still tied to physiology.

Indeed, the addresses had not touched on the specific relationship between women's role in the family and in public life, a question which was highly relevant. In 1897, the St. Petersburg city government denied women schoolteachers the right to marry; married women were not hired, and those who were already married were fired.[19] One can thus assume that those highly praised 139 graduates working in the city's primary school mentioned above were unmarried, and that some married graduates had perhaps been fired in 1897. Given that teaching was the primary career option open to women graduates of the Higher Courses, this ban effectively compelled a choice between family and career.[20] Leskov's observation thus appears germane after all, albeit with the important caveat that educated women did have legitimate career options.[21]

Though the figure of the woman student had lost much of its novelty by 1903, making the old prostitute-mother dyad outdated, she clearly remained a troublesome type, someone who did not quite fit into accepted social structures. Over the next decade, women students would become more rather than less troublesome, as thousands of women took advantage of the revolutionary changes in higher education. As public concern shifted in the wake of the revolution to the need for school and family reform, the social role of women's education would acquire new political significance. After all, who else but women would be charged with bringing progressive social and scientific values into the family?

FRUITS OF REVOLUTION

Women students actively participated in all phases of the 1905 Revolution. During the fall of 1904, they called for an end to the war with Japan, the convocation of a constituent assembly, and universal suffrage for both men and women.[22] In the aftermath of Bloody Sunday, students at the Women's Courses and the Women's Medical Institute began semester-long strikes.[23] That fall, in addition to the mass meetings held in all educational institutions, student resolutions called for the entrance of women into the university. In October 1906, women students were accorded the ultimate equality when two Bestuzhev students were executed in Kronshtadt for revolutionary activism.[24]

The revolution also marked a watershed in the history of women's education. Women's courses expanded their curriculum, often founding medical and juridical faculties, and new courses opened in many provincial cities including Kiev, Kazan, Kharkov, Odessa, Novocherkassk, and Tbilisi. In St. Petersburg alone, private courses offered a wide range of specializations—from natural science, agronomy, engineering, and architecture to law, pedagogy, and modern languages.[25] In addition, several private coeducational universities, with innovative new curricula and an elective system, were established. Most prominent were the celebrated Shaniavskii University in Moscow and the lesser known but equally important Psychoneurological Institute, founded by the psychiatrist V. M. Bekhterev in St. Petersburg.

The expansion of opportunity facilitated a veritable explosion in enrollment. In 1900–1901, 2,588 women students were enrolled in higher educational institutions throughout Russia. By 1906–1907, this figure had jumped to 10,493, and by 1915–1916, to 44,017.[26] Enrollments increased at the Bestuzhev Courses from 962 students in 1901–1902 to 4,351 students in 1908–1909.[27] The religious composition of the student body also changed. With the 3% quota on Jewish students largely disregarded until 1907–1908, the number of Jewish students jumped dramatically—a phenomenon suggestive of both the high number of Jewish applicants who had been rejected before 1905 as well as the expanding demand of Jewish youth for educational opportunity.[28] In the 1906–1907 academic year, 19% of the entering class at the Bestuzhev Courses was Jewish. This figure fell to 7% in 1908 and to only 4% in 1909.[29] The trend was similar in the Women's Medical Institute: in 1905–1906, some 10% of the entering class was Jewish, but by 1907, this figure had fallen back to 3%. By 1911, 73 of the 1,237 students (or 5.9%) were Jewish.[30] Although many of the educational reforms enacted during 1905 and 1906 were to be reversed by government decree, the floodgates had been opened. Women's courses around the country continued to admit larger cohorts of students and to expand their curricular offerings.

The revolutionary changes in women's education caused a serious disjunction between educational and career opportunity, because legal restrictions on the employment of women loosened slowly if at all. Only in 1906 were graduates of the St. Petersburg and Moscow Courses allowed to teach in the first four grades of male gymnasiums. Conditions at the Women's Medical Institute were slightly better, with its graduates receiving the same degree as male medical students, though without the right to government rank.[31] Most state-controlled careers remained closed, resulting in many incongruities, especially in the field of law. Even with juridical faculties operating in women's courses across the country, women were not admitted to the bar. The growing opportunity in an expanding private sphere could hardly take up the slack.

This contradictory state of affairs began to unravel. For women students, the first priority was to gain the admittance of graduates from higher courses into the state examinations necessary to receive an academic degree. With the connivance of a high-level official, the first three women accomplished this task in the spring of 1911. On the first day in office of the new conservative Minister of Education, Lev Kasso, this official placed their petition among routine papers, which Kasso signed without reading. As he could not later admit that he had acted so carelessly on his very first day, Kasso was forced to stand by the decision. Nevertheless, the three women had to face several other hurdles, including, ironically enough, the examinations of the male gymnasium, which they passed without difficulty. One of these pioneers, L. A. Mervart, recalls meeting with the head of the commission on state examinations, Professor V. V. Latyshev, several days before the scheduled examination period. Though he tried to dissuade her from taking the examinations—asserting that the "delicate female organism" was unsuited to withstand pressure—she was highly cognizant of the precedent she was establishing and reiterated her intention to take them. Latyshev then informed her that she was not scheduled to take the examinations that were indicated for her concentration in Germanic and Romance languages but instead must take the full course of study in history and philology, as well as Sanskrit and Lithuanian, which were not even taught at the courses. As it turned out, Mervart was a talented linguist—she had been studying both Sanskrit and Lithuanian in her spare time—and passed all fourteen of her examinations.[32]

Despite such successes, many avenues of employment remained blocked. Those women who passed the state law examinations, for example, were still not recognized at court.[33] Although the expansion of educational opportunity after 1905 gave thousands of women the chance to study and ultimately to participate in public life, the path to equality remained jammed with obstacles. Indeed, as feminist activists were also learning in their battle for women's suffrage, women could not always count on the support of their progressive male colleagues. Too often women's issues were neglected as secondary questions, inopportune at best.[34] This generalization held true in the most important battlefield for women students—the university.

WOMEN IN THE UNIVERSITY

In 1905, women students entered the universities for the first time since 1860, when they had briefly attended lectures at St. Petersburg University. Following the resolution of the Academic Union that August, many faculty councils called for the opening of male educational institutions to qualified women.[35] Despite these plans, the Ministry of Education claimed that the issue would be addressed in the new university charter and refused to sanction the enrollment of women as students.[36] For this reason, universities admitted women as unofficial auditors (*vol'noslushatel'nitsy*), who paid fees and followed a complete course of study. In May of 1908, however, the Ministry of Education announced that women must no longer take seats away from deserving "young people" (*molodye liudi*); new rules officially barred women from universities and expelled all of those currently enrolled. A tremendous public outcry ensured that those auditors who had already begun their studies would be allowed to complete them, but new admissions were strictly prohibited.

Though the exact number of women auditors is difficult to establish because many universities did not keep precise records, hundreds of women welcomed the chance to audit. Between the 1906–1907 and 1907–1908 academic years, the number of auditors in six universities almost doubled, from 923 to 1,690. At the high point of enrollment, in the 1907–1908 academic year, 688 women had enrolled in Kharkov University, 319 in Kazan, 308 in Moscow, and 208 in St. Petersburg. One contemporary estimated that by 1908, approximately two thousand women had enrolled in the universities, and twenty-five hundred in the specialized technical institutes. Thereafter, the number of auditors fell dramatically. By the fall of 1909, 250 remained in Kharkov, 34 in Kazan, 110 in Moscow, and 109 in St. Petersburg.[37]

Records exist on the social and religious background of ninety-six of the auditors enrolled in the 1906–1907 academic year at St. Petersburg University.[38] The largest single group consisted of the daughters of the lower urban estate (*meshchane*), a total of twenty-five; twenty were daughters of government officials, twelve of merchants, and eight of nobles. The others came from a variety of social backgrounds, often described in terms of the father's profession rather than his estate. These included engineers, medical doctors, and a member of the Third Duma. Even the daughter of the Minister of Education, Count I. I. Tolstoi, enrolled, and the daughter of Prime Minister Petr Stolypin applied for admission.[39] The mixed ethno-religious composition was particularly striking: Of those who listed a religion, forty-two were Russian Orthodox, thirty-eight Jewish, five Armenian, five Lutheran, two Roman Catholic, and one Old Believer. The age of auditors ranged from seventeen to forty-three years, with the vast majority falling between the ages of twenty and twenty-six (born 1880–1886). Most studied either law (39) or the natural (31) and physical (21) sciences, with a tiny minority in mathematics (4) and history and philology (1).

Although this biographical material does not include the auditors' reasons for applying to the university, a 1908–1909 national survey allows some general observations to be drawn. In those areas without a women's course, such as

Siberia, the reason was usually very practical: no other option existed. Similarly, some auditors simply wanted to study in those faculties not yet available at the local women's course, particularly law and medicine. In the capital cities, auditors instead cited the higher quality of male educational institutions and often had additional political reasons. Whereas some intended to demonstrate that women could work alongside men and match their academic achievements, a large number of Petersburg auditors in particular were determined to establish the principle of coeducation, hoping that a university education would entitle women to receive the same rights from their diploma as men. Overall, therefore, auditors had both practical and political reasons for applying to the university. They hoped to receive a better education but also to increase opportunities for women in general.[40] What they found in the university, however, was not quite what they had expected.

In the fall of 1906, when women began to appear in large numbers in St. Petersburg University, the lead article in a student newspaper heralded "the great step forward on the path towards progress," confident that the admission of women was destined to play "a tremendous role in the development of Russian culture and civil society." Recalling Meshcherskii's slanders and dismissing those who feared that educating women would lead to the collapse of the family, this student author argued that the admission of women would not lead to any moral decline—not in the university and not in the family. Educated women, he pointed out, make better mothers than uneducated women. The editorial concluded on an impassioned note: "The *studenchestvo* which always guarded general-human interests, which struggled for the equal rights of women before everyone else, will not lay down its arms until women have achieved full equality in the universities."[41]

Opinion surveys document that a large majority of students supported equal rights for women. In Iurev, 77% of students surveyed approved in principle the admission of women students, with support falling among more conservative students; only 40% of Octobrists and rightists voiced their support. At the St. Petersburg Technological Institute, 66% of students supported equal rights for women, and only 17% were actively opposed. Students were more ambivalent about the concrete meaning of equality. In these same surveys, supporters and opponents alike typically argued that women were made for family life rather than independent activity or labor. Education either better prepared them for this natural goal or else wrongly diverted them from it. Similarly, just as some believed that women students introduced debauchery into the university, others expressed apprehension that the standards of student life would harm the gentler sex. A common underlying concern was whether women would retain their femininity if allowed equal access to education or, more broadly, full legal equality.[42]

In light of the generally supportive opinions expressed, then, it is all the more noteworthy that male students apparently greeted their new comrades with reservation and sometimes even hostility. Women auditors consistently described their relations with male students in highly negative terms. Some students, they conclude, simply could not understand why women wanted to attend the university rather than women's courses; others seemed indifferent to the issue of equal access, whatever their professed support for the principle. Many who had initially supported the admission of women had also become less friendly once they realized that women were now their competitors. According to several auditors, male students did have one common characteristic—they all paid very close attention to their new "comrades." As one auditor at St. Petersburg University noted, students "are interested in the auditors. Each answer at an examination, each step [we take] becomes known to the entire university, and the normal inaccuracy of rumor does not fall in the favor of the auditor." In other words, anecdotes about the auditors were plentiful. Once the first curiosity had worn off, moreover, relations worsened; at best students were "polite," at worse, openly malevolent. A striking number of auditors concluded from their own experiences that a *studenchestvo* with high ideals no longer existed, and in its place were simply individual students; some were actively offensive and some were not.[43]

Women auditors also began a complex and ambiguous interaction with the university administration and professors, with conditions of study varying widely. In Moscow, for example, auditors were obligated to have entrance tickets, and if they failed to renew them on time before the beginning of the semester, they were required to obtain special permission each time they entered the university to attend a lecture. Examinations posed a special problem. Because auditors did not have the right to take exams, each professor decided individually whether to admit them. Many professors who gave examinations, however, refused to give the grades officially, instead jotting them down on a scrap of paper for the personal information of the auditor. One professor agreed to give exams privately at his home but not at the university, an offer which was rejected.[44] Although the same rules existed for male auditors, one woman auditor pointed out that men had the right to become students as soon as they had taken the required examinations, a right denied even to those women who had already graduated from women's courses or foreign universities. This double standard was enforced, she stressed, "only because, by some unforeseen accident, they had appeared on earth as women." [45]

When the May 1908 circular barred women from the universities, women auditors and their supporters mounted a public campaign in the press. In appealing to the Ministry of Education, members of the Duma, professors, and the public at large, they argued that women auditors had earned the right to a university education. The main thrust of the campaign was to document the high level of academic preparedness and achievement of the auditors, and, on this basis, to assert the right of women to equal status with men in the university. In a long supportive article, professor of law V. M. Gessen thus argued that the last two years had provided ample documentation of women's intellectual ability.[46] Professors around the country were also requested to evaluate the preparation, work ethic, and performance of women auditors. The results of the first 198 evaluations were overwhelmingly positive. Eleven professors (5%) determined that the preparation of women was partly inadequate usually due to the lower level of girls' gymnasiums in certain subjects, and only one (an ideological opponent of women's education) criticized their work ethic or performance. Many instead noted that auditors maintained higher average grades and were more serious than male students. A total of 174—including those with conservative political leanings—supported the right of women to become full students.[47]

In their endorsement of women's access to the university, professors did not cite intellectual ability alone. Indeed, if the twenty-fifth anniversary of the Bestuzhev Courses in 1903 had been celebrated as a symbol of Russia's cultural progress, the very existence of segregated educational institutions in 1908 could now signify Russia's backwardness. Women's courses were now described as a transitional step toward coeducational universities. At the core of professorial support was a conception of cultural progress that linked the education of women to the national good. Indeed, the education of women—the "backward" sex—seemed to exemplify the rising level of culture within Russia as a whole. For the state to limit access to education was in effect to constrict national progress. "On women lies the important task of educating children, future citizens," one professor thus wrote. "By preventing women from receiving a higher education equal to that of men, the state is committing a crime against contemporary culture. It is also committing a crime against the nation, lowering it as a whole to a half-level of education and human dignity." [48] In this view, a woman's right to education was a guarantee of social progress—and a political issue.

Anticipating common allegations that coeducation led to excessive familiarity between the sexes and sexual debauchery, other professors pointed out that the joint dedication to science provided an ideal environment for men and women to develop relations of mutual respect and cooperation which would have a positive impact on family values, social progress, and even scientific advancement (figure 6-1). One scientist pointedly held up Marie and Pierre Curie as the modern ideal of "scientific" partnership. Indeed, the educated woman now stood in contrast to the morally suspect male student. Some professors even argued that the presence of women in the university actually raised the moral level of male students and for that reason was altogether desirable.[49]

Although women auditors won the battle as individuals, receiving the right to finish out their tenure, they were highly cognizant of the insecurity of their status. When delegates gathered at a national conference of women auditors in St. Petersburg in October 1909, discussion focused on two central questions: the legal admission of women into universities on an equal footing to men and the admittance of women to state examinations. When delegates contacted various

FIGURE 6.1 This satire, entitled "Creation," depicts the conservative publicist M. O. Men'shikov "making" a *kursistka*. In the last scene, he condemns this "slut," who does not intend to study but gussies herself up in preparation for cuddling with students during lectures. *Satirikon* no. 25 (1908). (Courtesy University of Helsinki Slavonic Library)

members of the Duma to advance their cause, however, some Kadet deputies expressed concern that the question of female education would be linked to the question of university autonomy, which they clearly considered more important, and it was consequently suggested they limit their demands to the state examinations and focus their efforts on the Octobrists. The Octobrist politician Aleksandr Guchkov helpfully suggested they petition the tsar. Delegates were thus greeted with words of sympathy but not much else.[50] Though many politicians supported women's education in principle, women's educational equality was still perceived as a secondary issue.

When the draft of a new university charter was introduced into the Duma during the spring of 1910 (it did not include the admission of women), the specter of the woman auditor displaced the *kursistka* as the symbolic menace of right-wing rhetoric. In crude language, Vladimir Purishkevich, the newest leader of the extreme right, blamed the influence of women, Jewish students, and radical student leaders for what he considered the moral and political debauchery in the university. The agent of this degeneration was a certain Jewish woman auditor, who was a member of the Council of Elders of the juridical faculty of St. Petersburg University. (There was only one such woman.) "This Jewish woman," Purishkevich declared in the midst of general pandemonium, "carries the name of the juridical 'pussy' *[matka]*, and is in close physical relations with all the members of the Council." [51] Despite the eloquent defense of students in general (though not women auditors in particular) by many Duma members, Purishkevich was seconded by other deputies, who likened the university to a public place subject to police control.[52] In the eyes of some, the woman auditor was really just a streetwalker.

A NEW WOMAN?

The achievements of the 1905 Revolution in the sphere of women's education could not easily be reversed. Every year a new cohort of women crowded into and graduated from an ever-expanding number of women's courses. This fact undermined any unidimensional image or simplistic stereotype. With literary representations of the *kursistka* from previous decades clearly inadequate to the changed situation, and with compelling new ones elusive, the identity of the new woman student was something of an enigma. Speculation about her ranged widely.

Some older concerns remained. The philosopher Nikolai Berdiaev, for example, complained that women students were becoming too mannish and indeed copying male behavior.[53] For Anna Afanas'eva, a gymnasium student in St. Petersburg who had recently read some Nietzsche, such an androgynous image was less threatening. On May 28, 1907, she wrote in her diary: "Not long ago I was arguing with [my friend] Liza about the woman of the future. She said that there would not just be a superperson *[sverkhchelovek]* in general, but a superwoman *[sverkhzhenshchina]* and a superman *[sverkhmuzhchina]*. I suggested the opposite: the differences between the sexes are diminishing—even now it is noticeable." [54] The biologist I. I. Mechnikov argued, in contrast, that educated women were not developing into sexless beings along the model of worker-insects, as he had earlier feared and propagandized. Many women with a higher education retained a maternal instinct and a proclivity for matrimony, he noted, and often married in the course of their studies.[55]

Other commentators seemed more interested in the impact the new woman would have on society. Completely atypical and indeed representing social fears rather than ideals was the view of Aleksandra Kollontai. She described in approving terms the new type of contemporary *kursistka*, who was marked by modernism and had a sexual "past." As an independent individual paying her own way, she possessed the right to love as she chose and was destined to redefine the family and sexual relations.[56] The feminist leader Ariadna Tyrkova instead stressed women's activity in the public sphere. A strong supporter of equal education, full sexual equality, and a reformed family, Tyrkova believed that traditional "feminine" qualities would provide an important counterpart to the masculinity of government and the professions. Indeed, she cited maternal values as justification for women's engagement outside of the home.[57] Though exhibiting some continuity with earlier debates over the "third sex," this discussion was stamped by the new realities of post-1905 Russia, in which the educated woman was no longer a rarity. Its central themes were the social repercussions of educating women, the question of uniquely "female" qualities, and the transformative impact of the new woman on the family and society.

In this context of renewed social interest, women students became the object of several statistical investigations, which all sought to pin down the new generation of women students, their experiences, their goals, and their attitudes. In addition to the survey of female auditors mentioned above, one survey was designed for women students in Moscow, and two were conducted at the St. Petersburg Courses. However, the project encountered significant political resistance. While roughly twenty surveys of male students were conducted over this same period, only two of the four surveys of female students could even be brought to a successful conclusion—despite a much more limited investigative scope. The first two surveys, both of which failed, demonstrated that politics and sex were off limits, issues studiously avoided in subsequent polls. Despite these differences, the surveys were understood and interpreted at the time as a counterpart to the male surveys. Indeed, women students provided a stark contrast to the stereotype of the dissolute young man.

The survey of women auditors in the universities failed due to poor timing: it was sent out in the midst of the controversy over the decree barring women from the universities. Because it was received by auditors at a moment when their status was extremely precarious, many feared that it was some sort of "provocation" and consequently regarded such potentially controversial questions about membership in political parties and attitude towards religion with particular uncertainty. With auditors clearly fearing that their answers could be turned against them, only 178 questionnaires were returned to the organizers, and there was no response at all from auditors at Kharkov University (where the number of auditors fell from 688 in 1907 to 250 in 1909, a drop suggestive of difficult conditions there). The survey thus failed to accomplish even its most modest objective: to calculate the total number of women auditors.[58]

The second survey fared little better. Sponsored in 1908 by the Pirogov Society, it was designed to investigate the parameters of the sexual question for women students in Moscow. Fully cognizant of the unprecedented character of this project, one of its authors, the well-known physician Dmitrii Zhbankov, defended the scientific study of sexuality. Citing the imperative to subject all aspects of private and public life to open inspection, he argued that the explicit questions of the survey would not shock women students because modern urban life with its sexual violence and pornographic literature had already deprived them of their innocence. He also reworked the traditional arguments for "educating" women. In his view, the rational analysis of sexuality—by both the women respondents and scientists—would help to end false shame and lead to enlightened practices in personal and family life. In effect, the study of sex was educational: it would contribute to the transformation of the traditional patriarchal family into a progressive unit reproducing civic virtue.[59]

Although the survey had been approved by the directors of the various female educational institutions and students were willing to participate, it was abruptly forbidden by government order just as the forms were distributed. As the Moscow Governor-General explained in his letter to the Ministry of Education, the survey would have a "corrupting influence on the young generation." He then discussed the radical politics of women students in some detail, and enclosed (as documentation?) three confiscated questionnaires.[60] The Governor-General was not the only one to make this linkage. The relationship between sexuality and politics was also an integral part of the study itself.

The survey was divided into twenty-four sections with more then three hundred questions. Following the example of the surveys designed for male students, it was not limited to a narrow definition of the sexual question but sought to uncover the nexus between "conditions of life" and sexuality.[61] The first section addressed respondents' participation in the liberation movement of 1905–1907. They were asked whether they had participated in the "general cultural or political life" of the country, and how recent events had affected their private lives. These questions placed political and personal activity along a single interpretive axis, suggesting a polar relationship: did an emphasis on one lead to a deemphasis on the other? Subsequent sections probed the influence of family, school, literature, and daily life on factual knowledge about sex, sexual experience, and sexual desire. In contrast to the surveys for male students, few questions were devoted to venereal disease and masturbation.

The centerpiece was a section on attitudes toward love, sex, and marriage, questions mostly absent from the surveys for men. As inferred from the formulation of questions, the intention of this section was to gauge whether the new woman student had developed a new morality—in other words, to evaluate her fitness as a wife and mother. She was asked: Was love necessary for marriage and sexual relations? Did love and/or sexual life play a predominant role in your life? Would it be possible for you to love two men at the same time? Should women and men remain virgins until marriage? Was it possible to give oneself up under the influence of the moment? These questions suggest that the revolution in women's education had created some uncertainty regarding the sexual behavior of educated women. Would educated women chose sexual freedom over motherhood? [62] If the specter of young men ruining their health through masturbation and prostitutes had guided the formulation of questions for male students, its counterpart was the specter of modern educated women rejecting the traditional feminine values of love and motherhood.

One year after the interrupted sex survey, Bestuzhev students in the statistical seminar of Professor A. A. Kaufman designed, distributed, and analyzed a second questionnaire. Deliberately excluding all political and sexual questions, the students concentrated on the economic situation, academic life, and so far as possible, the "spiritual physiognomy" of the *kursistka*. [63] If the sex survey had searched for the modern woman in both her private and political life, this study instead focused on her public aspirations. The resulting portrait of the typical *kursistka* differed from that of the "disorderly" student. First, she tended to be slightly older (and depicted as more responsible): only 39.2% had enrolled immediately in the Bestuzhev Courses upon graduating from secondary school, and 59.2% of all respondents had worked after graduation, most as teachers or tutors. Quoting one respondent, Kaufman noted that "collisions with life" rather than the lessons of secondary school fostered their desire for higher education.[64] As one of the student statisticians also noted, the typical *kursistka* has engaged "in some form of professional activity, lived wholly or partly independently, and entered the higher school with a larger knowledge of life and experience than one having just completed a middle school." [65] Yet in striving for education, *kursistki* encountered extreme economic hardship forcing many (12.7%) to go without a daily dinner and an unknown number to curtail or interrupt their studies. The average living standard of the *kursistka* was slightly lower than that of the average student.[66] That such sacrifices were said to be made without personal ambition provided a stark (and much exploited) contrast to the new generation of students.

Although career opportunities had begun to open after 1905, the purpose of education remained somewhat unclear to most women students, with only 10.2% of respondents citing a purely professional interest. Kaufman concluded from this that "a general striving to develop a world view, an aspiration for public activism, attracted *many* women to the courses." A number of quotations documented this conclusion. Motives encompassed the desire "to be more useful to society," "the thirst to explain the life of man and to find its goal," "to develop a world view," and, in one case, the imperative "to leave home" and come "in general" to St. Petersburg and the courses.[67] The absence of professional career paths was thus translated into positive terms: the typical *kursistka* sought knowledge primarily for its own sake and endured tremendous hardship in the process.

Further evidence that the new woman student had retained her traditional values was found in her reading habits. The typical *kursistka*, it seems, rejected "pornographic" (i.e., modern) literature as "vulgar," and cited the great nineteenth-century writers Dostoevskii, Tolstoi, and Turgenev as both personal favorites and formative influences on her world view. Of contemporary writers, only Leonid Andreev and Anton Chekhov were listed among preferred writers.[68] While such general preferences tell us little about the specific interests and concerns of students at the time, they provided the finishing touch of a collective portrait, as Kaufman concluded:

> I think that this motif, *service to the people*, is the most characteristic for our students, and particularly for *Russian women students*, for whom the legitimate concern for daily bread has not degenerated into a corrupt idea of a *career*. . . . Without any doubt, [the survey has shown that] there is a strong core among *kursistki* standing on the right path: striving and able to combine *the aspiration to serve the people* with *serious scholarly interests* and *serious scholarly work* [emphasis in original].[69]

Kaufman's emphasis was surely directed against male students, then being admonished for their careerism and corruption. In the face of economic hardship and legal restrictions, the survey's authors argued that the *kursistka* had remained true to her intelligentsia heritage.[70]

Though other commentators rejected Kaufman's emphasis on generational continuity, this image of the woman student remained dominant in publicistic discussions through the end of the imperial period. In a 1914 article, the Marxist publicist Lev Kleinbort thus argued that a new generation of women students had appeared in 1905, who no longer limited their ambition to the pursuit of knowledge but aimed for the same legal and economic rights as men. While Kleinbort asserted that this new woman student was motivated by economic pressures and consequently studied harder and better in order to obtain the skills necessary for a job, his example evoked the image of women pursuing knowledge for its own sake. For some reason, he chose to contrast the behavior of male and female law students and observed that while men focused entirely on their diplomas and rarely attended lectures, women distinguished themselves by their high attendance at both lectures and seminars. Unfortunately, Kleinbort neglected to discuss the implications of the fact that women did not have the right to practice law.

Overall, Kleinbort's *kursistka* emerges as morally and ethically superior to the male student. Concluding with a discussion of the sexual question, Kleinbort emphasized the low interest of women students in erotic literature and their almost unanimous condemnation of prostitution, attitudes which he contrasted to those held by male students. "Golden female youth live by the same principles both within the walls of the school and outside of them," he pointedly stated. In their demand for the right to love, women did not claim the right to "strong sensations" but rather to a new kind of marriage and family. The new woman was a force of progress, Kleinbort concluded: "the *kursistka* is acquiring new habits, and, in turn, communicating them to the student."[71]

The historian of the *studenchestvo* Sergei Svatikov likewise perceived a generational change in 1905 and compared the experiences of male and female students since then. He noted how each had become socially and politically more heterogeneous, resulting in both increased political apathy and a higher interest in scientific and practical preparation.

> However, when you compare male and female youth, you can clearly and objectively see how high the purely idealistic orientation of women remains, how many girls strive for knowledge for the sake of knowledge and not for the sake of a diploma, how many search education not only for a means of economic survival or for the pleasures of pure thought, but also for the possibility to realize their "I," to make a new morality, [and] to give a new direction to the female mind and character. There is no need to idealize the woman student and one need not bow before her. It is necessary to respect her and see her as an equal comrade in life, science, and struggle.[72]

Two possible conclusions can be drawn from such observations: women students had retained their ideals either because of the restrictions placed on their professional activity or because of the particularities of their gender. Either way, the surveys were cited as evidence that education would strengthen rather than corrupt the feminine character.

FEMINISM, SOCIALISM, AND SCIENCE

Although the public image of the female student sometimes seemed a stark contrast to that of the male student, she was often criticized within the student community for her lack of solidarity and her preoccupation with her studies. Students especially complained about the indifference of women auditors to student politics (without acknowledging in any way their extremely tenuous position in the university).[73] Even when women students were praised (here by a male student) as "modest heroines" of the liberation movement, dedicating "all their power and even their lives to the altar of love for the people," it was always stressed that "the Russian woman did not consider it necessary to separate her own personal rights from the general slogans." [74] As the socialist left had theorized for decades, the liberation of the people would provide for the liberation of women as well, and feminism as such was particularist and egoistic. If public discussions depicted the *kursistka* as a force of moderation and morality, students thus focused on her duties as a public actor, that is, as a student. In the spring of 1914, St. Petersburg's leftist student newspaper *Student Years* sponsored an open forum on the "woman question." The debate progressively peeled away the layers of loyalties among students.

The forum was prompted by an article submitted by A. Poliashcheva entitled "The Woman Question at the St. Petersburg Higher Women's Courses." The editorial board appended a note stating its principled disagreement with the article and calling for more submissions.[75] For her part, Poliashcheva described in highly favorable terms a feminist study circle which had been founded the previous year at the Bestuzhev Courses. Its goal was to study the women's movement in Russia and abroad and to propagandize the idea of equal rights for women. She expressed her keen disappointment, however, at the general lack of interest of women students, and quoted some of their ironic responses: "Russian suffragettes? Have they broken any windows yet?" "Who are you? Man-haters? Well that's pretty dull." For Poliashcheva, the lesson was clear. Women students feared feminism and considered it somehow petty, not worthy in comparison to general human interests. They had become used to their inequality, she argued, and no longer noticed that one-half of the human race was deprived of rights simply because of gender. Distancing herself from the "militant" *(burnye)* English suffragettes, Poliashcheva reassured her audience that feminists intended neither to polarize the sexes nor to destroy the family—quite the contrary. While the subsequent debate was stormy, the issue of gender was lost amid the ideals of socialism and science.

The first replies, which marked International Women's Day, heralded Poliashcheva's article as a summons against apathy but subsumed the woman question under socialism. One article called upon women students to join their working-class sisters in the international struggle for the full liberation of all people from "political and economic slavery," while another asserted that the liberation of women depended on the liberation of humanity, making socialism, not feminism, the true solution.[76] The lead article of this same issue, written by the presumably male student B. Iller and entitled "The Liberation of the Woman," pursued a parallel line of argument. In its campaign for political, economic, professional, and cultural equality, Iller argued, the international socialist movement struggled "to transform the woman from a slave, toy, and beast of burden into a being equal to man, his comrade and his friend." Liberation required, however, a cultural and ethical revolution in male attitudes toward women, and indeed in their morals, habits, and marital relations. Iller identified three primary areas in which male students denigrated women as human beings:

swearing, obscene jokes, and prostitution. "When we swear, and, following [Maksim] Gorkii's expression, when the sacred pure word 'mother' is dragged through the mud, we humiliate and lower women," Iller admonished his readers.

> But the most frightful, the most loathsome act is when we go to a woman selling her body out of need, when we purchase a person. . . [we] mock our own 'principles'. . . . Remember comrades, so long as prostitution exists, so long as you use the female body for money, so long as you look upon a woman as a commodity, then the liberation of women remains but an empty phrase. . . . So long as the dark stigma of a buyer of women lies upon the conscience of man, he will not be able to gaze honorably into the eyes of his mother, sister, or beloved.[77]

Clean hands were necessary for the "sacred cause" (of socialism), he concluded; men must liberate women not only with their words but also with their deeds. While Iller was hardly unusual in his censure of male sexual vice, his article is interesting because it completely neglects the female side of the equation. With the liberation of women largely a male affair, the behavior and values of women are irrelevant.

If the initial articles had made the woman question a subtask of social revolution, the most passionate debate did not even concern women's rights but the relationship between science and life. A subsequent issue printed the letter of a female medical student. While feminism did not interest her, she did take issue with the repeated call for students to move out of "narrow academic life." Academic studies and particularly medicine, she stressed, were hardly opposed to life. "I, at the very least, have always believed that a connection exists and that we are moving along that path. . . . Our labor is not only serious but closely tied to life."[78] Her letter prompted an explosion of indignant and impassioned letters. One *kursistka* argued that life must take precedence over academic study, and recounted her mixed feelings when the first woman received a masters degree in Russian history. Her joy in the accomplishment was tempered by a sharp pain of realization that this talented woman had buried herself in an archive for several years and was herself alien to the real lives of her rural subjects. In this student's opinion, the new historian had produced a learned but dead work.[79] In a similar vein, another student lamented what she considered a decline of social values among the new generation of *kursitki*. In their preoccupation with petty personal issues, she complained, they had become alien to the principle of solidarity possessed by the old *studenchestvo* and organized workers. They lacked a social consciousness. She did not say whether they did possess a consciousness of gender.[80] In the last issue of that spring, an editorial criticized the opposition of science to life, and, quoting Marx, argued that knowledge must be used to serve mankind.[81]

Where then was the woman question among students? It had all but disappeared among questions of social revolution and human liberation, the nature of science and its relationship to life, and male sexual vice with its denigration of the generic woman. This slippage does not mean that gender was unimportant. There is some evidence, for example, that women students did take a particular interest in the life and protests of women workers.[82] It does suggest that sweeping generalizations cannot be made. Though women students clearly shared many goals related to the expansion of their educational and professional opportunity, as a group they were divided by numerous social, intellectual, professional, and political interests. In other words, a single "type" no longer existed, if indeed it ever had in the past. With their numbers counted in the tens of thousands rather than the hundreds, women students were fast becoming as heterogeneous as Russia's educated society. For them, the purpose of their education could not be subsumed under a single category, whether it be motherhood, political activism, or career.

Still, as it had for Elizaveta D'iakonova almost two decades earlier, the choice between family and personal development remained a stark one for some students. This theme forms the centerpiece of a one-act play, "A Stone in the Sea," by A. Khiterman, which appeared in a 1910 student literary collection.[83] The scene opens on a middle-class woman named Olia holding a baby in her arms. Dreaming about life outside of her home, she is thinking, "it is only necessary to break the window." Her husband, a physician, then returns from work and demands the complete attention of his wife. Olia attempts to leave him in order to become a full-fledged person, but she is briefly persuaded by his words about motherhood: "You are made to be a mother, a tender mother for adults and children. . . . When I see you breast-feeding our child, I am ready to sink to my knees and pray. . . . I see then the goddess of nature with her countless children." When she subsequently refuses sex as unpleasant, confessing that her dreams of passion had not been fulfilled, her husband rapes her, and the curtain closes on her screams.

With its violent ending, this short play is a tragic rewriting of Henrik Ibsen's *A Doll's House*. Like Nora, Olia aspires to independence and rejects the love of her husband as a form of possession. Yet the play has no real resolution. Only the brute force of the husband is victorious, since Olia never succumbs to "desire" during the rape. Unlike Nora, Olia fails to break with her "feminine tenderness" and becomes simply its victim. In Khiterman's scenario, personal independence and marriage are divided by an unbridgeable gulf. Other students agreed, though for very different reasons. Several works written by women students during World War I advanced an opposing ideal of femininity. Recounting, for example, the transformation of a student into a nurse or the "pure" love of a woman for her war-crippled husband, they contrasted the sterility of knowledge with the life-giving self-sacrifice of women for husband and country. In these cases, students became women through their ministration to men and father-land.[84]

By the turn of the twentieth century, the cause of women's education had won significant support within Russian educated society. While the traditional "gendering" of public and private space continued to shape images of the female student, endeavors to reform the family into an institution based on modern scientific and transparent moral values gave increased civic legitimacy to women's education. The 1905 Revolution marked a watershed in this process. As the number and variety of female educational institutions multiplied and the principle of higher education for women gained widespread legitimacy, women entered spheres once closed to them. The hybrid educational system that persisted until 1917, combined with the growing number of educated and working women in Russian society, prompted new questions about the character of the "new woman" and her equal rights, broadly construed.

In their visions of a new civic order, many liberals and professionals condemned the moral bankruptcy of male students but viewed the education of women as full of promise—if also of pitfalls. Even discounting the extreme words of Purishkevich, the equation of an educated woman with a prostitute had not disappeared. The sex survey of the Pirogov Society reflected the fear that women students would develop "modern" ideas concerning sexual freedom, reject love and marriage, and thus come to resemble their dissolute male comrades. But the specter of the sexually emancipated new woman was countered by a faith in the power of enlightenment to shape moral and intellectual character, and, in this way, to transform the school and the family. The education of women—the "backward" sex—symbolized the education of society, an association that built on a maternal metaphor. The enlightened woman was charged with nurturing and enlightening the next generation of sons. The public story of women students thus took its own path after the 1905 Revolution. Progressive society distinguished the *studenchestvo* according to gender and proclaimed the woman student a positive model for her dissolute male comrades. Yet for women students themselves, the new opportunities could not resolve many of the old questions. They were still faced with the difficult and often unacknowledged choices between career and motherhood, feminism and socialism, science and politics. Nevertheless, thousands of women had broken the window to the world.

CHAPTER SEVEN

"It Is Good to Die Young"

Heroic Ends and the Search for a New Story

Do not sob so senselessly over him,
It is good to die young!
Unrelenting vulgarity did not prevail
To cast even a shadow upon him,
Kneel before him,
Adorn his locks with a laurel!

— Nikolai Nekrasov, Untitled

In the decade before the 1905 Revolution, students proclaimed self-sacrifice in the name of the common good to be a worthy feat. While self-sacrifice usually entailed a heroic symbolic act—strike obstructions or fiery speeches leading to arrest—it also acquired a more literal understanding. Between 1897 and 1905, a series of student suicides entered the master plot of student radicalism. Through the narrative genre of hagiography and the staging of protest memorials and funerals, students unveiled the "real" story behind the individual circumstances: the perpetual struggle of idealistic and principled students against the despotism and arbitrariness of the state.

This tradition of "heroic" suicide traces its origins to the 1897 death of Mariia Vetrova, a student at the Bestuzhev Courses. Arrested in December 1896 for her involvement with an illegal populist group, she was held in preliminary detention until late January 1897, when she was unexpectedly transferred to the notorious Peter and Paul Fortress and placed in solitary confinement. On February 8, she set herself on fire with the kerosene from a lamp and died several days later. Her death was kept a secret for more than two weeks, and when the news finally went public, rumors spread that she had been raped by one of her guards. Refused permission to hold a memorial in her honor, students nonetheless gathered on March 4 at the Kazan Cathedral in central St. Petersburg, raised several wreaths, and sang the hymn "Eternal Memory." Hundreds were cited and sentenced to three days' incarceration.[1]

An underground brochure issued on the first anniversary of the memorial depicted a despotic government extinguishing the life of an idealistic and hardworking young woman. Stressing first the dissimulation of government officials, it chronicled the events leading up to the suicide. Why, it was asked, was Vetrova transferred to the prison reserved for hardened political prisoners and placed in solitary confinement? Since the family had been informed that Vetrova's offense was insignificant, was the explanation simply "moral torment"? Why was the suicide covered up for 16 days? Had Vetrova been raped? Or had she only suffered from "hallucinations" of rape, as prison officials claimed? Such rhetorical questions set the scene for the second theme of the brochure: the idealized life history of Vetrova. The illegitimate daughter of a peasant mother and an upper-class father, Vetrova grew up in an orphanage and became a school teacher. Thirsting for knowledge in order to serve the people, she had come to St. Petersburg in search of enlightenment two years earlier. Prison and death proved to be her unjust fate, a metaphor for the broader repression of students and progress in general.[2]

St. Petersburg's police chief later dismissed the suicide as the product of psychological disturbance and "erotomania," but also noted its great resonance: "Students looked [upon her as having] suffered for truth."[3] The image of political (and sexual) violence had indeed hardened the resolve of the protesters, seeing in her death all the components of a martyrdom—a political (religious) arrest, the subsequent violation of her person (and her purity), and self-immolation. Such a pattern also had a tradition in Russian radical culture. Several populist activists of both sexes had committed suicide while in prison or exile during the late 1870s and 1880s; the inhumane and arbitrary treatment of prisoners and occasional sexual violence, it was asserted, had also resulted in cases of insanity. The nexus between prison (as a site of unlimited arbitrariness) and suicide (as resistance) was made explicit in 1887, when the populist Mikhail Grachevskii burned himself to death as an open protest against prison conditions.[4] Vetrova's suicide merged with this tradition and gave a new symbolic form to the iconography of student protest. Over the course of the student movement of 1899–1905, the public memorial of suicide victims (like those of prominent cultural or political figures) became a forum for remembrance and protest. As in the case of Vetrova, suicide was rarely seen as the result of personal suffering or private tragedies, but as a martyrdom at the hands of a despotic state. At issue was not the motivation of the victim, but the public celebration of resistance, that is, the endurance of revolutionary struggle.

The next incident occurred in 1899, when a Moscow student committed suicide while in prison. Identified only as "Student Lieven" in the radical press, his death, like Vetrova's, was represented through the standard imagery of the student movement: the struggle of state and *studenchestvo*, arbitrary violence and moral right, power and dignity. Arrested for participating in a study circle, a minor offense, Lieven had been placed in solitary confinement for several months. After repeated requests for transfer into a common cell were denied, he too set himself on fire with kerosene. Praised in hagiographic terms as a theoretician with an interest in educating the people (he had planned to write popular books on the natural sciences), his funeral in Nizhnii-Novgorod became the occasion for a large demonstration.[5] Sergei Moiseev, then a gymnasium student and later a student activist, recalls his impressions:

> I read a proclamation for the first time—no words can describe its impact upon me. I went to the funeral. There were many people and wreaths with ribbons proclaiming. . . "Do not fear the broken body, it is not within their power to break the soul." I joined the crowd and an unforgettable feeling enveloped me. I did not understand and could not explain the social meaning of this demonstration, but I sensed something important. . . . With such impressions, I graduated gymnasium and entered the university that fall.[6]

When Nikolai Perovskii, a student leader in 1899 serving a three-year sentence of exile, shot himself, the reaction to the news back in St. Petersburg was similarly defiant. In a hectographed proclamation, his comrades and successors blamed the suicide on the "barbaric conditions of Russian life," which prevented all young people from fulfilling their true promise in service to the motherland. They also gave words to his act: "Perovskii has died; but with his death he has said to us: 'It is impossible to live this way. Fight, comrades, for a better future for Russia. Give her [Russia] more light. Destroy the yoke and darkness oppressing all which is alive.' "[7]

The émigré press also treated these suicides as evidence of the pathology of the regime. In the influential journal *Liberation,* a report on the 1903 prison suicide of Moscow student Vladimir Nikiforov detailed the psychological and physical cruelties he endured, his decline into a sickly youth with shattered nerves, and his repeated requests for a transfer out of solitary confinement. "The tragic death of V. L. Nikiforov does not appear as anything out of the ordinary in our torture chambers," commented the editor in a footnote. "By self-immolation. . . Grachevskii, Somov, Vetrova, and Lieven have all killed themselves. It is time for Russian society to lift its voice against the flagrant violence committed by the government. . . against those battling absolutism and lawlessness."[8] Nikiforov's story was both an allegory for the condition of Russian society and a call to arms.

The memorial of the political suicide reached its apogee in 1904 and 1905 with the suicides of two Petersburg students, Ivan Malyshev and Lev Iakovlev, whose funerals both became occasions for mass processions, singing, and revolutionary speeches. Red ribbons adorning funeral wreaths carried such slogans as "Do not be frightened of broken flesh, fear instead the breaking spirit," and "To him who untimely perished in the fateful battle." The course of events following Malyshev's death in October 1904 is particularly suggestive of suicide's resonance among students, because the memorial occurred against the advice and without the participation of student leaders. On the day of the funeral, some one thousand students gathered at the morgue to accompany the coffin to the cemetery. When they learned that it had been secretly moved the previous night, they tried to march to the cemetery but were forcibly dispersed by police. Describing Malyshev as "another victim of arbitrary rule," proclamations reminded students of Vetrova and their duty to honor the deceased by attending a "requiem service" at the Kazan Cathedral. This was, of course, an invitation to a demonstration, for the church would hardly approve of a requiem for a suicide, and the policy of the government was well known. Although revolutionary student groups issued contrary proclamations arguing that students should reserve their strength for the more important political battle ahead and not attend the memorial, several hundred students gathered at the appointed time and were dispersed by police.[9] For them, the honor of a comrade took precedence over the counsels of student leaders.

The power of this tradition can best be illustrated by a contrary example. In 1903, a woman medical student committed suicide out of "disappointment in the meaning of life," that is, for nonpolitical reasons. The response of her fellow students was nevertheless a spirited defense of active public engagement. In a long hectographed leaflet, her classmates first celebrate the meaning of life:

> This fact [of suicide] compels us to peer time and time again into the foggy distance of the future, where the "guiding lights" shine to us, as [Vladimir] Korolenko expressed it, symbolizing our ideals. Life draws us. Every living being thirsts for the immediate participation in life, the immediate application of its energies to life-creating labor. This thirst to be useful, this thirst for a meaningful participation in life drew us here under the roof of the [Women's Medical] Institute. . . . [B]efore all else, we all wish to be useful to the motherland, to humanity! . . . The sea of life is awakening social instincts in us, the instinctive thirst for struggle, for active participation in the struggle.

Following this passionate affirmation of living and struggling, the leaflet then turned to the "real" reason for the suicide of their young comrade:

> [She] complained of indifference, her inability to adapt herself to life— but don't these complaints ring with her anguish, that she was unable to unmoor herself from the shore of routine, [that she was unable] to seize the moment when the caressing waves were ready to whirl her into the open sea of the struggle for freedom and a better life?![10]

Existential doubt is absent from this text, replaced by a palpable optimism in the unlimited potential of the future. It was the failure of the suicide victim to vanquish the mundane by joining the revolutionary wave that had caused her suicide. The authors of the proclamation had in fact offered a different interpretation of "life." The victim had apparently suffered from the contradiction between ideals and daily life *(byt)*: in her suicide note, she had advised her sister not to ponder the meaning of life, so that she could live as a "happy animal." The proclamation, in contrast, defined life as service, struggle, and revolution, all of which dissolved the doubts and daily reality of the individual into the higher reality of the collective.

By 1905, the tradition of heroic suicide was well established within the masterplot of student radicalism. Contemporaries—both students and nonstudents—understood these deaths not in the context of an individual life, but as public events with political significance. Whatever the private anguish of the victims, the act of suicide was eulogized as a form of martyrdom and commemorated with the genre-specific hagiography and memorial. Despite the apparent unity of interpretation, two potentially contradictory conceptions of suicide coexisted within this tradition: suicide was the result of violence against the individual and an act of individual resistance to violence. The victim was often said to have suffered from a psychological disturbance caused by imprisonment and especially solitary confinement; otherwise such an act could hardly have been contemplated. Yet suicide was also proclaimed an act of resistance, an act that affirmed freedom in the midst of despotism. The revolution would reconstitute the relationship between psychosis and martyrdom.

EPIDEMIC SUICIDE AND THE REVOLUTIONARY EXPERIENCE

The specter of a new kind of mass suicide materialized at the height of revolution. In an article published in late 1905 in an influential medical journal, the outspoken physician Dmitrii Zhbankov described an epidemic of suicide that he linked to the "abnormal" cast of Russian life.[11] In a second article from 1906, he causally linked the "bloody epidemic" of suicide to the suppression of the revolution. Arguing that the old does not wish to yield its place to the new and citing the countless arrests, exiles, executions, and pogroms, Zhbankov did not veil his political critique. These conditions, he asserted, had disrupted the equilibrium of many Russians, destroyed their enjoyment of living, and kept them from placing any value on life itself. The outcome was suicide, mental illness, alcoholism, crime, murder, rape, and sexual promiscuity. "Is this not in the taste of the plague-stricken *Decameron?*" he wondered.[12] Zhbankov was not alone in this assessment. By 1906, other specialists were also warning of an "epidemic" of suicide, and by 1908, this term was well established in the press. Although the trend affected every social group, its most troubling dimension was the ever-increasing number of youthful victims. Only in its beginnings, moreover, did "epidemic" refer to a rash of cases at a specific time and place, for the term soon designated all cases in the Russian empire and would be used until the outbreak of war in 1914. In the politicized atmosphere of 1905 and 1906, epidemic suicide was first diagnosed as a symptom of political pathology, and this diagnosis would shape new cultural meanings for suicide as well as the emergence of a new kind of political suicide.

The relationship between revolutionary violence, psychosis, and suicide formed a central topic of discussion within the medical community. In September 1905, a national psychiatric conference unanimously resolved that "social-political factors acting in an oppressive fashion on the conditions of individual and social existence occupy a significant place in the etiology of nervous and psychiatric illness." [13] Citing their duties as medical professionals and citizens, many physicians asserted their specialized knowledge in the realm of "public health" and claimed a political voice on this basis. For the majority, the diagnosis was clear: the political regime was harming the collective well-being of Russian society. One physician explained:

> We see how often it happens, thanks to the direct efforts of our bureau-cracy, that one Russian citizen gets neurasthenia, another psychosis, [and] a third commits suicide. To place the struggle for the mental health of the Russian people in the hands of this same bureaucracy would mean to put a cross over this entire matter [e.g., as over a gravestone]. We are pleased that our civic-professional point of view coincides in the given instance with the general-civic [point of view] and altogether [we have] one thought, one desire, and one, sadly, as yet unattained dream, the immedi-ate convocation of the empowered representatives of the entire people.[14]

This quotation concludes a 1905 article by Doctor V. K. Khoroshko entitled, not insignificantly, "Hygiene of the soul" *(Gigiena dushi)*. By linking hygiene, a medical-sanitary term, to the soul, Khoroshko raised important questions concerning the role of social life in the development of psychosis and suicide and suggested a sociopolitical "cure."

Further investigation of this problem was propelled by the publication of a series of psychiatric case studies beginning in late 1905 that described a new kind of "revolutionary psychosis." The subjects were individuals who had usually experienced or witnessed episodes of extreme violence (such as students and workers), and whose symptoms clearly reflected the contemporary political environment. By 1907, concern had centered on the mental health of Russian society in general and the harm inflicted upon it by the violence of political reaction. With its focus on the causal relationship of political conditions and the development of mental illness, the analysis of revolutionary psychosis used case studies as metaphors for a broadly social trauma. The "real" cause of psychosis and suicide was not the experience or reasoning of the individual but a political pathology. Suicide was consequently represented as a social-psychotic act.[15]

As the discussion expanded out of the specialized press, the psychosis was often located less in the individual than in the social environment. In his article "Political Psychoses and Political Suicides," Natan Vigdorchik first summarized the medical debates in approving tones, concluding: "Political suicide and political psychosis—these are two paths along which all psychically weak and spiritually unbalanced individuals exit from the storm of the revolutionary epoch." Citing the worsening conditions of material life on the one hand, and the general atmosphere of blood and violence on the other, Vigdorchik agreed that the indirect influence of the epoch characterized both the forms of contemporary pathological suicide and the current epidemic. Although he devoted the bulk of his analysis to this "pathological suicide," Vigdorchik carefully distinguished a type of "normal suicide":

> Under certain circumstances, suicide appears to be the one objective-reasonable exit from a particular condition; under certain circumstances, suicide evidences not the weakness of mental organization but its strength and determination. . . . Nobody would term an individual mentally ill who wished to preserve his freedom and independence even unto death, or he who considered it shameful for his cause to give himself cowardly into the hands of the victors.[16]

Such cases, he noted without providing examples, were particularly common in the French Revolution of 1789 and the current Russian revolutionary situation. The scholar Lev Sheinis likewise identified an underlying sanity in some cases of suicide and quoted the eminent legal scholar Anatolii Koni in his support: "Life often constructs for man those circumstances according to which suicide appears to be its own kind of logical resolution, one which has nothing in common with [mental illness]." [17] Suicide could thus be a rational response to the pathological conditions of life. This dualism of pathology and rationality hid a potential contradiction. Was suicide the result of victimization or a heroic act of resistance?

Supplementing the growing weight of clinical evidence, statisticians also sought to illuminate the mental health of Russian society. Beginning in 1905, a new state agency and several independent specialists began a systematic collection of data related to suicide. Established under the Ministry of Education, the Medical-Sanitary Division led by Doctor G. V. Khlopin was empowered to oversee the collection and statistical analysis of documents related to the health of students of all ages in its jurisdiction, and in particular, to suicide. Working through bureaucratic channels, the division collected information about suicide, including school and police records, autopsy reports, and personal documents.[18] At the same time, three physicians began to provide independent statistical analyses. In compiling their data, N. I. Grigor'ev, G. I. Gordon, and Zhbankov collected newspaper accounts and compared them with official statistical sources. Not surprisingly, given the different sources, the studies produced widely disparate results and led to a political polemic. The size of the epidemic functioned as a measurement of conditions of life after 1905.

The results were indeed startling. In a study of suicide in St. Petersburg, Grigor'ev asserted that the suicide rate had tripled between 1906 and 1911, from 903 to 2,962 annual cases, and that official figures (532 and 1,165) accounted for approximately 60% of the real number of cases. Explaining the disjunction between official statistics and newspaper accounts as a failure of "bureaucratic methods," Grigor'ev diagnosed the old regime as both incompetent and pathogenic.[19] For his part, Gordon estimated the suicide rate from Grigor'ev's findings and found that his result, 370 suicides per 1,000,000 inhabitants, was the highest in Europe. Gordon's rejection of official statistics was explicitly political. In his eyes, their inaccuracy demonstrated the failure of the government to dam the tide of suicide and to formulate specific measures in response. It was, consequently, the civic duty of educated professionals such as himself to step forward.[20] In 1912, Zhbankov drew the political lesson of independent suicide statistics.

> In my first article about suicide (1906) we stated that if fundamental changes in our political and social life were not enacted, if violence and arbitrariness did not stop, then we should expect the further intensification of this epidemic of traumas and—as one of its dimensions—of suicide. And in actuality the value of life has fallen still further over the last years, and the trend to self-annihilation grows more and more. Herein follow several facts and figures that confirm this terrible phenomenon of Russian life.[21]

·The bureaucratic methods of the state came under particular criticism for obscuring the real dimensions and causes of suicide among students. As the official reports of the Medical-Sanitary Division began to appear in 1906, Khlopin first played down the problem of youth suicide, stressing that the problem was not worse than in Western Europe and expressing cautious optimism. While he began to express some concern about the "significant" increases by 1907, this very same report failed to list a single case among students from higher educational institutions.[22] By this time, as well, independent researchers were closely scrutinizing the official publications and providing alternative figures. One newspaper even pointed out the discrepancy between Khlopin's figure of twenty-seven suicide attempts among students (of all ages) in all of Russia during 1905 with that of the St. Petersburg city statistical office, which had registered twenty-six cases.[23] According to Dr. Gordon, the number of student suicides was much higher than Khlopin admitted. Not only had he had found 96 cases for 1905, but his total of 1,266 cases for the five-year period of 1905–1909 was more than twice that of Khlopin's figure of 563.[24] Gordon subsequently compared the suicide rate of Russian students to that of their Prussian counterparts and asserted that the Russian rate was approximately three times higher. He stressed, moreover, that while in Europe the suicide rate of youth under the age of twenty-five came to approximately 30% of the overall number of suicides, in Russia this group made up almost 60%. Clearly, the epidemic in Russia was not a mirror image of the Western experience.[25]

The independent statisticians working on the problem of suicide all stressed that their figures were not exact and must be viewed in relation to the flawed numbers provided by official bureaucratic sources. The dispute was less concerned with the actual number of cases than with the recognition of the existence of the epidemic and the failure of the government to address it. Yet to remedy the crisis, it was necessary to identify the causes and their cure. This proved particularly difficult with a phenomenon like suicide and a method like statistics. Although a statistical analysis will define a specific and generic "reason" for suicide (for example, a bad grade in school or a romantic misadventure), statistics in general are thought to illuminate correlations and trends that constitute the general causes for suicide (poverty, alienation, etc.). The progression from reasons to causes requires interpretation.

This process of interpretation was fundamental to the great resonance of the epidemic in Russian society. Apart from brief introductory statements, Khlopin largely declined to extrapolate general causes, referring generally to the low moral condition of the family and school. He instead provided dozens of charts and tables—literally thousands of statistical correlations based on time of year and time of day, age and sex, geography and method. Other commentators sought to distinguish the immediate reasons for a suicide from the causes propelling the epidemic; and most agreed that the basic cause lay in the abnormal conditions of life arising from the suppression of democracy. The epidemic spurred a discussion of these conditions of life, of what can be called "intermediate" causes—the structure of the school, the failure of moral upbringing in the family, the economic crisis, poverty, capitalism, pornographic literature, alcoholism, and even the acute sensitivity of the Russian character. Though statisticians used their figures as a political weapon against the government, their interpretations pointed to a larger social crisis. Statistics indicated that the environment of suicide was inextricably tied not only to political conditions but to a social malaise.

Psychological and statistical studies of suicide subverted the traditional story of student suicide as an epic struggle against absolutism. They instead recounted the systematic destruction of the social psyche by a pathological government, a process that was "documented" by the fact of suicide. Although suicide remained a highly political act, indeed even more so, it did not denote resistance so much as victimization. Yet even here, the political meaning of suicide remained ambiguous: if the conditions of life were pathological, could suicide then be a rational response to them? Could suicide be "normal"? The symbolism of youth suicide lent a further element of ambiguity, for it drew on old truisms. Arguing that the suicide rate among students had actually fallen during 1905 only to increase to epidemic levels after the revolution, Doctor I. E. Maizel' paraphrased Pirogov: "Youth are an extremely sensitive barometer, quickly reacting to currents of a political character."[26] The barometric reaction now entailed suicide rather than the political protests of earlier generations.

THE EPIDEMIC IN THE PRESS

Statisticians viewed the many suicides reported in the press as raw data, and their investigations consequently deduced a political and social pathology from the aggregate of suicide acts. Their findings were widely reported. Newspapers published interviews with specialists, the results of statistical and other studies, and the resolutions of medical conferences. In addition to acquainting the public with the specialized debates, the press excelled in depicting the private drama of suicide—the personal story in its particular context—and in distilling a broader message. If statistical studies extracted meaning from the patterns of suicide, then the press performed the opposite operation; cases of suicides were rewritten into modern parables.

With the new freedoms from censorship, increased literacy rates, and the growing diversity of the urban population, the daily newspaper was revolutionized in the aftermath of 1905. This period witnessed not only the appearance of respected liberal dailies, but also the tremendous success of the sensational "boulevard" newspaper and penny press.[27] In this new environment and most public of forums, the epidemic of suicide caught the public eye and became socially—even economically—relevant. Newspapers of all persuasions devoted considerable attention to the problem of suicide. In 1908, one journalist ironically commented: "A particular section has even appeared in newspapers, [called] 'Epidemic of Suicide.' It draws no more attention but certainly no less than the sports section."[28] This was not altogether an exaggeration, for the coverage was indeed extraordinary, and it took a variety of forms.

Like other miscellany of urban life—crimes, court cases, and executions— most suicides received brief mention in the daily chronicle of all newspapers, usually under the heading "Happenings" *(proisshestviia),* which should not be confused with the more important section, "Events" *(sobytiia).* The number of cases varied widely, from one or two incidents to well over twenty. The form of reportage was remarkably uniform, with each notice usually including the victim's name, age, and social status, the location of the incident and the method used, a laconically phrased explanation of the motive (occasionally drawn from the suicide letter), and a few descriptive details illuminating the setting or central characters. Particularly sensational cases of suicide merited more extensive coverage, which often lasted for several days and concluded with a description of the funeral. Sometimes the extent of the coverage varied widely, with one newspaper providing a short notice, and another several columns of interviews, rumors, and analysis. Although factual errors and discrepancies were quite common, the chronicle succeeded in its main task—the exposé of private drama. Newspaper stories did not dryly record the facts, they shaped them into recognizable and accessible stories.

Public input occurred in the feuilleton, the column, and the letter to the editor. In 1909 and 1910, for example, K. P. Slavnin published a serial column, "On the Battle with Suicide," which incorporated regular public and professional comment, particularly from students. It had been initiated in August 1909, when a polytechnic student, A. Goretskii, sent his suicide letter to Slavnin, who published it and founded an organization dedicated to the preservation of life.[29] Press coverage thus allowed for an unprecedented discussion of suicide. It transmitted the scholarly debates to the public, recounted innumerable private dramas, and facilitated the expression of public opinion. The newspaper shaped both the forms and the interpretation of suicide.

FROM A POVERTY OF MEANS TO A POVERTY OF VALUES

Poverty constituted one of the most important factors in urban suicide. In the estimate of Zhbankov, approximately 28% of all suicides were related to hunger, unemployment, and need.[30] According to Gordon, the percentage reached as high as 39% (compared with 5% in Prussia, he pointedly noted). This factor was not restricted to the lower classes: between 1902 and 1909, Gordon had also registered forty such cases among students.[31] The poverty of students was a well-known fact in Russia, and the many student surveys appearing in the years after 1905 lent a new statistical and moral actuality to it. Moreover, the classified sections of many newspapers were full of advertisements of students offering to give lessons, indeed, requesting work of any kind. Though long an established part of everyday life, by 1908, student poverty also became an essential component of the modern suicide epidemic.

Many newspaper reportages of suicide listed hunger as the primary cause and provided evocative human details. A short announcement entitled "Suicide of Student due to Need" thus recounted the events surrounding the death of Ivan Bogdanovich, a student at the Technological Institute. The previous month, it was reported, Bogdanovich had lost his stipend of fifteen rubles per month, and he had no other source of income; only three kopecks had been found in his pocket. "These circumstances affected him so strongly," the article concluded, "that Bogdanovich became gloomy and then killed himself." Another report on the same suicide added the following: "The deceased came to St. Petersburg from the provinces, where he most likely has family." [32] The image of three kopecks and parents expecting their son to come home lent the story an added poignancy. Another chronicle, "The Starving," briefly reported the attempted suicide from "extreme need" of Evgeniia Prislukhina, a 20-year-old Bestuzhev student. Taken to the hospital while still conscious, she had asked the doctor not to help her as "she had no means to live, and starvation threatened." [33] The reader was left to imagine the circumstances of her life.

In May 1908, the journalist V. Petrusevich reported his investigation of a suicide, which became the prototypical case. On April 25, 1908, a certain student A.B. had committed suicide without leaving any explanatory note. In an article published two weeks later, "Reasons unknown," Petrusevich recounted not the story of the suicide but his own search for the truth of this unexplained tragedy. He had visited the student's room, but found that it was distinguished by the singular absence of all personal objects. Everything, Petrusevich realized, had been sold off; there was nothing left to tell A.B.'s story. Then he accidentally came across a calendar on which small amounts of money had been noted in pencil. He had solved the "riddle." For the 115 days between January 1 and his suicide on April 25, the victim had spent a total of six rubles thirty-eight kopecks on twenty-six portions of soup, sixty-nine portions of bread, seven postage stamps, tea, and kerosene. He had been unable to pay his April rent of eight rubles. Petrusevich blamed Russian society for failing to support its youth and suggested that many suicides labeled "reasons unknown" had a similar explanation.[34]

In response to Petrusevich's article, a student wrote a letter to the editor in which he imagined the last months of A.B.'s life. A.B. had attempted to get help through student organizations but was placed on waiting lists and subjected to humiliating questions. He had sent seven letters looking for work, but had received no response. Unemployment prevented him not only from eating regularly, but also from buying enough kerosene for his lamp to study at night. In desperation, he had settled on suicide and had not bothered to leave a note—his experience had already shown that nobody gave a damn. Rather than asking for charity, this letter advocated self-help and requested that work opportunities be posted with the student labor bureau. For its part, the newspaper responded with its own interpretation of students' experience: as youth arrive "from the far corners of the provinces with an impassioned thirst for the light of knowledge and a firm hope for happiness, [they] instead receive a noose of cord and the luck to be registered. . . as a suicide statistic." [35]

The story of A.B. had proceeded through three stages of interpretation. Depicting himself as a concerned citizen, Petrusevich had recounted his own search for meaning in an unexplained suicide and castigated his indifferent fellow citizens. In his letter to the editor, the student had generalized the daily experience of poverty shared by students and blamed society's apathy. The newspaper had then extrapolated the universal story of students' journey to the city in search of enlightenment and the dashing of their hope, and Russia's, in hunger and suicide. While this pattern was readily available in many nineteenth-century novels, it also drew on the traditional autobiographical pattern of the Russian student— the idealized journey to the university in search of truth—and inverted the ending. Instead of consciousness, the student finds hunger, indifference, and death. Over the next years, these three strategies of interpretation became standard to the reportage of student suicide.

Shortly after the flurry of attention around A.B., N. Levitskii brought these themes together in an article published in Russia's most respected liberal daily. He prefaced his appeal with a quotation from a newspaper: "Student Kozlovskii slit his throat with a razor. The reason—extreme need." Using this example, he denounced the horrific economic situation of students, unable to pay tuition and often existing on the border of starvation:

> What are all of these great deprivations, diseases, and sorrows. . . other than a punishment for the desire to study? What after all is suicide and death from the harsh conditions of life other than a punishment for the striving towards enlightenment—the thirst for light and air both for oneself and for our long suffering motherland. . . ? And instead of the requested bread, we throw youth a stone, instead of quenching their thirst. . . we make for them a poison and a hell, such that youth perishes before our eyes.

This rhetorical contrast between students' indigence and their aspiration for intellectual and spiritual enlightenment became a potent metaphor for the fate of Russia as a nation after 1905. As Levitskii pointed out, the condition of the student reflected on the condition of society as a whole—the next generation of cultural leaders was dying from social apathy. Like Petrusevich, Levitskii had used the example of suicide to castigate society and call for reform.[36]

When the suicide statistics for 1908 were published in 1909, a series of newspaper commentaries built on these approaches. They all assumed the role of civic conscience and defined their task as the unveiling of the truth of suicide. Rejecting the official account, according to which only ten of the seventy-six student suicides had been the result of hunger, they focused instead on the forty-eight cases listed as "cause unknown." To understand, one commentator asserted, "it is necessary to recall the milieu in which our student youth live. In eighty-five cases out of one hundred, our students are people without means, absolutely indigent." The cause of many suicides is unknown, another admonished his readers, citing the countless work-wanted ads in the newspaper, "only due to our own indifference to the situation of students." A third likened youth thirsting for higher education to a "student proletariat." Under prevailing social conditions, he concluded, there is no place for many students to turn, except to the "noose, knife, poison, or bullet." A few months later, another commentary likewise described the new reality in urban centers. Quoting an advertisement, *"Kursistka,* proficient in German, French, and Latin seeks lessons and other work, including the position of chambermaid," the author cited analogous incidents: the *kursistka* fainting from hunger, the student who fell unconscious on the street, not from drunkenness as bystanders originally assumed, but from going several days without food. And when there is no place left to turn, the author reflected, only the bullet in the head remains. This article even played with the popular stereotype of the dissolute student in order to draw attention to the crisis. All of these commentators thus generalized a common student experience and called upon society to come to the aid of its children.[37]

In articulating their own experiences in letters to the editor, students drew on similar motifs. One letter (which the paper titled "Help"), asked for public assistance for the student labor bureau, and explained the kind of "education" students received each year in *Piter,* an affectionate slang for St. Petersburg:

> As is well known, *Piter* possesses wonderful attributes to attract those who thirst for light and knowledge. People of all ages and conditions, though primarily youth without any provision, come in great numbers from all ends of Russia. . . . Everyone, like moths, [approaches] the light and burns his wings. He thinks, "I have my youth and health, the passionate striving for knowledge, but there's not a penny in my pocket—well, it's nothing, [I can] overcome need." And so he goes to *Piter.* But there are thousands like him, leading to a certain denouement; for example, [to] throw yourself in the Neva.[38]

This student described two different cities—the hearth of culture and enlightenment and the untold coldness of the northern landscape and capital society. Suicide appears as the logical end point of the youthful dream for education and progress.

The hungry student as a metaphor for social apathy formed the theme of a 1907 short story by Vladimir Kokhanovskii entitled "Student Ivanov." The story opened with the following words: "For four years, student Ivanov, a lone and sickly young man of 24 years, had lived in poverty and hunger. Finally he grew tired and his thoughts became gloomy and hopeless." Kokhanovskii described the experiences of such a student: the cold apartment and unsympathetic landlady, the inability to find work or to study, and the alienation from friends. The tone of the story was ironic (though not unsympathetic), a narrative point of view that suggests that the motifs of student poverty had become stereotyped. But its central image was isolation and apathy, as the concluding scene powerfully evoked: "The shot with which Ivanov killed himself was muffled and did not wake the soundly sleeping people in the house. It also did not wake the sleeping neighbors. It sounded strange and solitary in the night; and then it became as quiet as before." [39]

In the reportage of suicide, letters to the editor, and works of fiction, poverty was commonly given a causal role in the suicide of students. Most representations of this association did not emphasize the economic or political dimensions of the problem, however, but the social one—the material poverty of students reflected the civic poverty of Russian society. In the fall and winter of 1909–1910, a series of student suicides in Kiev and St. Petersburg brought the many facets of this problem to the forefront of attention and introduced new elements of interpretative ambiguity. This process began with the 1909 suicide of a woman student in Kiev, whose suicide letter was published in newspapers across the country. This highly publicized case led in turn to a second suicide and inspired a group of Kiev students to publish a collection of all articles in the Kiev press on the suicide of students for the six-month period between October 1909 and March 1910. This 280-page book was entitled *To the Aid of Youth: A Collection of Articles, Letters, and Notes about Student Indigence and the Suicide of Students.* [40]

The book opens with the initial report on the suicide of Musia Ogunlukh in October 1909. She had thrown herself into the Dniepr River from Kiev's Chain Bridge. Appended to the subsequent entry was her suicide letter, which delegates from Kiev's student community had requested be published. Ogunlukh had addressed her letter "To Russian young women" *(K russkim devushkam).*

> To you my word: I am one of many and I fall as a sacrifice for many. My final word—damnation to the rich. . . . I can live no longer: the unending struggle took away my strength, my energy, my capacity for life, and most importantly, my faith in people. Where are those friends? Where are those comrades? Where are those well-wishers, who laugh with us when we are cheerful, when we do not need sympathy? There are no [real] friends, no dear comrades, only drinking buddies *[sobutyl'niki].*

Although she also blamed her loss of faith on the silence of one friend, whom she had twice asked to come to her aid in the days before her suicide, this betrayal had been the last in a series. Her ideal of student mutual aid had turned out to be a mirage. She then pointed to the broader lessons to be drawn from her experience:

> Now I cannot believe—but is it possible to live without faith? I exit life because I will not give in—compromise to me is worse than death: they want to kill our only dignity—our pride and self-esteem. I curse parents who have nothing except progeny: what right do they have to bring us into the world? If it is necessary, then this is my council to all you poor mothers: do not acquaint your children with the basic injunctions of

honor, justice, truth, and good. Teach them instead this worldly wisdom: "You are poor; therefore during your lifetime you must always grovel before the strong, and speak of them in the third person, 'they'—for they are the masters of the earth."[41]

From her long struggle with economic hardship, Ogunlukh extrapolated the spiritual poverty of the student community and Russian society as a whole. By contrasting the values of justice and truth with the power of money, she asserted that principles had become empty words before the realities of daily survival. While this suicide was the result of poverty, Ogunlukh characterized her act as a "sacrifice," an act of faith and resistance, and a cry for justice.

A month later, another Kiev student, Marusia Levandovskaia, also committed suicide, explaining only that she had tired of struggling for life. Her funeral was attended by some one thousand people, and her coffin, covered in white flowers, was carried by students and *kursistki* in a procession to the cemetery. Her suicide prompted three letters to the editor, each of which offered a different appraisal of her act. An acquaintance recounted his friendship with Levandovskaia since their youth in Kishinev and described her onerous work schedule, which had prevented her from making friends in Kiev. Recounting their last meeting, when he had reminded her of happy times in Kishinev, he recalled her words and mood: "Do you know—the horror of despair filled her voice—all of Kiev, our life seems to me like a cemetery of buried hopes, unrealized dreams. . . . Do you remember our dreams—the courses, student life, interesting and good people, comrades . . . ?" A moment later, she reminded her friend that Ogunlukh had also sought to escape from her "friends." For the author of the letter, the meaning was clear: both women had been victims of "poverty." Their hopes for education and progress had been dashed by their daily struggles, which had documented to them the spiritual impoverishment of society and *studenchestvo* alike.[42]

The subsequent two letters addressed the problem of poverty head on. The first, signed "Mother," argued that economic poverty alone was the reason for the rising number of suicides. Because society had not known of students' unending struggle to survive, she rationalized, nobody had stepped forward to help. "They perished not only from bitter need, but also from the consciousness that they were alone, that there was nobody to support them." She called on her fellow mothers to help save these starving young women with the creation of a charitable fund. In her view, physical nourishment would restore their spiritual faith as well.[43] In response to this letter, however, a Kiev student signed "Son" explicitly rejected material poverty as a sufficient explanation for suicide.

> Do you think that we are shooting ourselves, drowning ourselves, or poisoning ourselves due to hunger, because we often go without dinner, breakfast, or bread? In earlier years we also went hungry, but then we

weren't in a desert, then there was no spiritual hunger: we lived by our ideals, our belief in people and in a glorious future. Today we are alone; due to our conscience, we cannot go where our fathers *(Signposts)* call us. We do not want to live by bread alone. . . by petty-bourgeois values. . . . You are alien to us. . . . Musia and Marusia—these are victims. . . they have left, but the truth of their life remains.[44]

This student situated the epidemic of student suicide within the context of a new generational conflict. The failure of the revolution and the morally bankrupt alternative offered by the "liberal fathers" of *Signposts,* in his own words, caused the spiritual starvation of students. Musia and Marusia were the victims not of economic poverty but of the new bourgeois society.

A similar process occurred in St. Petersburg, where the economic context of suicide was likewise displaced by an overt political symbolism. The critical case occurred in December 1909, when the popular socialist student leader Veniamin Risel' (Comrade Genrikh) poisoned himself in the main university building and became a new kind of hero. Approximately one thousand students transformed Genrikh's funeral into a day-long demonstration with clear revolutionary symbolism. They draped the coffin with red ribbons, carried wreaths of red carnations, and followed the coffin through the city to the train station and the cemetery. Several hundred mounted police kept close watch and forbade students to sing, to carry the coffin by hand, or to pass by the university itself. The funeral was described in a newspaper:

At twilight, the coffin is put into the grave, and the voice of a student is heard: "Comrades! In just a moment our dear comrade 'Genrikh' will be left alone in the cold lonely cemetery. It was not long ago that his voice resounded among us, it was not long ago that he called us to glorious tasks. Comrade Genrikh: your memory will be preserved forever. When we lose heart and our spirit grows tired, then we will not forget your legacy. In the name of the entire *studenchestvo,* farewell comrade." Then another voice: "Thought is numbed, blood is congealed—a young life has perished." The body was then buried and a chorus sang "Eternal Memory."

Though the funeral was an affirmation of faith in the endurance of *studenchestvo* beyond the current epoch of darkness and despair, the funeral wreaths no longer quoted the defiant revolutionary slogans of years past. The most prominent ribbon instead evoked the words of the poet Nikolai Nekrasov, "It is good to die young." [45]

A second suicide, which occurred the following month, had a different political twist, for the student was not a radical but a moderate, a sympathizer with the Kadet party. His story became emblematic not of the decline of revolutionary spirit, as with Genrikh, but rather of the suppression of civil society. On January 16, St. Petersburg University student Aleksandr Krapukhin sent his suicide letter to Russia's most prominent liberal newspaper, which he thanked for its fair and principled reporting. He explicitly discounted material poverty as an explanation of his impending suicide and instead provided a political explanation:

> Every person has the right to order his life and personality. I die freely, consciously, and gladly. To the university, the spring of my life, and to my professors, the principled fighters for truth and right, my last grateful farewell. Please give my regards to the pupils at the school where I taught for three years. Material reasons were not the cause of my fateful denouement. I could always work on the side. It is difficult to live now in *Rus'*, when everything principled, civic *[narodnyi]*, and cultured is being destroyed without pity. I ask that humane people bury me.

By sending his letter to a newspaper, Krapukhin had clearly hoped for publicity. By stating that he would die "consciously," he further claimed a rational basis for his act. For its part, the newspaper posed a series of questions: "What did this unknown Aleksandr Krapukhin endure earlier, how did the experiences of his young life end in the words: 'It is difficult to live now in Rus'? What poisoned his soul? Who prepared this poison? Who? There is no answer." [46]

These were the questions on many commentators' minds that December and January of 1909–1910, for all sought to pin down the crisis. Across the political spectrum, the appraisal of these suicides highlighted the importance of the 1905 Revolution in the disintegration of the world view of the intelligentsia. More conservative commentators located the crisis within what they saw as a broader decline of values in modern society, springing, in its Russian variant, from the long-term hegemony of the radical intelligentsia. For them, both the revolution and the subsequent epidemic of suicide stemmed from the same nihilist evil. According to one particularly extreme view, the lies of leftwing parties had poisoned youth and destroyed their faith in God and tsar. [47] Many liberals and progressives instead perceived a process of disillusionment and confusion. Professor P. I. Kovalevskii, for example, focused on the "spiritual tragedy" of contemporary youth. Unlike such earlier periods as the 1860s, he explained, there were no longer any clear goals and ideals in whose name youth were willing to suffer. They had placed all of their hopes on the liberation movement, hopes that had proven chimerical. "The more impressionable representatives of the young generation could not bear the destruction of their ideals and decided that death was better than life," he concluded, "the unstable ones turned to drunkenness and dissipation." [48]

Krapukhin's story proved particularly sympathetic to the moderate press. In this example, Krapukhin's own words are quoted in order to make his suicide into an archetype of the era: "The tragic death of a new victim of these difficult times *[bezvremen'e]*, 'when everything principled, civic, and cultural is destroyed without pity,' compels us to return once again to this outstanding personality and to cite several of his biographical traits." This version of his story was a liberal variant of Vetrova's: The son of a priest, Krapukhin had spent three years as a rural schoolteacher, but, despite the importance of his service, the cultural isolation weighed on him. His high spiritual needs thus drew him to St. Petersburg, where he enrolled in the university and devoted himself to science. He went to all his lectures, spent entire days in the library, and was fulfilled. At first he had lived with his brother's family, where he was the favorite of the children, but recently he had taken his own apartment in order to prepare for the state examinations. His change in mood was linked to this move away from the family hearth, his observation of the miserable living conditions of workers, and his constant struggle with his own poverty. "It is said that A. Krapukhin followed the press with interest," the article concluded, "and that in recent times he constantly said—It is difficult to live in *Rus'*." [49] Whether this portrait of Krapukhin is accurate is immaterial, for his search for culture was a metaphor of the liberal path of cultural development, undermined by apathy and extremism.

In the case of Genrikh, the reportage typically linked his indigence to his political disappointment. Most articles mentioned that he had recently received an emergency loan of three rubles from a student organization and had ordered hot water without tea or sugar in the cafeteria before poisoning himself. One article recounted his recent complaints that society's political apathy had finally broken his rose-colored glasses. [50] Unlike Krapukhin, Genrikh did not become a symbol in the press at large; rather, his suicide resonated within the student community. [51] In the weeks after Genrikh's funeral, two students wrote letters to the editor of a Petersburg newspaper popular among students. Restating the well-established explanation, the first evoked the horror of student poverty, which he pointedly contrasted to Genrikh's principled struggle for knowledge and enlightenment and blamed on social apathy. His conclusion focused, however, on the irrelevance of students to the new society and even the death of the old *studenchestvo*: because they were no longer needed, he mourned, they were left to suffer in hunger, cold, and hopelessness. [52]

"If society relates to us with cold indifference, then it is acting fully logically," the second student retorted, "for with instinctive wisdom it feels in us an enemy, an enemy of that philistine spirit, which is the most characteristic trait of its spiritual physiognomy. And it is not mistaken. Do not forget, comrades, that this is the very same society in which [Vissarion] Belinskii died of hunger in complete isolation." [53] This student called upon his comrades to unite in a struggle against the philistinism and vulgarity (*meshchanstvo* and *poshlost'*) of society. In part, he had followed the logic of Nekrasov's poem quoted on the funeral wreath and at the beginning of this chapter, in which death is depicted as a liberation from the "unrelenting vulgarity" (*poshlost'*) of life. In seeking to resurrect the concept of the intelligentsia and *studenchestvo* as the antithesis of *meshchanstvo*, he identified the salvation of students in an active struggle against *poshlost'*. Yet he did not address a central question: did the suicides of Genrikh, Ogunlukh, and Levandovskaia represent a form of struggle and resistance, or defeat and victimization? Had the ideals of generations of students—and their last representatives in the persons of suicide victims—been buried in a graveyard, to take Levandovskaia's metaphor? Alongside the many faces of student poverty, the challenge of *poshlost'* was to become the second major theme within the epidemic of student suicide.

THE ETERNAL MASQUERADE

The "poverty of values" often had little relation to economic poverty. Indeed, the idea that it was simply "not worth it to live" *(ne stoit zhit', nechem zhit', nadoelo)* echoed increasingly often in both suicide letters and newspaper chronicles. Like destitution, disappointment would become a commonly acknowledged reason for student suicide. Newspapers were full of suicide letters ruminating on the meaningless of life:

> There are no sacred ideals in our daily life. [It is] sad, boring, and offensive [Nadezhda Dylova, 22, St. Petersburg Higher Women's Courses].[54]

> I am dying because I did not find the key to the solution of life. And it is simply not worth it to live like everyone else amidst the struggle for the trifles *[melochi]* of life. . . . Cognizance of one's powerlessness is not a sign of a weakness of mind or spirit [K. N. Grigor'ev, 27, Communications Institute].[55]

> I am tired and need to rest. I have endured an agonizing struggle between reason and feeling, and the former was victorious [Inna Poliakova, Moscow Higher Women's Courses].[56]

Sometimes the notes, such as the first one, implied that life was meaningless due to the absence of ideals in it, while others, such as the second one, pointed to a failed attempt to find a purpose in life. In asserting that reason rather than emotion had prompted her suicide, the third letter intimated a certain unreason in life itself. At the same time, its author likened death to sleep, as if it would provide an escape from reason. A common trait of these cases was the association of individual inadequacy (the inability to change the conditions of life) with moral strength (the desire not to be corrupted by life). Most also condemned not just contemporary social or political conditions but "life" as a whole. These suicides thus combined victimization with heroism, helplessness in the face of life with a principled determination to exit it.

Works of student fiction often grappled with similar issues. In his short story "Hollow," Iu. Golubai depicted the last hours of Alesha, a student who suffered from disappointment. "I am a cemetery, a walking cemetery," the hero ruminates. "My first deceased was faith. This death was hard, as if my father had died and left me an orphan. . . . Then the 'goal of life' died. That was also hard. Then an entire epidemic of death began. . . belief in science, art, socialist utopia, good and evil, justice. . . and now love. Only my body lives. And it wants death. It is tired of burying." [57] The central characteristic of both Alesha and his suicide is hollowness—the absence of meaning in his life and the absence of meaning in his death. Living had become impossible because the death of idealism had reduced life to mere bodily existence, and it was physical life which the bullet ended. In "Gloom (From Student Life)," D. Zherebkov likewise recounted the last hours of a student, who contemplates the contradiction between spiritual and animal life. In order to live, the hero decides, one must not think, yet then living is reduced to the "life of a dog" and the four walls of a kennel. In despair heightened by vodka, he hangs himself.[58]

In interpreting the new current of pessimism, students highlighted the role of the Revolution of 1905 in dismantling the common world view and community values of studenchestvo. One of the first articles on student suicide, which appeared in November 1906 in a student newspaper, explained several recent cases as the product of political reaction and violence and appealed to students to resist the "idol of death": "We are alive and young," it proclaimed, "We are mighty in the truth of our cause. . . . Before our eyes lies fog, the unclear outlines of our unknown future. But we must live—the people need us." [59] Such faith in both the "cause" and the collective "we" faded by the next year, when the student leader Aleksei Vilenkin conceded death's victory. Images of falling, loss, and decay governed his evaluation of students' mood just as they did suicide letters and short stories.[60] In retrospect, the meanings of these images seem both self-evident and obscure. On the one hand, they referred to the concrete failure of the 1905 Revolution to enact the desired political and educational reforms. On the other hand, they articulated a psychological loss of clarity, as the hero of a novel by Evgenii Chirikov so evocatively put it: "I did not lose the ideals with which as a youth I set upon my journey, but I lost the way, only the way." [61] Yet it remains to be explained what students really meant when they dismissed life as "boring," "a struggle for trifles."

"There are no guiding stars, no principles, no goal in life," students wrote, "there are no guiding lights." [62] The metaphor of "guiding lights" was originally formulated by the writer and activist Vladimir Korolenko, and it had been appropriated in 1903 by women medical students as a memorial to their comrade, whose failure to find them for herself, in their view, had led to her suicide. This case, discussed earlier in this chapter, offers an important parallel and contrast. Whereas the words of the suicide victim appear prescient from the point of view of 1910—she had contrasted the principles of justice and truth with the real "animal" nature of life—the pure faith of her comrades in the "guiding lights" belongs to a bygone age. These two conflicting perspectives were nonetheless central to the postrevolutionary suicide epidemic, because the metaphor of disappointment also built on the opposition of *bytie* (spiritual existence) to *byt* (everyday life) together with the concurrent critique of *poshlost'*. In 1903, the woman medical student had rejected the daily, meaningless grind of life, something that her politicized fellow students could not then grasp. An understanding of life based on the everyday (rather than on the historical unfolding of revolution) implies a conventional biographical plot: that is, in the case of a student, graduation, career, marriage, domestic life, and compromise (rather than self-education, consciousness, and principled struggle). For students after 1905, this opposition was played out on a temporal plane: the metaphors of decline all combine the idealization of a heroic past characterized by high ideals and common struggle *(bytie)* with the vilification of a prosaic present lacking any spiritual dimension *(byt)*.

This perspective is central, for example, to the interpretation of suicide advanced by the Moscow student T. L. Krivonosov. He opened his article with a panegyric to a past paradise, when students loved science and their university, when they studied for many years, preferring not to dive into the *"poshlost'* of worldly prose," and when they strove to make themselves into useful members of society. "Then students knew how to live," he reminisced, "[they] valued and loved their lives, and each of them knew and understood its meaning." In his view, the university had changed, and the typical student had a new slogan: "to finish with studies as soon as possible and to 'settle down' in life." In Krivonosov's view, the majority of students were now careerists, concerned only with arranging their personal advantage. While he acknowledged that such students could know "physical hunger," he insisted that "spiritual hunger" was the prerogative of a second type of student: the solitary ones *(odinokie)* who craved ideals and principles. "These students are the heirs to the glorious students of former years. . . the pitiful remains of the once glorious and healthy Russian *studenchestvo*." For Krivonosov, the principled rejection of *poshlost'*, which he defined through the *byt* phenomenon of careerism, thus characterized the heroic period of the *studenchestvo* and the current epidemic of student suicide. Though he likened suicide to a heroic act—a "cry of the soul" to the "indifferent street" and "apathetic crowd"—his solution to the epidemic looked backward. The debt that students owed to the victims was "to strive once again to ignite the bright flame of the active, principled and beautiful student life of the past." [63] In other words, to prevent suicide, it was necessary to combat *poshlost'* with the strength of common principle and a shot of nostalgia.

Despite differences in approach and conceptualization, many students advocated this solution. One article pointed out the contradiction of suicide as an answer to the absence of meaning in life. One need not vanquish life, he admonished, but only the absence of meaning. He imagined a future time, when "the wings of liberated thought [would make man] free and strong." Another argued that suicide was an attempt to remove the self from the conditions of life; the real task was to change these conditions: "We will develop in ourselves a glorious and true world view, so that we will not be the slaves but the creators of life, the gods of life." He hoped that science would provide the basis for this new world view. A third likened the current era to a long night and expressed optimism that morning would dawn. While each appealed to students to keep their faith and saw the solution in the development of a new world view, nobody had defined its contents.[64] One group of students actually organized a study group in order to search for new "guiding lights":

> In our days, in this dark epoch without principles, when it seems as if every spark of free thought is extinguished, when the majority of Russian youth are attracted to false values, when sport and physical development are ready to displace all ideals of spiritual life. . . we are founding the Circle of the Theory of Cognition. . . . We shall strive to unite the interested few only with ideas, the sincere aspiration to construct a scientifically based world view. . . . We do not need those who in twenty years will become philistines or fanatics. . . . We call only those who have not passed into the mire of everyday life, only those for whom an empty starry sky has more value than a muddy puddle full of fish.[65]

Another observer used a biological metaphor to reconceptualize the problem and defend the *studenchestvo*. Categorizing *poshlost'* as the trait of adults and idealism as that of youth, he argued that the struggle for principle would persist despite the inexorable corruption that followed graduation:

> It is often said that you [students] are now ardent champions of truth, you are firm defenders of justice and the downtrodden, but a little time passes—six or seven years—and you will enjoy a secure position, you will be surrounded by family, and. . . and all your knightly castles in the air will topple like a house of cards. . . . But this is natural! . . . What of it? The fact of the matter is that youth itself is not transient. . . . What does it matter if my soul begins to twist, if I bow to the idol of lies and avarice? We tire, others take our place. . . . Youth is eternal! [66]

In his view, the individual biological-biographical fate of students simply did not matter, for the supply of youth was constantly replenished. Yet this optimistic assessment of youth's heroic idealism sidestepped the problem of a new world view by stressing the inevitable process of compromise (figure 7-1).

The metaphor of aging proved to be double-edged. The writer Gorkii argued that unnamed modernist writers had poisoned the young generation with pre-

FIGURE 7.1 "Why the Russian Man is Apathetic" depicts the life cycle of the intelligentsia and provides a good illustration of students' conception of everyday life. Each pair depicts the stages of aspiration and reality: the child meeting the heroes of James Fenimore Cooper and Jules Verne—chased away by the school teacher; the gymnasium student meeting Chernyshevskii, Belinskii, and Pisarev—banished by the classics; the student meeting Marx and Lasalle—attacked by the policeman; the university graduate now free to read what he wants but beaten down by everyday life—wife, children, and the beginning of the cycle all over again. *Satirikon* no. 43 (1910). (Courtesy University of Helsinki Slavonic Library)

mature "age," leading to pessimism and suicide. "It was not so long ago that we were enraptured with [youth's] heroism, the spring-like beauty of its soul," he reminisced. "Over the last years [however,] youth have lived in a sickly atmosphere, poisoned by the venom of all kinds of doubt [and] saturated by the odor of death—rotting and putrid." According to Gorkii, "today's 'teacher of life' " (that is, the writer), was wrongly concerned with "individual freedom" and the mysteries of existence, rather than with the truly fundamental question, "Where do we go? *[Kuda idti?]*." For him, the choice was practical and political. One supported either socialist democracy or bourgeois capitalism. Gorkii called upon youth to return to the classics—Pushkin, Turgenev, Chekhov—to the "literature of younger *bogatyri*." [67]

Gorkii's solution also looked to an idealized past, when all of Russia's youth had banded together in a heroic struggle, or so it seemed, from the point of view of 1912. While some students continued to find vitality in the traditional heroes of the Russian intelligentsia, others found it difficult to glue the broken idols back together. Moreover, the role of modernism was hardly clear-cut: traces of modern writers are just as evident in the articles denouncing suicide as in the notes of suicide victims. Indeed, Gorkii had simply blamed suicide on the modernists' rejection of the didactic role of literature formulated in the 1860s (and now defended by Gorkii himself) but did not address the dynamics of students' disillusionment. As one critic pointed out, Gorkii had appealed to students to pick up their old banner but had neglected to give them an answer to the questions raised by modern literature and philosophy.[68] Nostalgia was his remedy, but in the eyes of this critic, hardly a sufficient one.

In 1912, Dr. Gordon and the Society for the Preservation of the People's Health attempted a more "scientific" approach to the problem. Just as earlier surveys had probed the political, economic, and sexual lives of student youth, a new survey was conducted in the hope of gauging their mood. The response was weaker than hoped: although 20,000 questionnaires had been distributed to men and women students across St. Petersburg, only 2,118 were returned. While this poor showing prevented the authors of the study from making definitive conclusions (and further highlighted students' boredom), Dr. E. P. Radin announced the results in 1913: 42.5% of respondents were suffering from disappointment and a high percentage had contemplated suicide. Radin identified two primary causes, what he termed "everyday" *(bytovye)* factors (such as poverty) and sociopolitical factors, and five archetypes: in declining order of frequency, disappointment in oneself; in life; in people; in the ideals of truth, good, and justice; and in beauty.[69]

Radin's conclusion was nonetheless optimistic. The various forms of suicide and pessimism shared a common cause, he asserted, for they were the temporary by-products of a still incomplete social transformation occurring in Russia: traditional categories of social identity based on birth were being replaced by those based on education, profession, and economic relations. Although the contemporary epoch was witnessing the creation of a new type of critically thinking individual, the arbitrary governance of the state together with the remnants of the old order in the school and the family were hindering his development and leading to suicide. To assist the birth of this new person and future citizen, Radin called for school reform, the treatment of the pupil with respect, the inculcation of moral discipline, and improved physical hygiene.[70] He defended a progressive vision. Students' pessimism was a product of the decrepit autocratic order.

Yet Radin's book leaves a more ambiguous impression, because he amassed not abstract statistical analyses but scores of extended quotations from the questionnaires, "the confession of youth" *(ispoved' molodezhi),* as he called them. Although Radin meant to document his thesis, the series of anonymous observations undermines the clarity of his vision. Those who were not disappointed, for example, often cited their low expectations as the reason. While few admitted to being a much-maligned "careerist," equally few enjoyed the security of world view provided by ideology or professional aspirations. The dominant voice was inevitably melancholy, as one *kursistka* stated: "I do not know whether it is honorable to live in such dark conditions, cognizant of one's powerlessness—or at once to end [it all]." [71] One meets throughout a profound dismay at the disjunction between words and action, ideals and reality, and the unending *poshlost'* of life itself:

> The entire world seems to me like some kind of masquerade. All around move living beings, perhaps nice ones [friends and family], but each of them, each without exception is in a mask, loathsomely whining in another's voice, loathsomely gesticulating with another's hands, loathsomely responding with another's soul—[they all] rush about with mouths stuffed with beautiful words about right, good and truth, beauty and justice. . . . And when one sees this, when one feels [the monotony], one wants to run and run. . . . Only there is no salvation. . . . The entire world, each corner of the provinces celebrates the eternal banal masquerade. . . . The masks are changed, the costumes are changed—and the ball continues without pause.[72]

Central to the liberal project was the reorganization of daily life—the reform of schools, families, hygiene—and it was daily life that students feared most of all in their confrontation with *poshlost'.*

The crisis of *studenchestvo* was, however, a crisis of the collective; only in particular cases was it a crisis of the individual as well. A tiny minority of students did commit suicide, and the particular experiences of disappointment inevitably evade the historian. Yet its motifs recur. Intending to close his study on a positive note with an appeal to students to choose life over death, Radin selected a quotation that actually highlighted the ambiguity inherent in suicide. A student recounted how he had bummed around Western Europe after 1905, earning his keep as a self-taught artist, and in this way had recovered his mental stability. He had appealed to others, who were also tormented by the grey "every-dayness" *(povsednevnost')* of life, to change their pattern, to move, to travel, to exit from themselves but not from life. "Search for the salvation of a bad life in life," he advocated, "only in a different key." [73] While his proposal was certainly positive and productive, he had advocated the escape from everyday life as the only solution.

The process by which a person decides to end his or her life is not accessible to the historian. Indeed, suicide is peculiar to mankind yet remains one of the great unknowns of human behavior. As the conscious decision to end one's self-consciousness, it both defines and subverts what it means to be human. Yet suicide is also a historical and public act. Its social meanings change over time and from place to place, as do its rates, methods, motivations, legal consequences, and interpretations. This chapter has examined the social meanings of suicide in a particular time and place and for a particular group of people. Rather than attempting to explain the phenomenon of suicide, it has focused on several conventions of expression that transgressed generic boundaries, appearing in short stories, medical studies, feuilletons, letters to the editor, and suicide letters. While the tracing of associations and metaphors can hardly resolve the unanswered question of suicide, it can illuminate its cultural landscape.

The history of student suicide in the early twentieth century falls into two general periods separated and defined by the Revolution of 1905. In the first period, the suicide of students was largely appropriated into the practices of the student movement. Through hagiography and the protest memorial or funeral, student radicals likened the dead to martyrs who had fallen in a battle with despotism. Their protests fulfilled three broad functions: to honor the comrade, to demonstrate the transfer of the revolutionary banner to another generation of fighters, and to affirm the endurance of the struggle. Although some students limited their participation to the first function, suicide resonated as a political act in which the private circumstances were less important than the public story. In the period following the 1905 Revolution, student suicide continued to draw on its heroic traditions, but it lacked a clear political lesson or, indeed, a master plot. As competing voices sought to define its real meaning, it became an object of dispute.

Suicide seemed to assume a new mass character right at the height of the revolutionary drama, and this politicized context helped to shape new interpretive strategies. Many psychiatrists and statisticians argued that the violence of revolution and later reaction had disrupted the health of Russian society as a whole, and that this disruption had led, in turn, to epidemic levels of suicide, psychosis, and crime. In advancing this notion of the pathogenic state, they claimed civic authority for themselves as the specialists best qualified to minister to the public health, broadly defined. As the prospect of political reform waned, their proposed cure focused on the reorganization of such social institutions as the school and the family, which, in their view, remained indelibly stamped by the old regime. This interpretation of suicide stands in the tradition of heroic suicide. In the new context, the state was pathogenic in addition to despotic, the victim was society rather than an individual, and the symptom was the suicide rate. Statistics inevitably drew attention to the social environment of suicide, however, and this attention was amplified in the new era of mass journalism. Indeed, the suicide of young people called into question the ability of specialists to heal society.

Two primary conventions governed the discussion of suicide in the press. The first accented the act of unveiling the truth of suicide. According to this model, suicide presented a psychological or sociological riddle which the journalist, the specialist, or the private citizen solves as a civic duty and a civic lesson. The second convention treated suicide as an allegory—the journey of the student to the city in search of enlightenment, which ends, however, in poverty, disappointment, and death. In both representations, student suicide came to articulate a wide range of social fears and political expectations. The poverty that seemed so clearly to be a factor in many cases itself became a powerful metaphor for the conditions of life after 1905. It implicated the government, which set tuition costs high and suppressed student mutual-aid organizations; it implicated society, which was unable or unwilling to care for its children; and it implicated a poverty of principles, which permeated not only state and society but also *studenchestvo*. As an allegory for Russia's experience, the story of student suicide likewise proved flexible. For some it exemplified the destructive force of revolution; for others, the suppression of culture and progress. Or had students simply renounced the principles of mutual aid, self-education, and service developed by their forebears, in favor of bourgeois individualism, personal pleasure, and careerism? Did suicide then evidence the decadence and decline of *studenchestvo* itself?

The words and actions of students compose a complex and contradictory tale. Many suicide notes did not, after all, express disappointment in ideals themselves but rather in the failure to translate them into life. Such suicides constructed death as the only honorable path, as an affirmation, not a denial, of principle. Their indictment of the spiritual poverty of *studenchestvo*, moreover, actually reinforced students' sense of belonging to a collective. The rediscovery of the protest memorial thus challenges any one-sided image of disintegration and decay. Yet the new memorials lacked the clear message of their predecessors and illustrate the difficulties students had in defining the collectivity they so clearly felt. The suicide was no longer a hero, who had fallen in a heroic battle with autocracy, but an individual, who had resisted life's corruption. If the sacrifice was a call to arms, who was the enemy: state or society? autocracy or bourgeoisie? Suicide did not have a clear story to tell.

CHAPTER EIGHT

Radicalism Reborn?

Students in Protest, War, and Revolution

We deeply believe that our *studenchestvo* has not fundamentally changed. Conditions have changed, the mood has changed, but not our convictions.

—*Proclamation of the Union of United Leftist Students, 1913*

Two years after the humiliating collapse of the 1908 strike, amid the surge of youth suicide, student protest again swept through Russia, only this time it led to the devastation of the universities and thousands of arrests. Beginning with a series of street demonstrations following the death of Lev Tolstoi in November 1910 and culminating in the mass resignation of Moscow professors in February 1911, these protests had far-reaching political consequences. The specter of renewed disorder in the universities contributed to a broad political crisis in the Duma, including the splintering of the Octobrist party and the growing political hegemony of the extreme right. It also underscored the contradictions of Russian liberalism, suspended in an untenable position between the revolutionary left and the authoritarian state.[1] From the perspective of many students, however, the protests marked the recovery of their "glorious traditions" by the "democratic" part of *studenchestvo,* the spiritual heir to the heroic generations of the past.

The reasons for this resurgence are complex. Most important, the general conditions that had led to the emergence of a student movement in the first place remained unaltered. Despite the efforts of professors to establish academic autonomy, the government continued to meddle in educational matters and to suppress student organizations. In interpreting this situation, students drew on their traditional vilification of "liberal compromise" and the concomitant advocacy of "active struggle" to condemn both the ineffectual resistance of the professoriate and the repressions of the state. This strategy built on the long-entrenched ideal of *studenchestvo* as the antithesis of bourgeois philistinism but made no pretense to the universality—to the inclusion of all students under its banner—that had been so important to the movement before 1905.

Although the new wave of protest thus demonstrated that scenarios depicting the decline and fall of *studenchestvo* into a bourgeois corporation along the German model had been premature, students as a collective did not develop a new story line. While the narrative of consciousness continued to be relevant to individual students seeking to understand their own experience of politicization, the absence of a collective story stamps the student movement in the years leading up to 1917. Many students clearly felt a sense of community binding them to their comrades and to the mythologized *studenchestvo* of past decades, but they could not identify a transparent basis for this community. As the social task of earlier years faded into nostalgia, student protest acquired an increasingly ritualized character.

AUTONOMY IN ASHES

Despite the absence of sustained nationwide protest, the two years between 1908 and 1910 witnessed a number of conflicts in academic centers across the country. Although many of these incidents concerned academic or corporate issues, others had an openly political agenda. Indeed, after the 1908 debacle, students rarely hesitated to acknowledge the political ramifications of their actions. In 1909, the protest of fifteen hundred Petersburg students against the execution of a Spanish anarchist by his government led to a diplomatic incident, the entrance of police into university buildings, and increased tension between students and professors.[2] In 1910, the current of unrest deepened. Nationwide protests erupted that spring over Purishkevich's attacks on the sexual degeneracy of students, and the death that fall of S. A. Muromtsev, the chairman of the First Duma, prompted a round of unauthorized memorial services.[3]

These incidents helped to engender and maintain a politicized atmosphere in the student community at large. Focusing much of their dissatisfaction on "liberal" professors, even calling them "lackeys of the state," student leaders increasingly advocated an overtly political and activist strategy predicated on an opposition to everything liberal. The submission of a new university charter to the State Duma in the spring of 1910 provided a case in point. Defining the universities as state institutions, the draft charter asserted the preeminent right of the state to defend its interests over the interests of scholarship or education. The assault against students was particularly sharp, with proposals advanced to raise tuition, cut financial aid, and prohibit extracurricular meetings. Despite the vocal and ultimately successful opposition of Duma moderates, students greeted the proposal as evidence that the conciliatory tactics advocated by professors had failed to check the aspirations of the state or to produce substantive positive results.[4]

After their initial disappointment with the 1908 strike, many students argued that its failure showed the irrelevance not of student protest but of limited academic protest. Articles in the student press pointed out that the goal of academic autonomy required the establishment of democracy in the country at large. On this basis, students were urged to unite in a coalition of democratic classes and parties to struggle for a combined academic and political transformation. This conception of "democracy" avoided the issue of class conflict by defining *studenchestvo* as an ethical group. It was even an "intellectual proletariat," one student asserted, because its impetuous youth, "Don Quixote–like heroism," and relative poverty placed it "at the extreme left of the bourgeois camp, now and then even drawing it closer to the proletariat." [5]

The death of Lev Tolstoi on November 7 ignited a new blaze of protest. Although most educated Russians admired Tolstoi as a great author and revered him as a principled fighter for his beliefs (whether or not they accepted his later religious teachings), he possessed special significance for students. Over the years, he had welcomed many students to his estate at Iasnaia Poliana and dedicated particular attention to the problems and aspirations of student youth. He had, moreover, openly praised the nonviolent methods and community values of the student movement of 1899 and later. For these reasons, students gathered across the country on November 8 to mourn the great writer and to choose delegations to attend the funeral at Iasnaia Poliana.[6]

Resolving to organize a memorial to the great "fighter for the embodiment [*voploshchenie*] of truth and justice," men and women students assembled that day at St. Petersburg University. The memorial proved to be a week of street demonstrations of a size not seen since 1905. Following a requiem service on November 9 at the Armenian Church in central St. Petersburg, a group of students sang the hymn "Eternal Memory" and tried to hold a demonstration at the nearby Kazan Cathedral. Throughout that afternoon, crowds congregating on Nevskii Prospect were disbanded by police. Without apparent coordination, the protests adopted one of Tolstoi's long-held causes, opposition to the death penalty, with a motto drawn from one of his articles, "We cannot be silent." Black flags proclaiming "Down with the Death Penalty" were even hoisted at the Psychoneurological Institute. Concerned about the quick growth of disorders, police entered the university on November 12 to the whistles and jeers of students and the dismay of professors. Believing their demonstrations to mark a general upsurge of political activism, students appealed to political parties to rally workers and began to refer to the active participation of the proletariat. Nothing of the sort occurred. Workers did not join the protests, nor were the major parties prepared to organize outside support for these unruly demonstrations.[7]

Though the protests subsided by the middle of the month, the mood was only superficially calm, because many students still faced short arrests and fines. When news of the maltreatment of political prisoners and the suicide of one reached St. Petersburg in late November, unrest bubbled back to the surface. Although street demonstrations were not held, police disrupted meetings at the Bestuzhev Courses, the university, and the Polytechnic Institute. Three-day strikes in honor of the political prisoners were held across St. Petersburg and observed as well in Moscow, Kharkov, and Kazan.[8] As the semester drew to a close, many students had been arrested, and calls for their immediate release evoked the principles of comradely solidarity. Before students dispersed for the winter holidays, a coalition committee was formed in St. Petersburg to lead renewed protest during the spring semester.[9]

The mood was equally confrontational in official spheres. For many conservatives, street demonstrations were a clear and loathsome sign of social revolution and, as such, mandated severe and uncompromising measures. With fears of renewed disorder guiding the formulation of policy, a January circular raised the stakes. Students were prohibited from meeting within educational institutions except in a supervised academic setting. Should this regulation be violated, the police had the right to enter the premises of the institution without permission from academic authorities, and any student cited would be immediately suspended. The new rules were a frontal assault on students' right to organize; they would effectively suppress mutual-aid societies and other groups. The news that students had been summarily exiled for their participation in the fall's demonstrations only inflamed the situation.[10]

Although the circular also infringed on the right of faculty to administer the university and was, therefore, a direct assault on academic autonomy, professors and students perceived little commonality in their separate predicaments.[11] While individual professors and many faculty councils formally registered their objections with the Ministry of Education, they were careful to distinguish their dissent from students' protests. The academic committee of the Technological Institute, for example, criticized the rules for reducing the authority of the director and the professoriate and for giving the director police functions. They were opposed because they violated academic autonomy and professorial authority, but not because they conflicted with constitutional norms.[12] While it would be a mistake to discount the genuine sympathy many professors had for their students, the fact remains that professors had petitioned the government for redress of grievances that were a direct consequence of government policy. By the middle of January, professors and the district curator were describing unrest as almost inevitable.[13]

When the new semester began in late January, the citywide Coalition Committee issued an appeal for an active semester-long strike, and on January 26, a series of strike resolutions were passed throughout the city. The quick intervention of police at the first signs of unrest resulted in further arrests, which propelled the movement. In referendums, the Women's Courses joined the strike with a vote of 2,329 to 1,174, whereas the Technological Institute voted not to strike. This decision was overturned when hundreds of university students were arrested. The strike soon spread across the country. As had often been the case before 1905, police tactics fostered student solidarity and escalated the confrontations. Moreover, students spoke openly of the political repercussions of their demands and universalized their grievances as violations of civil liberties, the rule of law, and human rights. Though limiting their demands to such apparently academic goals as the democratization of education and university autonomy, students understood their program as political in nature.[14]

In the wake of the strike votes, professors made a last minute attempt to dissuade students from striking. Asserting that scholarship and enlightenment were inherently forces of progress, no matter the policies of the government, the faculty council of St. Petersburg University blamed the "crude violence" of students for the crisis. The defense of academic autonomy was the task of professors, not students, the council stressed. Professors at the Bestuzhev Courses likewise described the strike as "harmful to the culture of the country," and expressed their hope that "in this difficult moment, students will find the necessary depth of understanding and moral feeling to save the courses from grave danger." [15]

Such appeals actually helped to shift the focal point of students' anger from the government as such to a demonized liberal professoriate. Liberal compromise, students argued, was equally to blame for the political degeneration of the last five years. As the protests intensified over the next week, students disrupted lectures with songs, whistles, political debate, and stink bombs. Strikers focused much of their disruption on popular professors, apparently in the hope of convincing them not to lecture. Nevertheless, such eminent liberal scholars as M. Ia. Pergament and L. I. Petrazhitskii asserted that it was their duty to continue teaching and consequently bore the brunt of the assault. The movement culminated on January 31, when 392 students were arrested inside the university. Despite the police stationed throughout educational institutions and the paucity of students in attendance, most professors continued to deliver their lectures. For student activists, this act symbolized the moral bankruptcy of a professoriate which claimed to defend the autonomy and sanctity of scholarship but was willing to lecture under police guard.

The experience of other educational institutions across St. Petersburg and the country was similar. At the first sign of disorder, police entered academic buildings, occupied strategic points, and escorted professors to their lectures. Although professors strenuously objected to these conditions, they blamed the government and the strikers equally, and most continued to lecture. With students being arrested, suspended, and expelled in unprecedented numbers, those institutions that had been slow to join the strike quickly declared their solidarity. In most schools, student opinion split into three groups. On the two extremes were those who actively supported the strike and a small but militant group on the far right that actively opposed it. The majority, angry at the restrictions of student organizations and sympathetic to the principle of solidarity, stood somewhere in the middle.[16]

The tactics of professors backfired for several reasons. First, the tremendous number of police stationed inside the schools (535 officers in St. Petersburg University alone—approximately one for every sixteen registered students), combined with the numerous arrests, counteracted any possibility of "moral persuasion." Second, the authority of the professoriate had been damaged by the experiences of recent years. In the eyes of students, the reforms of the revolutionary era had been progressively overturned, and each time faculty members had enjoined students to respect the sanctity of scholarship by not protesting, by allowing the professoriate to fight for autonomy instead. And finally, professors erroneously assumed that students shared an understanding of the university as an institution devoted to scholarship. In the eyes of many students, however, the restrictions on admissions and curriculum, the assault on student institutions, and the repression of free speech and assembly were destroying the university as they envisioned it.

This conflict formed the topic of an "Open Letter to Professors" from the university's Coalition Committee that sought to explain why students had rejected the counsels of their elders.[17] The story begins with the events of the previous fall:

> [When Tolstoi died] our demonstrations against the death penalty were the best wreaths we could lay at the grave of the great man, and you, our professors, were not with us on the streets. But you had condemned the death penalty in your lectures, and we wanted to believe that you sympathized with us. . . . And when you did not join the chorus of protest [against prison conditions] we still thought. . . that you were proud of us in your heart. . . . But gentlemen, people with real conviction do not behave in this manner!

Arguing that the moral personality was constructed in the daily struggle to enact principle into life, these students dismissed the "struggles" of their professors as representing a superficial and purely verbal commitment. Anger against the "hypocrisy" of liberal professors was particularly potent:

> Remember how you promised to take the defense of autonomy upon yourselves during the 1908 strike? Where is this defense? You have not refused to deliver your lectures in the presence of police. . . . The provocation and effrontery of the liberal-professor, Mr. Pergament, who, with a proudly raised head and disdainful smile, was escorted to lectures under a police guard, cost the *studenchestvo* dearly with 172 students arrested for obstructions. Professor Ivanovskii, who is not a liberal, has more right to deliver his lectures.

By agreeing to teach in such conditions, students argued, professors had lost their claim to the moral high ground. The letter concluded:

> If you will not fight for autonomy, if you have become used to the atmosphere of political lawlessness *[bezpravie]*, if you cannot show us other methods of struggle, then you do not have the right to interfere in our struggle for the political freedom of the country and for the autonomy of the higher school; and you do not have the least right to speak about your defense of "the eternal and immutable interests of scholarship." You may choose not to be with us, but you do not have the right to be against us.

This conflict reflected much more than a simple difference in tactics, for it exposed the age-old conflict between radical sons and liberal fathers.[18] Yet students also formulated their protest as a symbolic act: this time, the children intended to destroy what they perceived as the facade of cultural and political progress in Russia since 1905.

In many respects they succeeded. The protests led to the mass resignation of ninety-nine faculty members, including twenty-five full professors, from Moscow University. The destruction *(razgrom)* of the university, as it was called, began when Rector A. A. Manuilov and two of his assistants resigned their administrative positions in protest against the actions of police and the consequent "dual power" in the academy. Considering such behavior unacceptable for state employees, the Ministry of Education dismissed them from their academic posts as well. When the government refused to reinstate these respected scholars, other faculty members submitted their resignations—which were accepted. This demonstration of collegial solidarity was not intended to express sympathy for students, quite the opposite. The letters of resignation cited neither students' rights nor the mass arrests but only the violation of autonomy by the arbitrary dismissal of three professors and the unwanted presence of police in the academy. Students were blamed for calling the strike and provoking the police response.[19]

Students also suffered unprecedented losses. Over the course of the semester-long strike, 6,233 students were expelled or suspended around the country. By March, the daily number of students in attendance at St. Petersburg University fluctuated between eight hundred and thirteen hundred, or approximately 10–15% of total enrollment. About the same number of students (1,201) had been expelled or suspended. At the Women's Courses, many lectures were cancelled during March due to a full boycott, and those that did take place were delivered to less than twenty students. At the Women's Medical Institute, the strike was so successful that the Ministry of Education ordered the reopening of the institute and the expulsion of any student who did not attend classes. Despite the protest of the institute's director, who pointed out that most students had left St. Petersburg, all but twenty-four students were expelled and forced to reapply individually. Using this opportunity to reinstate the Jewish quota, the Ministry refused to readmit thirty-five out of seventy-three Jewish students, some of whom were in their final year of study.[20]

The university crisis of 1911 exposed tremendous fissures within Russia's educated society. The struggle between an authoritarian state and radical students placed moderate and liberal figures in an untenable position, unable either to mediate between the two extremes or to defend academic autonomy with legal methods. In a scathing attack on both the left and the right, Aleksandr Izgoev defended the liberal vision of a politically neutral university dedicated to "pure science." There were not two powers in the current political struggle, he argued, but three: the state, the revolution, and the "stratum of culture." Condemning those who viewed the university as a site of political struggle, Izgoev described its purpose as the education of public figures and the advancement of the cultural level of the nation, two preconditions for the creation of a democratic polity. Even in times of harsh repression, he argued, the university represented the most important hearth of culture, and student protest constituted a major hindrance to cultural progress. Professors were the true "masters" of the academy, Izgoev asserted, and the cause of students' "anticultural" attitude toward the university lay in their demand for equality with faculty. Academic autonomy required the submission of youth to their elders.[21]

Nikolai Iordanskii, the radical publicist who had been a student leader in 1899, also described the crisis in higher education as a conflict between fathers and children, but instead indicted Russian liberalism. In the aftermath of the 1905 Revolution, he argued, liberals (and in particular professors) believed that Russia had entered the path of Western constitutional development, but the events of 1911 had exposed the "tragedy of the liberal soul." Indeed, he noted, liberals were behaving as if a constitutional monarchy had actually been established in 1905, and on that basis they denied the legitimacy of students' political critique. "The question is not whether students occupy themselves with politics," Iordanskii asserted, "but whether after October 17, 1905, Russian citizens, and that includes students, have the right to participate in the political life of their country." Since liberal methods had failed to reverse the restrictions placed on independent political life in Russia, Iordanskii expressed his fundamental doubts that peaceful cultural development would lead to real political change.[22]

The importance of the "fathers and children" imagery was not lost on students. By celebrating the heroism of the strike with its many martyrs, students rejected a moderate path in favor of struggle for its own sake. The *studenchestvo* had once again "raised its voice in defense of human dignity."[23] Yet, as Izgoev had also pointed out, the strike was really only a form of "spiritual suicide." With their protest and sacrifices, students hoped only to reveal the complicity of the state and the duplicity of the professoriate. The strike was a rejection of everyday life in the academy. But symbolic suicide was hardly a more effective tactic of political change than liberal compromise. Though the 1911 movement marked the reemergence of student protest, it also demonstrated the depth of political stalemate in Russia. The path of reform had stumbled on the intransigence of the government and the seductive glory of heroism.

SCIENCE UNDER GUARD

Between 1911 and 1914, student protest became a recurring phenomenon in academic life. This movement took two dominant forms: symbolic one-day strikes and classroom protests. Citing ethical principles associated with the development of democratic social and political structures in Russia as a whole, students consistently described their protests as acts of political resistance against the police state and liberal compromise. Despite the limited scope and importance of student protest in these years, the government feared a repetition of 1910–1911 and thus acted with unprecedented force. By 1912, it had become typical for hundreds of police officers to be stationed at quick notice inside educational institutions. This practice would become even more common after 1914. In response, students began to stage short five-minute "flying meetings" *(letuchie skhodki)* with prepared resolutions. Although repression helped to maintain the politicized attitudes of students, it also prevented the development of a larger and more coordinated movement.

Symbolic protests occurred at least once every semester. On the first anniversary of the death of Lev Tolstoi, students across the country called a one-day strike in memory of both the writer and the protests of the previous year. For the next five years, November 7 was observed with either a strike or a memorial service. The shooting of workers at the Lena Goldfields in March 1912 also provoked both strikes and annual memorials, but relatively few students participated in street demonstrations.[24] While solidarity strikes indicated the ongoing desire among students to participate in the political life of their country, their circumscribed parameters also highlighted the limits of the movement. Students advanced political goals as the only means to achieve academic autonomy but then simply returned to their studies after each strike.

Student protest can be best understood in these years as one element of public opinion. The response of students to the most notorious controversy of this period, the 1913 trial of Mendel Beilis, a Jewish man accused of the ritual murder of an Orthodox child, is a case in point.[25] Protests occurred throughout that fall. Bestuzhev students sent a telegram to the defense team expressing their hope that the "defenders of truth" would "disperse the darkness of the blood slander." In condemning "the brazen slander of the Jewish people," students at St. Petersburg University asserted that the Beilis trial was "a device used by the government to inflame national enmity and to weaken the revolutionary spirit of the democratic masses." Professor D. P. Kosorotov, who had testified as an expert witness for the prosecution, was greeted on his return by mass protests of students. This pattern was repeated across the country, as students joined many other groups in denouncing the trial under the banner of democracy and human rights.[26]

Throughout 1912 and 1913, state interference in academic affairs was likewise met by prolonged and politicized unrest. When the government asserted its right to control faculty appointment by transferring popular professors to provincial universities and known conservatives to St. Petersburg, students protested the "outrage against the elementary rights of the higher school," likened the university to a police station, and called for a boycott of the appointed professors that even student Kadets approved. Throughout the spring semester of 1912, the lectures of two appointed professors, P. P. Migulin and V. A. Udintsev, were disrupted and often canceled, and those that did take place required police escorts to the auditoriums and guards within them.[27] The following fall, heckling continued in an environment of new appointments, the arrest of students, and an increased police presence which often included the "occupation" of the main corridor and staircases in addition to auditoriums. Students also took the opportunity to censure what they considered the "morally unscrupulous" decision of professors to tolerate their appointed colleagues. Once again, students and professors did not work together. While the police measures antagonized both parties, their tactical responses differed radically. Such respected professors as M. Ia. Pergament and D. D. Grimm resigned rather than submit to their arbitrary transfer to Iurev and Kharkov, respectively, but most professors registered their dissatisfaction bureaucratically. These confrontations once again underscored the political fragmentation of Russian society despite a common estrangement from the government.[28]

Though some students did compare the upsurge of activism to the newly energized workers' movement, the two groups never came together as they had in 1905. Party factions called on students to join the struggle of the people, but they had lost interest in student politics, quite rightly seeing it as an amorphous force resisting outside direction. Their proclamations were intended to attract individual students to their cause, rather than to politicize students as a group.[29] A short-lived Bolshevik-leaning student newspaper likewise called on "democratic" students to rally to Marxism as the only alternative to the petty-bourgeois decline of previous years. By encompassing every non-Marxist movement or interest in this "decline," however, this paper hardly aspired to be a force of unity.[30]

Instead, this role was assumed by various nonparty groups, which proposed to organize "democratic" students under the banner of general liberation: a free university in a free country. The proclamations of these groups typically condemned "scholasticism" and party polemics as destructive to the interests of democracy.[31] By the spring of 1913, an umbrella organization called the Union of United Leftist Students had formed, which advocated political means to achieve academic autonomy.[32] Other groups attempted to construct an infrastructure that would unite student economic organizations. Their goal was to improve students' economic situations and to promote spiritual unity, by which they meant to reunify the *studenchestvo* on the basis of such principles as self-help and solidarity. While some propagandized the cooperative movement, others worked to establish a legal basis for student economic organization, though with only limited success, given continued police interference.[33]

These currents found expression in new student newspapers, which were experiencing a revival after the repressions of 1911. The two most important publications were St. Petersburg's *Student Years* and Moscow's *The Student Cause,* both of which had a general democratic orientation (with the Moscow paper focusing more on economic issues). Founded in 1913, *Student Years* was run by an editorial board composed of delegates from most of St. Petersburg's higher schools. Although it strived to combine all "progressive" currents, the participation of Kadets was rejected by all the socialist groups, and the SDs refused to cooperate with the SRs. Nevertheless, its first issue evoked the slogan of 1905 in formulating its goal: "The problem of the century is the democratization of the system of life. In the sphere of education, this idea is expressed in the slogan 'the higher school for the people.' The democratic *studenchestvo* must enact this slogan into life." Despite the early disputes, *Student Years* survived until the wartime censor closed it down in 1915.[34]

Alongside the many signs of vitality, however, were reminders of the internal weakness of the new student movement. These flaws were exposed in the largest protests of this period, the "militarization" of the St. Petersburg Military-Medical Academy in the spring of 1913. As a medical school in the jurisdiction of the Ministry of War, the academy served a dual function: the education of military doctors and of doctors in general. Students who received scholarships were required to serve in the army. Conditions of study began to change, however, in November 1912. Henceforth, academy students were obligated to salute all officers, not just generals, as had previously been the practice. Resolving to reject this new regulation, students called a three-day protest strike. By February 1913, however, approximately thirty students had been punished for refusing to salute, and one student had even been wounded by an officer after he too had refused. In early March, another violent confrontation led students at the academy to declare a strike of indefinite length.[35]

At this point, a bombshell landed: a new charter was announced, which transformed the academy into a full military institution with its students subject to military discipline and duty. The curriculum was changed in order to expand offerings in military medicine and eliminate such civilian specializations as women's and children's medicine. Protests in support of the medical students spread across the country, with a total of forty-three educational institutions holding short strikes. After a heated debate, students at the Women's Medical Institute voted to allow their male comrades who had been forced to leave the academy to finish their education at the institute. Sympathy spread in society as well, with the St. Petersburg city government trying to raise money to help the affected students. Nevertheless, by the end of March, 432 of 764 students had returned to the academy under the new conditions, and the protests died down.[36]

Students depicted these protests as part of their larger struggle in defense of science. The strike resolution at St. Petersburg University, for example, condemned the "crude violence" of the state and its aspiration to transform "one of the most fertile grounds of science" into a "military barracks." [37] Convinced that the decrees constituted an attempt to convert students into soldiers, many students saw the specific events at the academy as emblematic of a broader goal to master the *studenchestvo*. Employing a disease metaphor, one medical student thus depicted the history of the academy in terms of the steady encroachment of the military principle (sickness) over the scientific ideal (health). Even as he hesitated to predict the final winner, he implied that both the professoriate and the *studenchestvo* were infected by diseases, whose only cure was active struggle.[38]

The ambiguous meaning of the protests found its symbol in the April suicide of a medical student, Veniamin Glotov. Although his suicide was depicted as an act of resistance, former students of the academy adopted the symbolism of death by calling themselves "the departed" *(ukhodnye)*. Note the language in this graveside speech:

> The students who have departed from the Academy have chosen me to say a final farewell to our dear comrade. . . . Your sensitive conscience did not allow compromise and impelled you to the defense of the *studenchestvo* and the Academy. With your death, you affirmed our righteous cause, the cause of struggle for the freedom of science. . . . Be at peace in your eternal sleep, dear comrade. . . . Your name will join those of other glorious student names, fighters who perished for the dignity of man. Sleep in peace; may the earth above you be lighter than was living and studying in rightless Russia.[39]

Student Years likewise commemorated this martyrdom to the despotic state with a black-rimmed photograph of Glotov accompanied by the message: "Veniamin Glotov has perished. . . . Overwhelmed by the weight of compromise, the dirt of life, and the purity of conscience, he fell. He could not endure a lie yet did not have the strength to struggle against it." It concluded with the ambiguous words, "Rest in Peace. . . we will still follow you" *(my eshche priidem k tebe)*.[40]

Glotov's suicide was rich with imagery—the death of conscience for continuing students, the death of an academy serving science, and the metaphoric death of the "departed comrades." Real students had been purged from the hearth of science, protest had failed to save the academy, and most students had returned to their studies. Yet the symbolic character of the strikes and the evocative power of suicide imagery underlined students' real powerlessness. Indeed, by casting suicide as an act embodying both the fall and the salvation, students affirmed martyrdom, in its most literal form, as their primary model of political behavior. The liberal leader I. V. Gessen argued that the suicide served as "a symbolic expression of the fall in mood" among students.[41] Apparently he was right: the opposition to the militarization of the academy was the last major student protest until 1917.

The government had learned an important lesson in 1911. To combat disorder, it was necessary to place science under police guard. These new realities were reflected in one student publication, which printed a "dictionary" of modern word usage. It began with "Autonomy: A word that is very difficult to translate into Russian," and ended with "University: A building into which students sometimes get to enter and sometimes the police."[42] An issue of the popular weekly *Modern Illustration* devoted to the theme of students employed the same motif: the last page showed a photograph of a soldier armed with a gun and bayonet standing guard in an undistinguished institutional hallway. The caption read: "In the Polytechnic Institute."[43]

PATRIOTISM AND PROTEST

When war was declared in August 1914, tremendous crowds of people all across Europe took to the streets in perhaps the greatest spectacle of mass patriotism ever displayed in the history of Europe. With few exceptions, socialist parties voted for war credits, affirmed their support for their nation, and renounced internationalism. Although the crowds were smaller and the socialist parties less enthusiastic, this general pattern held for Russia as well. But patriotism would wane in Russia by the spring of 1915, as the war undermined what remained of the moral and political authority of the monarchy.[44] The experiences of Russian students during World War I conform to this general pattern. Out of the initial patriotic fervor, signs of dissent grew in 1915. Closer examination suggests, however, that this shift was hardly abrupt. Even in 1914, students gave their loyalty less to the regime than to the nation, and it was this same loyalty that progressively undermined support for the government.

Even before the outbreak of war in 1914, significant numbers of students participated in patriotic demonstrations. Throughout March 1913, in connection with a congress devoted to the first Balkan war, hundreds if not thousands of students demonstrated against Austria and Germany under the banner of Slavic brotherhood. Singing the national anthem and holding the tsarist flag, they marched several times through the center of St. Petersburg defying the police order to disperse. The large number of demonstrators suggests that it was not just right-wing students, who participated.[45] This trend intensified in the fall of 1914, when students returned to their studies. In response to the first call-up of students that October, a crowd of students demonstrated in front of the Winter

Palace in support of the war. Several days later, at an assembly at Petrograd University, the rector conveyed the tsar's appreciation to the excited students, who shouted "Hurrah for the Emperor and army!"[46] At similar assemblies at other educational institutions, a vast majority of students expressed strong support for the war. Although the primary villain was Germany, several hundred students, many of them Armenian, also held a street demonstration against Turkey.[47]

Patriotism—and chauvinism—was also expressed in less conventional forums. On October 3 at Petrograd University, students heckled a professor of Roman law named B. F. von Zeller, crying "Down with the agent provocateur, who maintains dual citizenship." In his report on this incident, the rector explained that von Zeller, a Russian citizen of German descent, had been teaching in Berlin until the war had forced his return to Russia. In a sardonic tone, he noted that students seemed to think that he had become German simply by teaching there. The rumors of his split loyalties had been fueled by a slip of the tongue—during his first lecture, von Zeller had apparently said "we" *(u nas)* in reference to Germany.[48]

Patriotic manifestations in the classroom also raised politically ambiguous questions. A second incident was provoked by the statement of Professor Gribovskii asserting that both the student and labor movements had been funded by German and Austrian money. Condemning "such immoral and uncivilized tricks," one proclamation called upon students to rise in defense of their "cherished ideals" against such "slander." With another proclamation threatening to disrupt lectures if an explanation was not forthcoming, Gribovskii was persuaded to retract his words, and the disruptions ended.[49]

This incident underscores a fundamental ambivalence within student patriotism that stood at the heart of the original manifestations as well. After the assembly of October 10, when students had praised the tsar and his army, many students had remained in the auditorium to discuss the war. At this point, a call for an amnesty of all political prisoners was greeted with applause by some, and by accusations of treason by others. The assembly consequently divided into two hostile camps along more conventional political lines. With both groups claiming to support the war, some five hundred students left the auditorium singing revolutionary songs, and an unspecified number sang patriotic anthems. Later that afternoon, approximately seven hundred students gathered to affirm both their readiness to die for the motherland and their hope for a general amnesty. A second group of some one hundred fifty academists disrupted this meeting, arguing that patriotism should not be qualified by any conditions. Confrontations continued through the day. According to an Okhrana report, older students tended to oppose patriotic manifestations (though not the war) as anathema to student traditions, while younger students, apparently less concerned with these traditions, spoke of a "war of principles" between Russia and Germany.[50]

A similar conflict occurred in the Polytechnic Institute, where students refused outright to listen to speeches made by revolutionaries but likewise split into two opposing groups along conventional political lines. A student named Kamenskii voiced a widespread sentiment when he affirmed his willingness to fight in the Belgian army for Belgium's independence or the French army for the freedom of France, but to fight in the Russian army for the defense of the Russian state violated his principles. Similarly, proclamations affirmed the duty to go to war singing the "Marseillaise" rather than "God Save the Tsar." [51] While only a tiny minority of students actually opposed the war, many supporters were striving to reconcile it with their progressive political beliefs. As yet, there was no apparent conflict between the "hurrah" for the tsar and the national defense.

Through the end of 1914, students disregarded the appeals of the revolutionary parties. When the SD members of the Duma were arrested in November, student SDs and SRs called for mass protests, which did not occur. A small protest at the Women's Medical Institute was actually followed by a larger rally disavowing the original protest. Events at the university took a more serious turn due to police intervention. When lectures were disrupted on November 12, police detained 197 students, 195 of whom were later exonerated—they had been present in the classroom for the lecture, not for the protests. The memorials marking Tolstoi's death also took a more pacific form. At the university, Technological Institute, and Bestuzhev Courses, students gathered to sing "Eternal Memory" but staged no further protests. The numbers varied from only fifty technical students to some one thousand *kursistki*. [52] It is hardly surprising, given the general atmosphere, that students greeted antiwar proclamations of the student Bolshevik faction with a highly negative reaction, indeed, with actual enmity. [53]

Student patriotism took an increasingly civic form. Like students across the country, Petrograd students organized hospitals, distributed food, and allocated volunteer labor among charitable groups. While many technical students worked in Petrograd's war industries, many women students worked as nurses. [54] In late 1914, an "All-Student Committee for the Distribution of Aid to War Victims" was founded in Petrograd to coordinate student charitable donations and labor. According to an Okhrana report, it was run by "democratic" students who wanted to ensure that helping victims of war would not contradict the "old traditions." A similar concern dominated a December 1914 conference of student delegates from Petrograd schools and Iurev University. In addition to proposing the national coordination of student war aid, students discussed the potentially subversive question of the relationship of war aid to such "negative" and "harmful" phenomena as patriotic manifestations and chauvinism. [55]

By the spring of 1915, the repressive measures of the state began to politicize this civic sentiment. In February, several hundred students protested the closure of the Free Economic Society and the exile of SD members of the Duma. [56]

Many students associated with the war-aid committee were also critical of the "pseudonationalist" fervor of some conservative groups.[57] Tension heightened, however, when police were stationed in the university on March 4 (due more to the possibility rather than the actuality of disorder), and when five students were arrested and subsequently exiled with the active connivance of academists. For several weeks some six hundred police officers were stationed in the university to prevent any disruptions.[58] Given the "militarization" of their institution, students protested the intervention of police and the behavior of the academists, depicting both groups as having acted contrary to the principles of legality and decency. While academists argued that they were fulfilling their civic duty to the father-land, other students sent a delegation to the rector requesting a disciplinary court.[59] Although the school year ended without further incident, events had compelled students to ponder the relationship between patriotism and progressive politics. In a proclamation the next fall, more than fifty student groups reminded students about the spring's events and called for a purge of academism from the university (along with its chauvinism and collaboration with police) as the civic duty of all honorable students.[60]

With the formation of the Progressive Bloc in August 1915 and increasing signs of disintegration both at home and at the front, the politicization of civic attitudes in the university accelerated. That fall, one issue seemed to exemplify the inability of the state to orchestrate its own defense: the role of Jewish soldiers. At Petrograd University, a group of Jewish students distributed a proclamation and held a meeting demanding the same opportunities for military service as other students. Since the outbreak of war, they stated, the government had denied the Jewish population its most elementary human rights, had blamed the Jewish people for defeat, and had thereby created a poisoned atmosphere of extreme nationalism. As part of their general aspiration for equality, they demanded the right to fulfill their military duty in times of war by the same criteria used for students of Orthodox belief. According to an Okhrana report, this group drew little attention until academists began to heckle them, provoking in turn their defense by non-Jewish students and the escalation of the confrontation. Not insignificantly, this same report also noted the development of a "civic mood" among students.[61] Like other members of Russia's educated society, students were concluding that the government was an impediment to the war effort.

A complex interplay of civic-patriotic and political considerations was shaping attitudes toward the war. In a letter to a friend dated September 8, 1915, a Petrograd student recounted a discussion recently held in the apartment of a medical student. At issue was whether victory or defeat would lead to political progress in Russia. One person, adopting a "defeatist" position, argued that if Russia won the war, the people's faith in the tsar would be strengthened. Another countered that if Russia and her allies were victorious, closer relations with her democratic allies after the war would lead to political progress in Russia. When a third student suggested that only a German victory would topple autocracy, a fourth retorted that "victory" also meant German soldiers on Russian soil. In their final consensus, these students equated a German victory with ethical slavery and the triumph of militarism, and stressed the positive role of closer relations with the West in the development of Russian democracy.[62] In their path from patriotism in 1914 to civic protest in 1915, liberal and moderate-socialist students had grounded their endorsement of the war in "traditional" student principles and distinguished this support from loyalty to the government. Although protests became more frequent in 1916, and despite some antiwar propaganda, most continued to support the war, if with reservations.[63]

The war also brought a host of new problems to Petrograd, including a housing shortage due to the influx of refugees and migrants, as well as inflation and food shortages, all of which compounded the traditional problem of student poverty. A 1915 survey conducted at the Bestuzhev Courses found that the average monthly expenditures of students had risen from thirty-eight to forty-one rubles between 1909 and 1915 despite 80% inflation over this same period. Some 30% of students could no longer afford a full daily meal.[64] This situation inspired students from the university, Women's Courses, and Mining Institute to organize a cooperative. In the first two weeks of its existence in December 1915, twelve hundred students paid fifty kopecks each to become members.[65] The cooperative movement had a large number of proponents, and in Moscow, a newspaper was founded to propagandize it.[66] At the core of the movement was the traditional principle of self-help as self-education: economic need would compel students to pool their resources and then to develop the progressive values of initiative (samodeiatel'nost') and solidarity.[67]

Despite the pressures of the wartime censor, the student press also showed a striking vitality in 1916. Newspapers, journals, and article collections, reflecting everything from a nationalist to a socialist orientation, appeared throughout the country. Most claimed to represent "democratic" students, who, it was said, adhered to traditional student principles. Despite passionate and often contentious debates about the concrete task of the newest generation of students, these publications advanced a general program—the establishment of a republic in Russia and the concomitant democratization of education. While articles continued to describe the function of student organization as pedagogical—"a method of educating the followers of democracy," some stressed the importance of economic-professional organization (including the cooperative movement) as a new basis for a community ethos, while others envisioned a nonparty democratic front.[68]

"Democratic" students excluded "right-nationalist" and "liberal-bourgeois" students from their project. They argued that these "parts" of the student community either advanced a conservative political agenda or denied the need for a public role for students, and thus did not constitute part of studenchestvo. In an important sense they were correct, for neither group did in fact aspire to define a special path for students. Nationalist publications supported the war effort under the banner of either a united Slavdom or Russian autocracy, but did not advance a particular role for students.[69] Similarly, the sole "liberal" publication of 1916 concentrated its attention on the war effort as the civic duty of Russian society as a whole.[70] In contrast, a strong Jewish student press, which was divided into Zionist and national-democratic factions, did participate in the general debates.[71] At the core of the publicistic fervor was a very old dilemma: what was the *studenchestvo* and where was it going? Despite their strong participation in the war effort at home and their advocacy of broad principles of democracy, students were still searching for an all-encompassing ideal.

In an article entitled "The Forgotten," Mikhail Lederman lamented the lack of direction and purpose among students. Recounting the collective experiences of the previous ten years, he described how the pure idealism of the revolutionary years had degenerated into a kind of nihilism during the period of reaction. Instead of providing a new vision of the future, writers had glorified a cult of the body, initiating a second nightmare: "We began to search for truth, unsteadily and confusedly to resolve the 'accursed questions' of life and death. Tens and then hundreds became intoxicated on the heroism of departing from life, and audaciously set off [to find] truth [and] meaning in a land from which there is no return. . . . The demons of debauchery turned into the apostles of truth." Although the epidemic of suicide had ended, a positive new symbol of faith had not emerged. Lederman appealed, therefore, to writers, those "creators of thought," to help students find a path to the future.[72] This theme recurred in perhaps a score of articles over the course of 1916.[73] Even those who criticized the idea that students should ask their elders for guidance called for boldness of thought but did not offer any solution of their own.[74]

REVOLUTION

"Events of a tremendous political significance are building in Petrograd," Vladimir Khlebtsevich wrote to his brother on February 27, 1917. "Newspapers have disappeared, the trams have stopped since the 24th, yesterday and the day before shootings occurred along Nevskii, where crowds of workers were gathering. . . . Today is the most critical day—I heard that the Duma has declared itself a constituent assembly. . . . Everybody is expecting revolution." Like other Petrograd students, Khlebtsevich welcomed the labor protests of February 1917 and surely joined his comrades in the wave of meetings, where students heatedly discussed the crisis of government and the critical situation on the homefront. He supported the student strike in solidarity with the workers, though he may not have had the time to cast his vote because he was already working in a medical brigade serving the wounded. Yet Vladimir Khlebtsevich never had the chance to celebrate: that night, after writing to his brother, he was shot and killed while in an ambulance rushing to another scene of violence. Several days later Nikolai II abdicated his throne.[75]

The memorial service of Khlebtsevich that March became the occasion for a solemn celebration of the measured civic values of the February Revolution. A speech by Ekaterina Breshko-Breshkovskaia, the populist activist and "grandmother of the revolution," glorified him as a last innocent victim of the Romanovs, a reminder to the future that there should no longer be any victims of arbitrary rule. Petrograd students praised him as a true son of the intelligentsia, a follower of Herzen and Tolstoi, who could speak with peasants in their own language and study literature and mathematics.[76] The death of this student closed the chapter on tsarism and provided an opportunity to ground the new society in the traditional values of the intelligentsia.

In a series of meetings, students formally welcomed the revolution and, despite some ambiguities, seemed to acknowledge the primary political authority of the Provisional Government rather than the Petrograd Soviet of Workers' and Soldiers' Deputies. Enjoining their fellow citizens to work together on behalf of the entire country, Bestuzhev students sent addresses to both the Provisional Government and the Petrograd Soviet. Though polytechnic students seemed to locate primary authority in the Provisional Government, they also called upon it to work in unity with the Soviet. Before sending their declaration of loyalty to the Provisional Government, students at the Military-Medical Academy arrested the director and helped to set up a range of committees to oversee the administration of the "liberated" academy.[77] Their unilateral actions bespoke a potential contradiction in the new order.

Despite a number of logistical difficulties, the return to academic work occurred with great optimism.[78] The February Revolution seemed to promise the freedom of which generations of professors and students had dreamed. Students expelled for political reasons were readmitted, and those professors who had resigned in 1911 were offered back their old positions. In June, it was resolved that university admissions should be made without distinction of sex, nationality, or religion.[79] Students quickly took advantage of their new freedoms. During that spring, almost every conceivable group used the university as a meeting place, including student factions of the SDs, SRs, anarchists, radical democrats, and the peasant union.[80] Students likewise sponsored extracurricular courses on such topics as revolutionary history and methods of propaganda; the popular history professor Nikolai Kareev gave special evening lectures on the French Revolution of 1789 and the Paris Commune.[81] The only group excluded from the university was a certain "University Group of Anarchist Communists," which had used university buildings to shoot at the nearby military school and to type recipes for explosives. This curious organization sponsored a number of interesting events, including lecture courses on the history of anarchism, science and anarchism, and "Beethoven and the Anarchy of Music."[82]

While students saw the February Revolution as an opportunity to reorganize academic life, professors envisioned a higher school liberated from all political interference, whether in the form of ministerial meddling or student strikes.[83] Although information is sketchy, sources point to some friction between students and professors over the question of authority. In Moscow, an armed student militia organized in February continued to function well into March. Its head, a student named Brusilovskii, had stationed himself in the office of the prorector, where he directed the requisitioning of supplies, the assignment of auditoriums for mass meetings, and the arrest of former members of the police. He recognized neither the authority of the rector nor the jurisdiction of the Provisional Government. More often disputes arose because professors sharply delineated students' sphere of activity from their own. By the end of the semester, many institutions across the country were reporting serious unrest due to worsening student-professor relations. In some cases, students called strikes or other major protests when professors refused to admit them to faculty councils as voting members.[84] Overall, few substantive changes in the university order were carried out in the short period before October 1917, when political events made them irrelevant.

The October Revolution was largely a nonevent for Petrograd's students, because military and economic pressures had decimated the academic community. That fall, the university opened weeks late and functioned at a reduced level for a tiny number of advanced students. Only when the new Commissar of Enlightenment, Anatolii Lunacharskii, gave a lecture at the Bestuzhev Courses in December 1917 did students show signs of life. He was greeted with protests and, harkening back to old strike methods, threats of chemical obstructions.[85] Seeing the October Revolution as a Bolshevik coup d'état, most students argued that the legitimate democratic aspirations of the people had been betrayed by a new force of despotism.

CONCLUSION

Heroism and Everyday Life

An individual cannot be completely incarnated into the flesh of existing sociohistorical categories. There is no mere form that would be able to incarnate once and forever all of his human possibilities and needs, no form in which he could exhaust himself down to the last word, like the tragic or epic hero; no form that he could fill to the very brim, and yet at the same time not splash over the brim.

—Mikhail Bakhtin, "Epic and Novel,"
from *The Dialogic Imagination*

The importance of historical narratives lies both in what they exclude and in what they include. The story of consciousness was fundamentally a story of the heroic feat—it was epic in its scope, romantic or tragic in its many acts. For precisely this reason, it did not usually refer to everyday life, which, in its repetitive ordinariness, is the antithesis of the heroic. Nor did it include a concerted effort to revolutionize daily life. The 1905 Revolution marked the culmination and end of this collective story. For some students, the revolution initially seemed to fulfill their historical task as guides to the people. The union of students and workers in the university that October had fused consciousness with spontaneity, generating revolution. Even those who did not share this utopian vision believed that the times had changed. Citing the establishment of a parliament, the legalization of political parties, and class differentiation, students almost universally concluded that their role as political vanguard had ended.

The picture becomes more complex after 1905, in part because there was no longer a dominant story. From the triumph of capitalism to the fall into poverty and despair, every story that seemed at first to explain students' experiences proved inadequate. None of the new principles students advocated—civic-constitutional, professional, academic, cooperative, or democratic—proved able to capture the collective imagination. To be sure, the student community had become both politically and culturally more diverse. The disintegration of the story of consciousness had removed the mantle of commonality that had once allowed students to cloak real or potential differences. Simultaneously, the newly attained freedoms of organization and expression facilitated an unprecedented debate over identity, education, and politics in general. Yet the student community was not precisely in a state of crisis, as often claimed at the time. As shown by the countless newspapers, study circles, and mutual-aid societies constantly springing up despite police repression, it was in fact quite vibrant. What was missing was a myth of unity, a symbol of cohesion, and a feeling of coherence. Students mourned the absence of a meaningful new story.

The public image of students underwent a parallel transformation. Especially in light of the subsequent controversies, the degree to which students escaped criticism before 1905 is noteworthy. Progressive commentators occasionally chuckled at students' sense of historical self-importance, liberals chastised them for politicizing the university, and radicals regretted the parochial "student" nature of their movement. In other words, students' "spontaneity" or their seemingly irreverent attitude toward the educational institution drew fire, not their persons, behavior, or values as such. This practice reflected the common opposition to autocracy and the common hope placed on substantive political change within the liberation movement. More fundamentally, it echoed the self-representation of students themselves. Even such vocal critics as Petr Struve and Aleksandr Izgoev agreed that the student movement had played a critical role in educated society's own "rise to consciousness." Commonality disintegrated during the revolutionary years of 1905–1907. Confronted by protest and violence on the one hand and new ideas about constitutions, citizenship, classes, and parties on the other, individuals and groups were compelled to articulate their particular visions of political and social organization. In the aftermath of the revolution, students no longer basked in the benevolent gaze of their elders.

The fate of students' story of consciousness highlights the importance of the 1905 Revolution not only as a political event but as a cultural watershed. Though many of the controversies and concerns of postrevolutionary society predate 1905 (a short list would include crime, the writing of Artsybashev's *Sanin,* the modernist critique of the didactic role of literature, and the expansion of women's educational opportunities), the revolution was a marker dividing two distinct eras. It was a moment when long-held conventions and assumptions—such as the story of consciousness—suddenly no longer seemed as relevant. In this respect, a common language had been lost. Still, as both radicals and liberals tried to explain the outcomes of the revolution and to shape social values, they grasped the same symbol: the archetypical student.

The one-time heralds of revolution and targets of pogromic violence thus found themselves between the front lines of two opposing forces, Russian radicalism and Russian liberalism. In marked contrast to the earlier period, the revolutionary parties lost much of their interest in students after 1905, quite correctly seeing the student movement as a phenomenon beyond their direction and separate from what they perceived as the more important "class" struggle. Neither the 1908 strike nor the 1910 Tolstoi demonstrations and 1911 strike gained the support of organized revolutionary groups. Though parties continued to recruit among students, radicals denounced what they considered a new bourgeois order of political quiescence and careerism in the university. In their eyes, students had renounced conscious revolutionary struggle for their true class interests: they had joined the bourgeoisie. In fact, of course, this application of Marxist categories of historical development to the Russian context was just as "fictional" as the story of consciousness; students' brand of radicalism simply did not conform to the notions held by many revolutionaries.

For liberals, in contrast, students came to symbolize the excesses of revolution, not just in its political sense but also with the connotation of disorder. In 1911, Izgoev defended his vision of a politically neutral university by evoking the specter of 1905, when, as he put it, "the street seized the university" *(universitet ovladela ulitsa).*[1] This blended metaphor of revolution and disorder reflected an effort to reestablish clear boundaries between the university, the street, and the state that had collapsed during 1905 (and, by implication, 1911). In the process, many liberals—not just conservatives—increasingly linked protest with disorder and students with the street. This was hardly a coincidence. Students challenged liberalism's newly claimed cultural and political authority.

This challenge first occurred inside the academy, where student protest threatened autonomy and assaulted the moral vision of professors. Seeing both the state and the revolutionary tradition as thoroughly discredited, many liberals (and not just professors) asserted that political change could occur only through the creation and enactment of enlightened cultural values, from constitutional norms of political behavior to moral self-discipline in work and personal life. For this reason, they believed that the university in its dual educational and scientific role was an institution necessary to the cultural development of the Russian nation, regardless of the broader political climate. But Russian students did not stick to the role their professors envisioned for them. They were not to replay the story of Western students after 1848. In 1911, their shaken but intact faith in heroic action instead devastated the university. By prolonging their strike until science had been put under police guard, students destroyed any illusion of constitutionality, legality, or academic autonomy. While liberals understandably attacked the methods of students, their own methods had failed as well. Despite a concerted effort to construct legal procedures and constitutional limits, the government had continued to exercise arbitrary power in the university as in society as a whole.

The challenge to liberalism also lay within the controversy over students' morality and behavior. It was a truism in the last decade of the Romanov dynasty that youth was physically and morally sick. The evidence was suicide and venereal disease; causes included the family and the school. Calls for improvements in women's education as well as school reform reflected a general aspiration to regenerate these fundamental institutions and, in this fashion, to shape the civic values of the next generation. At the root of such endeavors was a faith in progress, enlightenment, and individualism, a faith that was also being undermined. While students' moral and political "fall" functioned as a metaphor for the end of revolution and as a pretext for intervention, it also implicated the complicity of educated society itself. With its negative assessment of daily life, suicide provided perhaps the most unsettling judgment of the liberal aspiration toward cultural progress. Was an individual suicide a victim of political reaction or of social apathy, or, indeed, a hero who had refused to be sullied by compromise? This ambiguity lent student suicide its disturbing resonance. It also demonstrated the ongoing hold of the categories embedded within the story of consciousness. That many students continued to value the heroic over the everyday, a central factor in both the 1911 protests and the revival of the suicide memorial, suggests that the psychological hold of the revolutionary tradition had not been broken. Whether liberalism would have made inroads against the traditions of student radicalism is ultimately unknown. The monarchy proved unable to make concessions, and the October Revolution disrupted the evolution of Russia's emerging civil society as a whole.

In the introduction, I stated my intention to tell the story of a story. In fact, of course, there were countless stories to be told, only some of which appeared on these pages, and my story—unlike the story of consciousness—lacks a clear resolution. The lives of my student-subjects took separate paths, each in its own way deviating from the established, predictable plots, including mine. Though stories are an intrinsic part of human cognition and of the historical landscape, they can never capture the human condition. Like other sociohistorical categories, they shape perception, give meaning to experience, and cut the chaos of reality into bite-sized pieces. Stories, after all, leave things out, make value judgments, and have beginnings and endings. Some of them eventually transcend into the lofty realm of myths. The story of student consciousness thus reached an end in its mythologization, when the individual and the accidental were melted down, when history was tempered into a triumphant monolith—at least according to the story.

The Making of the "Former People"

I am not a communist nor even a socialist, and I have not reconciled myself to much of what is now occurring, but it is necessary to look truth directly in the face. We, the former intelligentsia, the old *studenchestvo,* are fading, becoming decrepit. . . . A
new *studenchestvo* has arrived [and] a new intelligentsia is coming—fresh, impassioned, militant, untouched by our dog-like old
age. . . . It is necessary for us to make way for them, follow
them, and study life from them.

—*A Petrograd Student, 1920*

Soviet power was not fully instituted in higher education until well
into the 1920s, if even then. The years after the October Revolution witnessed a
struggle between professors and "old" students on the one hand, and the Soviet
state and "new" students on the other. While the modes of cooperation and
resistance of the professoriate have been described by historians, the formative
years of Soviet student culture remain to be documented.[1] An examination of
published materials suggests that students remained an oppositional force in the
universities and specialized institutes until the fall of 1922. During this period,
students formulated a political strategy based on three guiding principles: the
struggle for academic autonomy, cooperation with the professoriate, and the celebration of prerevolutionary "democratic" student traditions.[2] After October
1917, the "democratic" *studenchestvo* laid claim to its heroic heritage in a new
common cause. Yet in fighting for rather than against tradition, "old" students—
as they called themselves—soon found themselves relegated to the past. By 1922,
they had become the "former people" *(byvshie liudi).*

The campaign began in 1918 with the preparation by students and professors
of various reform projects for higher education, all of which were predicated on
the principle of almost total academic autonomy. The degree to which students
and professors resolved a number of once-contentious points is striking. While
students demanded and received a voice in the administration of the university,

they withdrew previous bids for the right to participate in such "scholarly" areas as faculty selection. Both groups agreed on the rights of students to elect a representative body and to control the distribution of financial aid and stipends. The only right accorded the state, which was expected to finance the university, was to review financial accounts.[3]

The student movement in Petrograd also revived. In 1918, the student council of each educational institution chose delegates for a citywide committee, which provided the organizational and ideological leadership of resistance under the banner of the "democratization of the higher school." When the government attempted to wrest control of financial aid the following year, the Petrograd committee partially counteracted the measure by organizing a boycott of the new state-sponsored organization. In 1920, students further succeeded in electing an anti-Soviet delegate to the Petrograd Soviet. In their struggle to retain control of legalized student economic and political institutions, students depicted themselves as defenders of Russian culture against the encroachments of an arbitrary new state power.[4]

For the new Soviet leaders, the university represented a bastion of old-regime values to be conquered and mastered by the new ruling classes and their presumed representative, the Communist Party. This was to be accomplished by curricular reforms, including the introduction of social science requirements (the study of Marxism and party history), and, more important, by changing the social composition of the student body. The first move was a 1918 decree reducing admission standards to a simple age requirement of 16 years. Although many students soon enrolled under the decree, their lack of preparation as well as the demands of the Civil War quickly reduced their numbers.[5] It was largely in response to this failure that the workers' faculties were founded in 1919. Designed as preparatory courses attached to universities for students of a worker or peasant background, they also served a second more obviously political function: they were to train the new generation of proletarian and peasant specialists. Within two years, the influx of these new students, who depended on the state for everything from financial aid to career advancement, combined with strict class-based admission requirements made students as a group more supportive of the new state. From a total of only three workers' faculties with 2,149 students in 1919, the number grew to eighty-four with 27,960 students in 1920–1921.[6]

Old students tried to convert these newcomers to the banner of student traditions. Sergei Zhaba, a longtime socialist student activist at Petrograd University, recounted how the Council of Elders attempted to foster a "spiritual connection" with the students of the workers' faculties as well as other incoming students. The primary strategy entailed the transmission of (old) student traditions through the observation of such anniversaries as the deaths of Lev Tolstoi and Nikolai Mikhailovskii and the Decembrist uprising. At parties, professors would speak on the historical meaning of the anniversary, after which students would give speeches and sing traditional student songs. Zhaba was vague as to the success of this tactic.[7]

With only a minority of students in the workers' faculties, most of whom were not party members, apparently taking an active role in student politics, the decisive moment came with victory in the Civil War, when Communist students entered the universities in force and initiated a concerted struggle for control of student institutions. As late as the spring of 1922, Communists remained in the minority in the Council of Elders of Petrograd University and the Military-Medical Academy. Only in the 1922–1923 academic year was the Communist victory secured, facilitated by the influx of new students, the graduation of old students, administrative measures limiting the activities of old students, and the arrest of many old student leaders.[8]

Over this brief period, two counterpoised groups had formed: the "old" and the "new" *studenchestvo*. In addition to reflecting real social changes, these terms acquired a polemical significance. The qualifier "old" gained multiple and multivalent meanings, depending on the point of view. On the one hand, the new Soviet state appropriated the heroic traditions of the *studenchestvo*. In 1918, Commissar of Enlightenment Lunacharskii distinguished two types of students: the half-hungry "proletarian" idealist and the privileged gentleman. With the intensification of class struggle after 1905, he argued, the idealist had given way to the gentleman, a trend he believed documented by the affiliation of many students with the Whites.[9] Even as he dismissed the contemporary generation as counterrevolutionary, Lunacharskii thus laid claim to the old, pre-1905, student traditions. On the other hand, the past as embodied by the old student also extended tentacles of corruption into the present and the future. In a 1924 call for vigilance, the Communist psychologist A. B. Zalkind noted the danger of "petty-bourgeois" contamination due in part to the mixing of old and new students.[10] This threat of infection was omnipresent in the 1920s, and it was now time for Soviet specialists to confront such familiar problems as political apathy, the physical and moral repercussions of student poverty, the specter of sexual promiscuity, and the disease of suicide, and to interpret them within the contradictions of the new society.

The interplay of heroism and decadence associated with the word "old" also characterized the attitudes of old students toward themselves. In the midst of defeat in 1922, Zhaba could still write: "At no time in prerevolutionary years had the *studenchestvo* sensed with such power its connection to the hearths of Russian culture, and its responsibility for their fate." In language reminiscent of earlier decades, he described the *studenchestvo* as an "oasis of democratic civic values" and the university as a "school of civic education." In his view, at least, students had again donned their heroic mantle in this new struggle for human "rights and dignity."[11] In contrast, Aleksandr Valentinov, another Petrograd student, argued that the events of October 1917 documented the failure of the intelligentsia and *studenchestvo* to enlighten and guide the people. In his fictionalized memoirs published in exile, he pictured the moral, intellectual, and political decadence of the last generation of students. According to his version of events, for example, students met the Bolsheviks' "seizure of power" by discussing how to find black-market sugar.[12]

A student movement deserving of the name disappeared in 1921–1922. When a new state power assumed the mantle of revolutionary leadership in October 1917, students could no longer locate themselves at the forefront of cultural and political progress. Despite the brief attempt of "old" students to defend democracy, the *studenchestvo* as an imagined community became a phenomenon of memory and myth. Having learned from the failures of its tsarist predecessor, the Soviet state viewed the student sphere as an especially important site of intervention. Instead of relying solely on an erratic repression, it was careful to legalize, regulate, and control the many institutions of the student subcultures. Not only were mutual-aid societies and representative institutions all given an official veneer, but activism was mobilized and channeled through the Komsomol, the Communist Youth League. If student radicalism had been a form of generational protest before 1917, apoliticism and a culture of entertainment—movies, dance, jazz—provided new symbols of self-identification and perhaps even protest after 1917.[13]

During this same period, the prehistory of student radicalism was appropriated into the official past of the new regime. This is hardly surprising, for many "old" Bolsheviks had received their first political education during student protests dating back to the 1880s. Indeed, in both theory and practice, the student subcultures had functioned for some individuals as a space for the development of "consciousness," and it was in this space that such young people as Vladimir Lenin were drawn to Marxism.[14] The rise of consciousness as a motive force of revolution became the subtext for a striking number of memoirs and histories which began to appear in the 1920s.[15] Typically, however, the "real" student movement was dated to the period before the "bourgeois revolution" of 1905, for in its aftermath, or so convention had it, most students became defenders of the bourgeois order. Soviet historians consequently never produced a synthetic history of student radicalism that included the period between 1907 and 1917, because it no longer fit into the established categories. Scattered articles instead examined the organizations and activities of student Bolsheviks and their struggle against "bourgeois" tendencies in the student community.[16] The history of student radicalism had merged into the mythology of the heroic feat, culminating in the rise of the Bolshevik Party as the bearer of consciousness.

Abbreviations

NZh   *Nauka i zhizn'*
NZhV   *Novyi zhurnal dlia vsekh*
Obr   *Obrazovanie*
OPNEP   *Obozrenie psikhiatrii, nevrologii i eksperimental'noi psikhologii*
Osv   *Osvobozhdenie*
OV   *Obshchestvennyi vrach*
PG   *Peterburgskaia gazeta*
PL   *Peterburgskii listok*
PS   *Put' studenchestva*
PSS   *Polnoe sobranie sochinenii*
PV   *Prakticheskii vrach*
PVk   *Pravitel'stvennyi vestnik*
RB   *Russkoe bogatstvo*
RD   *Rabochee delo*
RM   *Russkaia mysl'*
RR   *Revoliutsionnaia Rossiia*
RS   *Russkaia starina*
RSh   *Russkaia shkola*
RV   *Russkii vrach*
SlR   *Slavic Review*
SM   *Sovremennyi mir*
SR   *Soznatel'naia Rossiia*
SS   *Sovremennoe slovo*
StD   *Studencheskoe delo*
StG   *Studencheskie gody*
StM   *Studencheskaia mysl'*
StO   *Studencheskie otkliki*
StP   *Studencheskaia pravda*
StR   *Studencheskaia rech'*
Stud   *Studenchestvo*
StV   *Studencheskii vestnik*
StZh   *Studencheskaia zhizn'*
SZh   *Soiuz zhenshchin*
UZh   *Utro zhizni*
VE   *Vestnik Evropy*
VG   *Vrachebnaia gazeta*
VI   *Voprosy istorii*
VK   *Vestnik kooperatsii*
VkSZh   *Vestnik studencheskoi zhizni*
VRR   *Vestnik russkoi revoliutsii*
VS   *Vestnik studenchestva*
VStK   *Vestnik studencheskoi kooperatsii*
VSZh   *Vesti studencheskoi zhizni*
VV   *Vestnik vospitaniia*
VVy   *Veshnie vody*
ZhMNP   *Zhurnal Ministerstva narodnogo prosveshcheniia*
ZhORV   *Zhurnal obshchestva russkikh vrachei v pamiati N. I. Pirogova*
ZhS   *Zhivaia sila*
ZhV   *Zhizn' dlia vsekh*
ZZh   *Zaprosy zhizni*

Notes

INTRODUCTION

1. For the controversial work on the French Revolution and its interpretations, see François Furet, *Penser la Revolution Française* (Paris: 1978). On the problem of narrative in historical writing, see Hayden White, *Metahistory: The Historical Imagination in Nineteenth-Century Europe* (Baltimore: 1973).

2. On "stories" as a historical source, see Natalie Zemon Davis, *Fiction in the Archives: Pardon Tales and Their Tellers in Sixteenth-Century France* (Stanford: 1987).

3. Following the suggestion of Roland Barthes, I will not "demythologize" the story of consciousness but examine the making and functioning of it as a "cultural myth." See the revised edition of his *Mythologies* (Paris: 1970). Two scholars have examined the important place of narrative in Soviet Russia but have investigated the prerevolutionary roots only minimally; see Katerina Clark, *The Soviet Novel: History as Ritual* (Chicago: 1985) and James von Geldern, *Bolshevik Festivals 1917–1920* (Berkeley: 1993). On Muscovite Russia seen through the visor of one of its stories, see Daniel Rowland, "Biblical Military Imagery in the Political Culture of Early Modern Russia: The Blessed Host of the Heavenly Tsar," in *Medieval Russian Culture*, vol. 2, Michael S. Flier and Daniel Rowland, eds. (Berkeley: 1994).

4. On the revolutionary movement, including the role of students, see Norman M. Naimark, *Terrorists and Social Democrats: The Russian Revolutionary Movement Under Alexander III* (Cambridge, Mass.: 1983); Derek Offord, *The Russian Revolutionary Movement in the 1880s* (Cambridge, Eng.: 1986); Franco Venturi, *Roots of Revolution* (N.Y.: 1966); Allan Wildman, *The Making of a Workers' Revolution* (Chicago: 1967); and Reginald E. Zelnik, "Populists and Workers: The First Encounter between Populist Students and Industrial Workers in St. Petersburg, 1871–74," *Soviet Studies*, vol. 24 (1972).

5. On the formation of the student subcultures during the 1840s–1870s and their role in the production of revolutionaries, see Daniel Brower, *Training the Nihilists: Education and Radicalism in Tsarist Russia* (Ithaca, N.Y.: 1975). For two rich histories of higher education in tsarist Russia that include the student movement, see Samuel Kassow, *Students, Professors, and the State in Tsarist Russia* (Berkeley: 1989) and James C. McClelland, *Autocrats and Academics: Education, Culture, and Society in Tsarist Russia* (Chicago: 1979).

6. Benedict Anderson, *Imagined Communities: Reflections on the Origin and Spread of Nationalism*, 2nd ed. (London: 1991).

7. On the concept of intelligentsia (which dates to the same period as the *studenchestvo*), see Martin Malia, "What is the Intelligentsia?" in *The Russian Intelligentsia*, Richard Pipes, ed. (Cambridge, Mass: 1961).

8. Kassow in particular has shown the importance of *studenchestvo* to the student movement by providing many specific examples of students motivated by their belief in

studenchestvo rather than by an ideology or party. He defines *studenchestvo* by its "common language," which consisted of various "themes," most importantly, the sense of a student family, the obligation to uphold a common code of behavior, the sense of inadequacy before earlier generations of *studenchestvo*, and standards of ethics (*Students*, 8–11, 48–50). The problem in this otherwise useful approach is that Kassow does not analyze the contents of these themes, their change over time, or their changing functions. In his detailed exposition of the student movement, the ethos tends to have a static and abstract character.

9. Kassow (*Students*) and McClelland (*Autocrats*) discuss professors' views of the university in detail; Brower (*Training*) sets out the prehistory of students' concept of education.

10. The specific experiences of women students will be discussed in chapters 1, 3, and 6.

11. Reginald E. Zelnik, "Russian Bebels: An Introduction to the Memoirs of Semen Kanatchikov and Matvei Fisher," *The Russian Review* 35 pt. 1 (July 1976), pt. 2 (Oct. 1976); and Reginald E. Zelnik, trans. and ed., *A Radical Worker in Tsarist Russia: The Autobiography of Semën Ivanovich Kanatchikov* (Stanford: 1986).

12. Mark Steinberg, "Worker Authors and the Cult of the Person," in *Cultures in Flux: Lower-Class Values, Practices, and Resistance in Late Imperial Russia*, Stephen P. Frank and Mark D. Steinberg, eds. (Princeton: 1994).

13. Two excellent studies intentionally subvert the linear story of consciousness. Charters Wynn provides an upside-down view in his *Workers, Strikes, and Pogroms: The Donbass-Dnepr Bend in Late Imperial Russia* (Princeton: 1992). Joan Neuberger examines class definition through the prism of hooligan violence. See her *Hooliganism: Crime, Culture, and Power in St. Petersburg, 1900–1914* (Berkeley: 1993).

14. Leopold Haimson has shown this dialectic to be central to the development of Russian Marxism and Leninism in particular: *The Russian Marxists and the Origins of Bolshevism* (Cambridge, Mass.: 1955). Katerina Clark (*The Soviet Novel*) later described it as the structuring force of the socialist-realist novel.

15. The labor movement shared the rhetorical opposition of a conscious leadership to a spontaneous mass, political to economic (rather than academic) aspirations, and the plot of consciousness, but the parallel is incomplete, because "worker" was a modern identity, and the proletariat (not the *studenchestvo*) possessed the reins of history.

16. For a typical "party" work, see P. S. Gusiatnikov, *Revoliutsionnoe studencheskoe dvizhenie v Rossii* (Mos.: 1971). Kassow (*Students*) is unmatched in his careful reconstruction of the interaction of government, professors, and students in the making of the "university question," but he too appropriates the academic-political opposition.

17. Richard Pipes, *The Russian Revolution* (N.Y.: 1990), esp. 3–8. Unless one categorizes state bureaucrats (*chinovniki*) as "lower class," students did not in fact "come overwhelmingly from the lower classes," as Pipes claims. Students' social background is discussed at the end of this introduction.

18. Franco Moretti, *The Way of the World: The Bildungsroman in European Culture* (London: 1987), 4–5.

19. On *chastnaia zhizn'* and the problem of *byt*, or everyday life, see Svetlana Boym, *Common Places: Mythologies of Everyday Life in Russia* (Cambridge, Mass.: 1994), esp. ch. 1.

20. On the "Petersburg text" in Russian literature, see V. N. Toporov, "Peterburg i peterburgskii tekst russkoi literatury," in *Trudy po znakovym sistemam* 18 (Tartu: 1984).

21. RGIA, f. 733, op. 154, d. 471, l. 399.

22. On Russia's educational system, see Kassow, *Students;* McClelland, *Autocrats;* and Patrick Alston, *Education and the State in Tsarist Russia* (Stanford: 1969).

23. Accurate statistics on social background are unavailable because the mode of classification changed and estate categories were becoming less accurate gauges. See the official reports, *Otchet o sostoianii i deiatel'nosti Imp. S.-Peterburgskogo universiteta,* published annually.

24. For the 1905 enrollment figures, TsGIA SPb, f. 2075, op. 7, d. 5, ll. 1–2.

25. These figures refer to the five technical institutes in Russia administered by the Ministry of Education. V. R. Leikina-Svirskaia, *Russkaia intelligentsiia v 1900–1917 godakh* (Mos.: 1981), 15.

26. For general histories of women's education, see Ruth Dudgeon, "Women Students in Russia, 1860–1905" (Ph.D. diss., George Washington University, 1975); Christine Johanson, *Women's Struggle for Higher Education in Russia, 1855–1900* (Montreal: 1987); K. R. Shokhal, *Vysshee zhenskoe obrazovanie v Rossii* (SPb: 1910); A. N. Shabanova, "Zhenskoe vrachebnoe obrazovanie v Rossii." *IV* no. 5 (1913); and Jeanette E. Tuve, *The First Russian Women Physicians* (Newtonville, Mass.: 1984).

CHAPTER 1

1. N. I. Iordanskii, "Missiia P. S. Vannovskogo," *Byloe* no. 9 (1907), 100.

2. This report is unlike any other from the rector in its subject, length, and vehemence. RGIA, f. 733, op. 151, d. 48, ll. 108–115, esp. 115. The following discussion refers to this and another report (ll. 233–235).

3. Among the classics are Mikhail Bakhtin, *Rabelais and his World,* Hélène Iswolsky, trans. (Bloomington, Ind.: 1984); Natalie Zemon Davis, *Society and Culture in Early Modern France* (Stanford: 1975); and the collected essays of E. P. Thompson, *Customs in Common* (N.Y.: 1993).

4. N. Vasil'ev, "V 70ye gody (Iz moikh vospominanii)," *MB* nos. 6, 7 (1906): here no. 6, 217.

5. A. Pervushin, "Iz revoliutsionnogo proshlogo Gornogo Instituta," in *Na puti k pobede* (Len.: 1925), 127.

6. D. I. Pisarev, "Nasha universitetskaia nauka," in *Izbrannye pedagogicheskie sochineniia* (Mos.: 1951), 116.

7. A survey of gymnasium students several years later found Pisarev to be one of the *favorite* authors of 437 out of 933 respondents, and in sixth place overall after Tolstoi, Gorkii, Dostoevskii, Turgenev, and Chekhov. See K. Levin, "Chto chitaet i chem interesuetsia uchashchaiasia molodezh'?" *MB* no. 12 (1903): 104.

8. For an overview of recent scholarship on the reforms, see Ben Eklof, John Bushnell, and Larissa Zakharova, eds., *Russia's Great Reforms, 1855–1881* (Bloomington, Ind.: 1994).

9. See the pathbreaking study of this period in Russian culture by Irina Paperno, *Chernyshevsky and the Age of Realism* (Stanford: 1988); see also Abbott Gleason, *Young Russia: The Genesis of Russian Radicalism in the 1860s* (Chicago: 1980); Rufus W. Mathewson, *The Positive Hero in Russian Literature* (N.Y.: 1958); and Franco Venturi, *Roots of Revolution* (N.Y.: 1966).

10. N. A. Dobroliubov, "Kogda zhe pridet nastoiashchii den'?" in *Izbrannoe* (Mos.: 1986).

11. For extensive excerpts from the debates, see Isaiah Berlin, "Fathers and Children," in *Russian Thinkers* (N.Y.: 1979), 261–305.

12. D. I. Pisarev, "Bazarov," *Russkoe slovo* no. 3 (1862).

13. For the authoritative text, see Nikolai Chernyshevskii, *Chto delat'? Rasskazy o no-vykh liudiakh* (Len.: 1975).

14. On the history of the *raznochintsy,* see Elise Kimerling Wirtschafter, *Structures of Society: Imperial Russia's "People of Various Ranks"* (De Kalb, Ill.: 1994).

15. On the educational system and student politics in the nineteenth century, see Patrick Alston, *Education and the State in Tsarist Russia* (Stanford: 1969); Alain Besançon, *Education et société en Russie dans le second tiers du 19me siècle* (Paris: 1974); Daniel Brower, *Training the Nihilists: Education and Radicalism in Russia* (Ithaca, N.Y.: 1975); F. B. Kaiser, *Hochschulpolitik und studentischer Widerstand in der Zarenzeit* (Wiesbaden: 1983); and James C. McClelland, *Autocrats and Academics: Education, Culture, and Society in Tsarist Russia* (Chicago: 1979).

16. L. F. Panteleev, "Proisshestvie 29 sentiabria (1857g) mezhdu studentami (Moskovskogo) universiteta i politsiei," *MG* no. 4 (1908).

17. For a memoir account, see Vl. Sorokin, "Vospominaniia starogo studenta," *RS* 128 (1907). See also S. Ashevskii, "Russkoe studenchestvo v epokhe 60-kh godov," *SM* nos. 6–11 (1907); N. I. Pirogov, *Universitetskii vopros* (SPb: 1863); and Venturi, *Roots,* 220–231.

18. As quoted in Ashevskii, "Russkoe studenchestvo" no. 11, 114–117.

19. N. V. Shelgunov, "K molodomu pokoleniiu," in *Vospominaniia* (Mos.-Pet.: 1923), 290.

20. V. R. Leikina-Svirskaia, *Intelligentsiia v Rossii vo vtoroi polovine XIX veka* (Mos.: 1971), 316–318.

21. Western historians have investigated this question without, however, being able to establish a firm relationship between social background and radical politics. See Daniel Brower, "Student Political Attitudes and Social Origins: The Technological Institute of Saint Petersburg," *Journal of Social History* (Winter, 1972–1973).

22. Pisarev, "Nasha universitetskaia nauka," 56, 67–68, 176–177.

23. Petr Lavrov, *Historical Letters,* trans. and ed. James P. Scanlan (Berkeley: 1967).

24. All of these institutions have histories, with the *kruzhok* dating back to the 1820s. On the history of student circles, see S. P. Mel'gunov, *Iz istorii studencheskikh obshchestv v russkikh universitetakh* (Mos.: 1904). The Chaikovskii circle of the early 1870s most fully implemented this theory of moral upbringing; see Brower, *Training,* 202–205; and S. L. Chudnovskii, "Iz dal'nikh let (Otryvki iz vospominanii)," *Byloe* nos. 9, 10 (1907).

25. Vasil'ev, "V 70ye gody," no. 7, 57.

26. Pavel Miliukov, "Moi universitetskie gody," in *Moskovskii universitet 1755–1930: Iubileinyi sbornik* (Paris: 1930), 262.

27. Vasil'ev, "V 70ye gody," no. 6, 218.

28. G. B. Sliozberg, "Dorevoliutsionnoe russkoe studenchestvo," in *Sbornik vospominanii pamiati russkogo studenchestva* (Paris: 1934), 93.

29. The term belongs to Evgenii Anichkov. See his "Ustav 1884-go goda i studenchestvo na pereputi," in *Sbornik vospominanii,* 41.

30. V. B. [V. V. Bartenev], "Vospominaniia peterburzhtsa o vtoroi polovine 80-kh godov," *MG* nos. 10, 11 (1908): here no. 10, 169; and no. 11, 170–173.

31. M. A. Braginskii, "Dobroliubovskaia demonstratsiia 17go noiabria 1886g. v S.-Peterburge," *Byloe* no. 5 (1907): 307.

32. E. V. Geshin, "Shelgunovskaia demonstratsiia," *MG* no. 11 (1908): 27–32. On the demonstration and general mood, see also Iu. O. Martov, *Zapiski sotsial-demokrata* (Berlin: 1923), ch. 3.

33. Iordanskii, "Missiia," esp. 83, 131. Iordanskii was later an editor with *Sovremennyi mir* and Soviet representative to Italy.

34. *Ibid.,* 84.

35. *Ibid.,* 84.

36. *Ibid.,* 94–95.

37. *Ibid.,* 85–87. For the charter of the *Kassa* which was founded in 1882, see RGIA, f. 1405, op. 530, d. 1037, l. 58.

38. Excluding arrests for student protests, 121 Petersburg students were prosecuted for political crimes between 1894 and 1900. A minority of these arrests concerned propaganda among workers. RGIA, f. 1405, op. 530, d. 1037, ll. 3–61, esp. 53–61. This document collection also includes material on other urban regions.

39. Iordanskii, "Missiia," 86–98, esp. 86–91.

40. *Ibid.,* 89.

41. On the outreach of Marxists to workers as well as the strategies they used to interpret their experiences, see Allan K. Wildman, *The Making of a Workers' Revolution* (Chicago: 1967).

42. Marshall Berman, *All that is Solid Melts into Air: The Experience of Modernity* (N.Y.: 1982), 87–129.

43. Ann M. Lane, "Nietzsche Comes to Russia: Popularization and Protest in the 1890s," in *Nietzsche in Russia,* Bernice Glatzer Rosenthal, ed. (Princeton: 1986), 51–68.

44. Maksim Gorkii, *PSS,* esp. vols. 1, 2 (Mos.: 1949). See also Mary Louise Loe, "Gorky and Nietzsche: The Quest for a Russian Superman," in *Nietzsche in Russia,* 251–273. On his popularity, see Levin, "Chto chitaet," 104, 107–109.

45. Katerina Clark, *The Soviet Novel: History as Ritual* (Chicago: 1985), 52–67.

46. Mikh. Mogilianskii, "V devianostye gody (Vospominaniia)," *Byloe* nos. 23, 24 (1924). Mogilianskii's activities after the period described in his memoirs are unclear. According to a 1911 report of the St. Petersburg Chief of Police, he was involved in an assassination attempt on General D. F. Trepov in 1905. However, Samuel Kassow mentions in a footnote that Mogilianskii became a member of the liberal Constitutional Democratic Party, which would certainly be an ironic twist to his subsequent memoirs. Finally, a Soviet encyclopedia described him as a liberal publicist, a supporter of tsarism, an active opponent of Soviet power, and a Ukranian nationalist. For the police report, see GARF, f. 102 (DP IV), op. 100 (1908), d. 119 ch. 42, l. 239. See also Samuel Kassow, *Students, Professors, and the State in Tsarist Russia* (Berkeley: 1989), 104; and *Literaturnaia entsiklopediia,* vol. 7 (Moscow: 1934), 406–407.

47. *Mogilianskii, "V devianostye,"* (no. 23): 136, 139, 144, 151.

48. *Ibid.,* (no. 24): 137–139.

49. S. G. Strumilin, *Iz perezhitogo, 1897–1917gg* (Mos.: 1957), 76.

50. Mirra Ginsburg, ed. and trans., *A Soviet Heretic: Essays by Yevgeny Zamyatin* (Chicago: 1970), 5.

51. *Ibid.,* 9. For a parody of the genre, see the memoirs of the minor writer Aleksandr Serebrov [A. N. Tikhonov], *Vremia i liudi. Vospominaniia 1898–1905* (Mos.: 1960), 49–55.

52. V. M. Chernov, *Zapiski sotsialista-revoliutsionera* (Berlin: 1922), 97–139, esp. 97, 110, 117.

53. Unions of United *Zemliachestva* occupied the pinnacle of student organization in Moscow and Kiev. For a Justice Ministry memorandum on student organizations throughout Russia from 1894–1900, see RGIA, f. 1405, op. 530, d. 1038, ll. 1–18.

54. Chernov, *Zapiski,* 109–110, 115–119. Compare the memoirs of Iv. Kheraskov: "My university recollections concern the interesting period of the Russian student movement, when [the movement] outgrew its *zemliachestvo* stage and overflowed into the wide channel of mass actions that took ever more defined political colors relative to the nearness to

1905." See his "Iz istorii studencheskogo dvizheniia v Moskovskom universitete," in *Moskovskii universitet 1755–1930: Iubileinyi sbornik* (Paris: 1930), 431.

55. For a reprint of his statement, see *VRR* no. 2 (1901): 29–34.

56. Compare the experience of Sergei Moiseev, "Rech' obviniaemogo studenta," *Osv* no. 14 (1903): 235–239.

57. These quotations are from the congratulatory addresses sent by students and former students for the twenty-fifth anniversary celebration of the courses. See *Prazdnovanie dvadtsatipiatiletiia S.-Peterburgskikh Vysshikh zhenskikh kursov* (SPb: 1904), 84, 85, 87.

58. Mariia Miliukova, "Iz dalekikh vospominanii," RGB, f. 369, k. 397, d. 4.

59. *Ibid.,* ll. 2, 4.

60. *Ibid.,* ll. 11–12. She asked the police to return the "nonpolitical" part of her diary dealing with the birth of her son. Her request was refused.

61. *Ibid.,* ll. 2, 3, 4–5. Compare to the descriptions of the heroes of Soviet literature in Clark, *Soviet Novel,* 59–62.

62. *Miliukova, "Iz dalekikh vospominanii,"* ll. 18–19.

63. See D'iakonova's second diary, "Dnevnik na Vysshikh Zhenskikh kursakh, 1895–1899," published separately in 1904 and 1905 and reprinted in *Dnevnik Elizavety D'iakonovoi, 1886–1902,* 4th edition (Mos.: 1912), 175–493.

64. The curator of the academic district wrote two letters to her mother and finally received her approval. For copies of the letters, *Ibid.,* xxviii-xxix.

65. *Ibid.,* 228.

66. *Ibid.,* 193–195.

67. *Ibid.,* 234–239, 251–253, 328–332.

68. *Ibid.,* 246–250, 257–258.

69. *Ibid.,* 327, 354–355.

70. *Ibid.,* 479–489.

71. Stefan Zweig, *The World of Yesterday* (N.Y.: 1943), xi.

CHAPTER 2

1. For the correspondence and a copy of the notice, RGIA, f. 733, op. 151, d. 45, ll. 14, 37–38.

2. A. and V. G. Chertkov, *Studencheskoe dvizhenie 1899g.* (London: 1900), 5; and RGIA, f. 733, op. 151, d. 46, l. 132.

3. For statements of witnesses and victims, *Leningradskii gosudarstvennyi universitet v vospominaniiakh sovremennikov,* vol. 2 (Leningrad: 1982), 171–172 (note 2); and RGIA, f. 1405, op. 530, d. 1040, ll. 19–24, 29–33.

4. Nikolai Iordanskii, "Missiia P. S. Vannovskogo," *Byloe* no. 9 (1907): 98–100; and Mikh. Mogilianskii, "V devianostye gody (Vospominaniia)," *Byloe* no. 24 (1924): 121.

5. The police, in contrast, blamed the strike on the liberal press and student radicals. "S.-Peterburgskoe okhrannoe otdelenie v 1895–1901 gg. ('Trud' chinovnika otdeleniia P. S. Statkovskogo.)," *Byloe* no. 16 (1921): 126.

6. RGIA, f. 1405, op. 530, d. 1040, l. 14.

7. Mogilianskii ("V devianostye," 124) and Iordanskii ("Missiia," 102–103) recognized the political ramifications, but, like other student leaders, did not speak openly of them.

8. RGIA, f. 733, op. 151, d. 45, l. 21.

9. For examples, see Chertkov, *Studencheskoe dvizhenie,* 7; and RGIA, f. 1405, op. 530, d. 1040, l. 15–16.

10. Chertkov, *Studencheskoe dvizhenie*, 17.

11. RGIA, f. 1405, op. 530, d. 1040, l. 16; and f. 1410, op. 2, d. 56, l. 4.

12. Mogilianskii, "V devianostye," 125.

13. RGIA, f. 1405, op. 530, d. 1040, ll. 15, 17; and f. 1410, op. 2, d. 56, l. 4.

14. RGIA, f. 1129, op. 1, d. 63, ll. 1–6; and f. 733, op. 151, d. 45, ll. 75–77.

15. Iordanskii, "Missiia," 104–105. For the report to the tsar, see RGIA, f. 733, op. 151, d. 45, ll. 70–71; for the student's letter, see f. 1410, op. 2, d. 49, ll. 8–10.

16. For the announcement, see *PV* no. 41 (20.II.1899). On students' responses, see RGIA, f. 1410, op. 2, d. 57, l. 4; and Iordanskii, "Missiia," 104.

17. Bulletin of the fourteenth day in MISPbGU, f. RD, "Studencheskie volneniia 1899g." l. [58]. See also RGIA, f. 733, op. 151, d. 47, ll. 28, 34.

18. For proclamations, see TsGIA SPb, f. 139, op. 1, d. 8732, ll. 82–84, 92, 111, 114. On the *skhodka*, see RGIA, f. 733, op. 151, d. 47, ll. 13–14, 20, 98–99.

19. Students asked Vannovskii to intervene on their behalf, but he replied that his appointment was limited to St. Petersburg. RGIA, f. 733, op. 151, d. 47, l. 99; and Iordanskii, "Missiia," 123–124.

20. For a long excerpt from the Manifesto, see Chertkov, *Studencheskoe dvizhenie*, 35–38.

21. Mogilianskii ("V devianostye," 127–130) claims to have written the *Kassa*'s manifesto and vastly overstates its importance to the development of Russian Marxism.

22. It is unclear how students defended property rights. For the proclamation, see RGIA, f. 733, op. 151, d. 48, ll. 247–248.

23. RGIA, f. 733, op. 151, d. 48, l. 244. Leading student groups also denounced the *Kassa*'s manifesto; see MISPbGU, f. RD, d. "Studencheskie volneniia 1899g," ll. 2, 87.

24. Iordanskii, "Missiia," 103, 126–127.

25. Iordanskii, "Missiia," 125–126; Chertkov, *Studencheskoe dvizhenie*, 28–29; and RGIA, f. 733, op. 151, d. 48, ll. 116–118.

26. Two votes were held on March 16 and 17 with the margin growing closer: 950 to 46, and 825 to 601. (The figures are approximate, as there are discrepancies in the records.) G. M. Libanov, *Studencheskoe dvizhenie 1899g* (London: 1901), 59; and RGIA, f. 733, op. 151, d. 48, ll. 124, 242.

27. RGIA, f. 733, op. 151, d. 48, ll. 141, 177.

28. To be readmitted, students had to sign statements giving their word that they would not continue to protest. For an example, see TsGIA SPb, f. 139, op. 1, d. 8733, l. 38. See also the bulletins of the twenty-second, twenty-third, twenty-fifth, and twenty-sixth days (March 18–23), MISPbGU, f. RD, "Studencheskie volneniia 1899g," unnumbered.

29. These numbers are approximate and represent from just under 20% (university), to 34% (technological) and 59% (forestry) of enrolled students; TsGIA SPb, f. 139, op. 1, d. 8735, ll. 58–63; d. 8733, ll. 40, 68; and d. 8732, ll. 343–346. For lists of the arrested, see RGIA, f. 733, op. 151, d. 51; d. 52, f. 1405, op. 530, d. 1038, ll. 26–29; f. 1040, ll. 45–53; and f. 1405, op. 521, d. 450, ll. 266–285. See also Libanov, *Studencheskoe dvizhenie*, 77.

30. RGIA, f. 1410, op. 2, d. 52, l. 15.

31. RGIA, f. 1410, op. 2, d. 46, l. 2.

32. Unfortunately, this source does not indicate how this took place. *Iubileinyi sbornik Voenno-meditsinskoi akademii* (Len.: 1927), 102.

33. Dated April 7, 1899, RGIA, f. 1410, op. 2, d. 42, ll. 9–10.

34. RGIA, f. 1410, op. 2, d. 58, ll. 2–6.

35. RGIA, f. 1410, op. 2, d. 38, ll. 40, 48.

36. RGIA, f. 733, op. 151, d. 49, ll. 149–152; and f. 1405, op. 530, d. 1040, l. 76.

37. TsGIA SPb, f. 139, op. 1, d. 8735, l. 85; and d. 8733, l. 62. RGIA, f. 733, op. 151, d. 150, l. 99.

38. RGIA, f. 733, op. 151, d. 48, l. 275; and d. 61, ll. 9, 174.

39. RGIA, f. 733, op. 151, d. 150, l. 14. Compare the proclamation in Chertkov, *Studencheskoe dvizhenie*, 41–46.

40. Temporary rules were issued periodically to introduce a new policy without amending the official statute; their formulation is beyond the parameters of this study. For detailed analyses of the governmental reaction to the student movement, see Samuel Kassow, *Students, Professors, and the State in Tsarist Russia* (Berkeley: 1989). For these rules, see RGIA, f. 733, op. 151, d. 54, ll. 368–369; see also d. 57, d. 58, and l. 59, *passim*.

41. For Vannovskii's report, see RGIA, f. 733, op. 151, d. 244, esp. ll. 23–24.

42. RGIA, f. 733, op. 151, d. 150, ll. 266–276.

43. Libanov, *Studencheskoe dvizhenie*, 65; see also *RD* no. 2/3 (1899): 85, 108–111.

44. N. N., "Golos iz obshchestva," in Chertkov, *Studencheskoe dvizhenie*, 9–25.

45. P. E. Shchegolev, "Vstrechi s Tolstym," in *Leningradskii universitet*, 35–37; and "Tolstoi o studencheskoi stachke 1899g: Pis'mo N. M. Ezhova k A. Suvorinu," *LN* no. 69 (1961): 317–320. On Tolstoi's ongoing importance, see *Poslednie revoliutsionnye sobytiia v Rossii i Lev Tolstoi* (Berlin: 1901).

46. Chertkov, *Studencheskoe dvizhenie*, 55.

47. See the daily chronicle of events and the proclamations, RGIA, f. 733, op. 151, d. 61, ll. 100, 153–166.

48. Although some delegates desired a closer rapprochement between the "working masses" and the "intellectual proletariat," they believed that only a small number of students would progress so far as to join the workers' movement. RGIA, f. 733, op. 151, d. 62, ll. 14–16.

49. On the expulsion of Ekaterina Guseva, see RGIA, f. 733, op. 151, d. 62, ll. 55, 75–76, 104–106; and TsGIA SPb, f. 113, op. 1, d. 1178, l. 136; d. 1179, l. 46.

50. RGIA, f. 733, op. 151, d. 62, ll. 145, 169, 306; d. 66, ll. 28–32; and f. 1405, op. 530, d. 1039, ll. 21–23.

51. TsGIA SPb, f. 139, op. 1, d. 9044, ll. 13–25, *passim*. Other strike votes included: Mining Institute, 190 to 142; Institute of Communications, 230 to 100; Forestry Institute, 186 to 34. See RGIA, f. 733, op. 151, d. 242, l. 31. For an account by a drafted student, see L. S. [L. A. Sobolev], "Vospominaniia studenta-soldata," *Byloe* no. 5 (1906).

52. A notice posted in the university threatened to apply the Temporary Rules for any sign of disorder. MISPbGU, f. RD, d. 15.

53. "Togda i teper'," "Studencheskie revoliutsionnye pesni," The University of Helsinki Slavonic Library.

54. Signed "Gruppa universantov," RGIA, f. 733, op. 151, d. 66, l. 89.

55. Bulletin 6 (February 7), RGIA, f. 733, op. 151, d. 242, ll. 43–45. G. A. Engel' and V. A. Gorokhov, *Iz istorii studencheskogo dvizheniia 1899–1906* (Mos.: 1908), 24–25.

56. V. Levitskii, *Za chetvert' veka* (Mos.-Len.: 1926), 148–160; see also the daily chronology (February 8–19) compiled by the police, RGIA, f. 733, op. 151, d. 66, ll. 127–130; and an eyewitness statement, d. 65, l. 62.

57. On events in Moscow, see Mark Vishniak, *Dan' proshlomu* (N.Y.: 1954), 47–58; A. A. Titov, *Iz vospominanii o studencheskom dvizhenii 1901 goda* (Mos.: 1907); and I. Kheraskov, "Iz istorii studencheskogo dvizheniia v Moskovskom universitete (1897–1903)," in *Moskovskii universitet 1755–1930: Iubileinyi sbornik* (Paris: 1930), 431–450.

58. TsGIA SPb, f. 139, op. 1, d. 9044, l. 53–56; and RGIA, f. 733, op. 151, d. 64, ll. 114, 186, 240, 290.

59. RGIA, f. 733, op. 151, d. 242, ll. 46, 50, 65–68; and d. 243, ll. 116–120.

60. *RR* no. 2 (1901); *Iskra* no. 3, (1901); R. V. Ivanov-Razumnik, *Tiur'my i ssylki* (N.Y.: 1953), 19ff; and A. V. Tyrkova-Villiams, *Na putiakh k svobode* (N.Y.: 1952), 64ff.

61. N. V. Iukhneva, "Studencheskoe dvizhenie v Peterburgskom universitete i pervye demonstratsii 1901 goda," in *Ocherki po istorii Leningradskogo universiteta* (Len.: 1962), vol. 1, 138; P. S. Gusiatnikov, *Revoliutsionnoe studencheskoe dvizhenie v Rossii* (Mos.: 1971), 56–62; and *Ocherki istorii Leningrada* (Mos.-Len.: 1956), vol. 3, 204–211.

62. See bulletins 19 and 20, and the proclamation signed "Kruzhok studentov," which saw his appointment as a "sign of a better future," RGIA, f. 733, op. 151, d. 64, ll. 212, 287, 244.

63. The Technological Institute and Higher Women's Courses followed suit. RGIA, f. 733, op. 151, d. 65, ll. 154–156; and f. 560, op. 22, d. 243, l. 32. See also the intercepted letter of a student activist, GARF, f. 1167, op. 3, d. 2415.

64. Engel' and Gorokhov, *Iz istorii,* 41–42.

65. V. I. Lenin, "Otdacha v soldaty 183-kh studentov," *Iskra* no. 2 (1901).

66. Engel' and Gorokhov *(Iz istorii,* 48) imply that the laughter indicated a lack of political consciousness. Svatikov points out the irony; Sergei S. [Svatikov], "Istoricheskaia bibliografiia," *Byloe* no. 11 (1906): 308. On the fall's events, see RGIA, f. 733, op. 151, d. 290, ll. 145–146, 309, 328–330, 356–358, 439–440; d. 294, ll. 427–430; and d. 299, ll. 152–153.

67. On the academics and the politicals, see Titov, *Iz vospominanii,* 13–14; Vishniak, *Dan' proshlomu,* 57–58; and Kheraskov, "Iz istorii," 439–441.

68. On the reform projects, see RGIA, f. 733, op. 151, d. 294, ll. 212–219, 223, 285–313, 481–499.

69. For the resolution of February 5, see Engel' and Gorokhov, *Iz istorii,* 61–62; see also RGIA, f. 733, op. 151, d. 290, l. 469. On other institutes, see RGIA, f. 733, op. 151, d. 292, ll. 269, 284, 364, 376–379, 390, 435–436, 472.

70. For the proclamations of the *Kassa radikalov* as well as a final word from the *Kassa vzaimopomoshchi,* see RGIA, f. 733, op. 151, d. 288, ll. 240–241, 137; see also Engel' and Gorokhov, *Iz istorii,* 51–55.

71. TsGIA SPb, f. 113, op. 1, d. 1209, l. 178.

72. For their leaflet, see TsGIA SPb, f. 113, op. 1, d. 1209, l. 118.

73. Engel' and Gorokhov, *Iz istorii,* 64–65.

74. TsGIA SPb, f. 113, op. 1, d. 1209, l. 203; see also ll. 186, 189.

75. RGIA, f. 733, op. 151, d. 299, ll. 258, 260; and d. 292, ll. 218–219.

76. See the weekly reports, which list and describe many of these leaflets. RGIA, f. 733, op. 151, d. 299, ll. 226–357.

77. For the leaflets, see TsGIA SPb, f. 113, op. 1, d. 1209, l. 192; RGIA, f. 733, op. 151, d. 288, ll. 204–210; and d. 289, l. 46. For a curious memoir account, see N-in, "Vospominaniia anti-obstruktsionnista," *AS* (SPb) no. 1 (1909): 25–52, no. 2, 21–34.

78. TsGIA SPb, f. 113, op. 1, d. 1209, ll. 207, 211–212; and RGIA, f. 733, op. 151, d. 299, ll. 330–332.

79. For memoir accounts, see G. I. Chulkov, *Gody stranstvii* (Mos.: 1930), 13–25; "Studencheskie volneniia v 1901–1902gg," *KA* no. 89/90 (1938): 294–303; and Sergei E-v, "Iz istorii studencheskikh bezporiadkov," in *Sbornik vospominanii pamiati russkogo studenchestva* (Paris: 1934), 75–76. For a proclamation from exiled students, see RGIA, f. 1410, op. 2, d. 249, ll. 4a-5b. See also I. Kh. Lalaints, *Otpravka studentov v Sibir'* (Geneva: 1902); and the coverage in *Osv* nos. 9, 10 (1902), and no. 13 (1903).

80. For the Temporary Rules and material on specific trials, see RGIA, f. 733, op. 151, d. 298.

81. *Osv* no. 3/27 (1903): 39–40.

82. TsGIA SPb, f. 139, op. 1, d. 9594, ll. 49, 76–77; and RGIA, f. 733, op. 151, d. 639, ll. 125–132, 197.

83. Engel' and Gorokhov, *Iz istorii*, 78–79.

84. "Opekaemoe studenchestvo," *Iskra* no. 31 (1902); see also the leaflets, TsGIA SPb, f. 113, op. 1, d. 25, l. 163; and f. 139, op. 1, d. 9594, ll. 62–63. For a memoir account, see N. V. Doroshenko, "Vozniknovenie bol'shevistskoi organizatsii v peterburgskom universitete i pervye gody ee sushchestvovaniia," *KL* no. 2 (1931).

85. "Studenchestvo i revoliutsiia," *RR* no. 17 (1903).

86. On the formation of the *Partizany bor'by*, see Engel' and Gorokhov, *Iz istorii*, 97–98; the bulletin "Chto zhe nam delat'?" was reprinted in *Osv* no. 20/21 (1903): 367–368.

87. *Student* nos. 1, 2/3 (1903).

88. See the Conference's manifesto in *RR* no. 37 (1903): 18–20.

89. TsGIA SPb, f. 139, op. 1, d. 9594, ll. 113–114; and d. 9921, ll. 52–53. For a similar leaflet from the "Central Organization of Students," see RGIA, f. 1405, op. 530, d. 114, ll. 117–118.

90. Engel' and Gorokhov, *Iz istorii*, 3–5.

Chapter 3

1. Despite minor discrepancies, three memoirs form the basis of the following discussion. See the entries by V. N. Zverev, Mikheev, and A. A. Gapeev, in *Na puti k pobede: Iz revoliutsionnoi istorii Gornogo instituta* (Len.: 1925), 100–101, 102–105, 106–108.

2. These are the notes of Nikolai Skvalygin, who, according to the editor of this volume, had committed suicide and sent his notes to the editor, his childhood friend. Whether authentic or, as seems more likely, fictionalized, they retain their interest as a representation of the student turned spy. Adam Lel', *Zapiski studenta, 1900–1903* (SPb: 1908), 18.

3. *Ibid.*, 20–22.

4. This is possibly a reference to Ponomarev. *Ibid.*, 19–20.

5. I have not found the final determination. TsGIA SPb, f. 139, op. 1, d. 9594, ll. 24, 37–39.

6. S. G. Strumilin, "Iz perezhitogo," in *Leningradskii universitet v vospominaniiakh sovremennikov,* vol. 2 (Len.: 1982), 31–34.

7. TsGIA SPb, f. 113, op. 1, d. 1209, ll. 185, 187.

8. RGIA, f. 733, op. 151, d. 299, l. 255.

9. TsGIA SPb, f. 113, op. 1, d. 1209, l. 217.

10. TsGIA SPb, f. 113, op. 1, d. 1209, l. 192.

11. TsGIA SPb, f. 139, op. 1, d. 9044, ll. 25–28.

12. "Dennitsa" is an archaic word meaning sunrise. For information on the group, including membership (which did not exceed thirty individuals) and proposed charters, see RGIA, f. 733, op. 151, d. 466, ll. 1b–2, 16, 29, 31, 86, 118–129; and op. 155, d. 393. l. 352–353.

13. G. A. Engel' and V. A. Gorokhov, *Iz istorii studencheskogo dvizheniia* (Mos.: 1908), 100–103; Vladimir Voitinskii, *Gody pobed i porazhenii*, vol. 1 (Berlin: 1923), 10; and TsGIA SPb, f. 139, op. 1, d. 9921, ll. 5, 54–55, 77.

14. For the demonstrations of March 4, the numbers are, in order, 102/806, 72/550, 101/3078, and 57/1109. RGIA, f. 733, op. 151, d. 243, ll. 116–120, 127. On the demonstration of February 19, see d. 241, ll. 149–155.

15. Or 294 students—there is a discrepancy in the records. On the events of that spring, see TsGIA SPb, f. 139, op. 1, d. 8735; and f. 113, op. 1, d. 1207. For a breakdown by course and level of punishment, see RGIA, f. 733, op. 151, d. 52, ll. 39–72.

16. TsGIA SPb, f. 139, op. 1, d. 8734, ll. 4–16; and RGIA, f. 733, op. 151, d. 53, ll. 1–8.

17. There were 960 students officially enrolled, and some students were absent from St. Petersburg. The records of the interrogations include fewer than twenty cases of students opposing the strike. See TsGIA SPb, f. 113, op. 1, d. 1207, ll. 108–115, 129–152.

18. TsGIA SPb, f. 139, op. 1, d. 8735, ll. 86–88.

19. TsGIA SPb, f. 113, op. 1, d. 1207, l. 138. E. A. D'iakonova, *Dnevnik Elizavety D'iakonovoi, 1886–1902*, 4th ed. (Mos.: 1912), 382–388.

20. MISPbGU, f. RD, "Studencheskie volneniia 1899g," l. 105.

21. For two slightly different versions, see "Studencheskie revoliutsionnye pesni" in University of Helsinki Slavonic Library; and RGIA, f. 1410, op. 2, d. 60, l. 27.

22. D'iakonova, *Dnevnik*, 430; in contrast, almost all women medical students did take their examinations, see RGIA, f. 733, op. 151, d. 150, ll. 99–101, 116, 237, 335–339.

23. This concern remained for students at private women's courses. In one such case, a professor persuaded a student not to strike, and in agitation, she remarked: "The first compromise with conscience." See V. Povorinskaia, "Ottsy i deti nashikh dnei," *Obr* no. 7 (1905): 95–96.

24. See the proclamations from 1901 and 1902 in RGIA, f. 733, op. 151, d. 242, ll. 41–42; and TsGIA SPb, f. 113, op. 1, d. 1209, l. 184.

25. RGIA, f. 1405, op. 530, d. 114, l. 26.

26. For the protocol, see TsGIA SPb, f. 113, op. 1, d. 1210, ll. 6–8.

27. RGIA, f. 733, op. 152, d. 185, ll. 22–24. For the written notices of censure, see TsGIA SPb, f. 113, op. 1, d. 4, ll. 81–89.

28. TsGIA SPb, f. 113, op. 1, d. 1210, ll. 22–155, 412; for the returned examination cards with handwritten explanations on the back, see ll. 234–410.

29. TsGIA SPb, f. 113, op. 1, d. 1210, l. 51.

30. TsGIA SPb, f. 113, op. 1, d. 1210, l. 60.

31. TsGIA SPb, f. 113, op. 1, d. 1210, l. 50. Some students, such as the author of an anonymous letter to the director of the courses (l. 69), were not conservative and clearly agonized over their decision to attend classes: "Our sense of morality is suffering because necessity compels us to act contrary to decency *[vopreki poriadochnosti]* and to border a group whose views contradict our own. We do not know where to find support, and sometimes we are ashamed even before each other."

32. TsGIA SPb, f. 113, op. 10, d. 4, l. 80.

33. TsGIA SPb, f. 113, op. 1, d. 1210, l. 125.

34. TsGIA SPb, f. 113, op. 1, d. 1210, l. 122.

35. TsGIA SPb, f. 113, op. 1, d. 1210, l. 9; for other proclamations, see ll. 56, 103.

36. Many of these proclamations use "his" and "he" for an apparently grammatical reason—they refer to the masculine word for man/person, *chelovek*.

37. This is not to say that women students rejected the *studenchestvo*, but rather that they legitimized student protest in different ways. Elena Grot thus recalled in her memoirs: "Real comradely relations existed between students and *kursistki*, as if the entire Russian *studenchestvo* was one big family, being a member of which was considered a great honor." See her "V tumane proshlogo," *Nasha dan' Bestuzhevskim kursam. Vospominaniia byvshikh bestuzhevok za rubezhom* (Paris: 1971), 8.

38. This discussion refers to documents in RGIA, f. 733, op. 151, d. 45, ll. 1–10.

39. The comparison with hooliganism is a constructive one, because student "disorders" likewise relied on an audience to attain their "political" meaning. This audience included the police (as the representative of the official order) and even respectable society, which students vilified for its passivity and readiness to compromise. On hooliganism, see Joan Neuberger, *Hooliganism: Crime, Culture, and Power in St. Petersburg, 1900–1914* (Berkeley: 1993).

40. GARF, f. 102 (DP IV), op. 100 (1908), d. 119 ch. 42, ll. 231–281, esp. 243.

41. RGIA, f. 733, op. 151, d. 45, ll. 4, 7.

42. TsGIA SPb, f. 139, op. 1, d. 9924, l. 8.

43. Chernyshevskii *(What Is to Be Done?)* set the ethical standard with Aleksandr Kirsanov and Nastia Kriukova.

44. See the rector's report, TsGIA SPb, f. 139, op. 1, d. 9594, l. 5.

45. A survey of the sexual practices of Moscow students conducted in 1903–1904 confirms this impression. Of 1,504 responding students, 706 (46.8%) currently visited prostitutes, and an additional 344 (22.6%) had sexual relations with lower-class woman (servants, dressmakers, bar singers, etc.). M. A. Chlenov, *Polovaia perepis' Moskovskogo studenchestva i ee obshchestvennoe znachenie* (Mos.: 1909), 56.

46. Boris Gegidze, *V universitete: Nabroski studencheskoi zhizni* (SPb: [1903]).

47. TsGIA SPb, f. 139, op. 1, d. 9594, ll. 37–38.

48. P. Ivanov, *Studenty v Moskve: Byt, nravy i tipy* (Mos.: 1903).

49. "Kriticheskie otmetki," *MB* no. 3 (1903): 1; "Bibliograficheskii otdel," *Obr* no. 6 (1903): 106; and "Iz zhizni i literatury," *Obr* no. 12 (1903): 77–78.

50. Gegidze, *V universitete*, 5–8.

51. Svetlana Boym, *Common Places: Mythologies of Everyday Life in Russia* (Cambridge, Mass.: 1994), 29.

52. Gegidze, *V universitete*, 238–240.

53. *Ibid.*, 12–14.

54. *Ibid.*, 86–87.

55. *Ibid.*, 16–19.

56. *Ibid.*, 142–157.

57. *Ibid.*, 41–47.

58. *Ibid.*, 56–58.

59. *Ibid.*, 136.

60. *Ibid.*, 64–65.

61. "Kriticheskie otmetki," *MB* no. 9 (1903): 1–11.

62. N. Asheshov, "O sovremennoi molodezhi," *Obr* no. 12 (1903): 74–88.

63. Staryi student, "Nashe studenchestvo," *NZh* no. 1 (1904): 97–118.

64. Boris Frommett, *Ocherki po istorii studenchestva v Rossii* (SPb: 1912), 75–76.

65. See note 45.

66. Asheshov, "O sovremennoi molodezhi," 76.

67. D. K. O., "Studencheskoe dvizhenie i zadachi oppozitsii," and P. S. [Petr Struve], "Chto zhe teper'?" *Osv,* no. 56 (1904): 97–99. Criticism did not extend beyond regret for the strong Social Democratic influence among student leaders, the politicization of the university, and students' occasional political naiveté.

CHAPTER 4

1. On student protest in 1904, see RGIA, f. 1405, op. 530, d. 114, ll. 25–80, 129–132, 139; f. 733, op. 151, d. 645, ll. 42–43, 68–78; op. 152, d. 176, ll. 4, 6, 16, 19–21, 49, 57–63, 68–70,

104; TsGIA SPb, f. 139, op. 1, d. 10199, ll. 33, 44, 73, 144, 147; *Iubileinyi sbornik Voenno-Meditsinskoi Akademii* (Len.: 1927), 108; and *Osv* nos. 60–62 (1904).

2. The best general survey is the two-volume study by Abraham Ascher, *The Revolution of 1905: Russia in Disarray* (Stanford: 1988) and *The Revolution of 1905: Authority Restored* (Stanford: 1992); see also Laura Engelstein, *Moscow, 1905* (Stanford: 1982); Walter Sablinsky, *The Road to Bloody Sunday: Father Gapon and the St. Petersburg Massacre of 1905* (Princeton: 1976); and Gerald Surh, *1905 in St. Petersburg* (Stanford: 1989).

3. See the leaflet, TsGIA SPb, f. 139, op. 1, d. 10199, l. 175; the reports on a *skhodka* of technological students, d. 10198, l. 31, 33–34; and the resolution of music students, f. 2075, op. 6, d. 7b, l. 107.

4. For the inspector's report and the resolution, see TsGIA SPb, f. 139, op. 1, d. 10198, ll. 13, 46–47. For police reports, see f. 2075, op. 6, d. 7b, ll. 46–47; and GARF, f. 102 (DP OO), 1905, d. 3 ch. 26 ch. 1, ll. 1–5. For a memoir account, see Vladimir Voitinskii, *Gody pobed i porazhenii* (Berlin: 1923), vol. 1, 30–32; for a contemporary chronicle, see D. [A. A. D'iakonov], *1905 i 1906 god v Peterburgskom universitete* (SPb: 1907), 7–12.

5. Most votes were close: the faculty council of Petersburg University voted 29 to 23, Technological Institute 9 to 5, Women's Courses 21 to 19; the Women's Medical Institute voted unanimously. On responses to the strike among government officials and faculty, see RGIA, f. 733, op. 152, d. 176, ll. 120–123, 329–332, 342–381.

6. On revolutionary organizations that apparently evolved out of student groups, see TsGIA SPb, f. 2075, op. 6, d. 7a, ll. 20–24; and d. 7b, ll. 2–3, 135–136. For memoirs of students turned activists, see P. N. Karavaev, *V dooktiabr'skie gody* (Mos.: 1948), 17–22; Mark Vishniak, *Dan' proshlomu* (N.Y.: 1954), ch. 3; and K. S. Zharnovetskii, "Kronshtadskie vosstaniia v 1905–1906gg.," *KL* no. 3 (1925): 48–105. For memoirs of a student who did not get involved, see Sergei Kamenskii, *Vek Minuvshii* (Paris: 1958), 52, 68.

7. Three February bulletins written before government policy was clear reassured students of the political importance of their strike. RGIA, f. 733, op. 152, d. 176, ll. 168–169, 178. See also the agitational pamphlets of the United Student Organization of the RSDRP in *Listovki bol'shevistskikh organizatsii v pervoi russkoi revoliutsii 1905–1907gg* (Mos.: 1956), pt. 1, 237–242, 249–251.

8. TsGIA SPb, f. 2075, op. 6, d. 7b, ll. 25, 39–40; and f. 139, op. 1, d. 10198, l. 113.

9. Voitinskii, *Gody pobed*, 35–36.

10. Vera Dyleva-Ustvol'skaia, "Vospominaniia bestuzhevki," in *Leningradskii universitet v vospominaniiakh sovremennikov,* vol. 2 (Len.: 1982), 96–100.

11. Voitinskii (*Gody pobed,* 28–40) initially joined the Bolshevik faction but later became a Menshevik and emigrated after 1917.

12. F. I. Dan, "K nachalu akademicheskogo goda," *Iskra* no. 107 (29.VII.1905): 1.

13. P. S. Gusiatnikov, *Revoliutsionnoe studencheskoe dvizhenie v Rossii* (Mos.: 1971); and Samuel Kassow, *Students, Professors, and the State in Tsarist Russia* (Berkeley: 1989).

14. Petersburg students did not attend. GARF, f. 102 (DP OO), 1905, d. 3 ch. 77, l. 12. See the documents reprinted in A. Syromiatnikov, "Moskovskii universitet v oktiabr'skie dni 1905 g.," *KA* no. 1/74 (1936): 196–197.

15. On the *skhodka,* D'iakonov, *1905 i 1906,* 20–24; Voitinskii, *Gody pobed,* 46–51.

16. D'iakonov was a university student connected to the Coalition Council, who wrote a column on student life in 1905–1906 for the progressive newspaper *Rus',* which was published as a book in 1907. His intention was "to popularize the slogans of the revolution." See MISPbGU, f. RD, d. 23.

17. For the resolution, see TsGIA SPb, f. 14, op. 3, d. 16323, ll. 55–56.

18. Kassow, *Students,* ch. 6; and Ascher, *The Revolution of 1905,* vol. 1, 199.

19. For coverage of student debates and resolutions throughout St. Petersburg, see *Pravo* nos. 37, 38, 39, (1905): 3,068–3,074, 3,187–3,192, 3,261–3,267.

20. For the resolution of September 19, see TsGIA SPb, f. 14, op. 25, d. 36, ll. 18–19. For an account of the meeting, see D'iakonov, *1905 i 1906*, 28–32.

21. D'iakonov, *1905 i 1906*, 30.

22. On the sometimes contentious discussions of the admission of Jewish and women students, see D'iakonov, *1905 i 1906*, 24–27; TsGIA SPb, f. 14, op. 3, d. 16323, ll. 39–40; and GARF, f. 102 (DP OO), 1905, d. 3 ch. 26 ch. 1, ll. 17–18.

23. The nine popular professors included the political economist and former legal-Marxist M. I. Tugan-Baranovskii, the literary scholar S. A. Vengerov, the historian N. I. Kareev, as well as other generally well-known scholars and jurists, such as L. V. Khodskii, M. I. Sveshnikov, A. A. Isaev, V. I. Semevskii, E. V. Anichkov, and a certain Stakhovich. The seven under boycott included the villain of the 1903 disciplinary court I. Ia. Foinitskii, the influential government advisor A. I. Georgievskii, as well as D. P. Konovalov, Al. Vvedenskii, B. V. Nikol'skii, [M. M.?] Borovitinov, and [I. N.?] Zhdanov. TsGIA SPb, f. 14, op. 25, d. 36, l. 20.

24. These were Konovalov, who had alienated students with his police methods as director of the Mining Institute, and Nikol'skii, a professor of law involved with the far-right anti-Semitic organization Russian Assembly. D'iakonov, *1905 i 1906*, 34–35, 42–45; see also Petr Struve's heated criticism of the boycott, *Osv* no. 78/79 (1905): 497–498.

25. Kassow (*Students*, 258–259) argues that the choice of liberal rather than radical scholars reveals the political preferences of students. He does not take into account that students intended to counteract prior government actions and states erroneously that the boycott was canceled.

26. Voitinskii, *Gody pobed*, 75–76, 83–84, 89; D'iakonov, *1905 i 1906*, 42–45.

27. Each faculty elected 1 elder per 250 students (Juridical, 12; Natural Sciences, 3; Mathematics, 4; Philology, 2; Eastern Languages, 1), for a total of 22 elders. Of 677 votes cast in the Juridical faculty, for example, the SDs received 478 (9 elders), the SRs 85 (1 elder), the Kadets 105 (1 elder), and the "Wild Ones" 98 (1 elder). D'iakonov, *1905 i 1906*, 44–45, 52–56, 58–61, 64–65; Voitinskii, *Gody pobed*, 85.

28. D'iakonov, *1905 i 1906*, 44.

29. RGIA, f. 733, op. 153, d. 158, l. 1; TsGIA SPb, f. 14, op. 25, d. 36, l. 19; and A. S. Syromiatnikov, "Moskovskii universitet," 98–99.

30. Voitinskii, *Gody pobed*, 46.

31. GARF, f. 102 (DP OO), 1905, d. 3 ch. 26. ch. 1, l. 19; and *Pravo* no. 38, 3,188–3,189.

32. At the Mining and Communications Institutes and the Lesgaft Courses, outsiders were admitted with only a consultative voice. *Pravo* no. 37, 3,073; no. 38, 3,190. Ascher (*The Revolution of 1905*, vol. 1, 199–201) cites several cases when students limited the role of outsiders as evidence of their political moderation but does not examine the specific reasons in each case.

33. D'iakonov, *1905 i 1906*, 35–38. Compare the account of the police report stressing the presence of workers and the "extremist" orientation of the "exclusively" political debates. GARF, f. 102 (DP OO), 1905, d. 3 ch. 30, l. 3.

34. Voitinskii, *Gody pobed*, 55–56; D'iakonov, *1905 i 1906*, 35–38.

35. Voitinskii, *Gody pobed*, 56–63.

36. *Pravo* nos. 37–39 (1905).

37. GARF, f. 102 (DP OO), 1905, d. 3. ch. 30, l. 3; and RGIA, f. 733, op. 153, d. 158, l. 11.

38. GARF, f. 102 (DP OO), 1905, d. 3 ch. 26 ch. 1, ll. 21–26.

39. Report of October 1, D'iakonov, *1905 i 1906*, 46–49. Compare Voitinskii, *Gody pobed*, 63.

40. GARF, f. 102 (DP OO), 1905, d. 3 ch. 26 ch. 1, ll. 25–26. For an eye-witness account, see TsGIA SPb, f. 14, op. 3, d. 16323, ll. 63–64; and D'iakonov, *1905 i 1906*, 49–52. See also Surh, *1905*, 310–311.

41. By secret ballot, Moscow University students overwhelmingly reiterated their support for the meetings on September 24. Kassow, *Students*, 263–268.

42. For the police reports, see GARF, f. 102 (DP OO), 1905, d. 3 ch. 26 ch. 1, ll. 29, 31, 34–36, 38; TsGIA SPb, f. 2075, op. 6, d. 351, ll. 6–7; and op. 3, d. 3, l. 10.

43. RGIA, f. 733, op. 153, d. 158, l. 26.

44. Zotov prepared this twenty-one-page memoir on the basis of his diary, which is not part of the file. MISPbGU, f. RD, d. 10.

45. D'iakonov, *1905 i 1906*, 66–67.

46. RGIA, f. 733, op. 153, d. 158, l. 12.

47. Voitinskii, *Gody pobed*, 85–86.

48. *Ibid.*, 100.

49. For the police report, see GARF, f. 102 (DP OO), 1905, d. 3 ch. 26 ch. 1, ll. 34–36; see also D'iakonov, *1905 i 1906*, pp. 67–68; Voitinskii, *Gody pobed*, 98–102; and *Obshchestvennoe dvizhenie v Rossii*, vol. 2 (SPb: 1910), 98–99.

50. RGIA, f. 733, op. 153, d. 158, ll. 33–34, 37, 44–45.

51. RGIA, f. 733, op. 153, d. 158, ll. 63–64.

52. Beyond the pervasive anti-Semitism and the deliberate noninvolvement and even encouragement of local authorities, such suspicions have not been substantiated. For an overview of the violence, *Obshchestvennoe dvizhenie*, 96–104.

53. TsGIA SPb, f. 139, op. 1, d. 10199, ll. 190–199; RGIA, f. 733, op. 152, d. 176, ll. 124–125.

54. RGIA, f. 733, op. 152, d. 176, l. 145.

55. D'iakonov, *1905 i 1906*, 146–147.

56. *Moskva v dekabre 1905g. Sbornik statei*, (Mos.: 1906), 163–165, 184–187, 190.

57. It is unclear how the Black Hundreds were represented. *Moskva v dekabre 1905g*, 199.

58. N. K. Kol'tsov, *Pamiati pavshikh: Zhertvy iz sredy Moskovskogo studenchestva v oktiabr'skie i dekabr'skie dni* (Mos.: 1906), 55.

59. See V. Venozhinskii, *Politicheskaia zabastovka v S.-Peterburgskom universitete* (SPb: 1906); V. Aleksandrovich, *O studencheskoi zabastovke* (SPb: 1905); Student E. A., *Porugannyi khram nauki* (Mos.: 1906); and A. S. Budilovich, *Nauka i politika* (SPb: 1905). On right-wing political organization during the revolution, see Don C. Rawson, *Russian Rightists and the Revolution of 1905* (Cambridge, Eng.: 1995).

60. *Universitet i politika* (SPb: 1906). On the cover is the following quotation: "Freedom is a great cause, worthy of the sacrifice of life—life yes, but not science."

61. V. Ag-ov [V. K. Agafonov], "Vysshie uchebnye zavedeniia i revoliutsiia," *SR*, vyp. 1 (SPb: 1906), 46–57.

62. See the review of Ag-ov's article in *Stud* no. 2 (1906), 7–9.

63. On Jewish enrollment and admission policy in general, see TsGIA SPb, f. 14, op. 1, d. 10000.

64. D'iakonov, *1905 i 1906*, 72–79.

65. See the debate of September 7, 1906, *ibid.*, 80–87.

66. *Ibid.*, 78–79.

67. See the debate at the first session of the new Council in 1905, *ibid.*, 143.

68. A comparison of election results in various institutions over 1906 and 1907 suggests that Kadets may actually have been gaining. See *Stud* nos. 1–4 (1906) and *StM* nos. 1–3 (1907).

69. A. Vilenkin, "Universitetskii parlamentarizm," *Stud* no. 4 (1906): 4–7. See also a Moscow project reprinted in *Stud* no. 2 (1906): 11–12.

70. D'iakonov, *1905 i 1906*, 94–101.

71. See the exchange between N. Lenskii and E. Okunev, *StM* no. 1 (1907).

72. Al. Vilenkin, "O formakh studencheskoi organizatsii," *StO* no. 1 (1907).

73. "Razlozhenie skhodok," *StO* no. 2 (1907). See also the advocacy of "democracy" as students' new guiding principle, L. Sel'skii, *Obshchestvennaia zhizn' russkogo studenchestva i ee ocherednaia zadacha* (Kiev: 1907).

74. A. Kaigorodov, "Estestvennyi fakul'tet i kul'turno-nauchnye zadachi universiteta," *Stud* nos. 3, 4 (1906).

75. *Stud* no. 1 (1906): 10–11; no. 3 (1906): 41–44.

76. "S.-Peterburgskaia Studencheskaia Birzha Truda," *Stud* no. 2 (1906): 15–17.

77. *StZh* no. 1 (1906); *MS* no. 1 (1906); and *Stud* nos. 1, 3 (1906).

78. D'iakonov, *1905 i 1906*, 107–115. For two commentaries critical of Manuilov, see M. Aleksandrovich [M. A. Engel'gard], "Primenitel'no k podlosti" (khronika za nedeliu) *SR*, vyp. 4 (1906), 77–87; and V. A. Miakotin, "Khoziaeva universiteta," *NSO*, vyp. 2 (1906), 41–48.

79. The final vote was 4,000 to 15. D'iakonov, *1905 i 1906*, 118–124. See also *MS* no. 1 (1906): 13–14; "Zadachi universitetov," *Stud* no. 1 (1906): 2–6. On the reinstituted boycott of two professors, see D'iakonov, *1905 i 1906*, 81–82.

80. *Except for the dates of events described, reports of academic personnel and police have little in common. RGIA, f. 733, op. 153, d. 366, ll. 31, 34. For other examples, see GARF, f. 102 (DP OO), 1905, d. 3 ch. 26 ch. 1, ll. 54ff, passim; and TsGIA SPb, f. 113, op. 1, d. 13, ll. 2–13.*

81. Boris Frommett, *Ocherki po istorii studenchestva v Rossii* (SPb: 1912), 85.

82. RGIA, f. 733, op. 153, d. 366, l. 73.

CHAPTER 5

1. For excellent recent studies, see Laura Engelstein, *The Keys to Happiness: Sex and the Search for Modernity in Fin-de-Siècle Russia* (Ithaca, N.Y.: 1992); and Joan Neuberger, *Hooliganism: Crime, Culture, and Power in St. Petersburg, 1900–1914* (Berkeley: 1993).

2. E. V. Tarle, "Rol' studenchestva v revoliutsionnom dvizhenii v Evrope v 1848 godu," reprinted in *Sochineniia* (Mos.: 1957), vol. 1, 585–604, here 604. For a classic example of this general argument, see V. M. Friche, "Zapadno-evropeiskoe studenchestvo," the introductory article to *Osnovnye momenty studencheskogo dvizheniia v Rossii* by Rafael Vydrin (Mos.: 1908), 3–10. See also V. Maiskii, "Evoliutsiia nemetskogo studenchestva," *Obr* no. 5 (1909).

3. For a cross-section of opinion, see Ia. Danilin, ed., *Sanin v svete russkoi kritiki* (Mos.: 1908). On the popularity of *Sanin* among youth, see A. V. Peshekhonov, " 'Sanintsy' i 'Sanin,' " *RB* nos. 5, 6 (1908).

4. A. Vilenkin, "Nastroenie," *StR* nos. 1, 2 (1907).

5. M. Greidenberg, "Sanin (Itogi proshlogo i problemy budushchego)," in *Sbornik* (Kharkov: 1908), 174; see also 159–160, 164, 169.

6. "V kruzhke realistov," *StM* no. 2 (1907): 2.

7. For their charters, see RGIA, f. 733, op. 155, d. 393, ll. 284, 326.

8. *StO* no. 1 (1907): 2; no. 2 (1907): 2.

9. *StR* no. 2 (1907): 3.

10. *StO* no. 3 (1907): 3.

11. B. Tikhomirov, "Koe-chto o geroiakh M. Gor'kogo," *Griaduiushchii den'*, sbornik 2 (SPb: 1907), 139–145.

12. *StR* no. 1 (1907): 2.

13. *StR* no. 2 (1907): 3.

14. For the correspondence between the rector and the Ministry, and the various regulations of 1907–1908, see RGIA, f. 733, op. 154, d. 191.

15. Vad. Levchenko, "Krizis universitetskoi zhizni. (Mysli studenta)," *RM* no. 5 (1908).

16. For the police version of the actual events, see GARF, f. 102 (DP OO), 1905, d. 3 ch. 26 ch. 1, ll. 96–98, 101–102; see also an SR proclamation, f. 102 (DP IV), 1907, op. 99, d. 61 ch. 5, l. 18. For the press coverage, see *StO* nos. 1, 2 (1907).

17. "Po povodu tak nazyvaemogo 'popraveniia studenchestva,' " *StM* no. 1 (1907).

18. E. Charskii, "Zadachi universiteta," *StM* no. 1 (1907). See also M. Podshibiakin, "Staroe i novoe v studenchestve," *StR* no. 1 (1907): 2.

19. Rafael Vydrin, *Osnovnye momenty studencheskogo dvizheniia v Rossii* (Mos.: 1908).

20. RGIA, f. 733, op. 154, d. 159, ll. 5–7, 14–16, 22; and GARF, f. 102 (DP OO), 1905, d. 3 ch. 26 ch. 1, ll. 121–122, 130.

21. RGIA, f. 733, op. 154, d. 192, l. 59.

22. For the resolution, see TsGIA SPb, f. 14, op. 25, d. 40, ll. 33–34; for the police report, see GARF, f. 102 (DP OO), 1905, d. 3 ch. 26 ch. 2, ll. 174–175.

23. GARF, f. 102 (DP OO), 1905, d. 3 ch. 26 ch. 2, l. 164.

24. RGIA, f. 733, op. 154, d. 159, l. 192.

25. Writing under the pseudonym A. Iarmolovich, *Smert' prizrakov (Nadgrobnoe slovo nad poslednimi sobytiiami v S.-Peterburgskom universitete)* (SPb: 1908), 48.

26. Also called the "Dubinushka of 1908" after one of the best known revolutionary tunes in Russia. GARF, f. 102 (DP OO), 1905, d. 3 ch. 26 ch. 2, l. 186.

27. For the leaflets, see RGIA, f. 733, op. 154, d. 159, ll. 181–185.

28. The strike succeeded despite a vote (740 to 429) that hardly reflected a majority of the more than 2,000 students. TsGIA SPb, f. 492, op. 2, d. 9917, ll. 10–11.

29. RGIA, f. 733, op. 154, d. 159, ll. 94–110.

30. RGIA, f. 733, op. 154, d. 159, ll. 188, 190.

31. A. Z., "Chego khotiat studenty," *Rech'*, 2.X.1908.

32. For the notice from the faculty council requesting students to allow professors to defend autonomy, see TsGIA SPb, f. 14, op. 1, d. 10200, l. 27. The draft university charter (announced on October 4) was nonetheless closer to the reactionary 1884 charter than the August 1905 Temporary Rules. "V uchebnykh zavedeniiakh," *Rech'*, 7.X.1908.

33. V. A. Miakotin, "Tragediia vysshei shkoly," *RB* no. 10 (1908); see also I. Larskii, "Na granitse akademizma," *SM* no. 10 (1908); and M. Ia. Lazerson, "Studenchestvo i minuvshii akademicheskii krizis," *Obr* no. 4 (1909).

34. Quoted in Larskii, "Na granitse," 96.

35. See note 25.

36. Iarmolovich, *Smert' prizrakov*, 3.

37. *Ibid.*, 73–74.

38. *Ibid.*, 85–86, 83.

39. K., "Otluchat' ili ne otluchat'?" in *Chaika: Studencheskii literaturno-khudozhestvennyi sbornik* (SPb: 1909), 68.

40. During the 1908–1909 academic year, the mutual-aid society of the Polytechnic

Institute recorded 6,780 rubles dispersed and only 899 received. Boris Frommett, *Ocherki po istorii studenchestva v Rossii* (SPb: 1912), 95–97.

41. Raisa L., "K nastroeniiu sredi studenchestva"; Evg. Mikh., "Avtonomiia na iznanku!"; and I. Iashin, "Sovet starost"; all in *Chaika;* for an article describing the "new" *studenchestvo* in positive terms, see De-Mo, "O starom i novom studenchestve," *GP* no. 2 (1909).

42. Strumilin, " 'Nadgrobnoe slovo' studenchestvu," *GP* no. 3 (1909), 12–13. See also the student collection (particularly the article by Landov) *V zatish'e* no. 2, (1909); and B. Kovarskii, "Usluzhlivyi mogil'shchik," *GP* no. 2 (1909).

43. For the charter and program of the Academic Union, see *AS* no. 2 (1909): 35ff.

44. On right-wing politics and political organization in Russia, see Dietrich Löwe, *Antisemitismus und reaktionäre Utopie: Russischer Konservatismus im Kampf gegen den Wandel von Staat und Gesellschaft, 1890–1917* (Hamburg: 1978).

45. For the minutes of the disciplinary proceedings, see TsGIA SPb, f. 14, op. 25, d. 41, ll. 1–30, here 1–2; for the verdict, which failed to identify the culprits due to conflicting statements, see RGIA, f. 733, op. 154, d. 309, ll. 5–8.

46. TsGIA SPb, f. 14, op. 25, d. 41, ll. 3, 25–27, 29.

47. See the 1913 report of the Ministry of Internal Affairs on the history of the academist movement, RGIA, f. 733, op. 201, d. 357, ll. 28–35a, esp. 32.

48. RGIA, f. 1284, op. 187, d. 29, l. 50. The annual statement is between ll. 48 and 49.

49. On the reception of Stolypin, see Stud. Kanarskii, "Na avanpostakh," *VkSZh* no. 3 (1910): 12–13. For a defense of militant but nonparty academism, see K. I. Fediushin, "P. A. Stolypin i studenty," *IV* no. 5 (1914). For a more extreme view, see G. Kushnyr-Kushnarev, *Istoricheskii ocherk vozniknoveniia i razvitiia akademicheskikh organizatsii v Rossii* (SPb: 1914).

50. On German students, see Konrad H. Jarausch, *Deutsche Studenten, 1880–1970* (Frankfurt am Main: 1984); and Peter Krause, *"O du alte schöne Burschenherrlichkeit": Die Studenten und ihr Brauchtum* (Graz, Vienna, Cologne: 1979).

51. RGIA, f. 733, op. 155, d. 393, l. 355.

52. RGIA, f. 733, op. 155, d. 37, l. 3.

53. RGIA, f. 1284, op. 187, d. 155, l. 2.

54. RGIA, f. 733, op. 155, d. 392, l. 73.

55. RGIA, f. 733, op. 154, d. 397, l. 146.

56. The use of alcohol was a privilege contingent on orderly behavior. RGIA, f. 1284, op. 187, d. 206, ll. 29–30. On the opening and activities of the clubs, see *VSZh* no. 1 (1910): 6.

57. RGIA, f. 1284, op. 187, d. 155, ll. 2–4, 9–10; and d. 121, l. 13.

58. See the report on the dedication of a new club, *VSZh* no. 1 (1910): 6.

59. Music was provided for a male chorus. *AS* no. 1 (1909): 23–26.

60. "K chitateliam," *VSZh* no. 1 (1910): 2. "Izgoev o studenchestve," *VSZh* no. 3 (1910), and "Kritika nashikh kritikov," *VkSZh* no. 3/6 (1910).

61. *Rech',* 5.II.1909; see also the editions of February 14 and 20, 1909. On dueling among German students, see Kelvin McAleer, *Dueling: The Cult of Honor in Fin-de-Siècle Germany* (Princeton: 1994), ch. 4.

62. A. Belilin, "Neizbezhnost' akademizma," *VSZh* no. 1 (1910): 2–5.

63. On the history of the student survey, see the introduction in V. V. Sviatlovskii, ed., *Studenchestvo v tsifrakh* (SPb: 1909).

64. *Ibid.,* 66–67. See also M. V. Bernatskii, ed., *K kharakteristike sovremennogo studenchestva* (SPb: 1910), v–vi.

65. This was a common theme; see, for example, I. S. Simonov, *Shkola i polovoi vopros* (SPb: 1909).

66. For the survey, see M. A. Chlenov, *Polovaia perepis' Moskovskogo studenchestva* (Mos.: 1909), 14–27.

67. *Ibid.*, 36–40, 44–48. For further discussion of the sex surveys in particular, see Engelstein, *Keys,* 248–253.

68. A notable exception to this generalization was the Moscow sex survey itself.

69. Bernatskii, *K kharakteristike,* 42–55; D. I. Sheinis, *Evreiskoe studenchestvo v tsifrakh* (Kiev: 1911), 10–11, 15–16; and N. A. Kablukov, *Studencheskii kvartirnyi vopros v Moskve* (Mos.: 1908), *passim.*

70. Kablukov, *Studencheskii,* 5, 68–69.

71. See G. I. Gordon, "K voprosu o material'nom polozhenii nashego studenchestva," *VV* no. 7 (1914); and D. N. Zhbankov, "Izuchenie voprosa o polovoi zhizni uchashchikh-sia," *PV* nos. 27–29 (1908).

72. Kablukov, *Studencheskii,* 70.

73. A. Mastriukov, "Vopros 'prizvaniia' i rezul'taty ankety," *VV* no. 7 (1911): 169–170.

74. Chlenov, *Polovaia,* 31, 57.

75. D. P. Nikol'skii, "Sanitarno-gigienicheskie usloviia zhizni studentov Tekhnolog-icheskogo Instituta," in Bernatskii, *K kharakteristike,* 74–78, 80.

76. Boris Frommett, "Ob usloviiakh zhizni i o zabolevaemosti studenchestva," *VG* no. 22 (1911): 785.

77. Surveys usually queried political sympathy rather than party membership. Sviat-lovskii, *Studenchestvo,* 73.

78. Sheinis, *Evreiskoe,* 46.

79. Bernatskii, *K kharakteristike,* 16–18.

80. Bernatskii, *K kharakteristike,* 21–22; Sviatlovskii, *Studenchestvo,* 81–88; Sheinis, *Evreiskoe,* 46–53.

81. "Akademisty v tsifrakh," *StM* no. 10 (1911): 7; see also "K kharakteristike 'akademis-tov,'" *GS* no. 3 (1911): 10.

82. N. Zh., "Grustnye perspektivy," *StZh* no. 48 (1911): 3–4.

83. Bernatskii, *K kharakteristike,* v–viii.

84. *Ibid.,* 15, 39.

85. Contrast Chlenov (*Polovaia,* 97–103) with N. P. Malygin, "Iz itogov studencheskoi perepisi v Iur'eve," *ZhORV* no. 1 (1907): 21–22.

86. *Vekhi. Sbornik statei o russkoi intelligentsii,* (Mos.: 1909), i–iii.

87. A. S. Izgoev, "Ob intelligentnoi molodezhi," in *Vekhi,* 97–124. See also the article by Sergei Bulgakov ("Geroizm i podvizhnichestvo"), who portrayed students as archetypi-cal representatives of revolutionary heroism.

88. Portugeis wrote under a pseudonym, St. Ivanovich, "Novye vremena, novye pesni," *Sbornik vershiny* (SPb: 1909), 271.

89. Ol'ga Gridina, "Iazyk tsifr," *GK,* 6.XI.1909.

90. M. O. Gershenzon, "Tvorcheskoe samosoznanie," in *Vekhi,* esp. 90–93.

Chapter 6

1. V. V. Rozanov, "Homines novi," *Kogda nachal'stvo ushlo, 1905–1906gg* (SPb: 1910), 14–28, esp. 19–23. On Rozanov's philosophical views, see Laura Engelstein, *The Keys to Happiness: Sex and the Search for Modernity in Fin-de-Siècle Russia* (Ithaca, N.Y.: 1992), ch. 8.

2. For the classic texts advocating women's education, see N. I. Pirogov, "Voprosy zhizni," *Morskoi sbornik* (1856); and Mikhail Mikhailov, *Zhenshchiny: ikh vospitanie i znachenie v sem'e i obshchestve* (SPb: 1903). On the public debate, see Richard Stites, *The Women's Liberation Movement in Russia* (Princeton: 1978), pt. 2; and William G. Wagner, *Marriage, Property, and Law in Late Imperial Russia* (Oxford: 1994), 73–76, 83.

3. For a general summary of women's education, see Bonnie S. Anderson and Judith P. Zinser, *A History of Their Own: Women in Europe from Prehistory to the Present,* vol. 2 (N.Y.: 1988), 185–196. On the masculinity of science and the gender conflicts experienced by educated women, see Anthony Grafton and Lisa Jardine, *From Humanism to the Humanities: Education and the Liberal Arts in Fifteenth and Sixteenth Century Europe* (Cambridge, Mass.: 1986), ch. 2; Hiltrud Häntzschel and Hadumod Bußmann, *Bedrohlich gescheit: ein Jahrhundert Frauen und Wissenschaft in Bayern* (Munich, 1997); Londa Schiebinger, *The Mind has No Sex: Women in the Origins of Modern Science* (Cambridge, 1989); and Caroll Smith-Rosenberg, *Disorderly Conduct: Visions of Gender in Victorian America* (N.Y.: 1985), 245–296. The counter argument that the education of women would have a positive impact on the family was likewise common in the United States and Western Europe. See Judith R. Walkowitz, *City of Dreadful Delight: Narratives of Sexual Danger in Late-Victorian London* (Chicago: 1992), 63–65.

4. "Rech' Konservatora," *Grazhdanin* no. 78 (11.X.1901).

5. On the protests, see TsGIA SPb, f. 113, op. 1, d. 1209, ll. 34–60; and RGIA, f. 733, op. 151, d. 290, ll. 24, 52–66, 82.

6. *Prazdnovanie 25-letiia S.-Peterburgskikh Vysshikh zhenskikh kursov* (SPb: 1904).

7. *Ibid.,* 40.

8. *Ibid.,* 37.

9. *Ibid.,* 35–36.

10. See the addresses of the Academy of Sciences, St. Petersburg University, and former students from Irkutsk, *ibid.,* 33, 35, 64. For a similar view, see F. D. Batiushkov, "Zhenskii svobodnyi universitet," *MB* no. 12 (1903).

11. *Prazdnovanie,* 34.

12. *Ibid.,* 47, 51, 64, 73–75, 104.

13. "Obshchestvo Popechitel'stva o Vospitatel'nitsakh i Uchitel'nitsakh," *ibid.,* 67.

14. Women's Gymnasium E. P. Shaffe, *ibid.,* 78.

15. Institute of Communication-Engineering, *ibid.,* 45.

16. For twelve addresses from male students, see *ibid.,* 85–86, 104–106.

17. TsGIA SPb, f. 139, op. 1, d. 9594, ll. 25, 39.

18. For caricatures of the *nigilistka* that also contrast the virtues of motherhood with the dangers of education and nihilism, see Nikolai Leskov, *Nekuda* (1864), and Ivan Goncharov, *Obryv* (1869). On ideals of motherhood, see Jane T. Costlow, "The Pastoral Source: Representations of the Maternal Breast in Nineteenth-Century Russia," in *Sexuality and the Body in Russian Culture,* Jane T. Costlow, Stephanie Sandler, and Judith Vowles, eds. (Stanford: 1993).

19. According to Christine Ruane, this practice was widespread throughout the Russian empire. See her "The Vestal Virgins of St. Petersburg: Schoolteachers and the 1897 Marriage Ban," *The Russian Review* 50:2 (April 1991), and *Gender, Class, and the Professionalization of Russian City Teachers, 1860–1914* (Pittsburgh: 1994).

20. Of 2,229 graduates of the courses between 1882 and 1903, 840 were married and 820 were employed in some aspect of teaching. Information is missing for several hundred graduates. *S.-Peterburgskie Vysshie zhenskie kursy za 25 let, 1878–1903: Ocherki i materialy* (SPb: 1903), 150–153.

21. Perhaps because the Women's Medical Institute had opened so recently (1897) after the prolonged closure of its predecessor, most discussion of women's careers focused on pedagogy, although a maternal metaphor was sometimes used for women pursuing medical careers. On these women, see Mary Schaeffer Conroy, "Women Pharmacists in Russia before World War I," in Linda Edmondson, ed., *Women and Society in Russia and the Soviet Union* (Cambridge, Mass.: 1992); Barbara Alpern Engel, "Women Medical Students in Russia, 1872–1882: Reformers or Rebels?," *Journal of Social History* 12:3 (1979); A. N. Shabanova, "Zhenskoe vrachebnoe obrazovanie v Rossii," *IV* no. 5 (1913); and Jeanette E. Tuve, *The First Russian Women Physicians* (Newtonville, Mass.: 1984).

22. TsGIA SPb, f. 139, op. 1, d. 10199, ll. 65, 73.

23. On events at the courses, see TsGIA SPb, f. 113, op. 1, d. 1165; at the Medical Institute, see d. 1210, l. 233. On the arrest of women students for revolutionary activity, see f. 139 op. 1, d. 10198, ll. 141–142; f. 2075, op. 6, d. 71; d. 7a; and d. 7b.

24. For their obituaries, see P. Shaskol'skii, "A. Benediktova i A. Mamaeva," *Stud* no. 3 (1906): 4–5.

25. For histories of the major courses in Russia, see K. R. Shokhal', *Vysshee zhenskoe obrazovanie v Rossii* (SPb: 1910); see also S. G. Svatikov, "Russkaia studentka," *Put' studenchestva* (Mos.: 1916), 107–111. On the Women's Polytechnical Courses, see *Pervye zhenshchiny-inzhenery* (Len.: 1967).

26. These figures include students at private courses and institutes. Ruth Dudgeon, "Women Students in Russia, 1860–1905" (Ph.D. diss., George Washington University, 1975), 9.

27. *Vysshie zhenskie kursy v S.-Peterburge. Kratkaia istoricheskaia zapiska, 1878–1908gg.* (SPb: 1908).

28. On the growing number of Russian Jewish students studying in Germany and the problems they faced there and upon their return to Russia, see Jack Wertheimer, *Unwelcome Strangers: East European Jews in Imperial Germany* (N.Y.: 1987), 63–71.

29. A. A. Kaufman, ed., *Slushatel'nitsy S.-Peterburgskikh Vysshikh Zhenskikh (Bestuzhevskikh) Kursov (po dannym perepisi. . . 1909g)* (SPb: 1912), 4.

30. RGIA, f. 733, op. 201, d. 285, l. 40; and TsGIA SPb, f. 139, op. 1, d. 12,599, ll. 97–99, 116.

31. On the legal status and rights of graduates, see Shokhal', *Vysshee zhenskoe,* 147–151.

32. L. A. Mervart, "Kak Bestuzhevki sdavali gosudarstvennye ekzameny v 1911 godu," in *Sankt Peterburgskie Vysshie zhenskie (Bestuzhevskie) kursy (1878–1918gg.)* (Len.: 1965), 215–217.

33. S. M. Khlytchieva, "Vospominaniia iuristki pervogo vypuska," in *Sankt Peterburgskie Vysshie zhenskie (Bestuzhevskie) kursy,* 249–255.

34. On feminism in this period, including the strong support of feminists for women students, see Stites, *Women's Liberation,* 191–232; and Linda Edmondson, *Feminism in Russia, 1900–1917* (London: 1984).

35. M. I. Pokrovskaia, *O vysshem zhenskom obrazovanii v Rossii* (SPb: 1906), 14–15.

36. TsGIA SPb, f. 14, op. 1, d. 10000, l. 138.

37. I have not been able to confirm the number of women auditors at technical institutes; see Svatikov, *Put' studenchestva,* 108. For the detailed statistics on 1906–1908, see N. V. Chekhov, "Zhenshchiny v universitetakh," *SZh* no. 5 (1907): 9. For the 1909 figures, see RGIA, f. 733, op. 154, d. 309, ll. 40–44.

38. This file consists of biographical questionnaires filled out by students. Some are incomplete. TsGIA SPb, f. 14, op. 27, d. 514.

39. V. Shimkevich, "Opyt dvukh let," *SZh* no. 9 (1908): 12.

40. E. N. Shchepkina, "Zhenshchina v russkikh universitetakh," *VE* no. 9 (1912): 363–364.

41. A. S., "Zhenshchiny v universitete," *Stud* no. 2 (1906): 1.

42. V. V. Sviatlovskii, ed., *Studenchestvo v tsifrakh* (SPb: 1909), 101, 126–127; and M. V. Bernatskii, *K kharakteristike sovremennogo studenchestva* (SPb: 1910), 24, 27–28.

43. See Shchepkina, "Zhenshchina," 367–372, and the reports presented at a 1909 national conference of women auditors held in St. Petersburg, RGIA, f. 733, op. 154, d. 309, ll. 40–53.

44. RGIA, f. 733, op. 154, d. 309, ll.43–53.

45. Vol'noslushatel'nitsa, "O polozhenii vol'noslushatel'nits v universitete," *SZh* no. 5 (1907): 8. For other letters from auditors, see *SZh* nos. 3, 4, (1907), nos. 3, 5/6, 7/8 (1908).

46. V. M. Gessen, "O vol'noslushatel'nitsakh vysshei shkoly," *SZh* no. 5/6 (1908), 1–4.

47. It is difficult to assess whether this sample was at all representative, as participation was voluntary. For the survey, see *SZh* no. 5/6 (1908), 15; for the first results, see N. V. Chekhov, "Professura o vol'noslushatel'nitsakh," no. 9 (1908), 1–9. For other positive assessments, see M. N. Chubinskii, "Sovmestnoe obuchenie v vysshei shkole," *NS* no. 4 (1913); and M. M. Kovalevskii, "Vysshee zhenskoe obrazovanie," *VE* no. 6 (1911).

48. Chekhov, "Professura," 8.

49. *Ibid.*, 9, *passim.*

50. RGIA, f. 733, op. 154, d. 309, ll. 44–53.

51. Gosudarstvennaia Duma, Tretii Sozyv. *Stenograficheskie otchety* (3.III.1910), 2,897.

52. *Stenograficheskie otchety* (8.III.1910), 9–15. On student reactions, see RGIA, f. 733, op. 154, d. 698, l. 3; and "Protest studenchestva!" *StZh* no. 9 (1910): 8–11.

53. N. A. Berdiaev, *Novoe religioznoe soznanie i obshchestvennost'* (SPb: 1907).

54. Anna Afanas'eva, "Iz dnevnika gimnazistki," in *Revoliutsionnoe iunoshestvo, 1905–1917gg* (Len.: 1924), 109.

55. See the review of Mechnikov's *Etiudy optimizma*, Moskvichka, "Tretii pol," *SZh* no. 4 (1908): 9–11.

56. A. M. Kollontai, "Novaia zhenshchina," *SM* no. 9 (1913): 166–179.

57. A. V. Tyrkova, "Izmenenie zhenskoi psikhologii za poslednee stoletie," *Trudy pervogo vserossiiskogo s"ezda po obrazovaniiu zhenshchin,* vol. 1 (SPb: 1914), 1–5.

58. Shchepkina, "Zhenshchina," 361–362.

59. Several women physicians, school teachers, a writer, and twelve women students participated in the formulation of questions. D. N. Zhbankov, "Izuchenie voprosa o polovoi zhizni uchashchikhsia," *PV* nos. 27–29 (1908): 474, 486–491.

60. The three questionnaires follow the letter dated December 17, 1908. RGIA, f. 733, op. 154, d. 314, ll. 1, 2–25.

61. Zhbankov, "Izuchenie,"489, 503, 505.

62. All three respondents admitted sexual desire but privileged love over sex, confined sex to a marriage of love, and hoped to have a family and children; only one wished to combine marriage with public life. RGIA, f. 733, op. 154, d. 314, ll. 6–8, 14–16, 22–24.

63. A. A. Kaufman, "Russkaia kursistka v tsifrakh," *RM* no. 6 (1912): 63–64. For the complete results, see Kaufman, ed. *Slushatel'nitsy S.-Peterburgskikh Vysshikh zhenskikh (Bestuzhevskikh) kursov (po dannym perepisi . . .)* (SPb: 1912).

64. Kaufman, "Russkaia kursistka," 67.

65. Kaufman, *Slushatel'nitsy,* 11.

66. Kaufman, "Russkaia kursistka," 68–71; *Slushatel'nitsy,* 50–51.

67. Kaufman, "Russkaia kursistka," 76–77; *Slushatel'nitsy,* 79–83.

68. While Dostoevskii was preferred to Tolstoi as a writer, Tolstoi (the moralist) had

had a greater impact on personal development. Kaufman, "Russkaia kursistka," 84–88; *Slushatel'nitsy*, 110–124.

69. Kaufman, "Russkaia kursistka," 93.

70. For a similar conclusion, see A. A. Kaufman, *Slushatel'nitsy Petrogradskikh) vysshikh zhenskikh (Bestuzhevskikh) kursov na vtorom godu voiny* (Pet.: 1916).

71. L. N. Kleinbort, "Sovremennaia molodezh': Russkaia kursistka," *SM* no. 10 (1914), esp. 18–19, 31–33, 37–40. Compare to his "Sovremennaia molodezh' (Prezhde i teper')," *SM* no. 10 (1914).

72. Svatikov, *Put' studenchestva*, 110–111.

73. *Ibid.*, x. See also S. Sh., "Evreiskaia kursistka," in *Nash put'. Sbornik, posviashchennyi interesam evreiskogo studenchestva* (Pet.: 1916), 33–35.

74. Student Gosh, "Zhenshchina-grazhdanin," *StG* no. 2 (1913): 10–12.

75. A. Poliashcheva, "Zhenskii vopros," *StG* no. 8:1 (1914): 3–4.

76. "Pomnite!" and N. Aktiv, "Gde otvet?" *StG* no. 10:3 (1914), 1, 2.

77. B. Iller, "Osvobozhdenie zhenshchiny," *StG* no. 10:3 (1914): 1–2.

78. Medichka, "Pis'mo v redaktsiiu," *StG* no. 12:5 (1914): 3.

79. E. Kritskaia, "Pis'mo v redaktsiiu," *StG* no. 13:6 (1914): 4.

80. *StG* no. 13:6 (1914): 3.

81. *StG* no. 14:7 (1914): 1.

82. RGIA, f. 733, op. 155, d. 1191, l. 7.

83. A. Khiterman, "Kamen' v more," *Otkliki: Studencheskii literaturnyi sbornik* (Mos.: 1910), 61–68.

84. Nina Karatygina, *Krov' zhivotvoriashchaia, Sbornik* (Pet.: 1916). Kursistka N. O. Nefed'eva, "Moia pervaia liubov'," *Studencheskii sbornik* (Pet.: 1915), 115–146. It is interesting to note that Nefed'eva wrote in a masculine voice.

CHAPTER 7

1. N. Rostov, "Samoubiistvo M. F. Vetrovoi i studencheskie bezporiadki 1897g.," *KS* no. 2 (1926); see also Nik. Iordanskii, "Missia P. S. Vannovskogo," *Byloe* no. 9/21 (1907): 94–96.

2. *Pamiati Mar'i Fedos'evny Vetrovoi* (SPb: 1898), 3–22, in RGIA, f. 1410, op. 2, d. 30, ll. 46–57.

3. GARF, f. 102 (DP IV), op. 100 (1908), d. 119 ch. 42, l. 235.

4. Vera Figner, *Memoirs of a Revolutionist* (De Kalb, Ill.: 1991), 193–194.

5. *Listki svobodnogo slova* no. 8 (1899): 24–25.

6. "Rech' obviniaemogo studenta," *Osv* no. 14 (1903): 236.

7. Dated March 25, 1901. RGIA, f. 733, op. 151, d. 64, l. 213.

8. "Novaia drama v tiur'me," *Osv* no. 10 (1903): 179–180.

9. TsGIA SPb, f. 2075, op. 6, d. 7b, ll. 155, 158; RGIA, f. 733, op. 152, d. 176, ii. 19–22; and f. 1405, op. 530, d. 114, ll. 120–127.

10. TsGIA SPb, f. 139, op. 1, d. 9593, l. 157.

11. D. N. Zhbankov, "Travmaticheskaia epidemiia," *PV* nos. 32–35 (1905).

12. D. N. Zhbankov, "O samoubiistvakh v poslednee vremia," *PV* nos. 26–29 (1906): 437–438.

13. V. K. Khoroshko, " 'Gigiena dushi' i biurokratiia," *RM* no. 12 (1905): 139.

14. Khoroshko, " 'Gigiena,' " 138. On the politicization and professionalization of psychiatry, see Julie Brown, "Revolution and Psychosis: The Mixing of Science and Politics in Russian Psychiatric Medicine, 1905–1913," *SlR* no. 3 (1987).

15. For the first case studies, see F. E. Rybakov, "Dushevnye razstroistva v sviazi s tekushchimi politicheskimi sobytiiami," *RV* no. 51 (1905), no. 3 (1906). On the broader debate, see "Korrespondentsii," *OPNEP* no. 7 (1906). For further analysis of this issue, see Laura Engelstein, *The Keys to Happiness: Sex and the Search for Modernity in Fin–de–Siècle Russia* (Ithaca, N.Y.: 1992), 257–264.

16. N. A. Vigdorchik, "Politicheskie psikhozy i politicheskie samoubiistva," *Obr* no. 12 (1907), 59–60.

17. Lev Sheinis, "Epidemicheskie samoubiistva," *VV* no. 1 (1909): 150.

18. The first report summarized records from before 1905, and subsequent reports were published in annual volumes under the same title. G. V. Khlopin, "Samoubiistva, pokusheniia na samoubiistvo i neschastnye sluchai sredi uchashchikhsia russkikh ucheb-nykh zavedenii," *ZhMNP* no. 3 (1906): 1–81.

19. From 1906 to 1911, Grigor'ev registered 13,085 cases, compared with 6,968 official cases. N. I. Grigor'ev, "Samoubiistva i pokusheniia na samoubiistvo v Peterburge," *RV* no. 6 (1913): 188. For official statistics, see the annual *Ezhegodnik S.-Peterburga;* and S. A. Novosel'skii, *Statistika samoubiistv* (SPb: 1910).

20. G. I. Gordon, "Sovremennye samoubiistva," *RM* no. 5 (1912): 75.

21. He had collected 16,989 newspaper accounts of suicide. D. N. Zhbankov, "K statistike samoubiistv v 1905–11 godakh," *PV* nos. 34–38 (1912): 520.

22. The reason for the omission was incomplete data. G. V. Khlopin, *Samoubiistvo, pokusheniia na samoubiistvo i neschastnye sluchai sredi uchashchikhsia russkikh uchebnykh zavedenii*. Series. 1907 (SPb: 1908), i–vii.

23. *PL,* 23.IV.1908.

24. Gordon, "Sovremennye samoubiistva," 83. For Khlopin's complete statistics, see *Samoubiistvo,* 1909 (SPb: 1911), ii. Only for 1907 did he acknowledge his data as incomplete.

25. G. I. Gordon, "Samoubiistva molodezhi i ee nervno-psikhicheskaia neustoichivost'," *NZhV* no. 9 (1912): 107–108. Unfortunately, there is no comparable study for Western Europe, though suicide rates were also increasing, especially among secondary school students. Primary sources touching on this problem include Emile Durkheim, *Suicide: A Study in Sociology* (N.Y.: 1951); Paul Friedman, ed., *On Suicide (Discussions of the Vienna Psychoanalytic Society—1910)* (N.Y.: 1957); and Louis Proal, *L'éducation et le suicide des enfants* (Paris: 1907).

26. I. E. Maizel', "O samoubiistvakh sredi uchashchikhsia," *VV* no. 8 (1908): 161.

27. Jeffrey Brooks, *When Russia Learned to Read* (Princeton: 1985); and Louise McReynolds, *The News Under Russia's Old Regime* (Princeton: 1991). On the representation of suicide in the English press and for an analysis of "journalistic realism," see Michael MacDonald and Terence R. Murphy, *Sleepless Souls: Suicide in Early Modern England* (Oxford: 1990), 301–337.

28. *Poslednie novosti,* 29.V.1908.

29. *NR,* 10.VIII.1909.

30. D. N. Zhbankov, "Sovremennye samoubiistva," *SM* no. 3 (1910): 29.

31. G. I. Gordon, "Golodnye samoubiistva," *ZhV* no. 4 (1912): 671–672, 675.

32. *PL, PG,* 17.III.1908.

33. *GK, NR,* 3.XII.1908. See also the case of F. Barkanovich, *Rech', Slovo, NV, PL,* 4.VI.1909.

34. V. Petrusevich, "Prichiny neizvestny," *Rus',* 7.V.1908.

35. *Rus',* 19.V.1908.

36. N. Levitskii, "Memento mori," *Rech',* 15.VII.1908. See also *NR,* 26.VIII.1909.

37. "Uzhasy zhizni," *PL*, 21.V.1909; G. I. Gordon, "Samoubiistvo v Vysshikh uchebnykh zavedeniiakh v 1908g," *SS*, 19.V.1909; Igrek, "Studencheskii proletariat," *Novyi golos*, 23.V.1909; and N. Dneprov, "Odna is mnogikh," *GK*, 9.X.1909.

38. "Pomogite (Sredi studenchestva)," *NR*, 16.XI.1909. See also N. A. Skvortsov, "V bitve s zhizn'iu," *StD* no. 7 (1912): 155–157.

39. Vl. Kokhanovskii, "Student Ivanov," *Obr* no. 12 (1907): 31–54. For variations on this theme, see N. Nikandrov, "Byvshii student," *SM* no. 3 (1909): 71–88; Semen Fomin, "Student Bylinin," *StZh* no. 21 (1910): 8–9.

40. *Na pomoshch' molodezhi: Sbornik statei, pisem i zametok o studencheskikh nuzhdakh, i samoubiistvakh uchashchikhsia* (Kiev: 1910).

41. *Ibid.*, 1–2.

42. *Ibid.*, 39–40, 45–46.

43. *Ibid.*, 46–47.

44. *Ibid.*, 47–48.

45. *NR*, 15.XII.1909. See also the account in *Rech'*, 15.XII.1909. For the full poem that was written in response to Pisarev's accidental drowning death, see N. A. Nekrasov, *Sobranie sochinenii*, vol. 2 (Mos.: 1965), 252–253.

46. "Esche odin," *Rech'*, 17.I.1910; the newspaper sent a wreath to his funeral: "To Aleksandr Krapukhin, friend and reader." *Rech'*, 20.I.1910.

47. *Zemshchina*, 24.I.1910. See also K. K-n, "Naprasnye 'rozy'," *S.-Peterburgskie vedomosti*, 19.I.1910.

48. *PL*, 27.I.1910. Other well-known educators and physicians drew similar conclusions: see V. M. Bekhterev, *NV*, 9.III.1910; P. Ia. Rozenbakh, *PG*, 17.III.1909; and D. S. Zernov, *PG*, 10.III.1910.

49. "Biografiia studenta Krapukhina," *SS*, 18.I.1910.

50. *Rech'*, *PL*, *NR*, 13.XII.1909.

51. In his memoirs, N. P. Antsiferov does not mention poverty as a cause but recalls that the suicide remained the subject of many rumors. See his *Iz dum o bylom* (Mos.: 1992), 180–181.

52. *NR*, 18.XII.1909.

53. *NR*, 28.XII.1909.

54. *Slovo*, 11.IV.1909.

55. *PG*, 27.XI.1908.

56. *Birzhevye vedomosti*, 20.IV.1908.

57. Iu. Golubai, "Pusto," *Gaudeamus* no. 2 (1911): 2–3.

58. D. Zherebkov, "Mgla (Iz studencheskoi zhizni)," *StZh* no. 43/19 (1910): 8–9; see also M. Nemov, "Nechaianno," *StZh* no. 1 (1910): 13–15; and G. Brazilevich, *Studentsamoubiitsa: Sbornik* (SPb: 1910).

59. M. Al'bin, "Zhit'!" *StZh* no. 1 (1906): 1.

60. A. Vilenkin, "Nastroenie," *StR* no. 2 (1907): 2–3.

61. Cited in Vasilii Miasnikov, "Dumy o nashem studenchestve," in *Utro Zhizni: Studencheskii literaturnyi al'manakh* (Khabarovsk: 1914), 4.

62. Compare K. P. Slavnin, "K bor'be s samoubiistvom," *NR*, 17.VIII.1909; and Miasnikov, "Dumy," esp. 4, 8.

63. T. L. Krivonosov, " 'Odinokie' i ikh 'poslednee slovo'," *StZh* no. 22 (1910): 2–5.

64. G. Murashev, "Motivy sovremennosti," *StD* no. 4/11 (1912): 108–112; L. Slutskii, "O samoubiistvakh," *StM* no 7 (1911): 5–7; and S. Ganzen, "O 'kholode' zhizni," *GP* no. 8 (1913): 14–16.

65. "Sredi studenchestva," *NR*, 26.X.1909.

66. N. W., "Molodost' bezsmertna," *StM* no. 10 (1910): 3–4.

67. Maksim Gorkii, "Izdaleka," *ZZh* no. 7 (1912): 386–387, 392. This view was very common; see also A. Gladkii, "Vzgliad khudozhnikov na zhizn' i samoubiistvo," *VV* no. 6 (1913); and F. E. Rybakov, *Sovremennye pisateli i bol'nye nervy* (Mos.: 1908).

68. Vladimir Vagner, "Samoubiistvo i filosofskii pessimizm," *ZZh* no. 49 (1912): 2,811–2,816.

69. E. P. Radin, *Dushevnoe nastroenie sovremennoi uchashcheisia molodezhi* (SPb: 1913).

70. Radin (*ibid.*, 108–117) was influenced by Durkheim; however, he blamed suicide more on the incomplete nature of the transformation to modernity rather than on modern forms of social organization.

71. *Ibid.*, 47.

72. *Ibid.*, 39–40.

73. *Ibid.*, 117–118.

Chapter 8

1. On the broader social and political crisis, see Leopold H. Haimson, "The Problem of Social Stability in Urban Russia, 1905–1917," *SlR* 23:4 (1964) [Part One]; 24:1 (1965) [Part Two]; and Geoffrey A. Hosking, *The Russian Constitutional Experiment: Government and Duma, 1907–1914* (Cambridge, Eng.: 1973).

2. GARF, f. 102 (DP IV), op. 100 (1908), d. 119 ch. 42, ll. 271–272; and TsGIA SPb, f. 14, op. 25, d. 43, ll. 1–3.

3. For an overview of student activism across Russia, see "Studencheskie dvizheniia v 1910-m godu," *StM* no. 6 (1911): 2–5.

4. For an analysis of the proposal sympathetic to students, see Rafael Vydrin, "Nakanune novogo universitetskogo ustava," *SM* no. 1 (1910). See also the proclamation, RGIA, f. 733, op. 201, d. 168, l. 5.

5. "K voprosu o 'krizise' studenchestva," *StZh* no. 22 (1910): 2.

6. For photographs of the funeral, see *GS* no. 10 (1910).

7. RGIA, f. 733, op. 201, d. 168, ll. 20–24; see also the reports in the Moscow newspaper, *GS* nos. 9–13 (1910).

8. TsGIA SPb, f. 569, op. 13, d. 331, ll. 20–24, 39–40, 43–44, 48; f. 113, op. 10, d. 63, ll. 1–2, 8–9; and RGIA, f. 733, op. 201, d. 205, ll. 50–81, *passim*.

9. *GS* no. 13 (1910): 6. For the notes of one student on the "angry and dissatisfied mood," see GARF, f. 1167, op. 1, d. 5433. On the composition and later arrest of the council, see GARF, f. 102 (DP IV), 1911, d. 146 t. 1, l. 327.

10. On the arrest, expulsion, and exile of students after the rules were published, see *GS* nos. 1/14–3/16 (1911).

11. For an anonymous letter to the rector advising him to resign or become a powerless appendage of the bureaucratic regime, see TsGIA SPb, f. 14, op. 25, d. 39, ll. 4–5.

12. RGIA, f. 733, op. 201, d. 216, ll. 67–70; see also the protocol of the faculty council of the Women's Courses, which opposed the new rules, f. 733, op. 155, d. 49, l. 197–202.

13. RGIA, f. 733, op. 201, d. 205, ll. 128–129.

14. TsGIA SPb, f. 113, op. 10, d. 63, l. 16; and RGIA, f. 733, op. 201, d. 217, ll. 101–02, 112, 128.

15. TsGIA SPb, f. 14, op. 1, d. 10475, l. 72; and f. 113, op. 10, d. 63, l. 11.

16. On the situation at the Bestuzhev Courses, where 134 students signed a petition advocating the resumption of studies, and at the Technological Institute, see RGIA, f. 733,

op. 201, d. 217, ll. 101–105, 128–131; and d. 216, ll. 52–53, 66–88, *passim,* 109. On a moderate group at the Mining Institute, see f. 25, op. 1, d. 5964, ll. 6–10.

17. RGIA, f. 733, op. 201, d. 168, l. 27–30.

18. For leaflets on this theme, see RGIA, f. 733, op. 201, d. 216, ll. 81, 114.

19. This crisis is discussed extensively in *Ezhegodnik gazety Rech' za 1911g* (SPb: 1912).

20. For statistics on expelled and suspended students around the country, see RGIA, f. 733, op. 201, d. 206, ll. 166–168. On the Women's Medical Insitute, where 1,213 of 1,237 students were suspended, see TsGIA SPb, f. 139, op. 1, d. 12599, ll. 97–99; and RGIA, f. 733, op. 201, d. 285, ll. 2–6, 45–47.

21. A. S. Izgoev, "Krizis vysshei shkoly," *RM* no. 3 (1911). Compare with A. A. Isaev, *Zabastovki uchashchikhsia* (SPb: 1912).

22. Nikolai Iordanskii, "Otsy i deti," *SM* no. 2 (1911). See also V. A. Miakotin, "Dliashchaiasia tragediia," *RB* no. 3 (1911).

23. See the proclamation of the Coalition Committee, RGIA, f. 733, op. 201, d. 216, l. 81.

24. In one demonstration, seventy-three students were arrested; on the protests, see RGIA, f., 733, op. 201, d. 336, ll. 119–121; and d. 357, ll. 5–10.

25. On the trial, see Hans Rogger, "The Beilis Case: Anti-Semitism and Politics in the Reign of Nicholas ll," *SlR* 25:4 (1966).

26. For an overview, see *StG* no. 6 (1913): 4. See also TsGIA SPb, f. 569, op. 13, d. 360, l. 136–141; f. 14, op. 25, d. 48, l. 28–38; and RGIA, f. 733, op. 201, d. 403, l. 109–114.

27. RGIA, f. 733, op. 201, d. 336, ll. 81–82; and TsGIA SPb, f. 139, op. 1, d. 13149, ll. 1–26, *passim.*

28. RGIA, f. 733, op. 155, d. 462, ll. 27–48; op. 201, d. 403, ll. 3–10, 31–38, *passim*; and TsGIA SPb, f. 569, op. 13, d. 457, l. 33.

29. RGIA, f. 733, op. 155, d. 462, l. 23; f. 733, op. 201, d. 404, ll. 4–5; and d. 357, l. 5.

30. *UZh* no. 1 (1914).

31. For representative proclamations, see RGIA, f. 733, op. 201, d. 357, l. 6; and d. 404, l. 3.

32. For their first proclamation, see TsGIA SPb, f. 14, op. 25, d. 48, l. 2.

33. Boris Frommett, "Rossiiskoe studenchestvo i kooperatsiia," *VK* no. 2 (1911); and GARF, f. 102 (DP OO), 1914, d. 59 ch. 57, ll. 14–18.

34. For the Okhrana reports on the newspaper's editorial board, see GARF, f. 102 (DP OO), 1914, d. 59 ch. 57, ll. 16, 19–21.

35. *StD* no. 4 (1912): 125, 127 (the pages are sequential but misnumbered); and *UZh* no. 1 (1914): 16. On events across the country, see "Kak otozvalos' studenchestvo i obshchestvo na sobytiia v Voenno-Meditsinsk. Akad.," *StG* no. 3/4 (1913): 27–30.

36. See the Okhrana reports, RGIA, f. 1405, op. 530, d. 859, ll. 34–44, 51.

37. RGIA, f. 733, op. 201, d. 403, l. 90.

38. Student Voprosov, "De profundis," *StG* no. 1 (1913): 17–19; and Stud. Vopr-ov, "Reforma, studenchestvo, i professura," *StG* no. 2 (1913): 21–22.

39. TsGIA SPb, f. 14, op. 25, d. 48, l. 21. On the graveside protests and police intervention, see RGIA, f. 733, op. 201, d. 403, ll. 95, 103.

40. *StG* no. 5 (1913): 4.

41. I. V. Gessen, "Vnutrenniaia zhizn'," *Ezhegodnik gazety Rech' na 1913g* (SPb: 1914), 21.

42. The Russian *avtonomiia* is, of course, of foreign origin. *Studencheskii sbornik "Gaudeaumus"* (Kharkov: 1913), 7–8.

43. *Sovremennaia illustratsiia* no. 9 (September 21, 1913): 144.

44. Hubertus F. Jahn, *Patriotic Culture in Russia during World War I* (Ithaca, N.Y.: 1995).

45. One police report states, for example, that students formed "the predominating element" among the ten to twelve thousand participants in a March 24, 1913 manifestation. TsGIA SPb, f. 569, op. 13, d. 1055, ll. 26, 39, 49–50, 57.

46. RGIA, f. 1405, op. 530, d. 883, ll. 50–51.

47. TsGIA SPb, f. 569, op. 13, d. 1055, ll. 67–69. On student attitudes toward the war in general, see L. N. Kleinbort, "Molodezh' i voina," *SM* no. 11 (1914).

48. No further disruptions were reported. TsGIA SPb, f. 569, op. 13, d. 1182zh, l. 29; and f. 14, op. 1, d. 10873, ll. 14–15.

49. RGIA, f. 733, op. 201, d. 403, ll. 181–184.

50. RGIA, f. 1405, op. 530, d. 883, ll. 49–53.

51. RGIA, f. 1405, op. 530, d. 883, ll. 55–56.

52. GARF, f. 102 (DP OO), op. 244 (1914), d. 59 ch. 57, ll. 66, 68–73, 80–82; RGIA, f. 733, op. 155, d. 1191, ll. 24–25; op. 201, d. 505, ll. 5–9; and f. 1405, op. 530, d. 883, ll. 64–76.

53. This evaluation of an Okhrana report is probably accurate, because the Okhrana tended to overestimate, not underestimate, the radicalism of students. GARF, f. 102 (DP OO), op. 245 (1915), d. 59. ch. 57, l. 3.

54. "Studenchestvo i voina," *StV* no. 1 (1915): 6–7. See also the petition of a Moscow student to postpone her exams; she worked several 24-hour shifts each week in a field hospital in addition to attending medical school: RGIA, f. 733, op. 156, d. 131, l. 33.

55. GARF, f. 102 (DP OO), op. 245 (1915), d. 59 ch. 57, ll. 3–6.

56. RGIA, f. 733, op. 201, d. 509, ll. 6–10; f. 1405, op. 530, d. 906, ll. 16–20; and GARF, f. 102 (DP OO), op. 245 (1915), d. 59 ch. 57, ll. 8–9.

57. On the defense of Russo-German *zemliachestva* and the criticism of attempts to wipe out the "German" influence in the university, see *StG* no. 15 (1915): 5, 6.

58. The disorders occurred when students gathered in a hallway talking about the case of Colonel Miasoedov, executed for treason on flimsy evidence. RGIA, f. 733, op. 201, d. 506, ll. 26–28; and TsGIA SPb, f. 569, op. 13, d. 1182zh, ll. 79–91.

59. See the academists' report to the Minister of Interior, RGIA, f. 733, op. 156, d. 143, ll. 33–34; on the student delegation, see f. 1405, op. 530, d. 906, ll. 23–24.

60. GARF, f. 102 (DP OO), op. 245 (1915), d. 59 ch. 57, ll. 45–46.

61. TsGIA SPb, f. 14, op. 25, d. 49, I. 7; and RGIA, f. 733, op. 201, d. 506, l. 62. For the Okhrana report, see GARF, f. 102 (DP OO), op. 245 (1915), d. 59 ch. 57, ll. 42–44.

62. This letter was intercepted by the Okhrana. GARF, f. 102 (DP OO), op. 245 (1915), d. 59 ch. 57 lit. B, ll. 4, 11, 12. For a proclamation of polytechnic students blaming the state for military failures, see d. 59 ch. 57, ll. 28–29.

63. On protest in 1916, see TsGIA SPb, f. 569, op. 13, d. 1182zh, l. 115–119; and GARF, f. 102 (DP OO), op. 246 (1916), d. 59 ch. 57, ll. 1–5, 15, 17.

64. A. A. Kaufman, ed., *Slushatel'nitsy Petrogradskikh vysshikh zhenskikh (Bestuzhevskikh) kursov na vtorom godu voiny* (Pet.: 1916), 1, 8.

65. *StG* nos. 19, 21 (1915); and *ZhS* no. 1–3 (1916): 91–93. For the Okhrana report, see GARF, f. 102 (DP OO), op. 245 (1915), d. 59 ch. 57, l. 43.

66. *VStK* no. 1 (1916): 1.

67. "Pro Domo sua," *VStK* no. 4/5 (1916): 3. See also the anthology, S. G. Svatikov, ed., *Put' studenchestva* (Mos.: 1916).

68. Compare the Moscow newspaper *VStK* for the spring of 1916, and its successor *VS* (especially nos. 4, 5, 7), for the 1916–1917 academic year, with M. M. Rosin, "Puti v studenchestve," *ZhS* no. 1–3 (1916): 77–81.

69. Many of the conservative publications were not edited by students, although they did include student contributions. See the newspapers *Severnyi gusliar'* (1914–1915) and *VVy* (1914–1918); and the books *Molodaia Rus': Studencheskii sbornik* (Pet.: 1916) and *Studencheskii sbornik* (Pet.: 1915).

70. This one-time publication, *Voina i Petrogradskaia vysshaia shkola* (1916), was halted by the censors, and I have been unable to locate a copy. My comments are based on the reviews in *ZhS* no. 1–3 (1916): 85–88.

71. *Evreiskii student* (1914–1918); *Evreiskoe studenchestvo* (1914–1917); and *Nash put'. Sbornik, posviashchennyi interesam evreiskogo studenchestva* (Pet.: 1916).

72. Mikhail Lederman, "Zabytye," *StM* no. 1 (December 1915): 25–26.

73. In addition to the publications already cited, see the student journal *Put' studenchestva* nos. 1–6 (1916).

74. *Nash put'*, 57–58; and *ZhS* no. 1–3 (1916): 80.

75. Documents about the life and death of Khlebtsevich, including his poetry, are collected in three files: GARF, f. 2315, op. 1, d. 287; MISPbGU, f. RD, d. 29; and TsGIA SPb, f. 14, op. 27, d. 101, ll. 85–115. On the participation of students in the Revolution, see TsGIA SPb, f. 14, op. 27, d. 64, ll. 1, 4, 7; RGIA, f. 733, op. 201, d. 518, ll. 63–65, 75, 79, 102; and the Okhrana report dated February 25, GARF, f. 102 (DP OO), op. 247 (1917), d. 341 ch. 57, l. 43.

76. GARF, f. 2315, op. 1, d. 287, ll. 6–11.

77. Many resolutions were printed in *VVy* no. 20/21 (February/March 1917): 99. See also *Iubileinyi sbornik Voenno-meditsinskoi Akademii* (Len.: 1927), 20.

78. On the quartering of soldiers in educational institutions and other logistical problems, see TsGIA SPb, f. 14, op. 27, d. 67, l. 22; f. 492, op. 2, d. 13879, l. 3, and *passim*.

79. Required preparation was the equivalent of the boy's classical gymnasium. TsGIA SPb, f. 14, op. 27, d. 54.

80. For the register of authorized student meetings held at the university from September 22, 1914 through May 12, 1917, see TsGIA SPb, f. 14, op. 27, d. 397.

81. TsGIA SPb, f. 14, op. 27, d. 117, ll. 38, 40.

82. For the report on this incident and some of the group's posters, see TsGIA SPb, f. 14, op. 27, d. 67, ll. 55–59, 61.

83. See the speech of Moscow University's rector, *VVy* no. 4/5 (1917): 25–27.

84. On the situation in Moscow, see GARF, f. 2315, op. 1, d. 26, ll. 73–74, 83. For the situation across the country, see ll. 114, 125, 128, 140, 147, 154; and *VV* no. 6/7 (1917): 79–80.

85. *StP* no. 1 (1918): 11.

Conclusion

1. A. S. Izgoev, "Krizis vysshei shkoly," *Russkaia mysl'* no. 3 (1911).

Epilogue

1. See Sheila Fitzpatrick, *The Commissariat of Enlightenment* (N.Y.: 1971), and *The Cultural Front: Power and Culture in Revolutionary Russia* (Ithaca, N.Y.: 1992), 37–90; and James C. McClelland, "Bolsheviks, Professors, and the Reform of Higher Education in Soviet Russia, 1917–1921," (Ph.D. diss., Princeton University, 1970).

2. For an overview by a participant, see Sergei Zhaba, *Petrogradskoe studenchestvo v bor'be za svobodnuiu vysshuiu shkolu* (Paris: 1922).

3. *Polozhenie o Rossiiskikh universitetakh, proekt* (Mos.-Pet.: 1918); and the students' version, *Osnovnye polozheniia po voprosu o reforme vysshei shkoly, priniatye studenchestvom Petrogradskogo universiteta* (Pet.: 1918).

4. *Evreiskii student* no. 31/32 (February 1918): 58; and Zhaba, *Petrogradskoe*, 15–22, 35–36.

5. *Iubileinyi sbornik Voenno-meditsinskoi Akademii* (Len.: 1927), 13–14.

6. *Desiat' let stroitel'stva rabfakov: Sbornik statei* (Mos.-Len.: 1929), 36, 37, 144. See also *Itogi i perspektivy rabochikh fakul'tetov* (Len.: 1925).

7. Zhaba, *Petrogradskoe*, 24, 26. According to a 1914 Okhrana report, Zhaba was associated with the "Group of United Socialists." See RGIA, f. 1405, op. 530, d. 883, ll. 56–57. For an opposing perspective, see N. A. Bukhbinder, "Studencheskaia organizatsiia pri pet. kom. R.S.-D.R.P. (bolsh.)," *KL* no. 6 (1923).

8. Zhaba, *Petrogradskoe*, 26–51; *Iubileinyi sbornik*, 22–24, 26–29.

9. A. V. Lunacharskii, "Dva studenta," *StP* no. 1 (1918): 3–5. See also his "K Uchashchimsia," *Narodnoe prosveshchenie* no. 1 (1918).

10. A. B. Zalkind, *Ocherki kul'tury revoliutsionnogo vremeni* (Mos.: 1924), 133–134.

11. Zhaba, *Petrogradskoe*, 54–56, 61.

12. A. Valentinov, *Poslednie studenty (Zapiski studenta)* (1922). The victory of Soviet power led to a similar crisis of conscience among other members of the "old" educated society. See P. A. Sorokin, "Otpravliaias' v dorogu," *Utrenniki*, vol. 1 (Pet.: 1922), 10.

13. On the early years of the Komsomol, see Isabel A. Tirado, *Young Guard! The Communist Youth League, Petrograd 1917–1920* (Westport, Conn.: 1988); on the struggle in secondary education, see James C. McClelland, "The Utopian and the Heroic: Divergent Paths to the Communist Educational Ideal," in *Bolshevik Culture: Experiment and Order in the Russian Revolution*, Abbott Gleason, Peter Kenez, and Richard Stites, eds. (Bloomington, Ind.: 1985), 114–130. On popular culture in the 1920s, see Richard Stites, *Russian Popular Culture: Entertainment and Society Since 1900* (Cambridge, Eng.: 1992), 37–63.

14. The Soviet historian P. S. Gusiatnikov even provides a list of some seventy-five names belonging to this "glorious cohort of fighters"—students who later became important figures in the "Leninist Party" and Soviet state. See his *Revoliutsionnoe studencheskoe dvizhenie v Rossii* (Mos.: 1971), 224–225.

15. Various subgenres also developed, including that of the gymnasium student who had already achieved consciousness before even entering university. See, for example, Valentin Dunaev *Na zare iunosti* (Mos.: 1927); and V. I. Orlov, "Iz perezhitogo," in *Piatyi god: sbornik* (Mos.: 1925).

16. This is a generalization. The degree to which historians adopted this model as well as the quality of scholarship varied, as it does everywhere. An additional historiographical trend (which dominated works published in emigration and developed in the Soviet Union after the 1920s) bypassed political dogma by focusing on the scientific life of the prerevolutionary university. See, for example, Iu. N. Emel'ianov, ed., *Moskovskii universitet v vospominaniiakh sovremennikov* (Mos.: 1989). Many university histories (listed in the bibliography) have a dualistic quality, with sections on student radicalism referring to the revolutionary tradition and sections on academic life highlighting the high quality (and continuity) of Russian and Soviet universities. Some historians likewise focused on the development of state policy and the professoriate.

Selected Bibliography

ARCHIVAL SOURCES

St. Petersburg

I. Rossiiskii gosudarstvennyi istoricheskii arkhiv (RGIA)

        Fond 560: Ministerstvo finansov
        Fond 733: Ministerstvo narodnogo prosveshcheniia
        Fond 1129: V. T. Sheviakov
        Fond 1284: Ministerstvo vnutrennikh del
        Fond 1405: Ministerstvo iustitsii
        Fond 1410: Veshchestvennye dokazatel'stva, Ministerstvo iustitsii

II. Tsentral'nyi gosudarstvennyi istoricheskii archiv g. S.-Peterburga (TsGIA SPb)

        Fond 14: S.-Peterburgskii universitet
        Fond 113: Vysshie zhenskie (Bestuzhevskie) kursy
        Fond 139: S.-Peterburgskii uchebnyi okrug
        Fond 436: Zhenskii meditsinskii institut
        Fond 478: Politekhnicheskii institut
        Fond 492: Tekhnologicheskii institut
        Fond 569: S.-Peterburgskii Gradonachal'nik
        Fond 990: Elektrotekhnicheskii institut
        Fond 2075: S.-Peterburgskii General-Gubernator

III. Muzei istorii S.-Peterburgskogo gosudarstvennogo universiteta (MISPbGU)

        Fond RD: Revoliutsionnoe dvizhenie

Moscow

I. Gosudarstvennyi arkhiv Rossiiskoi Federatsii (GARF)

        Fond 102 (DP OO): Departament politsii, Osobyi otdel
        Fond 102 (DP IV): Departament politsii, IV deloproizvodstvo
        Fond 111: S.-Peterburgskoe okhranoe otdelenie
        Fond 124: Ministerstvo iustitsii

Fond 1167: Veshchestvennye dokazatel'stva, Ministerstvo iustitsii
Fond 2315: Vremennoe pravitel'stvo

II. Rossiiskaia gosudarstvennaia biblioteka, Otdel rukopisei (RGB)

Fond 269, k. 397, d. 4: Mariia A. Miliukova, "Memuary"

THE STUDENT PRESS

Journal/Newspaper (Date and Place of Publication)

Note: "*" indicates that I have either not located or not read the
newspaper.

Bal'naia gazeta (1911–1912, SPb)
Evreiskii student (1914–1918, Pet.)
Evreiskoe studenchestvo (1914–1917, Mos.)
Gaudeamus (1911, SPb)
Golos molodoi Rossii (1906, SPb)
Golos politekhnika (1909–1913, SPb)
Golos studenchestva (1910–1911, Mos.)
Listok studentov-psikhonevrologov (1911–1913, SPb)
Meditsinskoe obozrenie (1909, SPb)
Molodaia Rossiia (1906, SPb)
Molodaia Rossiia (1912, Kiev)
Molodaia zhizn' (1906, SPb)
Molodaia zhizn' (1912–1913, SPb)
Molodye sily (1906, SPb)
Otkliki nashei zhizni (1912–1913, SPb)
Politekhnik (1912–1913, SPb)
Put' studenchestva (1916, Pet.)
Severnyi gusliar' (1914–1915, Pet.)
Studencheskaia gazeta (1906, Mos.)
Studencheskaia gazeta (1913, SPb)
Studencheskaia mysl' (1901–1902, SPb)
Studencheskaia mysl' (1907, SPb)
Studencheskaia mysl' (1910–1911, Kiev)
Studencheskaia mysl' (1915–1916, Pet.)
Studencheskaia pravda (1918, Pet.)
Studencheskaia rech' (1907, SPb)
Studencheskaia zhizn' (1906, SPb)
Studencheskaia zhizn' (1910–1911, Mos.)
Studencheskie gody (1913–1915, SPb-Pet.)
Studencheskie izvestiia (1907, Mos.)
Studencheskie otkliki (1907, SPb)
Studencheskii listok (1913–1918, SPb-Pet.)*
Studencheskii mir (1910, Mos.)

Studencheskii vestnik (1915, Pet.)

Studencheskoe delo (1912–1913, Mos.)

Studencheskoe ekho (1907, SPb)

Studencheskoe slovo (1913, Mos.)*

Studenchestvo (1906, SPb)

Student (1903, Geneva)

Student-medik: Organ akademistov (1908–1911, SPb)*

Utro zhizni (1914, SPb)

V zatish'e (1908–1913, SPb)

Veshnie vody (1914–1918, Pet.)

Vesti studencheskoi zhizni (1910–1913, SPb)

Vestnik studencheskoi kooperatsii (1916, Mos.)

Vestnik studencheskoi zhizni (1908, SPb)

Vestnik studenchestva (1907, Mos.)

Vestnik studenchestva (1916, Mos.)

Voina i Petrogradskaia vysshaia shkola (1916, Pet.)*

Zhivaia sila (1916, Pet.)

Zhizn' studentov psikhonevrologov (1913–1914, SPb)

STUDENT LITERARY-CRITICAL COLLECTIONS

Akademicheskii sbornik. 2 vols. SPb: 1909.

Chaika: Studencheskii literaturno-khudozhestvennyi sbornik. SPb: 1909.

Griaduiushchii den'. 2 vols. SPb: 1907.

Literaturno-khudozhestvennyi sbornik. SPb: 1903.

Literaturnyi sbornik izdannyi studentami Imp. S.-Peterburgskogo universiteta v pol'zu ranenykh burov. SPb: 1903.

Molodaia Rus': Studencheskii sbornik. Pet.: 1916.

Nash put': Sbornik posviashchennyi interesam evreiskogo studenchestva. Pet.: 1916.

Obshchestudencheskii literaturnyi sbornik. Mos.: 1910.

Otkliki: Studencheskii literaturnyi sbornik. Mos.: 1910.

Sbornik. Kharkov: 1908.

Stazhery: Studencheskii al'manakh. SPb: 1913.

Studencheskii al'manakh. SPb: 1911–1912.

Studencheskii kruzhok politicheskoi ekonomiki. SPb: 1905.

Studencheskii sbornik. 2 vols. Kharkov: 1907–1908.

Studencheskii sbornik. Vyshnii Volochek: 1909.

Studencheskii sbornik. Pet.: 1915.

Studencheskii sbornik "Gaudeamus". 3 vols. Kharkov: 1913–1916.

Studenchestvo—Zhertvam voiny, Sbornik. Mos.: 1916.

U gorna: Sbornik 1. SPb: 1907.

Utro zhizni: Studencheskii literaturnyi al'manakh. Khabarovsk: 1914.

Vserossiiskii studencheskii sbornik. Kharkov: 1911.

PERSONAL ACCOUNTS

Afanas'eva, Anna. "Iz dnevnika gimnazistki." In *Revoliutsionnoe iunoshestvo, 1905–1917gg.*
Vol. 1. Len.: 1924.

Antsiferov, N. P. *Iz dum o bylom.* Edited and annotated by A. I. Dobkin. Mos.: 1992.

Arsen'ev, N. S. *Dary i vstrechi zhiznennogo puti.* Frankfurt: 1974.

Belousov, I. "Iz vospominanii o 1905 gode." *KS* no. 20 (1925).

Bogomazova, Z. P., T. D. Katsenelenbogen, and T. N. Puzyrevskaia, eds. *Pervye zhenshchiny-inzhenery.* Len.: 1967.

Braginskii, M. A. "Dobroliubovskaia demonstratsiia 17 noiabria 1886g v S.-Peterburge." *Byloe* no. 5 (1907).

Brandt, A. A. *List'ia pozheltelye: Peredumannoe i perezhitoe.* Belgrade: 1930.

Bukhbinder, N. A. "Studencheskaia organizatsiia pri Pet. Kom. RSDRP(b)." *KL* no. 6 (1923).

Burenin, N. E. *Pamiatnye gody.* Len.: 1961.

Chernov, V. N. *Zapiska sotsialista-revoliutsionera.* Berlin: 1922.

Chudnovskii, S. L. "Iz dal'nikh let (Otryvki iz vospominanii)." *Byloe* nos. 9, 10 (1907).

Chulkov, G. I. *Gody stranstvii: Iz knigi vospominanii.* Mos.: 1930.

D'iakonova, E. A. *Dnevnik Elizavety D'iakonovoi, 1886–1902.* 4th edition. Mos.: 1912.

Divil'kovskii, A. "Staroe studenchestvo na sluzhbe revoliutsii (Iz vospominanii)." *Pechat' i revoliutsiia* no. 3 (1924).

Doroshenko, N. V. "Vozniknovenie bol'shevistskoi organizatsii v Peterburgskom universitete i pervye gody ee sushchestvovaniia." *KL* no. 2 (1931).

Dunaev, Valentin. *Na zare iunosti.* Mos.: 1927.

Egorov, I. V. *Ot monarkhii k oktiabriu.* Len.: 1980.

El'iashevich, V. B., A. A. Kizevetter, and M. M. Novikov, eds. *Moskovskii Universitet 1755–1930: Iubileinyi sbornik.* Paris: 1930.

Emel'ianov, Iu. N. *Moskovskii universitet v vospominaniiakh sovremennikov, 1755–1917.* Mos.: 1989.

Engel', G. A. "1905 i studencheskoe dvizhenie v Peterburge." *KL* no. 2 (1925).

Fediushin, K. I. "Petr Arkad'evich Stolypin i studenty (Otryvki iz vospominanii)." *IV* no. 5 (1911).

Figner, Vera. *Memoirs of a Revolutionist.* De Kalb, Ill.: 1991.

Gegidze, Boris. *V universitete: Nabroski studencheskoi zhizni.* SPb: 1903.

Geshin, E. V. "Shelgunovskaia demonstratsiia (Vospominaniia sovremennika)." *MG* no. 11 (1908).

Iordanskii, N. I. "Missiia P. S. Vannovskogo." *Byloe* no. 9 (1907).

Iubileinyi sbornik Voenno-meditsinskoi akademii. Len.: 1927.

Ivanov, P. *Studenty v Moskve: Byt, nravy i tipy.* Mos.: 1903.

Ivanov-Razumnik, R. V. *Tiurmy i ssylki.* N.Y.: 1953.

Kamenskii, Sergei. *Vek minuvshii.* Paris: 1967.

Karavaev, P. N. *V dooktiabr'skie gody.* Mos.: 1948.

Kurbskii, V. *Ocherki studencheskoi zhizni (Iz dnevnika byvshego studenta).* Mos.: 1912.

L. S. [L. A. Sobolev]. "Vospominaniia studenta-soldata." *Byloe* no. 5 (1906).

Lel', Adam. *Zapiski studenta, 1900–1903.* SPb: 1908.

Levitskii, V. *Za chetvert' veka.* Mos.: 1926.

Martov, Iu. O. *Zapiski sotsial-demokrata.* Berlin: 1922.

Mavrodin, V. V., and V. Ezhov, eds. *Leningradskii Universitet v vospominaniiakh sovremennikov.* Len.: 1982.

Mel'gunov, S. P. *Vospominaniia i dnevniki.* Paris: 1964.

Mogilianskii, M. M. "Na rubezhe stoletii." *Golos minuvshego na chuzhoi storone* no. 4/xvii (1926).

———. "V devianostye gody." *Byloe* nos. 23, 24 (1924).

[Moiseev, Sergei]. "Rech' obviniaemogo studenta." *Osv* no. 14 (1903)

Na puti k pobede: Iz revoliutsionnoi istorii Gornogo instituta. Len.: 1925.

Nasha dan' bestuzhevskim kursam. Vospominaniia byvshikh bestuzhevok za rubezhom. Paris: 1971.

Nestroev, G. A. "K istorii studencheskogo dvizheniia v Rossii." *KS* nos. 28, 29 (1926).

Orlov, V. I. "Iz perezhitogo." In *Piatyi god: Sbornik.* Mos.: 1925.

———. "Studencheskoe dvizhenie 1901 goda." *KA* no. 75 (1936).

Osorgin, Mikhail. "Posolon." In *Sbornik vospominanii pamiati russkogo studenchestva.* Paris: 1934.

Panteleev, L. F. "Proisshestvie 29 sentiabria (1857g) mezhdu studentami (Moskovskogo) universiteta i politsiei." *MG* no. 4 (1908).

Posse, V. A. *Moi zhiznennyi put'.* Mos.: 1929.

Rostov, N. "Samoubiistvo M. F. Vetrovoi i studencheskie bezporiadki 1897g." *KS* no. 23 (1926).

Sankt Peterburgskie vysshie zhenskie (Bestuzhevskie) kursy, 1878–1918. Len.: 1965.

Sbornik vospominanii pamiati russkogo studenchestva kontsa XIX, nachala XX vekov. Paris: 1934.

Serebrov, Aleksandr [A. N. Tikhonov]. *Vremia i liudi. Vospominaniia 1898–1905.* Mos.: 1960.

Shubakov, N. "V Iasnoi poliane." *Tekushchaia zhizn'* no. 1 (1909).

Sorokin, Vl. "Vospominaniia starogo studenta." *RS* 128 (1907).

Strumilin, S. G. *Iz perezhitogo, 1897–1917.* Mos.: 1957.

Svobodov, A. "Gor'kii i studencheskoe dvizhenie 1901g." *KS* no. 35 (1927).

Titov, A. A. *Iz vospominanii o studencheskom dvizhenii 1901ogo goda.* Mos.: 1907.

Tyrkova-Villiams, A. V. *Na putiakh k svobode.* N.Y.: 1953.

V. B. [V. V. Bartenev]. "Vospominaniia peterburzhtsa o vtoroi polovine 80kh godov." *MG* nos. 10, 11 (1908).

Valentinov, A. *Poslednie studenty (Zapiski studenta).* Berlin: 1922.

Vasil'ev, N. "V 70ye gody (Iz moikh vospominanii)." *MB* nos. 6, 7 (1906).

Vernadskii, G. "Iz vospominanii." *Novyi zhurnal* no. 100 (1970).

Vishniak, M. V. *Dan' proshlomu.* N.Y.: 1954.

Voitinskii, V. S. *Gody pobed i porazhenii.* Berlin: 1923.

Voronkov, M. I. *Iz zhizni dorevoliutsionnogo studenchestva.* Mos.: 1947.

Zaionchkovskii, P. A., ed. *Moskovskii universitet v vospominaniiakh sovremennikov.* Mos.: 1956.

Zamyatin, Yevgeny. *A Soviet Heretic: Essays by Yevgeny Zamiatin.* Edited and translated by Mirra Ginsburg. Chicago: 1970.

Zhaba, Sergei. *Peterburgskoe studenchestvo v bor'be za svobodnuiu vysshuiu shkolu.* Paris: 1922.

Zharnovetskii, K. S. "Kronshtadskie vosstaniia v 1905–1906gg." *KL* no. 3 (1925).

OTHER PRIMARY SOURCES

Ag-ov, V. [V. K. Agafonov]. "Vysshie uchebnye zavedeniia i revoliutsiia." *SR* vyp. 1 (SPb: 1906).

Aleksandrovich, M. [M. A. Engel'gard]. "Primenitel'no k podlosti." Khronika za nedeliu. *SR* vyp. 4 (1906).

Aleksandrovich, V. *O studencheskoi zabastovke.* SPb: 1905.

Anivtsev, N. *Studencheskie pesni.* SPb: 1914.

Arsen'ev, K. "Polozhenie del v vysshei shkole." *VE* no. 3 (1911).

Artsybashev, M. P. "Sanin." *SM* nos. 1–4 (1907). Reprint. *Sobranie Sochinenii.* Vol. 1. Mos.: 1994.

Asheshov, N. "O sovremennoi molodezhi." *Obr* no. 12 (1903).

Ashevskii, S. "Russkoe studenchestvo v epokhe 60-kh godov." *SM* nos. 6–11 (1907).

B. G. "V. I. Sergeevich i studencheskie bezporiadki v 1899 godu." *IV* no. 1 (1911).

Berdiaev, N. A. *Novoe religioznoe soznanie i obshchestvennost'.* SPb: 1907.

Bernatskii, M. V., ed. *K kharakteristike sovremennogo studenchestva.* SPb: 1910.

Brazilevich, G. *Student-samoubiitsa: Sbornik.* SPb: 1910.

Budilovich, A. S. *Nauka i politika.* SPb: 1905.

Chekhov, N. V. "Professura o vol'noslushatel'nitsakh." *SZh* no. 9 (1908).

———. "Zhenshchiny v universitete." *SZh* no. 5 (1907).

Chernyshevskii, N. G. *Chto delat'? Rasskazy o novykh liudiakh.* 1863. Reprint. Len.: 1975.

Chertkov, V. G. *Russkie studenty v osvoboditel'nom dvizhenii.* Mos.: 1908.

———, and A. Chertkov. *Studencheskoe dvizhenie 1899g.* London: 1900.

Chlenov, M. A. *Polovaia perepis' Moskovskogo studenchestva i ee obshchestvennoe znachenie.* Mos.: 1909.

Chubinskii, M. N. "Sovmestnoe obuchenie v vysshei shkole." *NS* no. 4 (1913).

D. [A. A. D'iakonov]. *1905 i 1906 v Peterburgskom universitete.* SPb: 1907.

D. K. O. "Studencheskoe dvizhenie i zadachi oppozitsii." *Osv* no. 56 (1904).

Dan, F. I. "K nachalu akademicheskogo goda." *Iskra* no. 107 (1905).

Danilevskii, A. Ia. *Sbornik iubileinyi: Imp. Voenno-meditsinskoi akademii.* SPb: 1902.

Danilin, Ia., ed. *Sanin v svete russkoi kritiki.* Mos.: 1908.

Desiat' let stroitel'stva rabfakov. Sbornik statei. Mos.-Len.: 1929.

Dobroliubov, N. A. *Izbrannoe.* Mos.: 1986.

Durkheim, Emile. *Suicide: A Study in Sociology.* N.Y.: 1951.

Dymov, Osip. "Samoubiitsa." *NS* no. 5 (1912).

Engel', G. A. and V. A. Gorokhov. *Iz istorii studencheskogo dvizheniia 1899–1906g.* Mos.: 1908.

Friedman, Paul, ed. *On Suicide (Discussions of the Vienna Psychoanalytic Society—1910).* N.Y.: 1957.

Frommett, Boris "Dukhovnye zaprosy sovremennogo studenchestva." *ZhV* no. 1 (1911).

———. "Ob usloviiakh zhizni i o zabolevaemosti studenchestva." *VG* nos. 22, 23 (1911).

————. *Ocherki po istorii studenchestva v Rossii.* SPb: 1912.

————. "Rossiiskoe studenchestvo i kooperatsiia." *VK* no. 2 (1911).

Gardenin, Iu. "Studenchestvo i revoliutsiia." *Sbornik statei Antonova i dr.* Vyp. 1. Mos.: 1908.

Gershuni, G. A. *Reforma Generala Vannovskogo.* 1902.

Gessen, I. V. "Vnutrenniaia zhizn'." *Ezhegodnik gazety Rech' na 1913g.* Spb.: 1914.

Gessen, V. M. "O vol'noslushatel'nitsakh vysshei shkoly." *SZh* no. 5/6 (1908).

Gladkii, A. "Vzgliad khudozhnikov na zhizn' i samoubiistvo." *VV* no. 6 (1913).

Gordon, G. I. "Golodnye samoubiistva." *ZhV* no. 4 (1912).

————. "K voprosu o material'nom polozhenii nashego studenchestva." *VV* no. 7 (1914).

————. "Samoubiistva molodezhi i ee nervno-psikhicheskaia neustoichivost'." *NZhV* no. 9 (1912).

————. "Samoubiitsy i ikh pis'ma." *NZhV* no. 2/28 (1911).

————. "Sovremennye samoubiistva." *RM* no. 5 (1912).

Gorkii, Maksim. *PSS.* Vols. 1, 2. Mos.: 1949.

————. *Mat'.* 1906. Reprint. Len.: 1970.

————. "Izdaleka." *ZZh* no. 7 (1912).

Gosudarstvennaia Duma. *Stenograficheskie otchety.* Tretii sozyv. SPb: 1908–1912.

Grigor'ev, N. I. "Samoubiistva i pokusheniia na samoubiistvo v Peterburge v 1911g." *RV* no. 6 (1913).

————. "Samoubiistvo v S.-Peterburge za pervuiu polovinu 1910g." *VG* no. 36 (1910).

Gusel'shchikov, M. "Iz studencheskoi ankety." *RB* no. 6 (1910).

Iarmolovich, Aleksei. [A. K. Lozina-Lozinskii]. *Smert' prizrakov.* SPb: 1908.

Imperatorskii Sankt Peterburgskii Universitet. *Otchet o sostoianii.* SPb: 1898–1914.

————. *Protokoly zasedanii soveta.* SPb: 1905–1914.

Iordanskii, N. I. "Krizis intelligentsii." *SM* no. 2 (1908).

————. "Ottsy i deti." *SM* no. 2 (1911).

Isaev, A. A. *Zabastovki uchashchikhsia.* SPb: 1912.

Itogi i perspektivy rabochikh fakul'tetov (1919–1924). Len.: 1924.

Ivanovich, St. [S. O. Portugeis]. "Novye vremena, novye pesni. K likvidatsii raznochintsa." *Sbornik vershiny.* SPb: 1909.

"Iz otcheta o perliustratsii del politsii za 1908 god." *KA* no. 28 (1928).

Izbienie russkoi molodezhi. Dokumental'nye podrobnosti poslednikh studencheskikh bezporiadkov v Peterburge, Moskve, i Kieve. Berlin: 1902.

Izgoev, A. S. "Krizis vysshei shkoly." *RM* no. 3 (1911).

————. *Russkoe obshchestvo i revoliutsiia.* Mos.: 1910.

Kablukov, N. A. *Studencheskii kvartirnyi vopros v Moskve.* Mos.: 1908.

Kanina, V. G. "Dvadtsatipiatiletie Vysshikh zhenskikh kursov v S.-Peterburge." *IV XCV* (1904).

Karatygina, Nina. *Krov' zhivotvoriashchaia, Sbornik.* Pet.: 1916.

Kaufman, A. A. "Russkaia kursistka v tsifrakh." *RM* no. 6 (1912).

————. *Slushatel'nitsy S.-Peterburgskikh vysshikh zhenskikh (Bestuzhevskikh) kursov na vtorom godu voiny.* Pet.: 1916.

————. *Slushatel'nitsy S.-Peterburgskikh vysshikh zhenskikh (Bestuzhevskikh) kursov po dannym perepisi (ankety). . . 1909g.* SPb: 1912.

Khlopin, G. V. "Samoubiistvo, pokusheniia na samoubiistvo i neschastnye sluchai sredi uchashchikhsia russkikh uchebnykh zavedenii." *ZhMNP* no. 3 (1906).

Khlopin, G. V., N. G. Ushinskii, and E. A. Neznamov. *Samoubiistvo, pokusheniia na samoubiistvo i neschastnye sluchai sredi uchashchikhsia russkikh uchebnykh zavedenii.* Series. SPb: 1906–1916.

Khoroshko, V. K. " 'Gigiena dushi' i biurokratiia." *RM* no. 12 (1905).

Kleinbort, L. N. "Molodezh' i voina." *SM* no. 11 (1914).

———. "Sovremennaia molodezh' (Prezhde i teper')." *SM* no. 10 (1914).

———. "Sovremennaia molodezh' (Russkaia kursistka)." *SM* no. 9 (1914).

Kokhanovskii, V. "Student Ivanov." *Obr* no. 12 (1907).

Kollontai, A. M. "Novaia zhenshchina." *SM* no. 9 (1913).

Kol'tsov, N. K. "Akademicheskaia molodezh'." *RB* no. 3 (1909).

———. *Pamiati pavshikh: Zhertvy iz sredy Moskovskogo studenchestva v oktiabr'skie i dekabr'skie dni.* Mos.: 1906.

Kovalevskii, M. M. "Vysshee zhenskoe obrazovanie." *VE* no. 6 (1911).

Kushnyr-Kushnarev, G. *Istoricheskii ocherk vozniknoveniia i razvitiia akademicheskikh organizatsii v Rossii.* SPb: 1914.

Lalaints, I. Kh. *Otpravka studentov v Sibir'.* Geneva: 1902.

Larskii, I. "Na granitse akademizma." *SM* no. 10 (1908).

———. "Reforma nadzora." *SM* no. 8 (1911).

———. "Universitetskie sobytiia." *SM* no. 1 (1908).

Lavrov, Petr. *Historical Letters (1868–69).* Translated and edited by James P. Scanlan. Berkeley: 1967.

Lazerson, M. Ia. "Studenchestvo i minuvshii akademicheskii krizis." *Obr* no. 4 (1909).

[Lenin, V.] "Otdacha v soldaty 183-kh studentov." *Iskra* no. 2 (1901).

Levchenko, Vad. "Krizis universitetskoi zhizni (Mysli studenta)." *RM* no. 5 (1908).

Levin, K. "Chto chitaet i chem interesuetsia uchashchaiasia molodezh'?" *MB* no. 11 (1903).

Libanov, G. M. *Studencheskoe dvizhenie 1899 goda.* London: 1901.

Likhacheva, E. *Materialy dlia istorii zhenskogo obrazovaniia v Rossii.* SPb: 1899–1901.

Listovki bol'shevistskikh organizatsii v pervoi russkoi revoliutsii 1905–1907gg. 3 vols. Mos.: 1956.

Lunacharskii, A. V. "Dva studenta," *StP* no. 1 (1918).

———. "K Uchashchimsia." *Narodnoe prosveshchenie* no. 1 (1918).

Maiskii, V. "Evoliutsiia nemetskogo studenchestva." *Obr* no. 5 (1909).

Maizel', I. E. "O samoubiistvakh sredi uchashchikhsia." *VV* no. 8 (1908).

Malygin, N. P. "Iz itogov studencheskoi perepisi v Iur'eve. . . ." *ZhORV* no. 1 (1907).

Margolin, D. *Spravochnik po vysshemu obrazovaniiu.* Pet.: 1915.

Martov, L., P. Maslov, and A. Potresov, eds. *Obshchestvennoe dvizhenie v Rossii.* 4 vols. SPb: 1910.

Mastriukov, A. "Vopros prizvaniia i rezul'taty ankety." *VV* no. 7 (1911).

Materialy k istorii russkoi kontrrevoliutsii. SPb: 1908.

Mel'gunov, S. P. *Iz istorii studencheskikh obshchestv v russkikh universitetakh.* Mos.: 1904.

———. *Studencheskie organizatsii 80–90gg. v Moskovskom universitete.* Mos.: 1908.

Meshcherskii, V. P. "Rech' Konservatora." *Grazhdanin* no. 78 (11.X.1901).

Miakotin, V. A. "Dliashchaiasia tragediia." *RB* no. 3 (1911).

———. "Khoziaeva universiteta." *NSO* vyp. 2 (1906).

———. "Tragediia vysshei shkoly." *RB* no. 10 (1908).

Mikhailov, M. L. *Zhenshchiny, ikh vospitanie i znachenie v sem'e i obshchestve.* SPb: 1903.

"Moskovskoe studenchestvo i professura nakanune Fevral'skoi revoliutsii." *KA* no. 58 (1933).

Moskva v dekabre 1905g. Sbornik statei. Mos.: 1906.

Na Pomoshch' molodezhi: Sbornik statei, pisem i zametok o studencheskikh nuzhdakh, i samoubiistvakh uchashchikhsia. Kiev: 1910.

"Nashe studenchestvo." *NZh* no. 1 (1904).

Nekrasov, N. A. *Sobranie sochinenii.* Vol. 2. Mos.: 1965.

Nikandrov, N. "Byvshii student." *SM* no. 3 (1909).

"Novaia drama v tiur'me." *Osv* no. 10 (1903).

Novosel'skii, S. A. *Statistika samoubiistv.* SPb: 1910.

"Opekaemoe studenchestvo." *Iskra* no. 31 (1902).

Osnovnye polozheniia po voprosu o reforme Vysshei shkoly, priniatye studenchestvom Petrogradskogo universiteta. Pet.: 1918.

P. S. [Petr Struve]. "Chto zhe teper'?" *Osv* no. 56 (1904).

Peshekhonov, A. V. " 'Sanintsy' i 'Sanin.' " *RB* nos. 5, 6 (1908).

Pirogov, N. I. *Universitetskii vopros.* SPb: 1863.

———. "Voprosy zhizni." *Morskoi sbornik* (1856).

Pisarev, D. I. *Izbrannye pedagogicheskie sochineniia.* Mos.: 1951.

———. "Bazarov." *Russkoe slovo* no. 3 (1862).

Pokrovskaia, M. I. *O vysshem zhenskom obrazovanii v Rossii.* SPb: 1906.

Polozhenie o russkikh universitetakh: Proekty. Pet.: [1918].

Poslednie revoliutsionnye sobytiia v Rossii i Lev Tolstoi. Berlin: 1901.

Povorinskaia, V. "Ottsy i deti nashikh dnei." *Obr* no. 7 (1905).

Prazdnovanie 25-letiia Vysshikh zhenskikh (Bestuzhevskikh) kursov. SPb: 1904.

Proal, Louis. *L'éducation et le suicide des enfants.* Paris: 1907.

Purishkevich, V. M. *Materialy po voprosu o razlozhenii sovremennogo russkogo universiteta.* SPb: 1914.

Radin, E. P. *Dushevnoe nastroenie sovremennoi uchashcheisia molodezhi po dannym Peterburgskoi obshchestudencheskoi ankety 1912 goda.* SPb: 1913.

Rozanov, V. V. "Homines novi." In *Kogda nachal'stvo ushlo.* SPb: 1910.

———. "O studencheskikh bezporiadkakh." In *Religiia i kul'tura.* SPb: 1899.

Rybakov, F. E. "Dushevnye razstroistva v sviazi s tekushchimi politicheskimi sobytiiami." *RV* no. 51 (1905), no. 3 (1906).

———. *Sovremennye pisateli i bol'nye nervy.* Mos.: 1908.

S.-Peterburgskie Vysshie zhenskie kursy za 25 let, 1878–1903: Ocherki i Materialy. SPb: 1903.

S.-Peterburgskii universitet v pervoe stoletie ego deiatel'nosti, 1819–1919. Pet.: 1919.

"S.-Peterburgskoe okhrannoe otdelenie v 1895–1901 gg. ('Trud' chinovnika otdeleniia P. S. Statkovskogo)." *Byloe* no. 16 (1921).

Sel'skii, L. *Obshchestvennaia zhizn' russkogo studenchestva i ee ocherednaia zadacha.* Kiev: 1907.

Shabanova, A. N. *Ocherk zhenskogo dvizheniia v Rossii.* SPb: 1912.

———. "Zhenskoe vrachebnoe obrazovanie v Rossii." *IV* no. 5 (1913).

Shchepkina, E. N. "Zhenshchina v russkikh universitetakh." *VE* no. 9 (1912).

Sheinis, D. I. *Evreiskoe studenchestvo v tsifrakh.* Kiev: 1911.

Sheinis, Lev. "Epidemicheskie samoubiistva." *VV* no. 1 (1908).

Shelgunov, N. V. "K molodomu pokoleniiu." In *Vospominaniia.* Mos.-Pet.: 1923.

Shimkevich, V. "Opyt dvukh let." *SZh* no. 9 (1908).

Shokhal', K. R. "K voprosu o dopushchenii zhenshchin v universitety." *RSh* no. 11 (1912).

———. *Vysshee zhenskoe obrazovanie v Rossii.* SPb: 1910.

Simonov, I. S. *Shkola i polovoi vopros.* SPb: 1909.

Sorokin, P. A. "Otpravliaias' v dorogu." In *Utrenniki.* Vol. 1. Edited by D. A. Lutokhin. Pet.: 1922.

Sovremennaia illiustratsiia no. 9 (September 21, 1913).

Staryi student. "Nashe studenchestvo." *NZh* no. 1 (1904).

"Studenchestvo i revoliutsiia." *RR* no. 17 (1903).

Student E. A. *Porugannyi khram nauki.* Mos.: 1906.

Svatikov, S. G., ed. *Put' studenchestva.* Mos.: 1916.

Sviatlovskii, V. V. *Studenchestvo v tsifrakh.* SPb: 1909.

Syromiatnikov, A. S. "Moskovskii universitet v Oktiabr'skie dni 1905 goda." *KA* 74 (1936).

———. "Studencheskie volneniia v 1901–1902 gg." *KA* 89/90 (1938).

Tarle, E. V. "Rol' studenchestva v revoliutsionnom dvizhenii v Evrope v 1848 godu." In *Sochineniia.* Vol. 1. Mos.: 1957.

Teplov, Vasilii. "Piatidesiatiletie vysshego zhenskogo obrazovaniia v Rossii." *VV* no. 9 (1910).

"Tolstoi o studencheskoi stachke 1899g: Pis'mo N. M. Ezhova k A. Suvorinu." *LN* 69 (1961).

Trudy pervogo vserossiiskogo s"ezda po obrazovaniiu zhenshchin. Pet.: 1914.

Trudy soveshchaniia ob ekonomicheskikh nuzhdakh studenchestva. SPb: 1909.

Universitet i politika. SPb: 1906.

Vagner, Vladimir. "Samoubiistvo i filosofskii pessimizm." *ZZh* no. 49 (1912).

Venozhinskii, V. *Politicheskaia zabastovka v S.-Peterburgskom universitete.* SPb: 1906.

Vekhi: Sbornik statei o russkoi intelligentsii. Mos.: 1909.

Verzhbitskii, V. G. *Materialy po istorii Rossii v periode kapitalizma.* Mos.: 1976.

Vigdorchik, N. A. "Politicheskie psikhozy i politicheskie samoubiistva." *Obr* no. 12 (1907).

Vorovskii, V. "Bazarov i Sanin. Dva nigilizma." In *Literaturnaia kritika.* Mos.: 1971.

Vydrin, Rafael. "Nakanune novogo universitetskogo ustava." *SM* no. 2 (1910).

———. *Osnovnye momenty studencheskogo dvizheniia v Rossii.* Mos.: 1908.

Vysshie zhenskie kursy v S.-Peterburge. Kratkaia istoricheskaia zapiska. SPb: 1900.

Vysshie zhenskie kursy v S.-Peterburge. Kratkaia istoricheskaia zapiska, 1878–1908. SPb: 1908.

Zalkind, A. B. *Ocherki kul'tury revoliutsionnogo vremeni.* Mos.: 1924.

———. *Revoliutsiia i molodezh'.* Mos.: 1925.

Zhbankov, D. N. "Izuchenie voprosa o polovoi zhizni uchashchikhsia." *PV* nos. 27–29 (1908).

———. "K statistike samoubiistv v 1905–11 godakh." *PV* nos. 34–36, 38 (1912).

———. "O samoubiistvakh v poslednee vremia." *PV* nos. 26–29 (1906).

———. "Sovremennye samoubiistva." *SM* no. 3 (1910).

————. "Travmaticheskaia epidemiia." *PV* nos. 32–35 (1905).

Zweig, Stefan. *The World of Yesterday.* N.Y.: 1943.

SELECTED UNIVERSITY HISTORIES PUBLISHED IN THE SOVIET UNION

Bovykin, V. I., and O. Latysheva. "Moskovskii universitet v revoliutsii 1905–1907 godov." *VI* no. 4 (1955).

Degot', V. "K voprosu o roli studenchestva v revoliutsionnom dvizhenii." *KS* no. 2/87 (1932).

Eimontova, R. G. *Russkie universitety na grani dvukh epokh.* Mos.: 1985.

Georgieva, N. G. "Sovetskaia istoriografiia studencheskogo dvizheniia v Rossii na rubezhe XIX-XXvv." *VI* no. 10 (1979).

Gusiatnikov, P. S. *Revoliutsionnoe studencheskoe dvizhenie v Rossii.* Mos.: 1971.

Iakovlev, V. "Politika tsarskogo pravitel'stva v universitetskom voprose." *Vestnik Leningradskogo universiteta* no. 2 (1969).

Ivanov, A. E. "Universitety Rossii v 1905g." *IZ* no. 88 (1971).

————. "Demokraticheskoe studenchestvo v revoliutsii 1905–1907gg." *IZ* no. 107 (1975).

Istoriia Leningradskogo politekhnicheskogo instituta. Len.: 1957.

Istoriia Leningradskogo universiteta. Len.: 1969.

Istoriia Moskovskogo universiteta. Mos.: 1955.

Kondrat'ev, K., ed. *Leningradskii Universitet.* Len.: 1963.

Kupaigorodskaia, A. P. *Vysshaia shkola Leningrada v pervye gody sovetskoi vlasti, 1917–1925.* Len.: 1984.

Leningradskii meditsinskii institut k xxx-letiiu deiatel'nosti, 1897–1927. Len.: 1928.

Mavrodin, V. V., ed. *Leningradskii Universitet 1819–1944.* Mos.: 1955.

————. *Istoriia Leningradskogo universiteta: Ocherki.* Len.: 1969.

Ocherki po istorii Leningradskogo universiteta. 5 vols. Len.: 1962–1984.

Orlov, V. I. *Studencheskoe dvizhenie Moskovskogo universiteta v 19om stoletii.* Mos.: 1934.

Rappoport, M. L. *Za sto let: Revoliutsionnaia istoriia Leningradskogo Technologicheskogo instituta.* Len.: 1928.

Shalaginova, L. I. "Studencheskoe dvizhenie nakanune i v dni Fevral'skoi revoliutsii." *VI* no. 2 (1967).

Shchetinina, G. A. *Studenchestvo i revoliutsionnoe dvizhenie v Rossii.* Mos.: 1987.

————. *Universitety v Rossii i ustav 1884g.* Mos.: 1976.

Sladkevich, N. G. "Peterburgskii universitet v 1905 g." *Vestnik Leningradskogo universiteta* no. 3 (1955).

————, and G. A. Tishkin. *Peterburgskii universitet i revoliutsionnoe dvizhenie v Rossii.* Len.: 1979.

Tkachenko, P. S. *Moskovskoe studenchestvo v obshchestvenno-politicheskoi zhizni Rossii vo vtoroi polovine XIX veka.* Mos.: 1958.

Index